Marcius D. Raymond

Gray Genealogy

being a genealogical record and history of the descendants of John Gray, of

Beverly, Mass., and also including sketches of other Gray families

Marcius D. Raymond

Gray Genealogy
*being a genealogical record and history of the descendants of John Gray, of Beverly, Mass.,
and also including sketches of other Gray families*

ISBN/EAN: 9783337284763

Printed in Europe, USA, Canada, Australia, Japan

Cover: Foto ©Andreas Hilbeck / pixelio.de

More available books at **www.hansebooks.com**

GRAY GENEALOGY,

*Being a Genealogical Record and History of the
Descendants of*

JOHN GRAY, OF BEVERLY, MASS.,

And Also Including

SKETCHES OF OTHER GRAY FAMILIES,

BY

M. D. RAYMOND.

TARRYTOWN, N. Y.
1887.

To the Memory of his Grandmother,

MABEL GRAY RAYMOND,

This Volume is affectionately Dedicated by

THE AUTHOR.

INDEX

LIST OF ILLUSTRATIONS.

INTRODUCTION.

It should be stated at the outset that this volume does not include, and was not intended to include the complete record of a Family that has filled a prominent place in English history for so many centuries. Such a work would indeed be a herculean task, and it would be an ambitious historian who should essay it with the expectation of accomplishment during a lifetime.

The compiling of a genealogy and history of the branch of the Gray family to which the writer is akin, was incidentally undertaken with the view of preserving some interesting personal statistics which had come into his possession, and which were thought worthy of preservation. They referred especially to his ancestors in that line, and at the first, a much less extended record was contemplated, but a continuance of investigation gave increased scope to the work adding new lines in various directions, until it has embraced sketches of many of the early and most numerous Gray families in America, besides mention of some whose direct connection with the different branches does not appear.

The difficulties in the way, and the limitations of time and expense, have hindered the full realization of his desires, but the writer has industriously gathered up interesting family facts from many sources, and while some have eluded the most earnest research, those which are garnered as the result of these labors, will at least furnish interesting data for the future historian, and may not be considered an unworthy contribution to that end. The writer has found the work of fascinating interest and only regrets that he could not have followed it to its fullest, most complete conclusions.

The seeming long delay in the completion of this volume has doubtless been a disappointment to many, but other busy activities and exacting duties have necessarily taken much of the time and attention of the writer while he has been engaged upon this work, and much more is included in it than was at first intended. The end, continually in sight, has continually evaded him, and the temptation to extend research to other and inviting fields, has not easily been put aside.

With a kindly greeting to all of kith and kin, and all of the name of Gray, and especially to those who have cordially assisted in the work, this volume is issued, in the hope that it may be found worthy of preservation and be the means of increased interest in the history of an ancient and honorable family.

Tarrytown-on-Hudson, N. Y., May, 1887.

M. D. RAYMOND.

The name Gray, is of *local* origin, that is, following the name of a *place* in Burgundy, France. In the Department of Haute-Saone, there is now a town called Gray. The name was originally Croy. A Norman Chief named Rolf, or Rollo, or Raoul, invaded France with his Norwegian followers and established himself there in the 9th Century. A descendant, or at all events a member of the same family, became Chamberlain to Robert, Duke of Normandy, and received from him the Castle and honor of Croy, from which his family assumed the name of DeCroy, which was afterwards changed to DeGray, and at last to Gray without the prefix.

Gray instead of Grey is adopted in this work, it being the orthography in use in this branch of the family, as it is almost universally in the different branches in this country. In England and Ireland, however, in the titled families, Grey still obtains, while in Scotland it is Gray. However, this slight difference makes but a narrow line of demarcation between different branches of a family all evidently descended from one parent stock and of one origin.

The Grays unquestionably came over to England with William the Conqueror in 1066, for among the names of those inscribed at Battle Abbey, after the decisive battle of Hastings, as worthy to be remembered for valiant services there rendered, was J. de Gray. Nesbit's Heraldry says: "In an old manuscript of Arms in the reign of William the Conqueror, are the Armoreal bearings of Paganus de Gray, equitum signifer to King William." Again we quote from the same high authority: "Gray, Earl of Kent, Chief of the ancient and illustrious house of Gray, so dignified in the reign of Edward IV., from whom are descended and branched the Barons of Rotherfield, Codmore, Wilton, Ruthem, Groby, and Rugemont, the Viscount of Lisle, the Earl of Stamford, the Marquis of Dorset, and the Duke of Suffolk,—all of that surname derived from the honour and Castle of Gray, (or

Croy as some write,) in Picardy, their patrimony before the Conquest."

In regard to the Grays of Scotland being of the same family we have again the testimony of Nesbit's Heraldry: "Gray Lord Gray in Scotland, same Arms as My Lord Gray of Wark and Chillingham, England. Motto, Anchor Fast Anchor. The first of this line was a son of Gray in Chillingham, Northumberland, England, who came to Scotland in the reign of Alexander II., (about 1230,) and gave his allegiance to that King, receiving possessions in Roufield shire of Roxburgh. His issue has continued still in Scotland." His son, Sir Andrew Gray, joined King Robert Bruce when he ascended the throne. The Grays in Ireland, generally designated as Scotch-Irish, are doubtless the descendants of that branch of the family.

The Grays were closely allied with the Royal house of England and were near the throne. Edward IV. married Elizabeth Gray the widow of Sir John Gray who was slain at the second battle of St. Albans, 1461. On the death of King Edward, her son, the young Prince Consort, and her son Lord Gray, were both executed in 1483, by that bloody usurper, the notorious Richard III.

Burke's Peerage says: "The family of Gray is of great antiquity in Northumberland. Henry de Gray obtained from King Richard I., (1190) the manor of Turoc in Essex. Sir John Gray, Knight of Berwick, 1372, was father of Sir Thomas of Berwick and Chillingham. Sir Edward de Gray married dau. and heiress of Henry heir apparent of William."

The union of the Grays with the royal line of Tudor was by the marriage of the Duke of Suffolk, with Mary, daughter of Henry VII., sister of Henry VIII., and widow of King Louis XII., of France, who had died Jan. 1, 1515. The tragic fate of their daughter, Lady Jane Gray, who reigned for a brief hour an unwilling Queen, has attracted the attention and enlisted the sympathies of the world. The story of her pure and beautiful life and of her heroic death will long illumine the pages of one of the most eventful periods of English history. Her execution, 1554, was soon followed by that of her father, the Duke of Suffolk, and his brothers, Lord John and Lord Thomas Gray.

The Grays were not restored to their rights and court favor until the accession of James I., 1603. Since then they have repeatedly distinguished themselves in politics, literature, and the learned professions, and still continue prominently represented among the titled nobility in England, Scotland and Ireland. In modern times they have furnished poets, statesmen, and military commanders in the British realm.

The Gray Family in America is numerous, widespread, and consists of many diverse branches. They were among the Pilgrims of New England, the Quakers of Pennsylvania, were also early settlers of Virginia and other Southern States. Within the first century—from 1620 to 1720—researches made warrant the estimate that at least twenty different families of Grays, or different branches of the same family, had emigrated to this country and made their homes in the New World. As early as 1622, two brothers, Thomas and John Gray, had become proprietors of the island of Nantasket in Boston Harbor by purchase from the Indians. At an early period there were also Grays at Salem, Boston, Plymouth, and Yarmouth, and in the provinces of Connecticut and Maine. It is a historic fact worthy of mention, that Mrs. Desire Kent, daughter of Edward Gray, who came over in the Mayflower, had the honor of being the first woman who landed at Plymouth Rock. Abraham Gray is mentioned as among the Pilgrim refugees at Leyden, Holland, in 1622.

Of the later emigrations there were several, notably that of a family of Grays who settled at Worcester, Mass., 1718. There are also numerous families that trace back no farther than two or or three generations in this country. This multiplicity of branches of the family adds greatly to the difficulty of tracing any one particular line, as they are often found in the same vicinage with the same names, and the confusion so made is some times almost inextricable. For the benefit of the general information so imparted, and for the aid of others who may be inclined to make further investigations, considerable of space is given in the appendix to this volume to the publication of such data of these different branches as has been gathered in researches made for the genealogical facts of the particular family of Grays a sketch of whose history is herewith published.

That the Grays in this country have proved themselves worthy of their distinguished ancestry is abundantly evidenced. Among its honored representatives are a U. S. Senator, a Justice of the U. S. Supreme Court, the Governor of a State, and many names prominent in the learned professions, while they furnished their full quota of patriot soldiers in the Revolution, and again in the war for the Union.

The Grays of this line have some strongly marked characteristics. They are often men of stalwart stature, personal prowess and commanding presence; courageous, patriotic, natural leaders among men, withal lovers of peace, not given to self-assertion, modest as well as brave, inclined to philosophical speculation, and rather reserved than effusive. A strong type of character distinctly perpetuated.

———

JOHN GRAY (1.)

The original pilgrim of this branch of the Gray family, and the time of his arrival, do not so clearly appear as might be desired. The absolute data of record run back directly to the marriage of John Gray with Ruth Hebbard at Beverly, Mass., Apr. 28, 1704, their "intention of marriage" having previously been published "March ye 26th." The only authority prior to that is an an ancient Family Record of John Gray, grandson of John of Beverly, "Faithfully copied by his youngest son Reuben Gray," which is a very interesting document, the basis of all the investigations made, and found correct in almost every minute particular so far as it has been tested by official records as to the statements set forth. That quaint old record says, "My grandfather was born in the eastern part of New England. Died about A. D. 1713." As a matter of fact the 1st church records of Beverly give the date of his death as Feb. 29, 1712. This old record then says, "My grandmother, Ruth Hebbard, was born in Windham, Conn., and died there. My father John Gray was born in Beverly, in the province of Massachusetts. Died in Sharon, Conn., A. D. 1761, aged about 53 years," which is nearly correct. Again, "My mother, Anne Hebbard, was born in Windham, Conn., May, 1706. Died in Sharon, May, (28) 1746." Then follows a list of his brothers and sisters with dates of birth, marriage and death, all of which have been proved to be correct from town and church records. This all to substantiate the following important statement also by him made: *"My great grandfather moved from England among the former settlers. Had six soms."* A memorandum left by the late Dr. John F. Gray of New York, who had much interest in family matters, and who was a man careful and exact in his statements, says: "Grandfather (the John Gray whose record is above quoted) told me his great grandfather, our ancestor, John Gray (1), came direct from England. Been in British Navy; had lost an arm, was a pensioner, half-pay. Lion couchant his family crest. My grandfather inherited a sleeve button made after the death of the half-pay ancestor from the thimble he wore over the stump of his arm." This is a well authenticated tradition in the family, the full particulars of the loss of the sleeve button above referred to being handed down.

Not being able to disprove the foregoing statements, on the contrary something of record being found which might substantiate them, not the least of which is the fact that all the other statements made in the said record of John Gray have been found well authenticated, they are accepted as correct data, though less full than might be wished. It is not slight collateral proof that there were living at Beverly a George and an Isaac Gray, cotemporaneous with John, and a Joseph Gray was killed near there by the Indians in 1711, of whom no connection can be found elsewhere, and the strong presumption is that they were brothers. That would account for four of the six sons of John Gray (1).

The compiler of this work frankly admits that he was at first strongly of the opinion that the Beverly Grays were from Salem, there having been several families of that name there at an early day with numerous descendants, and the close proximity of the two places, formerly one, (Salem) gave strength to that assumption; but a careful and exhaustive research there made, including all public documents and records, family and otherwise, absolutely dispelled that belief, and convinced the writer most thoroughly that the statement of John Gray aforesaid was made upon absolute knowledge of the facts in the case, and it is therefore accepted, unquestioned. It only remains to be added that the character of the descendants of this line warrants the claim of such an ancestry.

JOHN GRAY (2.)

Of his birth, we only know that it was in "the eastern part of New England," probably about 1680, as he was married as already stated to Ruth Hebbard, at Beverly, Mass., Apr. 28, 1704. She was the daughter of John and Ruth Hebbard, and born Aug. 6, 1683. At this point the record of John Gray is again of interest. It says that Ruth Hebbard was born in Windham, Conn. At first this seems confusing because there were several families of Hebbards at Beverly, but the records of Windham give many of that name also there. Probably they were kindred. The records of Beverly show that the widow Ruth Gray married Benjamin Webster, Nov. 8, 1712. That she returned to Windham and died there, we have the statement of her grandson John Gray (3), while the fact that her son, John Gray, appears as there residing, is further evidence. Mr. Gray had died young, leaving two children, Ruth Gray b. Jan. 5, 1704, and John Gray (3) b. May 17, 1707. His life was brief with but little outward promise that he was to be the progenitor of such a numerous and vigorous race. Of the daughter, Ruth, there is no further trace. Of his supposed brothers, the records of Beverly concerning them and their descendants will appear in another place.

JOHN GRAY (3.)

Born in Beverly, Mass., May 17, 1707, he was less than five years old when his father died, and within a year his mother had remarried. The town records of Windham, Conn., show that John Gray was married at that place to Anne Hebbard, Feb'y 26th, 1728. Probably she was akin to him, being of the same name as his mother, and of the place of her nativity. The following children were born to them, the names and dates being copied from the town records of Windham, Lebanon, and Sharon, Conn.:

>ANNE, b. in Windham, Conn., Nov. 18, 1729; mar. Abraham Mudge, at Sharon, Jan. 26, 1753; d. near New Concord, Canaan, Columbia Co., N. Y., June 22, 1776.

JOSEPH, b. June 12, 1732, in Windham, Conn.; d. Mar. 29, 1796, in Greene, Chenango Co., N. Y.

ADAH, b. in Windham, Mar. 18, 1734; d. in Litchfield, Conn., Nov. 1765.

NATHANIEL, b. in Lebanon, Conn., Mar. 17, 1736; d. in Sherburne, Chenango Co., N. Y., June 24, 1810.

JOHN, b. in Lebanon, Conn., Dec. 13, (N. S.) 1739; d. in Sherburne, N. Y., Sept. 22, 1822.

RUTH, b. in Sharon, Conn., June 4th, 1744; mar. Elder David Mudge; d. July, 1815.

JERUSHA, b. in Sharon, Conn., Apr. 2, 1746; d. Apr. 21, 1746.

Anne Hebbard Gray died in Sharon, Conn., May 28, 1746, and John Gray (3) mar. second, the widow Catherine Gardner, of Sharon, Sept. 18, 1747, by whom were the following children :

SILAS, b. in Sharon, Conn., May 8, 1748; d. at Princetown, Schenectady Co., N. Y., April, 1820.

SARAH, b. in Sharon, Apr. 4, 1750; mar. Oliver Bates at Berlin, N. Y.; was a member of the Baptist Church at that place in 1798; after the death of her husband, she removed with her son, Oliver Bates, Jr., to Genesee Co., N. Y.

DARIUS, b. in Sharon, June 18, 1752; d. in Sharon, Aug. 12, 1816.

WILLIAM, b. in Sharon, May 22, 1754; d. in Sharon.

DANIEL, b. in Sharon, June 4, 1756; d. in Berlin, Rensselaer Co., N. Y., May 23, 1830.

JAMES, b. in Sharon, Aug. 3, 1759.

The dates and places of birth above given indicate frequent migrations. Between 1734 and 1736 John Gray must have removed with his then little family from Windham, where he had united with the Congregational Church in 1729, to Lebanon, a town adjoining on the south and in the neighboring county of New London. There he remained for several years, during which three children more were added to the family, when they took up the line of march for Sharon, Litchfield Co., on the western border and near the north line of the State of Connecticut. The first record of real estate purchased by him there is of the date of Feb. 1, 1743; 6 acres of Margaret Goodrich, £12. July 7, 1746, it is recorded that he bought 20 acres of David Hamilton, price, £400. The history of Sharon says, "John Gray first settled in the Valley, and his house stood upon the bank near the Valley Store, a little east of Henry Hotchkiss' house. In 1748 he sold his place to Abel Wood and removed to the Mountain." He appears to have sold for considerable less than cost, receiving only £260. He had lost his wife there, and probably the lowlands, though more fertile, as generally in a new country, proved unhealthy. "The Mountain" so-called, was two or three miles eastwardly, on a high plateau, and about two miles from the present village of Sharon. It was then supposed that it would be the center of the town; and it was so laid out and did remain so for many years. He then bought 100 acres of John Mills, "west of Ebenezer Jackson," for which he paid £300; deed recorded June 9, 1748. Sold the same to John Pardee, May 7, 1754, for £1200. He then purchased a farm just "east of the Gould place," where he continued to reside until his de- cease in 1761. That he bravely took up arms in defence of the frontier settlements is evidenced by the fact that his name ap- pears as a member of Capt. Williams' Co., at Fort Massachu- setts, (Pittsfield, Berkshire Co.,) in 1755. In the inventory of his personal estate are noted, 1 gun, 1 "swoard." If preserved, what priceless mementos they would have been.

The records of the Probate Court show that the widow Cath- erine Gray was appointed guardian to Darius, William, Daniel and James, "all sons of John Gray late of Sharon, dec'd," April 25, 1763. Silas Gray chose his brother John for guardian Feb. 7th, 1764. Sarah Gray chose David Foster for her guardian, June 18, 1764. The inventory of his personal estate as filed shows a footing of £46.10s.1d., beside what was set off to the widow, while there were "sundry charges" of £20.7s, besides the court charges of £2.7s.4d. There is no record of any will or of any division or sale of real property; but in any case the estate evidently was not insolvent. Darius was the only son who con- tinued permanently to remain in Sharon, and he probably be- came the owner of the homestead.

There is no record of the death of the widow, Catherine Gardner Gray, and no trace of her later than the proceedings of the Probate Court, to which reference has been made. And strange to relate, the most thorough and repeated search, made by the writer, and by others, in all known private and public burial places from one end of Sharon to the other, failed to disclose the grave of John Gray, or of either of his wives, or of his children. And none of their descendants, some of whom continued to reside in that town, have knowledge of the place of their burial. It was a disappointment and surprise not to be able to find it.

The location of the old home "on the Mountain," however, is distinctly determined. The well defined ruins, a grass-grown mound,—the foundation walls of the primeval house there erected, now in an open field barren of all other signs of habitation, near by an old roadway long since deserted,—there is the place around which cluster forgotten memories, forgotten loves, forgotten traditions, and unwritten history that well might stir the heart to quicker beat at thought of them. There John Gray lived, there his family of stalwart sons and fair daughters gathered under the roof-tree of his home; there he toiled, there died; there the drama of his life, which had been full of labor and trial, and earnest effort, ended; and that spot, however bleak and barren, can never be common ground to one of his descendants.

John Gray of Sharon was one of that sturdy race of pioneers who proved his claim alike to ancestry and to posterity. He was the father of men and women of strength and character, and must have possessed the germ and realization of them in himself. Scarcely fifty-four, he had condensed the energies of a life-time into that period. He had pushed on to the borders of civilization and helped there to lay enduring foundations for the good of all future time. The spirit of the true Pilgrim was in him; he knew neither fear nor discouragement; and while not a line is carved nor a stone is raised to his memory, his descendants will do him honor to the remotest generations. The noble hills of Sharon keep ceaseless vigil where he sleeps while they look out upon the promised land.

JOHN GRAY (4.)

Born in Lebanon, Conn., Dec. 13, 1739, he removed with his father's family to Sharon, Conn., in 1743, and was the youngest son living at the death of his mother in May, 1746. Conceiving that he was neglected by his stepmother, when a mere lad he seceded from the paternal union, and after trudging on several miles over the hills he was met by the pastor of the parish, (the Rev. Cotton Mather Smith, eminent for his piety and his learning, for half a century ministering to the Church at Sharon, and also father of Gov. John Cotton Smith of Connecticut,) to whom he frankly confessed his design and the reason for it. The pastor kindly raised him to his horse, and took him to the Selectman, who, with the consent of the father, bound him till of age to his Reverend benefactor, who said that there was the material to build a valuable man ; and he drilled him to work and to study, teaching him Latin and other branches of learning in his own library.

The boy grew up to manhood under such good influences, and on Nov. 16, 1763, he married Betsey (Elizabeth) Skeel, who was born at New Milford, Dec. 15, 1745. The birth-places of the children indicate that they continued to reside in Sharon until 1768, about which time they must have removed to Canaan, Columbia Co., N. Y., where they made their home for some twelve years or more in what is known as Frisbie Street, he being engaged in the milling business on a site where there is still a mill, with a good water privilege there. He was probably also engaged somewhat in farming, as the "ear-mark" of his flocks is on the town records date of Feb. 27, 1773.

The Revolution found him a staunch patriot, and the old records show that he was chosen to the responsible position of member of the Committee of Public Safety for King's District, which comprised several of the adjoining towns, on May 6, 1777, and served during that year. It is said of him that when the army was in need he would slaughter and send to it his last bullock. And when the advance of Burgoyne's army required more volunteers at the front, he promptly shouldered his musket, and leaving his wife and young family trembling with apprehension, marched to meet the enemy, participating in the battle of Stillwater and the triumph of Saratoga.

John Gray and "Elizabeth his wife" had taken letters from the Church at Sharon, and united with the Church at New Concord on removing to Canaan, but owing to doctrinal differences, he having become a Restorationist, was separated from it, though still a rigorous Sabbatarian, and one of the Informing officers appointed to see that the laws regulating the observance of the Sabbath were strictly enforced, on May 1, 1781. He afterwards also held the same office in the town of Sherburne, N. Y.

He must have removed to Florida, Montgomery Co., N. Y., as early as 1782, as a son was born to him there of that date. From that place he removed to Sherburne, Chenango Co., N. Y., in 1793, he and and one of his sons, John Gray, Jr., being of the original twenty pioneer families who settled that place. An old map of the first survey of that quarter of the township shows his name as having drawn Lot No. 12, 130 acres, in the division of the lands. It proved to be a valuable tract, and the present beautiful and prosperous village of Sherburne is located almost wholly upon it. Mrs. Bicknell, an old lady still residing there, well remembers when Mr. Gray's log house was standing in what is now the centre of the business part of that town, corner of East and North Street, and opposite the Soldiers' Monument. He was a public spirited citizen, interested much in all that pertained to the welfare of the growing settlement, and was influential in securing the extension of the Cherry Valley Turnpike, in those early days a very important thoroughfare, through to Sherburne.

As heretofore stated, the starting point of this Genealogy was a record kept by John Gray (4.) There are two of these memorandums, one being in the form of a diary with yearly entries. The latter is a unique document, and is here given entire :

JOHN GRAY'S DIARY.

Nov. 16, 1813.—My wife and I have this day lived together half a century. Have had 12 children; 3 are gone, 9 remain living. We have had 62 grandchildren, 49 of whom remain living. We have had 4 great grandchildren, all living.

My great grandfather moved from England among the former settlers; had six sons. I live in remembrance of more than one-third part of the time since the first settlement of New England. I remember four wars; two with France, one glorious and one foolish with England. The world that I was born into has almost all left me and I now live in a a world of strangers.

Nov. 16, 1814.—My wife and I have lived together another year. Have added to our progeny 3 grand children and 1 great grandchild, since dead.

Nov. 16, 1815.—We have lived together another year, in which have been born 1 grandchild and 3 great grandchildren; 1 dead.

Nov. 16, 1816.—We have lived together another year, in which have been born 3 grand children and 3 great grandchildren.

Nov. 16, 1817.—My wife and I have lived together another year, which makes fifty-four. In this last have been born 2 grandchildren and 1 great grandchild.

Nov. 16, 1818.—We have lived together another year, in which have been born 2 grandchildren and 4 great grandchildren; 1 dead.

Nov. 16, 1819.—We have lived together another year, in which have been born 2 grandchildren and 2 great grandchildren.

Nov. 16, 1820.—We have lived together another year, in which have been born 2 grandchildren and 2 great grandchildren.

Nov. 16, 1821.—We have lived together another year, in which have been born 1 grandchild and 4 great grandchildren.

This closes the diary of John Gray, so significant in its brevity and comprehensiveness, dignified, yet so full of pathos and tenderness. The harp of life was broken. At a good old age, in his 83d year, Sept. 22, 1822, he was gathered to his fathers, and was buried in the Sherburne Quarter Cemetery, near his brother Nathaniel, who had preceded him. His aged and beloved wife, who followed him March 10, 1824, was buried by his side, in the same resting place of the dead.

A granddaughter, who remembers him well, describes him as a venerable man, erect of form, and with long silvered hair. He was conscientious, philosophical, a man of thought, and lived a most exemplary and useful life. He was an earnest, devoted Christian, and in a letter written to one of his sons describing a great revival which took place in Sherburne in 1820, he used the following language, significant of his glowing hope and strong desire : "Thus may Christ go on conquering and to conquer until all shall become subject to Him."

CHILDREN OF JOHN AND BETSEY GRAY.

JERUSHA, born in Sharon, Conn., Aug. 29, 1764 ; died in Florida, Montgomery Co., N. Y., Sept. 10, 1786.

BETSEY, born in Sharon, April 13, 1766; mar. Abraham Raymond, (brother of Newcomb and James Raymond, all of Kent, Conn., and among the proprietors and first settlers of Sherburne, N. Y.,) May 5, 1783. Children:

Mercy, b. Apr. 18, 1785; David, b. May 21, 1787; Ebenezer, (Rev.) b. Mar. 3, 1789; John, b. Feb. 10, 1791; Abigail, b. Apr. 21, 1793, mar. Rev. Alvin T. Smith and journeyed over the Rocky Mountains on horseback as a Missionary to the Indians in Oregon, in 1840; Cynthia, b. Mar. 28, 1795; Lodema, b. Mar. 18, 1797; Electa, (1) b. Apr. 3, 1799; Josiah, b. April 10, 1801; Benjamin Newcomb, b. Feb. 20, 1804; Lodema, (2.) b. Dec. 21, 1805; Electa, (2) b. Jan. 3, 1808; Semantha, b. Feb. 8, 1811.

Betsey Gray Raymond had the honor of being the first woman among the settlers of Sherburne, and for several months was the only woman there. She and her husband were both charter members of the Congregational Church of that place, he being one of the first two Deacons chosen. He died at Sherburne, May 12, 1830; she afterwards removed to Victor, N. Y., where she died April 21, 1839.

MABEL, born in Sharon, Nov. 10, 1767, mar. Aug. 10, 1785, Newcomb Raymond, son of David, of Kent, Conn., he son of Abraham of Kent and Norwalk, Conn., son of Thomas, son of John (2), son of John (1), son of Richard Raymond of Beverly and Salem, Mass., 1630, of Norwalk 1660, and afterwards of Saybrook, Conn., where he died 1692. The following children were born of this marriage: Sarai Raymond, b. June 2, 1786; Jerusha, b. Feb. 16, 1788; Harvey, b. Mar. 23, 1790; Irad, b. June, 22, 1792; Alfred (1), b. June 1st, 1794; Anna, b. Mar. 7, 1796; Alfred (2), b. Nov. 4, 1798; Laura, b. Nov. 26, 1800; Augustine, b. Nov. 1. 1802; George B., b. Aug. 15, 1808.——Alfred Raymond (2) mar. Sarah Gardiner, dau. of Henry Gardiner son of William Gardiner of the Gardiners of Gardiner's Island, at Sherburne, N. Y., April 13, 1826. Children: Ruth, b. Jan. 9, 1827; William H., b. Sept. 9, 1828; Angeline, b. Feb. 19, 1831; Marcius D., b. Apr. 8, 1833; Edgar and Edwin, twin brothers, b. January 19, 1836; Alfred Gray, b. Mar. 1, 1837; Sarah C., b. Sept 7, 1839; Hervey, b. Nov. 4, 1841; LaMont Gardiner, b. Apr. 8, 1845; Amelia Newton, b. Nov.17, 1847. Sarah Gardiner d. Feb. 6, 1849. Alfred Raymond mar. 2nd, Mrs. Nancy Purdy. He d. Dec. 3, 1880; she d. Feb. 26, 1879. ——Marcius D. Raymond son of Alfred, mar. Elnora H. Purdy, Sept. 19, 1855, at Sherburne, N. Y. Child: Lizzie May Raymond, b. Springfield, O., May 4, 1858; mar. Joseph E. See, at Tarrytown, N. Y., Apr. 19, 1882; son, Raymond Gardiner See, b. Tarrytown, Feb. 14, 1883.

MABEL GRAY.

Mabel Gray Raymond was a woman of many attractive and lovable qualities. Her memory is precious to all who knew her, and is treasured as a priceless legacy by her descendants. An aged relative, Mrs. Amanda Gray Lee, of Cedar Mountain, N. C., now in her 94th year, who well remembers her, says of her, date of Feb. 11, 1886: "In person Mabel Gray was of medium size, and well proportioned, with fair complexion and dark hair and eyes. She was a woman of strong intellect and independent character; a great reader, and possessed of unusual conversational powers; genial in manner, and entertaining alike to old and young; which engaging gifts she continued to retain even when a confirmed invalid, as was the case during the later years of her life. She was a general favorite, and when a child one of the greatest of treats to me was a visit to Aunt Mabel." She was one of the original members of the Congregational Church of Sherburne, at which place she continued to reside until her decease, Feb. 11, 1826. Her husband, Newcomb Raymond, a patriot soldier of the Revolution, an upright man and a devout Christian, died in 1852 aged 89 years. "E'en the ashes of the just, smell sweet and blossom in the dust."

> JOHN (5), b. in Canaan, N. Y., Dec. 15, 1769; d. at Forestville, N. Y., April 24, 1859.
>
> EDWARD (1), b. in Canaan, N. Y., Sept. 24, 1771, d. same place and year.
>
> NATHANIEL, b. in Canaan, Aug. 4, 1773; d. at Savannah, Ill., 1855.
>
> ALFRED (1), b. in Canaan, Mar. 24, 1775; d. in same place, Oct. 17, 1775.
>
> ANNE, b. in Canaan, Oct. 8, 1776; mar. William Ryneck; d. at Lincklaen, N. Y., Aug. 1, 1838, leaving two sons and six daughters.
>
> ALFRED (2), b. in Canaan, July 29, 1778; d. at Montreal, Canada, Sept. 3, 1820.
>
> EDWARD (2), b. in Canaan, June 20, 1780; d. at Alexander, Genesee Co., N. Y., June 13, 1830.
>
> REUBEN, b. in Florida, N. Y., Aug. 15, 1782; d. at Elmira, N. Y., 1860.
>
> MARGARET, b. in Florida, N. Y., Jan. 15, 1785; mar. Wm. Burns, from Scotland; had a son and two daughters.

JOHN GRAY.

JOHN GRAY (5.)

Born in Canaan, N. Y., Dec. 15, 1769, his boyhood was mainly spent there, and living in that eventful Revolutionary period, and on the border ground, almost within hearing of the battles of Stillwater and Saratoga, in which his father participated, he must have been thoroughly imbued with the patriotic spirit of those stirring times, for at the age of fourteen he enlisted in Col. Willett's command, and did duty on what was then the western frontier of the State, until the cessation of hostilities. He had already attained to the ordinary stature of a man, and was physically competent to bear arms. Such a boyhood well prepared him for a cheerful and loyal discharge of all the duties of citizenship.

On the removal of his father's family to Florida, N. Y., 1781–2, he made that place and Duanesburgh his home until his removal to Sherburne, Chenango County, N. Y., about 1794–5. He married Diantha Burritt, daughter of the Rev. Blackleach Burritt, a Congregationalist Minister who used to take his musket into the pulpit for defence, and for ready joining in offensive warfare, if need be, who was captured by the British near White Plains, N. Y., and for a long time confined in the notorious Sugar House Prison at New York. It is worthy of record here in this connection, that while the Patriot Pastor was so incarcerated, being sick almost unto death, he was kindly ministered unto by William Irving, father of Washington Irving, and to whom he afterwards gave a quaint certificate vouching for his loyalty and setting forth the facts of the case, he (Irving) evidently being under the impression that his residence in the city during the war might expose him to proscription on the part of the now victorious Patriots. The document is published in Vol. I., of Washington Irving's Biography, and reference is made to the fact in the Burritt Family Record.

The marriage took place at Winhall, Vt., May 26, 1793, the father of the bride officiating. The bans published at the close of the morning sermon, a sermon for the occasion was prepared in the intermission, and the marriage ceremony was performed at the close of the afternoon service. It had been decided by the family, after the father had gone to "the meeting," (early, as was his custom,) that as sisters were there from a distance,

and the horse-back journey from Duanesburgh, N. Y., made by the
expectant bridegroom for the visit, was a long and tedious one,
it was best that the union be then and there consummated, not-
withstanding that the bride to be was then engaged in teaching
school. A witness of the scene said he well remembered the weep-
ing of the bride in it all. When asked by her child in after
years why this was, she replied, " I deeply felt my unfitness
through youth and inexperience, for the responsibilities and trials
awaiting a maiden of eighteen years." Her husband and children always "rose up and called her blessed," for her faithful and
loving wifehood and motherhood, trained as she was in the
school of those times to be a true helpmeet to her husband in
life's responsibilities. Quite naturally their five sons were all
staunch Republicans, Temperance and Anti-Slavery men, and
though not called themselves to defend our National liberties in
war, were ever the promoters of the good things of peace times,
and when the strife to preserve our federal compact inviolate
came, gave their benediction to their sons, who fought for the
Union, made and sealed by the blood of their ancestors.

The bride and groom evidently soon set their faces in the direction of their to be new home in the wilderness, at Sherburne,
N. Y., where the enterprising husband had already secured an
interest, being one of the thirteen original Proprietors of a
Quarter of a township in the fertile and beautiful valley of the
Chenango, the first settlement of which was made in 1793. Mr.
Gray was a prominent citizen of the thriving town, in the church
as well as in public affairs, and in 1813 he took a seat upon the
bench as Associate Judge, being so chosen by the unanimous
action of both parties—a significant tribute to his integrity and
worth as a man.

Judge Gray removed with his family to Chautauqua Co., N. Y.,
in 1819, and continued to reside there until his decease, which
took place April 24, 1859. The following brief " in memorian"
sketch is from the pen of William Cullen Bryant, in the N. Y.
Evening Post:

"Judge Gray, the father of Dr. John F. Gray of this city, died
on Saturday last, at Forestville in Chautauqua County, in his
ninety-first year. He was a remarkable example of mental activity and bodily health preserved to a late old age—cheerful,
benevolent, and enjoying life to the last. Another link has been

struck from the chain of living testimony, which but a few years ago, seemed to bind us so firmly to the men of the Revolution. The last years of his life were passed in retirement at his residence at Forestville, interrupted only by occasional visits to his son in New York. Of the hundreds who are bound to Dr. Gray by the tender ties of physician and patient, there are few who will not long remember the commanding form, scarcely bent by age, the silver lock and the serene and benignant countenance, that used to appear from time to time in his crowded rooms, as if to remind us how grand and how beautiful old age may be,

> " 'When watched by eyes that love him, calm and sage,
> Slow fade his late declining years away.' "

CHILDREN OF JOHN GRAY (5) AND DIANTHA BURRITT HIS WIFE.

NATHANIEL, b. in Duanesburgh, N. Y., Nov. 7th, 1794; d. at Silver Creek, N. Y., Jan., 1872.

BLACKLEACH B., Rev., b. in Sherburne, N. Y., Mar. 31, 1797; d. Canandaugua, N. Y., Feb. 18, 1870.

DIANTHA (1), b. in Sherburne, July 22, 1799; d. July 28, 1800.

ALFRED W., Dr., b. in Sherburne, April 15, 1802; d. at Milwaukee, Wis., Jan. 8, 1873.

JOHN F., (6), Dr., b. in Sherburne, Sept. 23, 1804; d. June 5, 1882.

PATRICK W., Dr., b. in Sherburne, Nov. 18, 1806; d. at Elmira, N. Y., Dec. 18, 1865.

DIANTHA, 2d, b. in Sherburne, March 8, 1809.

SAMUEL B., b. Oct. 10, 1812; d. Nov. 14, 1812.

JOHN F. GRAY (6.)

Dr. John Franklin Gray was born in Sherburne, N. Y., on September 23, 1804, and was the fourth of five sons of John Gray, one of the first settlers in that town. When he was fifteen years old his father moved to Chautauqua County. There were no good schools in that part of the State then, but young Gray was very industrious in his studies and obtained a good education. At an early age he chose medicine as his profession, but as his father's means were limited, he had to earn the money for obtaining his medical education. He first entered the office of Dr. Haven, of Hamilton. He stayed there for two years, and afterward went to Dunkirk, N. Y., where he opened a private school, studying medicine all the time under Dr. Williams. In 1824 he went to New York, entered the College of Physicians and Surgeons and obtained his degree in 1826. Soon after his graduation Dr. Gray opened an office, and was successful from the first.

He married a daughter of Dr. Amos G. Hull, a prominent physician of that city. Soon after his marriage, Dr. Gray learned of Hahnemann's medical theories through Hans B. Gram, a Danish doctor, who was born in Boston of Danish parents and educated in Denmark. He heard Dr. Gram lecture, but was not convinced. He then reluctantly consented to let Dr. Gram treat one of his patients whose case had resisted his own skill. Dr. Gram had remarkable success, not only with that patient but with others, and Dr. Gray was converted to Homœopathy. He announced his intention openly, of practicing according to that system, and in consequence lost his profitable practice, and all his professional friends. He endured many hardships and much ill treatment for his devotion to Homœopathy. He studied German so that he might become more familiar with Hahnemann's works, and opened a correspondence with that distinguished physician that continued till Hahnemann's death.

Dr. Gray soon made many converts among his acquaintances and relatives. His brother-in-law, Dr. A. Gerald Hull, was one of the first, and two of his brothers followed soon after. Dr. Gray was the first to propose the formation of a National Society of Homœopathists, and in 1844 the American Institute of Homœopathy was organized. Previously, in 1834, aided by

Dr. Hull, he had commenced the publication of the first Homœ-opathic journal, *The Examiner*, to which he was a frequent contributor. He was also the author of "The Early Annals of Homœopathy," published in 1863. It should be stated in this connection, that Dr. Gray was the first convert to Homœopathy in this country, and was for a long period its most distinguished advocate.

Dr. Gray was an accomplished classical scholar. He received the honorary degree of Doctor of Laws from Hamilton College in 1871. He was always an earnest advocate of a high standard of medical scholarship, and was instrumental in having the law passed establishing the State Board of Medical Examiners. He was chosen President of the first Board of Examiners, and always kept the position.

Dr. Gray was a member of the "Society of the Cincinnati," having been admitted July 4th, 1860; he was the Physician of the Society from July 4th, 1878, until his death, June 5th, 1882, and by a general order issued, the members of the Society were requested to attend his funeral at Dr. Hall's Church, Fifth Ave-and 55th St., New York, on Thursday, June 8th. Dr. Gray was also a member of the N. Y. Historical Society.

Dr. Gray was strong in his attachment to his family and kindred, and all memories of such association were by him fondly cherished. The place of his birth and the home of his early years was ever to him an object of much interest, and the anniversary of his leaving it to go out into the world of strangers was always by him remembered, the day of "Removal" being next sacred, in his family calendar, to days of Birth, and Burial. His description of a visit made by him to Sherburne, after nearly fifty years of absence, and his recognition of a kinsman there, not seen in all that long period; then young, now a gray haired veteran; by a strong resemblance in his eyes to those of his mother, the Doctor's dear "Aunt Mabel," was a striking evidence of the strength of such attachments in him. While there he also looked after the graves of his ancestors with pious care, and attended to the preservation of memorial stones that had been set up. It pleased him to find that while times had changed, old forms and customs still remained; on the Sabbath he heard the same prayers uttered, the same songs sung, and the same doctrines preached as when a boy. And it gratified him that it should be so.   Half a century of busy, active life in the great metropolis, fame fairly won, and a professional career rarely equalled in the full measure of its success, had not changed the simplicity and sincerity of his nature. The old loves were still the strongest.

And at the last, after investigating with deep philosophical insight the facts of science, and after all analytical and metaphysical research, in the true child-like spirit of the humble, believing disciple, he trusted only and wholly in Christ as his Redeemer, Saviour. To which fact, his beloved pastor, Dr. John Hall, gave ample testimony in his funeral discourse, in the presence of the great and notable assemblage which had gathered to do honor to the memory of the eminent and beloved physician, Dr. Gray.

DESCENDANTS OF DR. JOHN F. GRAY (6).

Dr. Gray married Elizabeth W. Hull, in New York, Sept. 25, 1826, by whom were the following children :

ELIZABETH W., daughter of Dr. John F. Gray, (6), b. 1827; mar. Dr. Lewis T. Warner, 1848; d. Sept. 1865; he d. 1882. children:

GERALD GRAY WARNER, b. May 9, 1851.

JOHN FRANKLIN GRAY WARNER, b. July 21, 1859; d. July 29, 1860.

MARY WARNER, b. 1861; mar. Henry H. Sherwood, of San Francisco, Aug. 18, 1885.

LOUISE WARNER, b. Oct. 1865; mar. Chas. Loring Brace, Jr., of Dobb's Ferry, N. Y., Jan. 14, 1885, and resides at Minneapolis, Minn.

JOHN F. S. GRAY, Dr., (7), b. in New York, July, 1840 ; mar. Anna Howell, 1865. Following children:

GERALD H., b. Sept. 20, 1866; member of class of '89, Harvard College.

JOHN F., (8), b. Dec. 18, 1867; pupil with Rev. Edward Everett Hale, at Roxbury, Mass.

EDWARD F., b. Apr. 1869; d. Oct. 14, 1877.

ELIZABETH WILLIAMS, b. July 18, 1870.

MARY, b. Sept. 1871; d. Jan. 1873.

MARY L., daughter of Dr. John F. Gray, (6), b. 1846; mar. Benjamin Knower, of New York, 1873; d. April 13, 1879, leaving no children.

Also there were the following deceased children of Dr. John F. Gray (6) : John, Josephine, John 2d, Geraldine, aged 19 years, and Edward, who died aged 16, while at Harvard Preparatory School.

NATHANIEL GRAY.

The eldest son of John Gray (5), he was born at Duanesburgh, N. Y., Nov. 7th, 1795, and soon after removed with his parents to Sherburne, Chenango County, N. Y., where his father was one of the pioneer settlers. He married Harriet Dewey, at Lisle, N. Y., in Feb., 1824, and removed to Chautauqua Co., N. Y. He was elected Member of Assembly, and served in the State Legislature during the session of 1833. He was also several times chosen Supervisor of his town, and evinced much aptitude for public affairs, and an uprightness that gave him large respect and confidence.

Mr. Gray was a man of great sincerity, strong convictions, and was a devoted Christian. His pastor, speaking at his funeral, said: "Our departed friend had been for over half a century a professed follower of Jesus, having joined the Church as a young man. I can say that it was always a good thing for me to commune with him. You well know, how long after infirmity might have been thought to excuse him, he attended regularly on the services of God's house, and took his part among Christ's people, in witnessing for Jesus, in teaching the Word in the Bible Class, and in other duties of a Christian. I remember well his peculiar pleasure in attending the meetings held for Sabbath School children, and his earnest endeavors to give interest, and a useful direction to all such occasions. And the children always loved to see and hear him as he spoke to them in cheerful and instructive words. Naturally Mr. Gray was of a somewhat doubting and desponding turn, but his faith was able usually to rise above the depression incident to such a temperament. I remember well how earnestly once an old and true friend of his, Rev. Nathaniel Smith, inquired of me after his former friend and dear co-worker in the vineyard, Nathaniel Gray."

Such was the tenor of this good man's life. Singularly pure and upright, universally and highly esteemed, he had a constitutional inheritance which subjected him at times to religious melancholy and depression of mind. Withal he had good musical talent, which he cultivated to some extent for especial use in Sabbath School work. He was a man of sensitive nature, and many admirable qualities; a brother beloved. He left no children. His wife, who survived him, died January 5, 1877.

BLACKLEACH BURRITT GRAY.

Rev. Blackleach Burritt Gray, second son of Judge John Gray (5), was born at Sherburne, N. Y., March 31, 1797. He bore the name of his maternal grandfather, Rev. Blackleach Burritt, a man who was notorious in his day as a preacher and a patriot. Educated at Hamilton College, and Auburn Theological Seminary, in September, 1829, he was licensed to preach by the Buffalo Presbytery, and was ordained and installed first as pastor of the Presbyterian Church at Sheridan, Chautauqua County, New York, where his father resided. He preached at Sheridan from May 12, 1830, until Oct. 9, 1833, when he was called to the Presbyterian Church at Byron, Genesee Co., N. Y.; preaching there until April, 1837, he was called to the Presbyterian Church at Jamestown, Chautauqua Co., N. Y., where he officiated until 1840, when he removed to Brighton, Monroe Co., N. Y., and had the charge of the Presbyterian Church at that place for the period of ten years.

About the year 1850 he was called to the Presbyterian Church at Seneca Castle, Ontario Co., N. Y., where he preached for nearly eighteen years, when from feeble health and infirmity of years, he resigned his charge in his seventieth year, and retired from the ministry, removing to a home which his son, Gen. John B. Gray, of St. Louis, had provided for him at Canandaigua, N. Y.

There, in his declining years and feebleness, he was most pleasantly and comfortably situated in the bosom of his family and amid Christian friends, until he was attacked by typhoid fever, and after an illness of several weeks, died on Feb. 18, 1870, aged 73 years. As a layman and pastor for fifty years, he labored earnestly and faithfully in the cause of Christ, and his ministrations were most successful in the conversion of sinners. Many men, much more distinguished by worldly honors, have accomplished much less for the salvation of souls.

He was married at Auburn, N. Y., Sept. 25, 1829, to Miss Mary N. Arnett, daughter of William and Mary Arnett. She was his faithful companion and judicious counsellor, whose sympathizing heart and hand did much to sustain and encourage him through his arduous labors, and in raising his family. She survived him for ten years, and died at the home of her son, Gen. John B. Gray, at Saint Louis, May 12, 1880, aged 76 years.

B.V.B. Gray

25.

JOHN BURRITT GRAY, Gen., b. at Sheridan, N. Y., June 25, 1831; mar. Mary F. Morehouse, at Springfield, Ill., Nov. 15, 1854. Children:

LILLIE HULL GRAY, b. Aug. 13, 1856; mar. Richard P. Hanenkamp, Jr., at St. Louis, Mo., Dec. 18, 1878. Children: Ethel Hanenkamp, b. Jan. 30, 1880; d. Sept. 18, 1882. Ralph Gray Hanenkamp, b. Nov. 26, 1883; d. Apr. 12, 1884.

MINNIE GRAY, b. Nov. 12, 1858; d. Aug. 16, 1860.

His first wife having died, at Auburn, N. Y., Nov. 5, 1861, John B. Gray married 2d, Caroline L. A. Favis, Aug. 31, 1877.

SAMUEL ORTON GRAY, son of Rev. Blackleach B. Gray, b. Jan. 28, 1834; d. Jan. 9, 1835.

MARY DIANTHA GRAY, b. July 12, 1835; d. Feb. 10, 1837.

MARY DIANTHA GRAY, 2d, b. at Jamestown, N. Y., June 12, 1838; mar. Henry J. Peck, at Seneca Castle, N. Y., Oct. 18, 1859. Children:

FRED B. PECK, b. Aug. 18, 1860.
JAMES I. PECK, b. Aug. 10, 1863.
MARY GRAY PECK, b. Oct. 21, 1867.

WILLIAM ARNETT GRAY, son of Rev. Blackleach B. Gray, b. at Brighton, N. Y., June 10, 1840; mar. Lydia A. Keevil, June 12, 1880. Issue:

ALICE GRAY, b. Oct. 20, 1881.

William A. Gray has been connected with the American Express Company in various positions of trust for the past twenty years, and is still in the employ of that Company, at Cleveland, Ohio.

JAMES RICHARD GRAY, son of Rev. Blackleach B. Gray, b. at Brighton, N. Y., April 9, 1844. His first marriage was with Sarah H. Scott, at Kansas City, Mo., July 20, 1870, of which marriage were born:

MARY P. GRAY, b. March 6, 1871.
JOHN B. GRAY, Jr., b. July 10, 1874.

Mr. Gray's first wife died Oct. 5, 1875, and his second marriage was with Margaret Hutchison, at St. Louis, Mo., May 12, 1880, of which marriage were born:

FRED GRAY, b. Oct. 9, 1881.
ROY GRAY, b. May 12, 1883.
RICHARD GRAY, b. Mar. 10, 1885.

JOHN BURRITT GRAY.

Gen. John Burritt Gray, the eldest son of Rev. Blackleach B. Gray, born at Sheridan, N. Y., June 25, 1831, on becoming of age removed to Saint Louis, Mo., where he was engaged in business for some ten years prior to the war. The call to arms did not find him debating the question of his loyalty, but with all the ardor of a patriotic nature he espoused the Union cause, and from the first gave to it strong and courageous support.

He was associated with Gens. Lyon, Schofield, and Frank P. Blair, in organizing and drilling the loyal men of the State of Missouri during the summer of 1861. In November of that year, he accepted a staff position with Gen. Halleck as Lieut. Col. and A. D. C., and was assigned to duty with Gen. Scofield. In the summer of 1862 he was commissioned Colonel of the 1st Infantry M. S. M., and also Brigadier General of the Missouri Militia. He served with his Regiment, and by seniority as Col. commanded a Brigade in the field for several months, and until the spring of 1863, when he accepted the position of Adjutant General of Missouri, which he held until the close of the war.

His duties were onerous and responsibilities great. The State was divided almost equally as to loyalty and disloyalty, and there was a neighborhood or partisan warfare throughout its borders, compelling the maintenance of a small army of its own which co-operated with the United States troops in suppressing the Rebellion. About one hundred Regiments of this force made their returns and reports direct to Gen. Gray, in addition to the business of a hundred more Regiments of Missouri Volunteers, which were in the service of the United States; so that his position was different, and more difficult than that of the Adjutants General of the loyal States, whose duties consisted mainly in organizing their respective volunteers and turning them over to the authorities.

Gen. Gray sought service in the field, but circumstances prevented it; the loyal old Governor, (Gamble) insisted upon his taking the chief position upon his staff, which he accepted, and doubtless so rendered his country as much service as he could have given had he commanded a fighting brigade or division on the field.

John B Gray

At the close of the war, Gen. Gray prepared and presented to Congress the claim of Missouri for reimbursement of monies expended on behalf of the United States in supporting troops, and after two years' work succeeded in collecting and paying into the State Treasury upwards of seven millions of dollars in settlement of that claim. In 1867 he declined the office of Postmaster of St. Louis, tendered him by President Johnson, and he was afterwards offered the position of Third Auditor of the Treasury by President Grant. His name was also prominently mentioned in connection with other and higher office, but he declined public service, preferring to engage in the activities of business affairs. For several years past he has been connected with the American Patent Brake Co., of which he is the Vice President, with headquarters now in New York.

JAMES R. GRAY.

James R. Gray served with credit in the war for the Union, as 1st Lieutenant of the 7th Missouri Volunteer Cavalry, and upon the staff of General Davidson in the Arkansas campaign, receiving honorable mention from the General in his reports, especially in the battle resulting in the capture of Little Rock. He served with Gen. Davidson during some two years of the war, when he resigned on account of ill health. Nearly ever since he has occupied, and still holds the position of Clerk of the Circuit Court of St. Louis.

ALFRED WLLIAM GRAY.

Alfred William Gray, M. D., third son of John Gray (5), was born in Sherburne, N. Y., April 15, 1802, and spent his youth and early manhood in that place. His father was for many years Associate Judge of Chenango County, and prominent among the early settlers there. His mother was the daughter of a Presbyterian clergyman of note, and a lady of character and culture.

Dr. Gray's early education was acquired in the public schools of the County, and after graduating from them he was placed under the care of a valued friend of the family practising medicine in the neighborhood. From the office of that physician, after a tutorship of four years, he passed the examination of the Chenango County Medical Society, and received the degree of Doctor of Medicine. He afterwards practised his profession at Sacketts Harbor, N. Y., and there married Valeria Elizabeth Dodd, in 1823.

He was appointed Surgeon in the N. Y. State Militia, by Gov. De Witt Clinton, and after a few years' service, he resumed private practice at Jamestown, Chautauqua County, N. Y., from whence he removed to Milwaukee, Wis., in 1856, where he practised his profession until the time of his death, Jan. 8, 1873.

Dr. Gray was a skilful Surgeon, and while residing at Jamestown, he successfully performed the very difficult and hazardous operation (the second of the kind it is said that was performed in the United States,) of removing an ovarian tumor,—a very large one,—assisted only by one of his medical students. Years afterwards, in remarking upon his emotions on that occasion, he stated that before the patient went on the table, he shook like a leaf in the wind, for he was about to cut where, if the knife swerved a hair's breadth, it might be fatal. " But *after prayer* with the patient, I was as steady as a rock, and I could then have cut her into pieces without a quiver, if it had been necessary to do so."

Dr. Gray was a devoted Christian, and his faith in God was something wonderful. He was a man of pronounced religious principle, and a light in the Presbyterian faith, in which church he officiated as pastor for a period of two years during his residence in Chautauqua Co., N. Y.

DESCENDANTS OF DR. ALFRED W. GRAY.

DEBORAH, b. 1825; d. at the age of five years.

JOHN, b. 1827; d. at six months old.

MARY E., daughter, of Grand Rapids, Mich., b. at Watertown, N. Y., July 18, 1830; mar. Danford Miller Crosby, Esq., at Jamestown, N. Y., June 14, 1849, and resides at Grand Rapids, Mich. Children:

> ALFRED WILLIAM, b. at Jamestown, N. Y., Apr. 3, 1850, now residing at Round Rock, Texas.

> HATTIE VALERIA, b. at Ionia, Mich., Jan. 12, 1857; mar. Amos De Courcey Greene, at Grand Rapids, Mich.; children : Alfred De Courcey, b. July 31, 1878; Cora Valeria, b. Apr. 13, 1884.

JANE A., daughter, b. July, 1831 ; mar. to James Foote, at Jamestown, N. Y., Nov. 5, 1850; d. in Oct., 1862. Children :

> MINNIE E., b. Dec. 1, 1851; mar. Dr. Geo. E. Morgan, 1869; resides in New York.

> VALERIA, b. Mar. 30, 1854; mar. Henry Treadwell of New York.

> HARRIET, b. Aug. 16, 1856; mar. William Treadwell, of New York.

> HARRY.

FRANCES GRAY, daughter, of Cambridge, N. Y., b. in Sheridan, Chautauqna Co., N. Y., Dec. 8, 1833; mar. to Rev. Henry G. Blinn, Nov. 5, 1850. Children:

> KATE GOODWIN, b. in Jamestown, N. Y., Jan. 31, 1852; mar. Russell Cole, July 4, 1871, at Cambridge, Washington Co., N. Y. Alfred Thomas Cole, son, b. July, 1874, d. Aug. 20, 1880. Mr. Russell Cole died same year, and Mrs. Cole mar. 2d, Christian Emil Lohmann, Oct. 10, 1882. Mr. Lohmann, is a native of Copenhagen, an architect and artist. Present residence, Chicago.

ALFRED BARRETT BLINN, b. in Tecumseh, Mich., Feb. 11, 1859; d. Sept. 17, 1863, at Cohoes, N. Y.

FRANCIS GRAY BLINN, Dr., b. in Tecumseh, Mich., Jan. 23, 1861; mar. Louise Bloeden, at South Saginaw, Mich., May 26, 1883; now practising medicine at Lansing, Mich. Anna Minnie, daughter, was b. in Chicago, Ill., Mar. 7th, 1884.

VALERIA, daughter, b. at Panama, Chautauqua Co., N. Y., Mar. 14, 1836; mar. Rev. Thomas Sherrard, at Milwaukee, Wis., June 21, 1860. Children:

HENRY GRAY, b. at Centralia, Ill., Aug. 6, 1861; Professor of Classics, at Detroit, Mich.

MARGARET P., b. at Centralia, Ill., Mar. 20, 1863; mar. Prof. Charlton T. Lewis, of New York, June 30, 1885.

EVELYN BARRETT, b. Aug. 26, 1864, at Centralia, Ill.; residence, Tecumseh, Mich.

VALERIA GRAY, b. Mar. 19, 1867, at Brooklyn, Mich., d. Feb. 22, 1877.

HARRIET WINIFRED, b. at Brooklyn, Mich., Jan. 25, 1869.

THOMAS HINDMAN, b. at Brooklyn, Mich., May 17, 1874.

Rev. Thomas Sherrard died at Brooklyn, Mich. Aug. 10, 1874.

HARRIET, daughter, b. at Panama, N. Y., Mar. 31, 1838; mar. Dwight W. Jackson in 1858; d. at Brooklyn, Mich., Sept. 10, 1873.

ALFRED GRAY, b. Dec. 1840; killed by a barrel of wet ashes falling upon him in July, 1844.

NATHANIEL A., Dr., of Milwaukee, Wis., b. at Portland, N. Y., Mar. 8, 1842; mar. Letitia Dunn, at New Lisbon, Wis., 1866.

NATHANIEL A. GRAY.

Nathaniel A. Gray, M. D., of Milwaukee, Wis., son of Dr. Alfred W. Gray, was born in Chautauqua Co., N. Y., March 8, 1842, and received his earlier training in the Academy at Jamestown, N. Y. Leaving that State in 1856, with his parents, who emigrated westward and took up their abode in Milwaukee, he entered as a pupil in the High School of that city, completing his literary studies in 1861.

Medical culture having been his objective point, he commenced his career under the tutelage of his father, an eminent and skilful physician, with whom he remained four years, and then completed his medical studies at Bellevue and N. Y. Homœopathic Hospitals, where he received his degree of M. D., in 1867.

Dr. Gray was married at New Lisbon, Juneau County, Wis., Feb. 29th, 1866, to Letitia Dunn, a native of Portage City, Wis., the daughter of Andrew and Sarah Dunn, two of the early pioneers in Wisconsin's Territorial history.

To Nathaniel and Letitia Gray have been born four children, as follows:

Sarah Elizabeth Gray, b. Apr. 23, 1867.
Nathaniel Gray, b. June 8, 1869; d. Aug. 20, 1870.
Alfred William Gray, b. Sept. 26, 1873.
Walter K. Gray, b. Nov. 28, 1878.

Dr. N. A. Gray has a large practice, and deservedly takes high rank in the medical profession of Milwaukee. He was for several years Secretary of the Homœopathic State Medical Society of Wisconsin, and has been officially connected with the Asylum for the insane in that State.

PATRICK WELLS GRAY.

Dr. Patrick Wells Gray, fifth and youngest son of Judge John Gray (5), was born in Sherburne, N. Y., Nov. 18th, 1806. Removing with his father's family to western New York, in 1819, he afterwards studied medicine with Dr. Beebe, of Erie, Pa., and graduating at an allopathic school entered upon the practice of medicine.

Dr. Gray married Amy Wentworth Graves, at Erie, Pa., Sept. 29th, 1830, after which he took up Theology, graduating at Oberlin College, and was ordained and installed in the Presbyterian ministry, at Randolph, Pa. Subsequently he was stationed at Hamburg, N. Y., preaching at these places some five years, after which, in 1842, he resumed the practice of medicine, having, in the meantime, by study and careful investigation, become converted to the Homœopathic school. At that time he removed to Buffalo, then having a population of twenty or twenty-five thousand. He was the pioneer of Homœopathy there, and continued the practice of his profession in that city some ten years. Being afflicted with a throat and bronchial affection which was aggravated by Lake winds, Dr. Gray removed from Buffalo to Elmira, N. Y., in 1852, where he continued in a large and lucrative practice until his decease, Dec. 18, 1865. His wife, Mrs. Amy W. Gray, survived him some three years.

DESCENDANTS OF DR. PATRICK WELLS GRAY.

CARROLL E. GRAY, b. in Madison, Ohio, July 23, 1831.

HARRIET DIANTHA GRAY, b. in Portland, N. Y., March 9th, 1835; mar. Wellington Gray Lee, son of Joel Lee and Amanda Gray Lee, and great-great-grandson of John Gray (3) of Sharon, in London, England, June 5, 1862. He d. in New York, 1881. Her present residence is at Hornellsville, N. Y. Children: An infant daughter died in London, England, May 7, 1863.

JOHN F. GRAY LEE, b. Aug. 5, 1867; d. Aug. 16, 1867.

WELLINGTON GRAY LEE, b. Apr. 11, 1869.

THEODORE W. GRAY, b. in Westfield, N. Y., Aug. 29, 1837; d. at Randolph, Pa., Aug. 1, 1840.

ROLLIN B. GRAY, Dr., b. in Randolph, Pa., June 4, 1840.

ELLA ELIZABETH GRAY, of Hornellsville, N. Y., b. in Buffalo, N. Y., Aug. 2, 1846.

Carroll Eugene Gray

CARROLL EUGENE GRAY.

Carroll Eugene Gray, son of Dr. P. Wells Gray, was born in Madison, Ohio, July 23d, 1831. While in his youth his parents located at Buffalo, N. Y., where he received a common school education, completing an academical course in Jamestown, N. Y.; following commercial pursuits till 1868, when he began the study of, and engaged in both the management and construction of illuminating gas works. In 1873 he removed to St. Louis, Mo., interesting capital of that city in local gas and water companies, promoting and building works in Missouri, Texas, Colorado, Illinois, Indiana and Kansas.

In 1883 Mr. Gray moved to Chicago, undertaking by preference, work in the north-west, bearing a creditable name throughout that region, both as a Gas and a Hydraulic Engineer and Builder. During this period of seventeen years the subject of this sketch has constructed some eleven gas works, and nine water works, and in some of the more prominent towns of the west. His two elder sons are now succeeding him in the business, Mr. Gray declining large contracts in future.

Mr. Gray married Emma E. Wilton, of Kent, England. Children:

PAULINE E. GRAY, b. in London, England, Sept. 24, 1859; mar. Frank L. Deming, St. Louis, Mo.

CARROLL E. GRAY, Jr., b. in London, England, Sept. 7th, 1862.

THEODORE WELLS GRAY, b. in New York city, Aug. 4th, 1865.

JOHN ROLLIN GRAY, b. in Cleveland, Ohio, June 13th, 1868.

AMY WENTWORTH GRAY, b. in Lawrence, Kansas, Nov. 2d, 1872.

HATTIE E. GRAY, b. in St. Louis, Missouri, Nov. 30th, 1876.

The present residence of Mr. and Mrs. Gray and family is at Fergus Falls, Minn.

34.

ROLLIN B. GRAY.

Dr. Rollin B. Gray, youngest son of Dr. Patrick Wells Gray, was born in Randolph, Crawford Co., Pa., June 4th, 1840. Graduated in medicine in 1865, and also received the degree of M. D., from the Homœopathic College of New York in 1871. He served as a Lieutenant in a Missouri Regt. for two years and three months in the War for the Union; was in the first engagement of the war, at "Camp Jackson," and also at Fulton, Calloway Co., Mo. Detached duty at St. Louis, during balance of service.

Dr. Gray engaged in practice with his uncle, Dr. John F. Gray, of New York, until August, 1866, when he removed to Brooklyn, N. Y., where he built up a large and lucrative clientele. Was elected President, for three successive years, of the "Long Island Medical Society," which consists of members of both the Homœopathic and Allopathic Schools of Medicine. Returned to practice in connection with Dr. John F. Gray in New York, 1877, where he remained until the latter's death, in June, 1882.

Dr. Gray was married in 1867 to Lillie D. Whitney, of Brooklyn, N. Y., by whom are the following children:

ANITA GRAY, b. Apr. 29, 1868.
MARIAN GRAY, b. Oct. 26, 1869.
LILLIAN GRAY, b. Jan. 5, 1871; d. Apr. 12, 1876.
ELIZABETH GRAY, b. June 12, 1872; d. Mar. 9, 1873.

Dr. Gray and family now reside in the city of New York, where he is actively engaged in the practice of his profession.

DIANTHA ELOISE GRAY SACKETT

DIANTHA ELOISE GRAY-SACKETT.

Mrs. Diantha Eloise Gray-Sackett, youngest daughter of Judge John Gray (5) and Diantha Burritt his wife, was born at Sherburne, N. Y., Mar. 8, 1809, of which place she still has many pleasant recollections, although she removed from there with her parents in 1819, to Chautauqua Co., N. Y. Miss Gray at an early age manifested a desire and an aptness for teaching, and when older, chose it for her life work. This led her and her parents to seek her best qualifications for it. Troy Seminary was the only one in the State that held out anything for girls better than did the "Select Schools," with their medley of studies unillustrated and half taught, or the Academies here and there. The goal of her ambition however before her, she tried to make good use of these advantages supplemented by instruction from tutors, both in the country and in New York city. Finding light literature interfering with her lessons and course of study, she resolutely put it all aside till she should have "done with school." 1134321

In 1829 her motives were changed, and thenceforth that of *duty* to serve God and her generation were the impelling force in devotion to her calling. Gradually the conviction that it was a paramount claim on her to set aside ordinary teaching for efforts to raise the needed interest and the means to establish a permanent school in which the many young lady converts of those days of revivals (1830–1836) might be received and helped to become as polished corners of the Temple.

So impressed, and after a year in visiting Christian leaders of the then existing schools, and pastors of churches, she became satisfied of the feasibility of the scheme, and relinquishing her own school for its prosecution, in the spring of 1837 she went to Le Roy, N. Y., to aid in laying the foundations of such an institution. Though not at first the realization of all her views and hopes, the result was a prosperous and excellent Seminary, and finally, through the gift of its devoted Founder, Mrs. E. E. Ingham Staunton, of the entire investment, a really public institution, a free will offering on the altar of advanced and Christian education. As the Ingham University, it recently celebrated its Semi-Centennial Anniversary.

Miss Gray was married June 25, 1839, to Rev. H. A. Sackett, and for about 11 years shared with him his pastoral responsibilities in Franklinville, N. Y., and in Groton, N. Y. Among those duties she found that of teaching a school of twenty to forty young ladies, longing for advantages they could not find otherwise; in the 1st, as Home Mission Parish, and in the 2nd, a call to care for the Female Department of the Academy.

Thus providentially Mr. Sackett became himself so intensely interested by what he saw of the necessity of more accessible means of culture, especially to fit many daughters of the church for usefulness, that he at last decided it duty to suspend, for the necessary time, his ministerial work, and give himself to that of building up a College for women, of equal value, and in the *way* so many had been provided for young men.

After six years of inestimable labor the Elmira College came into existence, mainly through their united and most earnest efforts. They felt themselves called of God to this work, and ever rejoiced in it as such, though so great had been its prostrating power, that Mr. Sackett could not return to the ministry he so loved.

Afterward they opened a school at Stonington, Conn., that they might educate their only daughter at home, and at the same time make one more contribution to the cause of Christian education. This attained, they found rest and a quiet home in Cranford, N. J., where Mr. Sackett died Dec. 30, 1879, and where Mrs. Sackett still resides. A woman of rare fortitude, faith, courage, culture, character, and high endowments; esteemed and beloved, the centre of many strong ties of kindred and affection.

ELIZA DIANTHA SACKETT, daughter of Rev. and Mrs. Sackett, born Sept. 7th, 1840, resides with her mother at Cranford, N. J.

NATHANIEL GRAY.

Nathaniel Gray, son of John Gray (4), was born near New Concord, in Canaan, Columbia Co., N. Y., Aug. 14, 1773. He married at Sherburne, N. Y., Sept. 5, 1797, Sarah Butler, who was born at Weathersfield, Conn., Apr. 30, 1771. Mr. and Mrs. Gray afterwards removed to German, Chenango Co. N. Y., then to Evans, N. Y., and from there to Savanna, Ill., where Nathaniel Gray died at the residence of his son Reuben H. Gray, April 10, 1845, having lived an exemplary and useful life. Mr. Gray was a farmer, and an influential man, both in the church and in political circles. He was an Elder in the church, and usually held some public office.

Mrs. Gray died at the residence of her son, Rev. Calvin Gray, at Mt Carroll, Ill., Apr. 1852.

DESCENDANTS OF NATHANIEL GRAY.

PAMELIA GRAY, b. in Sherburne, N. Y., Sept. 4th, 1798; mar. Patrick Hamilton, June 2, 1844; d. May 1st, 1851, at Dowagiac, Mich.; no children.

MILAN GRAY, b. in Sherburne, N. Y., Jan. 4th, 1800; d. at Evans, N. Y., Sept 17th, 1822.

FRANCIS GRAY, b. at German, N. Y., Mar. 26, 1803; d. June 5, 1807.

CALVIN GRAY.

Rev. Calvin Gray, son of Nathaniel Gray, and grandson of John Gray (4), was born at German, N. Y., Sept. 1, 1805, and June 7, 1842, married Abigail North Spaulding, at Franklinville, Cattaraugus Co., N. Y., she having been born at Lisle, Broome Co., N. Y., May 14, 1815. He had consecrated his life to the Christian Ministry, taking a private course of study with Dr.

Stillman of Dunkirk, his health not permitting him to enter upon
a regular classical course. His first preaching was at Ripley,
N. Y., and from thence he went to Arcade, Wyoming Co., and
was then a Home Missionary at South Wales and West Aurora,
Erie Co., N. Y.

In 1844 he went to Carroll County, Ill., as a Home Missionary, where after several years of hard, incessant labor his health giving out, Mrs. Gray then engaged in teaching as the support of
the family. In 1867 he removed to Geneva, Kansas, where he
preached as pastor for five years, and for five years as a self sus-
taining Missionary. He then went to Fort Dodge, Iowa, to spend
his remaining days with his eldest son, Rev. Lyman C. Gray,
then pastor of the First Presbyterian Church, of that place,
and there he continued to reside until his decease, which took
place Mar. 20, 1885, in his 80th year. And so this veteran of
the church militant, after nearly half a century of faithful service laid down his well worn armor, than which none knightlier
was ever worn by man. Mrs. Gray, who still survives, writes,
date of Mar. 18, 1886, " My dear husband was a great sufferer
for years, but a murmur never escaped his lips. He often used
to say, 'What should I do without the Bible?' and when his eyes
became dim so that he could not read, it was daily read to
him."

The following is a list of the children and grandchildren of
Rev. and Mrs. Calvin Gray:

LYMAN CALVIN GRAY, Rev., b. at South Wales, N. Y., Oct.
26, 1843 ; mar. Mollie Scripps, in Astoria, Ill., June 9,
1871. Graduated at Knox College, Ill., and at Auburn
Theological Seminary, N. Y. Has labored for several
years as a Home Missionary in Northern Iowa, and as
pastor of the Presbyterian Church at Fort Dodge, at
which place he continues to reside, although temporarily, on account of ill health, obliged to stop preaching
and engage in other avocation. He has invented a
very ingenious Postal Cabinet of great utility, and is
Manager of the company organized for its manufacture. It has high official and personal endorsement,
and is practicable for various uses. Rev. and Mrs.
Calvin Gray have the following children:

39.

WILLIAM CALVIN GRAY, b. at Auburn, N. Y., June
19, 1872.
GEORGE HENRY GRAY, b. at Auburn, N. Y., Feb.
14, 1874; d. Mar. 5, 1879, at Ft. Dodge, Iowa.
JAMES JOHNSON GRAY, b. at Ft. Dodge, Iowa,
July 8, 1876.
JOHN LYMAN GRAY, b. at Ft. Dodge, Iowa, Nov.
8, 1878.
HARLEY WINTER GRAY, b. at Fort Dodge, Iowa,
Dec. 10, 1880.
MARY CARLTON GRAY, b. at Fort Dodge, Iowa,
Jan. 4, 1886.
CARLTON RINEWALT GRAY, b. at Mt. Carroll, Ill., Jan. 7th,
1847; d. Sept. 26, 1847.
LINUS SHEPARD GRAY, b. at Mt. Carroll, Ill., July 25, 1849;
d. June 21, 1850.
HENRY NORTH GRAY, b. at Mt. Carroll, Ill., July 7, 1851;
mar. Tillie Mattoon, Oct. 1, 1872, in Geneva, Kansas,
who was b. at Canton, N. Y., Feb. 4, 1845. Is a
farmer, and active in Bible Readings and Sabbath
School work. Children :
LUCY ABIGAIL GRAY, b. at Geneva, Kas., Sept. 1,
1873.
CARLTON NORTH GRAY, b. at Geneva, Kansas,
Oct. 28, 1875.
CENA TILLIE GRAY, b. at Geneva, Kas., Mar. 24,
1878.
MARY SOPHRONIA GRAY, b. at Geneva, Kansas,
Nov. 17, 1879.
CHARLES BURNETTE GRAY, b. at Geneva, Kansas,
Sept. 6, 1881; d. May 27, 1882.
EDDIE and ETTIE GRAY, twins, b. Apr. 2, 1884;
Eddie d. Aug. 18, and Ettie, Aug. 19; both
buried in one grave, in Geneva Cemetery, on
Aug. 20th, 1884.
ROSCOE SPAULDING GRAY, son of Rev. Calvin Gray, b. at
Mt. Carroll, Ill., Apr. 7th, 1857. Has removed to
San Francisco, California. Is engaged in reporting
and newspaper work.

REUBEN H. GRAY.

Reuben H. Gray, son of Nathaniel Gray, was born at Eden, N. Y., Mar. 3, 1816. He married Abby Dewey, at Evans Centre, N. Y., Dec. 30, 1838. Moved west, located at Savanna, Ill., and engaged in the mercantile business. Died Sept. 15, 1871, after a short illness, leaving a family of four children, as follows:

> HELEN GRAY, b. Mar. 19, 1840; mar. May 3, 1866, Francis Karney, at Mt. Carroll, Ill. ; have following children: Myrtle, b. Apr. 16, 1867. Reuben, b. June 2, 1869. Nellie, b. Nov. 7, 1871. May, b. May 11, 1873. Frances, b. April 8, 1876. Lois, b. Feb. 10, 1879. Reside near Savanna, Ill.

> GEORGE GRAY, second child of Reuben H. Gray, born at Evans, N. Y., Dec. 31, 1843, married Sarah Heiser, at Savanna, Ill., Oct. 26, 1869, d. Dec. 4th, 1871, leaving one child,

> > GEORGE GRAY, b. 1870,

> who now lives with his mother, near Stromsburg, Neb.

> SARAH GRAY, daughter of Reuben H. Gray, born at Savanna, Ill., Dec. 12, 1851, married W. I. Bowen of that place, Oct. 26, 1881, and still resides there, having one child, George Leland Bowen, b. Aug. 21, 1883.

> ALBERT GRAY, fourth and last child of Reuben H., was born Feb. 12, 1856; d. Oct. 5, 1862.

John F. Gray

ALFRED GRAY.

Alfred Gray, son of John Gray (4), was born in Canaan, Columbia Co., N. Y., July 29, 1778. He married for his first wife, Sarah Hudson, of Cherry Valley, N. Y., by whom he had two children, a son and a daughter. After the death of his first wife, at Cherry Valley, on July 14th, 1805, Mr. Gray removed to Sherburne, N. Y., where, in 1806, he married Mary Olmstead, from Ridgefield, Conn., by whom he had three sons and four daughters. Descendants by first marriage:

> JOHN HUDSON GRAY, Dr., son of Alfred Gray, b. at Cherry Valley, N. Y., Oct. 1st, 1802; mar. Lucinda Felton, Aug. 17, 1828. Dr. Gray removed to Schuyler Lake, Otsego Co., N. Y., and at the time of his decease, Feb. 26, 1847, he enjoyed an extensive practice, and had won a reputation which bid fair to render him a formidable rival of his former preceptor, the celebrated Dr. Delos White, of Cherry Valley. The widow Lucinda Felton Gray, died at Schuyler Lake, Mar. 26, 1881. Children:
>
>> JOHN FELTON GRAY, b. Dec. 7, 1830.
>>
>> SARAH ANN GRAY, b. Nov. 19, 1833; mar. Robert M. Durfy, Oct. 4, 1854; Robby Durfy, son of, d. Nov. 15, 1859. Robert M. Durfy d. Jan. 12, 1862. Sarah Ann Gray Durfy d. Jan. 31, 1878.
>
> SARAH ANN GRAY, b. Feb. 15, 1805; d. June 5. 1820.

JOHN FELTON GRAY.

John Felton Gray, only son of Dr. John Hudson Gray, still continues to reside at Schuyler Lake, N. Y., where he was born Dec. 7, 1830. Commencing as a clerk he worked his way up, and for several years was engaged in the mercantile business. Has been five times chosen Supervisor of his town, and has been Chairman of the Board of Supervisors of Otsego County. Has also served his third term as Justice of the Peace. Last few years has been engaged in settlement of estates, and in attending to his own business affairs. In independent circumstances; a bachelor.

CHARLES M. GRAY.

Charles M. Gray, son of Alfred and Mary Olmstead Gray, and grandson of John Gray (4), was born at Sherburne, N. Y., June 13, 1807, and married Mary Ann Haines, at Philadelphia, Nov. 24, 1832. With his young wife he removed to Chicago the following year, 1833, where he extensively engaged in the manufacture of grain cradles, and in 1847 he became associated with Cyrus H. McCormick, in the manufacture of reapers, under the firm name of McCormick & Gray.

In 1854 Mr. Gray was elected Mayor of Chicago, and his administration of the affairs of that city commanded the approval of the better element of both parties. A Chicago paper says: "It may almost be said, that during his term of office was inaugurated that system of public improvements which has given all essential facilities to intramural commerce, and made the city itself the pride and glory of a State."

Soon after the expiration of his term of office as Mayor he was appointed General Freight Agent of the Michigan Southern & Northern Indiana R. R., and in the duties of his new position, in the language of another, " Mr. Gray brought to the solution of the problem a varied and successful business experience, a broad intellectual force that was phenominal and a robust integrity that has commanded the admiration of every man with whom he came in contact. In this task he was so successful that it does no injustice to others to repeat the statement so frequently made, that Charles M. Gray was the father of the railway freight system of the United States." After the consolidation with the Cleveland & Erie R. R., in 1869, Mr. Gray retained his position in Chicago, and remained as Asst. Gen. Freight Agt. of the consolidated line up to the time of his death.

Mr. Gray died at his residence in the city of Chicago, of which he had been for more than half a century an honored resident, Oct. 17, 1885, having been prostrated over a year previous by a shock of apoplexy, from which he did not fully recover. The following just and beautiful tribute to the deceased is from the Chicago *Tribune:* " It is not lavish praise of this man to say, that the purity of his life, his great intellectual force, and his uncompromising integrity, constitute a trinity of virtues that

Cemfrag

finds few equals and no superiors among men. To her who for more than fifty years has cherished him in sickness and in health, he has given a love and a devotion that seemed to strengthen with each advancing year. His last words of encouragement and advice, like a ray of sunshine through the breaking clouds will strengthen her footsteps and warm and beautify the pathway which she must now tread alone. Loving feet will follow him to the grave. Loving hands will fashion the sod over his last resting place, and loving eyes will sanctify it with their tears. In this busy world of commerce sturdy lives will halt in their restless activity to catch one further inspiration from the great soul that has gone to its final rest."

Again: "The funeral of Capt. Chas. M. Gray, took place from the family residence on Wabash Avenue. Among the most conspicuous floral offerings was a magnificent design representing a freight car, made up of tube-roses, immortelles buds, blush roses and other flowers, from the associates of the deceased on the Lake Shore & Michigan Southern R. R. The parlors and halls were crowded with friends who came to pay their last mark of respect for the departed, and only a small portion of those who had come could gain admission to hear Bishop Cheney read the burial service. There was a great throng of citizens, many of them old friends of Capt. Gray."

The following sketch of his family was furnished by Mr. Gray date of Juiy 23, 1884, and is a sad summary: "We have had three children, viz: Remington, Reuben, and Mary. The last one died when only two years old; the eldest son died when 18 years old. The other son, Reuben C. Gray, died in Virginia, where he had purchased a farm, in 1882, aged 46 years. He had no children; his wife died before he did."

Mr. Gray was greatly interested in the "Gray Genealogy," and did much to encourage and facilitate its publication. Even during his illness he did not cease his cordial co-operation. Under date of Oct. 16, 1884, he wrote: "Since I last wrote you I have had a shock of apoplexy that has left me partially paralyzed; but thank the good Lord, I have the right hand with which to write you once more. Your letters are of great interest to me, and I hope you are still progressing with the family record of the Grays."

GEORGE M. GRAY.

George M. Gray, youngest son of Alfred Gray, and grandson of John Gray (4), was born at Sherburne, N. Y., July 25, 1818. Soon after, his father's family removed to Victor, Ontario Co., N. Y., and from thence he went to Chicago, Ill., whither his elder brother had preceded him, arriving there June 22, 1834, being then a lad of sixteen summers.

He was engaged in various pursuits, up to 1851, when he was appoined General Western Agent of the first through Railway line connecting the East with Chicago, now known as the Lake Shore & Michigan Southern line. Mr. Gray remained in that service until 1866, when he at once became associated with the Pullman Sleeping Car Company, with which he is still connected.

From 1854 until 1864, Mr. Gray was also a silent partner in the wholesale hardware business, under the firm name of Tuttle, Hibbard & Co. He was married to Maria L. Johnson, of Bangor, Maine, in 1839, who still survives. Residence Chicago. No children.

> MARY M. GRAY, daughter of Alfred Gray, was born in Sherburne, N. Y., Jan. 1, 1813; mar. Lemuel W. Hard at Pittsford, Monroe Co., N. Y., Mar. 12, 1832; children:
>
> > CAROLINE J. HARD, b. Apr. 13, 1834; married to Chas. C. Sears, Dec. 1852. Living children: Maggie H., Stella B., George R., and Harry A. Sears.
> >
> > SARAH ANN HARD, b. May 31, 1837 ; married to Russell A. Britton, Feb. 1865.
> >
> > CHAS. DELOS HARD, b. Dec. 20, 1838; married Mae Fisk, Oct. 1874; children: Carl Bowen Hard, Leila Hayden Hard, George Gray Hard, Bessie Chester Hard.
> >
> > ALFRED AUGUSTUS HARD, b. Sept. 10, 1841; mar. Elvene L. Curtis, Aug. 4, 1874.
> >
> > GEORGE C. HARD, b. June 22, 1843; mar. Emily Louise Hughes, 1868 ; d. Feb. 27, 1883; children: Carrie Gray Hard, b. Oct. 1869; Lem A. Hard, b. Oct. 1879.
> >
> > DENSMORE D. HARD, b. July 21, 1845.
>
> Mrs. Hard now resides at Cleveland, O.

JANE E. GRAY, daughter of Alfred Gray, b. in Sherburne,
N. Y., mar. John Ogden of Milwaukee, Wis., Sept. 21,
1836. Living issue:

> JOHN G. OGDEN, mar. Sarah S. Atkins, Oct. 16,
> 1873. William Gray Ogden, son of, b. Oct.
> 20, 1883.
> GEORGE W. OGDEN, mar. M. E. Noxon, Oct. 28,
> 1873. Marion Gray Ogden, daughter of, b.
> Feb. 20, 1875.
> HENRY M. OGDEN, mar. Minnie J. Matthews, Jan.
> 21, 1885.
> ABIGAIL OGDEN, unmarried.

All residents of Milwaukee, Wis.

BETSEY GRAY, daughter of Alfred Gray, married S. S.
Chamberlain, and lives at Lockport, Ill., and has two
sons married and in business at Joliet, Ill.

SARAH ANN GRAY, daughter of Alfred Gray, was born at
Victor, Ontario Co., N. Y., April 20, 1820; mar. to
Horace Chase, at Hatley, Ill., Oct. 4th, 1837. Re-
moved to Milwaukee, Wis., same year, where she died
Aug. 5, 1852. Issue, seven infant children, deceased;
one daughter living, viz:

> ELLA CHASE, b. Jan. 24, 1849, in Milwaukee; mar.
> to Dr. Horace Enos, of Chicago, Ill., May
> 24, 1870; children: Horace Chase Enos,
> b. July 17, 1871. Charles Reade Enos, b.
> May 19, 1873. Juliette Cora Enos, b. Apr.
> 2, 1876.

Mr. Chase was b. in Derby, Orleans Co., Vt., Dec. 25, 1810.
Came to Chicago May 19, 1834, and soon afterwent to Mil-
waukee, at that time an Indian trading post, and a part of the
Territory of Michigan, and there he still continues to reside.

Alfred Gray resided at Sherburne and Earlville, N. Y., where
he was engaged in the mercantile business, until 1818, when he
removed to Victor, N. Y. He died at Montreal, Canada, while
there on business, in 1820. His widow married Capt. Rowley,
of Pittsford, N. Y., and there resided until 1833, when the family removed to Illinois, where she died in Oct. 1864. Mrs. Gray
was the daughter of Jared Olmstead son of Samuel Olmstead,
one of the original proprietors of Ridgefield, Conn., 1708. She
was *one of three at a birth*, (triplets), born May 21, 1786.

46.

EDWARD GRAY.

Edward Gray, son of John Gray (4), was born in Canaan, N. Y., June 20, 1780. He married Elizabeth Mudge, born 1781, daughter of Elder John Mudge, the first pastor of the Baptist Church at Sherburne, N. Y., who was born at Sharon, Conn., 1755. Mr. Gray continued to live at Sherburne until 1825, when he removed with his family to Alexander, Genesee Co., N. Y., where he died June 13th, 1830. She died in Feb., 1864.

The following incident in his early life, copied from the History of Sherburne, evidences a vigor of independence and a muscular virility of no little forcefulness. It is in the account of the first school kept, or attempted to be kept, in that then frontier settlement: "A pedagogue by the name of Gardner was employed to teach it; when exercising a class in spelling he put the word book—the scholar spelled it b-u-k—the teacher pronounced it right. Edward Gray, son of John Gray, disputed this. The master, in order to maintain the dignity of his station, undertook to correct him corporeally; a scuffle ensued, from which the teacher came out second best. The result was, the school was broken up for the remainder of the winter."

The following is a list of the descendants of Edward and Elizabeth Gray:

> CHAUNCEY GRAY, eldest son of Edward Gray, b. in Sherburne, N. Y., 1805; mar. Belinda Skinner, at Sherburne, 1825. Children:
>
>> BETSEY, b. 1826; mar. Wm. Woodhouse Dana, at Elba, N. Y., 1843; d. 1868. Had a son, Wm. W. Dana, now residing at Ripon, Wis.
>>
>> EUNICE, b. 1827; mar. Abram Fields, at Wales, N. Y., 1851. Residence, Winona, Wis. Children: Lucius Smith Fields, b. 1842; mar. Ida M. Lake, at Buffalo, N. Y., 1864; d. 1875, leaving a son, who resides with his grandmother, Mrs. Eunice Gray Fields. Amanda Lucinda Fields, b. 1844; d. 1854; Julius Augustus, b. 1847; d. 1848; Margaret Elizabeth, b. 1848; d. 1849; Daniel Deloren, b. 1853; d. 1877; Martha Sophia, b. 1858; d. 1860.

MARILLA, b. 1829; d. 1830.

MARY CHARITY, mar. Thomas Lake, at Fredonia, 1846; had six children, four living.

HOMER GRAY, b. 1832; went off with a drover, 1844, from Bethany, N. Y., and has not been heard from but once since, and that indirectly, in 1853, when he was reported to be in California, and doing well.

SARAH JEANETTE, b. 1838; mar. William Cyrenus Oakes, at Buffalo, 1856; had eleven children; eight living; she d. at Salamanca, N. Y., June 30, 1881. She had united with the Baptist Church at Dunkirk, 1866, and it is said of her that she was a true Christian woman, faithful and trustful to the end. She has a son residing at Salamanca, and a 'daughter, Mrs. Belinda Rockwell, at Kane, Pa.

Chauncey Gray was a coppersmith by trade, also something of a musician. A shadow of mystery covers his life, and a melancholy tragedy closed it. From lack of application, or untoward circumstance, or right purpose, he did not get on in the world. A darksome fate seemed to pursue him; he could not withstand the forces of evil, which sad to relate, made him his own destroyer. Crushed and overborne by the tempter, in an evil hour, reason dethroned, he fell by his own hand, and his life went out in darkness. This tragic event occurred at his residence on Eagle St., Fredonia, N. Y., in March, 1850, where he had been living since about 1844. Let the mantle of charity fall softly over his unmarked grave!

The widow Belinda Gray afterwards married Mr. Buckland Gillett, of that place, and after his death removed to Salamanca, where she died at the residence of her daughter, Mrs. Sarah J. Oakes; a woman much respected.

JOHN M. GRAY, b. in Sherburne, N. Y., Feb. 1808. Was a wagon-maker by trade. Married Almira Daniels at Brookville, N. Y., in 1829, who died June, 1836, leaving two children; a daughter who d. 1855, and a son,

MARCUS GRAY, of Batavia, N. Y., b. at Alexander, N. Y., June 2, 1831; mar. May 8, 1851, to Margaret Devine; children:

GEO. E. GRAY, Dr., b. Apr. 15, 1852;
graduated from University of Mich-
igan, July 1, 1880; in practice at
South Pueblo, Col.
MARTIN GRAY, son of Marcus Gray, b.
Feb. 29, 1855; mar. Katie Broe;
one son,
BENJAMIN GRAY.

John M. Gray mar. 2d, Caroline Wyman, by whom he had
one daughter, Emma Gray, now Mrs. Williams, of Alexander,
N. Y.

John M. Gray mar. 3d, Catharine Miner, by whom were three
children; Elizabeth Gray, died when three years old. Mrs. Gray
d. 1847.

SILAS GRAY, b. April, 1843; d. Apr. 1861.
HELEN GRAY, b. Nov. 26, 1846; mar. Oct. 22,
1861, to Levant Sisson. Residence, Medina,
N. Y.

John M. Gray mar. 4th, Eunice Mead. Mr. Gray died Sept.
23, 1874.

MARILLA GRAY, b. at Sherburne, N. Y., Jan. 22, 1809;
mar. Asa McOmber; d. Aug. 7, 1856, at Gaines, N.
Y.; descendants:

MARION (McOmber) Knickerbocker, b. Aug. 6th,
1829; residence, Gaines, N. Y.
JULIA (McOmber) Hoyt, b. Nov. 27, 1832; resi-
dence, Gaines, N. Y.
GEORGE McOMBER, b. May 27, 1834; drowned
in Canandaigua Lake, N. Y., Sept. 12, 1876.
He married Harriet Bunnell, at East Bloom-
field, N. Y., Feb. 27, 1857; children: Asa, b.
Apr. 7, 1859; George, Jr., b. July 24, 1862;
d. Mar. 24, 1885; Julia, b. Mar. 15, 1866;
all born at East Bloomfield, N. Y. Mrs.
McOmber and her two surviving children re-
side at Chicago.
MERRITT McOMBER, b. Apr. 23, 1836, at Gaines,
N. Y.; mar. Charlotte J. ——; children:
Carrie L., b. Sept. 22, 1862; mar. Mr.
Maxson, at Gaines, N. Y.; Fred, b. Feb. 6,
1868. Mr. McOmber mar. 2d, Melinda
L.——. Residence, Manchester, N. Y.

49.

CHARLES McOMBER, b. June 26, 1838; d. July
15, 1841.
JANE (McOmber) Hatch, b. Dec. 13, 1840; residence, Gaines, N. Y.
EMMA, b. Nov. 12, 1842; d. Aug. 21, 1843.
FANNIE, b. Apr. 7, 1844.
FRED McOMBER, b. at Gaines, N. Y., Jan. 23, 1846;
mar. Minnie M. Graham, at Berrien Springs, Mich.,
May 15, 1872; one child, Graham Oertel Mc-Omber, b. July 30, 1875. Mr. McOmber is publisher
of the Berrien Springs *Era*, and Sec'y and Gen.
Passenger Agt. of the St. Joseph Valley R. R.
EUNICE, b. Nov. 26, 1848; mar. Sept. 28, 1865, Ferdinand D. Oertel, of Chicago; he d. Sept. 30, 1882;
mar. 2d, Thos. B. Dohan, Chicago, Apr. 21, 1885.
SIDNEY GRAY, b. 1806, and d. in Sherburne, N. Y., 1819.
EDWARD GRAY, Jr., b. in Sherburne, N. Y., 1815; mar. at
Lockport, N. Y., 1841; d. 1865; no descendants.
REUBEN GRAY, b. in Sherburne, N. Y., 1817; mar. in 1843;
lived at Warsaw, N. Y.; d. at Oakley, Wis., at the residence of his sister, Mrs. Matteson, Jan. 19, 1881.
FRANK GRAY, son of Reuben Gray, b. at South
Warsaw, N. Y., Aug. 27, 1856; unmarried.
CHARLOTTE GRAY, daughter of Edward Gray, b. in Sherburne, N. Y., June 19, 1820; mar. Saul Matteson, at
Brookville, N. Y., Apr. 29, 1841; residence, Oakley,
Wis.; one son, Chas. E., a Union soldier; three daughters, Delia E., Ida M., and Marion; two children dec'd.
BETSEY GRAY, b. at Sherburne, N. Y., Apr. 13, 1822; mar.
Geo. Cadman, at Batavia, N. Y., 1844; he d. 1860;
she d. 1882; nine children.
CAROLINE GRAY, daughter of Edward Gray, b. in Sherburne,
N. Y., Aug. 10, 1824; mar. Ichabod Waldron, at East
Pembroke, N. Y., Feb. 19, 1845; residence, Albion,
N. Y.; six children.
ELIZA E. GRAY, b. at Brookville, N. Y., July 8, 1828; mar.
Almiron Wade, Mar. 20, 1843; he d. 1855; a son,
WILLIAM WALLACE WADE, b. Aug. 21, 1851; mar.
Minnie Garrett, Dec. 5, 1874.
Mrs. Wade mar. 2d, David Dodge, Jan. 28, 1858; children:
ROYAL DILSON DODGE, b. June 3, 1859; mar. Oct.
17, 1878, to Mary Christmon.
JENNIE L. DODGE, b. Aug. 11, 1861; mar. John
H. Ernesse, Dec. 17, 1878.
GEORGE BROWN DODGE, b. Mar. 22, 1867.
Mrs. Dodge resides at East Pembroke, N. Y.

REUBEN GRAY.

Col. Reuben Gray, youngest son of John Gray (4), was born in Florida, Montgomery Co., N. Y., Aug. 15, 1782. Removed to Sherburne, N. Y., with his father's family, in 1793, and married Rebecca Belcher at that place, 1806. He continued to reside in Sherburne until after the death of his mother, in 1824, his parents having made their home with him during the later years of their lives. He served in the war of 1812, as Captain in Col. Mead's Chenango County Regiment, and was afterwards Colonel of a Militia Regiment. That Col. Gray was a man of literary taste and poetic sentiment, as well as a soldier gallant and brave, in whom the fires of patriotism not dimly burned, is evidenced by a few stray leaflets of his composition that have been preserved. The following extract from a pastoral poem entitled "Farewell," and expressive of his deep feeling on being obliged to give up his loved home by reason of having become surety for another, has in it a touch of pathos and tenderness, a love and appreciation of nature, a smoothly flowing rhyme and rhythm, and a true poetic fervor, worthy of more ambitious verse. It was written at Sherburne, date of 1821:

> Farewell, each pleasing scene,
> Ye radiant fields of purest green,
> Ye trees that once I called my own,
> Each plant that by this hand was sown.
>
> Farewell, ye babbling silver brooks,
> How oft I've traced your winding nooks,
> Seen you drop tears from mossy stone!
> Say, will you weep, your lover gone?
>
> (Laugh not, ye proud,) farewell, dear plough,—
> The bleating flock and lowing cow,
> Thou lowly hut, my home, farewell!—
> Those who ne'er felt can ne'er tell
>
> Nor even feel that pang of heart
> Which he must feel who's torn apart
> From HOME—there still in dreams I rove,
> And feast on scenes God bade me love.

The following quaint letter from Col. Gray to a kinsman, is characteristic, and almost a complete biography in itself:

SHERIDAN, N. Y., Jan. 18th, 1847.

Dear Sir:—Yours of the 29th of July last, duly rec'd. Do not attribute my neglecting so long to answer you, to a desire on my part to break off the correspondence. I am old and sometimes negligent in promptly writing, but have always yet "had the last word" in a correspondence. You wish me to inform you whether Calvin and Charles are the sons of my father's former or later brothers. They are my brother's sons. Calvin Gray is of the Presbyterian stamp. He went to the N. W. part of Ill. Charles M. Gray still lives in Chicago. He is the son of Alfred Gray, who died about 1820. Jas. T. Gifford married my sister's daughter. Philo Hatch, likewise. I had two sisters that married brothers—Newcomb and James Raymond. Children of both live in or near Elgin. I believe that I have told you all I know of our relatives west of Michigan. No, I have not. I recollect a niece, Abigail Raymond, who married a Mr. Smith attached to a Missionary establishment, and went to Oregon six years since.

I should like to fill out my sheet, but have nothing at present in my head, unless I go into *self-ology.* Well, then, let us at that! My age, I believe that you have—if not, say 64. Wife, one; children, none. My "better half" is rather the largest part of me, for she is tall and fat; myself part. rather short and lean. We have been one near forty-one years. I expect that, (though hard to acknowledge,) I may now be fairly set down as one of the "has beens;" for I was once young, am now old. I was once rich, (not very), now I am poor. As to poverty, I came as honestly by it as I have by my age, and have as little cause to regret one as the other. I have health, and a little farm of seven acres from which I make my "bread in the sweat of my face." I am a Christian, 'tho I do not belong to any sect. I am a Whig, yet my coon's tail is not so long as to make me forget that I am more of an *American* than anything else. I am far from being a political abolitionist; yet I do not like negro slavery—'tis a curse to any State that has it.

Alack ! I had like to have got talking about politics, but never mind, I'll say no more about it; only let us be honest, be our party what it may. I just thought that you must live in a good climate for raising silk, and, as we do something at it, I will enclose you a skein of the article. I don't think it will add to the postage; if it does you can take your revenge by sending me a big letter! Finally, a little more about what I have been: I once had command of a company of militia; was on the lines a few months in that capacity in the last war. I have once had the command of a regiment. Accept our respects to yourself, family, and other friends.   REUBEN GRAY.

MR. S. R. GRAY, Barry, Ill.

Col. Gray afterwards removed from Sheridan to Elmira, N. Y., where he died in 1860, leaving no children. His character and personality are of increased interest from the fact that but for his care in preserving his father's record and diary, and his additions thereto of family facts from his own researches, this Genealogy could not well have been written, and much valuable data would have been lost.

ADDENDA.

In closing up this branch of the family, the following addenda of statistics received too late for proper position is here placed:

Mrs. Pauline E. Denning, daughter of Carroll E. Gray, was married May 29, 1879. Children: Harry Lee, b. Mar. 19, 1880, d. Oct. 28, 1883; Ned Gray, b. Nov. 24, 1883.

Betsey E. Gray, daughter of Alfred Gray and granddaughter of John Gray (4), mar. S. S. Chamberlin of Lockport, Ill., Jan. 19, 1841. Children: Geo. N., b. Dec. 20, 1851, mar. Ella E. Munger, Dec. 5, 1876; living issue, Frederick Munger Chamberlin b. Aug. 30, 1877, and Tessie Frances Chamberlin b. Sept. 20, 1880. Residence of Geo. N. Ceamberlin and family, Joliet, Ill. Chas. G. Chamberlin, b Jan. 30, 1859, mar. Emma Taylor Apr. 5, 1880. Living issue, Eva L., b. May 24, 1881. Residence, Lockport, Ill.

NATHANIEL GRAY.

Nathaniel Gray, second son of John Gray (3), born in Lebanon, Conn., March 17, 1736, removed with his father's family to Sharon, in 1743, where he grew up to a stalwart manhood, inured to toil, and participating in the labors and privations of that then frontier settlement. The robust virtues of courage and patriotism had a sturdy growth amid such surroundings, and the call to arms during the French War found this hardy young man ready for service. The following interesting incident is related of him in that connection, in the History of Sherburne, N. Y., published by his grandson, the late Joel Hatch: "Mr. Gray having been honorably discharged, returned home. The next season Abraham Raymond of Kent, entered the service, and was marched upon the same ground, which was near the south end of Lake Champlain, in the vicinity of lake George and Crown Point. He was there taken sick and unable to get home without assistance. With the spirit of the good Samaritan, Mr. Gray mounted his horse and went to his rescue, riding some two hundred miles, through woods and wilds, exposed to hostile bands of French and Indians, then in open war with the Colonies, and known to be lurking around. He found Mr. Raymond weak and feeble, unable to mount a horse without assistance. Riding behind and supporting himself as well as he could, they rode a few miles and halted. By frequent short journeys, rests, and careful nursing, he gradually increased in strength, and finally arrived home in safety." Kent, which was the home of the Raymonds, adjoins Sharon, the home of the Grays, and thus early we have evidence of the intimate friendship existing between the families, which resulted in several intermarriages and in close relations during that and succeeding generations, and until the present time.

The records of the old historic Oblong Church, in the town of Amenia, formerly Amenia Precinct, Dutchess Co., N. Y., near by the western boundaries of Kent and Sharon, Conn., show, in the quaint language of good old Dominie Knibloe, for half a century the faithful pastor of that early founded church, that "Nathaniel Gray was married *with* Deborah Lathrop, daughter of Deacon Meltiah Lathrop, in the evening, Feb. 15, A. D., 1763."

The next record of Nathaniel Gray appears in connection with the purchase and sale of land by him at Mt. Ephraim, town of Richmond, Berkshire Co., Mass., adjoining Canaan, N. Y., date of Nov. 14, 1763. He also sold land there in 1764, and 1765. The record of the last transaction by him at that place is as follows: "Nathaniel Gray of Dover Plains, sold land to Simeon Smith of Sharon, May 30, 1766." While residing at Richmond a son, Elijah Gray, was born, on March 12th, 1764. He must have removed to Dover Plains prior to Sept. 24, 1765, as a second son, Elisha Gray, was born there on that date. The Oblong Church records show that "Nathaniel Gray and wife had their sons Elijah and Elisha baptized Aug. 10, 1766; dau. Ruth bapt. Dec. 21, 1766; dau. Eunice bapt. Mar. 1, 1768 at Dover."

Dover Plains adjoined Amenia on the south, and doubtless Mr. Gray and family had removed thither from Richmond, Mass., so as to be near the Lathrops, who were living in that vicinity. But the hand of death soon overshadowed the household, striking down the young mother, and leaving husband and children and home desolate. Deborah Lathrop Gray died June 13, 1770, and the memorial stone at her grave in the burial place at Dover Plains is noted in the history of Dutchess County as one of the oldest there still preserved. The following inscription was copied from the stone by the writer in 1885 :

In Memory of
D E B O R A H,
Wife of Nathaniel Gray,
Died June 13, 1770, Æ 31.
Here in this tomb interred lies,
A friend that was most dear;
Although Pale Death hath closed her eyes,
Her Memory still is here.

She was born in Tolland, Conn., Aug. 11, 1739. Her father, Deacon Meltiah Lathrop, was a man of prominence in public affairs as well as in the church. He afterwards removed to Canaan, Columbia Co., where he was a member of the Committee of Public Safety for Kings District in 1777, and where he died Sept. 5, 1787, in his 73d year, and was buried, about one mile from New Concord (in the town of Canaan) in a neighborhood burying ground, near the residence of the late De Witt C. Brown, where his memorial stone is still to be seen.

After the death of his wife, Mr. Gray removed to Kent, Conn., where he married Bethiah Newcomb Raymond, widow of David Raymond, Dec. 30, 1773. There were two children born of this second marriage, as appears on the public records of that place: "Deborah, daughter of the above named persons, was born Oct. 31, 1774. Departed this life September 23, 1775. Bethiah, daughter to the above named persons, was born July 4, 1776." The widow Raymond brought to his family three sons, Abraham, Newcomb and James Raymond; and three daughters, Mercy, Sarai and Hannah, the former of whom afterwards married Major Abram Dixon, while Sarai married Elijah Gray, the oldest son of her step-father.

Mr. Gray was a prominent member of the Congregational Church at Kent, where he continued to reside until after the Revolution, when in company with others of kindred he removed to Duanesburgh, Albany Co., N. Y., where they resided for several years, and until the removal to Sherburne, Chenango Co., N. Y., in 1793. Nathaniel Gray was one of the foremost pioneers of that settlement, and the purchase of a quarter of the township for the little colony was negotiated by and through him, for which purpose he made two journeys to the city of New York, and the title passed through him to the eleven original proprietors, of whom he was one. In the division of the lands by lot, the first choice of plots was by universal consent conceded to him, and on an old map of the original survey, a copy of which is in the possession of the writer, his name appears as proprietor of lot No. 1, 133¾ acres. There he continued to reside until his decease in 1810, and on a plot of that ground, given by him for a public burial place, and so still maintained to this day, called the Quarter Cemetery, he was buried.

Mr. Gray was one of the charter members of the Congregational Church of Sherburne, and was its Senior Deacon. The History of Sherburne says of him: "Nathaniel Gray was the first Justice of the Peace appointed in the town. He was not a man of brilliant talents, but had the faculty to win from all veneration and respect. His counsels were received as words of wisdom, and his opinions as law. The religious and moral atmosphere which he diffused around all his actions, gave him a commanding influence over men, which few in any community possess. He was the Patriarch of the settlers — a man without an enemy—a burning and shining light in the church."

A living grand-daughter, Mrs. Amanda Gray Lee, of Cedar Mountain, North Carolina, now in her 94th year, gives the following recollection of him, date of Feb. 11, 1886 :

"Of tall and commanding figure, well proportioned, he was a man of fine presence. His eyes were dark blue, hair brown, complexion fair. He always wore a smile when speaking, and was genial in manners, though very firm and strict in his views of right, including religious duties, especially that of observation of the Sabbath. He was Deacon in the church and Justice of the Peace. He was called 'Justice of the Peace and Peace Justice,' because he always advised parties to settle their differences without invoking the law, offering to waive his fee if they would settle. When cases did come before him they were decided according to their merits without fear or favor."

The following inscription on his tombstone is an epitome of his character and evidences the estimation in which he was held :

"The sweet remembrance of the just
Shall flourish while he sleeps in dust."
Here lies the body of
NATHANIEL GRAY,
Born the 17th of March 1736,
Died the 24th of June, 1810.
Having previously explored this country, he, in the winter of 1793, while it was yet a wilderness, took up his abode and cultivated this field, a small portion of which his remains still occupy. Before his departure from this life he had the satisfaction to see "the wilderness blossom like the rose." He was a devoted man and a pious Christian. Influenced by the divine precepts of that religion which he not only professed but practised, he acquitted himself of his duties to his family and society with truth and sincerity.
On the right lies the body of
BETHIAH,
his wife;
Born Feb'y 26, 1735,
Died August 19, 1811.
They were happily united in their views of here and hereafter, and cheerfully walked hand in hand in humble hope of obtaining the reward appointed for the elect—eternal bliss.
"Blessed are the dead who die in the Lord."

ELIJAH GRAY.

Elijah Gray, oldest son of Nathaniel and Deborah Lathrop Gray, born at Richmond, Berkshire Co., Mass., Mar. 12, 1764, married Sarai Raymond, daughter of his step-mother, Bethiah Newcomb Raymond Gray, at Florida, N. Y., in 1788, and removed to Sherburne, N. Y., in 1793, of which he was one of the pioneer settlers. He lived with his father and occupied part of his farm. Abram Dixon, a son of Major Abram Dixon and nephew of Elijah Gray, thus describes a visit to that primitive Gray homestead, winter of 1794-5: "Deacon Gray, (who was my step-grandfather,) and his son Elijah Gray, (whose wife was my mother's sister,) had built a double log house, one part of which was occupied as a school house six hours a day. We found the school in full blast, under the care of Elisha Gray, brother of my uncle Elijah, who at the same time occupied the same room as a dwelling for his family, consisting of his wife and three children: Nathaniel, about my own age, and Amanda and Hannah, and it served as kitchen, parlor, dining and sleeping room, except that we, the children, were sent up the ladder into the loft, to bed!"

After the death of his father and step-mother, Elijah Gray removed with his family to Sheridan, Chautauqua Co., in 1813, and died at Jamestown, N. Y., in 1847. Mr. Gray and his wife were among the founders and original members of the Congregational Church at Sherburne, N. Y.

DESCENDANTS OF ELIJAH GRAY.

NATHANIEL GRAY, b. Nov. 1, 1789; d. at Sherburne, N. Y., Oct. 8, 1811. It is said of him that he was "a young man of great promise" and high endowments. His early death was cause for deep regret to a large circle of friends and relatives.

AMANDA GRAY LEE, b. at Florida, N. Y., Nov. 23, 1792; mar. Joel Lee, of Sheridan, N. Y., March 17, 1814; he d. May 15, 1836; she resides at Cedar Mountain, North Carolina.

PERSIA, mar. Mr. Powell, and d. 1870.

MARILLA GRAY, b. in Sherburne, 1803, d. at Elgin, Ill., 1882; unmarried.

JULIETTE CLARINDA GRAY, born in Sherburne, N. Y., Sept. 20, 1809; mar. Eber Keyes, Aug. 23, 1831; died at Busti, Chautauqua Co., N. Y., Oct. 24, 1844. Children: Addison Keyes, b. Nov. 23, 1832, d. Aug. 16, 1834; Lydia Kidder, b. Apr. 4, 1834; married John H. Becker, Feb., 1864, and has three children, Florence, Eber and Kate; Ellen Gray, b. Feb. 14, 1839, mar. Alfred Wallin, 1868; Addison Ashley Keyes, late Ed. Albany *Express*, Albany, N. Y., b. Oct. 3, 1842, married Mary Agnes Bradley, Jan. 27, 1865; children, Edward Ashley Keyes, b. Apr. 27, 1866, Mary Ella, b. Apr. 9, 1868, Juliette ·Gray, b. Nov. 24, 1870, and Anna Rowena, b. Dec. 31, 1872. Mr. Eber Keyes died at Elgin, Ill., June 18, 1883, in his 85th year.

JOSEPH DIXON GRAY, b. in Sherburne, N. Y., May, 1807; married Mary Warren. Children:

> AUSTIN GRAY, b. 1831, killed by the Indians in California, 1854. Was remarkable for stature, (6 feet ten inches in height), strength and courage.
>
> OSCAR D. GRAY, born April 6, 1833; married, but no children; resides at Waterloo, Iowa. Was a soldier in the war for the Union, and acquitted himself with honor.
>
> MARY GRAY, only daughter, married Geo. Flanders, of Boston. She now resides in Kansas City.

Mr. J. D. Gray's first wife died in 1854, and for his second wife he married Lucy M. Boardman, at Waterford, Erie Co., Pa., Sept. 29, 1856. Children:

> CHARLES AUSTIN GRAY, b. April 5, 1858; married in 1880, Etta Babcock, of St. Paul, Minn. Resides at Waterville, Minn.

Mr. Joseph Dixon Gray died at Fayette, Iowa, March 1st, 1876. His widow, Mrs. Lucy M. Gray, is Matron of the Iowa Hospital for the Insane, at Independence, Iowa.

ADELAIDE LEE STRONG STANCLIFF,
AMANDA GRAY LEE, CAROLINE LEE STRONG.
RAYMOND ELY STANCLIFF.

AMANDA GRAY LEE.

Amanda Gray Lee, daughter of Elijah Gray, was born at Florida, N. Y., Nov, 23, 1792; moved the following year with her parents to Sherburne, N. Y., and has the distinction of being the only living representative of that band of pioneers and pilgrims who were the early settlers of that place. The following biography is furnished by one of her descendants:

"Her childhood was spent there, in the beautiful Chenango Valley, the enjoyment of whose fields and woods she shared with the birds and squirrels, and appreciated as fully as they. It could probably have been said of her, with as much truth as it ever is of any one, that she rivalled the birds, for she was a natural singer, and in after years developed a voice remarkable for power combined with sweetness of tone. It was sometimes mistaken for a flute. On arrival at young womanhood she was a prominent and popular member of a circle of forty cousins, of whom a large number could be called together on short notice.

"In 1813 her father removed with his family to Sheridan, Chautauqua Co., N. Y., where she married, in 1814, Joel Lee, and where all her children were born. Left alone with a family of eight, on the death of her husband in 1836, she brought them up in such a way as to give them a love for home so strong that her children were always glad to return. One of her sons-in-law, who wrote the dedication in a Bible, the joint gift of her children, quoted the passage, 'Her children shall rise up and call her blessed.'

"She has lived under the administration of every President of the United States, and, beginning with Jefferson, has personal recollection of the prominent events and general character of each one since, having always taken much interest in politics, and everything concerning the welfare of the community and country. A church member for over a half century, she evidently tries to lead a life consistent with her profession, and apparently has good reason to hope that when removed from this life, she will enter into the rest that is promised to the faithful.

"She is now in her 94th year, in good health, with a considerable degree of strength, and the possession of all her faculties."

OLIVE LEE, b. Dec. 25, 1814; died Feb. 19, 1833.

WELLINGTON LEE, b. Dec. 18, 1815; married in London, England, June 5, 1862, to Harriet E. Gray, daughter of Dr. Patrick W. Gray; died in New York City, March 21st, 1881.

Wellington Lee was an eminent Civil Engineer, and was the inventor and builder of the first successful Steam Fire Engine in America. He also raised the ships sunk in the harbor of Sevastopol in the Crimean War.

DANIEL URIEL LEE, of Ashville, N. C., b. Sept. 17, 1817; mar. March 1, 1846, Elizabeth B. Thorne; mar. 2d, May 12, 1859, Irene A. Lee; mar. 3d, July, 1868, Mary Larned Blashfield.

Daniel U. Lee volunteered in the 3d Iowa Battery, in Debuque, in Sept., 1861. The Battery took the field in the Army of the Southwest, under Gen. Curtis, in the Pea Ridge campaign. At that battle he was Chief of the line of Caissons, and was promoted to a Lieutenancy from that date. The Battery took part in Sherman's first attempt on Vicksburg, at taking of Arkansas Post, and afterward posted in garrison at Little Rock, Arkansas, to the end of the war. He was an efficient officer, and was especially commended by Gen. Sigel for his action at the battle of Pea Ridge.

T. C. LEE, oldest son of Daniel U. Lee, enlisted in an Ohio regiment at Newark, Ohio, in July, 1861, at the age of 15 years and one month. He served 7 months in Missouri; was discharged for disability, which proved not permanent, and after a rest of three months, he re-enlisted in the 145th Regt. Pa. Vols., at Erie, Pa. Went to the Army of the Potomac and took part in all the battles after Antietam. He carried the colors at Fredericksburgh and brought them off; was wounded at Bristoe Station, at Gettysburg, took part in three bayonet charges on second day's fight, and was wounded at Petersburg. He was made 1st Lieutenant at Gettysburg, and remained with his Regiment till the close of the war.

CAROLINE LEE, b. June 23, 1819; mar. Martin Strong, Oct. 4, 1842; residence, Waterford, Pa. Children:

> ADELAIDE LEE STRONG, b. Waterford, Pa., Nov. 12, 1843; mar. Ely M. Stancliff, Nov. 14, 1871, of Erie, Pa. Issue:
>
>> RAYMOND ELY STANCLIFF, b. Nov. 27, 1878.
>
> LEON STRONG, b. Sept. 15, 1845; residence, Fort Dodge, Iowa.
>
> SARA STRONG, b. Oct. 27, 1847; residence, Waterford, Pa.
>
> ROB ROY STRONG, b. Nov. 3, 1854; residence, Omaha, Nebraska.

ELENORA LEE, b. June 7, 1821; d. Sept. 20, 1823.

ELIAS BAUDINOT LEE, b. Aug. 1, 1823; mar. Caroline E. Douglas, Mar. 14, 1851.

Major Elias Baudinot Lee enlisted in the war for the Union in Co. A, of the 211th Regt. Pennsylvania Volunteers. He raised the Company in Meadville, Pa., where he resided, and was elected as Captain, 1864. The 211th had prominent part in the taking of Fort Steadman. Capt. Lee was in command of the Regiment in the final assault on Petersburgh, April 2, 1865, and was shot from the breastworks which he had mounted for example to his men. Waving his sword over his head he called his men to "Come on!" when he received a mortal wound from the sharpshooters. He died April 5th, 1865. His remains were sent home to Meadville, Pa., and buried with military honors, a large concourse of citizens following to the grave, among them the two brothers and a sister of the deceased. The demonstration was becoming the obsequies of a prominent citizen soldier, and was a mark of the esteem in which he was held by his patriotic fellow citizens. He had been promoted to Major of his Regiment a few days before his death, though his commission had not reached him.

> SARA ALMIRA LEE, b. July 9, 1826; mar. James Martin Porter, Sept. 5, 1844; d. Aug. 22, 1870, at Aiken, S. C.
>
> HELEN LEE, b. Sept. 29, 1832; mar. Jas. G. E. Larned, May 9, 1859; residence, Cedar Mountain, N. C., at which place she holds the position of P. M.

ELISHA GRAY.

Elisha Gray, son of Nathaniel and Deborah Lathrop Gray, was born at Dover, Dutchess Co., N. Y., Sept. 24, 1765. He married Martha (Patty) Burritt, daughter of Rev. Blackleach Burritt, and was among the pioneers and original proprietors of Sherburne, N. Y., in 1793. He afterwards removed to Spring-ville, Pa., and from thence to Madison, Lake Co., Ohio. He died in the summer of 1823, at Talmadge, Summit Co., Ohio, while on his return from Kentucky, where he had been on a vis-it to his son Alanson. Mrs. Gray died at Madison, Ohio, in June, 1851. Issue:

MELISSA GRAY, b. 1791; married Selic Fairchild; no children.

ALANSON GRAY, son of Elisha, b. May 4, 1793, married Ruth Cowgill, of Mason Co., Ky., by whom were two daughters, viz: Melissa and Ruth, the former born 1818, and the latter, 1819. The mother died when Ruth was a few days old. Melissa mar. Orville Rankin, at Greencastle, Ind., and had several sons and daughters. Ruth married a Mr. Atchison at Greencastle, and had sons and daughters. Jan. 2, 1821, Alanson Gray married for his second wife, Jane R. Tarvin, of Campbell Co., Ky., by whom he had seven sons and four daughters, to wit:

JOHN TARVIN GRAY, b. Sept. 14, 1821, at Kenton, Ky.		
ELISHA BURRITT " " Apr. 20, 1823,	"	"
ALFRED WHITMAN " " Sept. 27, 1825,	"	"
MARTHA JANE " " Jan. 2, 1827,	Carthage,	"
ALANSON " " Apr. 2, 1830,	"	"
SALLIE STANTON " " July 6, 1832,	"	"
OLIVER HAZZARD " " Aug. 8, 1833,	"	"
PHILANDER RAYMOND " Jan. 14, 1837, Campbell Co. "		
RICHARD TARVIN GRAY," Mar. 1, 1839,	"	"
SALLIE ARMSTRONG " " Mar. 19, 1841,	"	"
NANCY W., " " Sept. 15, 1843,	"	"

Mrs. Alanson Gray, b. Jan. 2, 1801, in what is now Kenton Co., Ky., about thirteen miles south of Covington, was a daughter of Richard Tarvin, and granddaughter of George Tarvin, who came from England with his parents and settled near Fredericksburg, Va. They were a fine stock of people, noted for solid moral and christian worth.

63.

Alanson Gray died in Campbell Co., Ky., Nov. 12, 1858.
Mrs. Gray died Dec. 18, 1869, and was buried near her birth-
place.

JOHN T. GRAY, married, June 22, 1848, Cynthia, daughter of
Philander Raymond, and grand-daughter of James Ray-
mond and Melissa Burritt Raymond, who was a sister of
Mr. Gray's grandmother, Martha (Patty), Burritt Gray.
She was born in Sherburne, N. Y., and educated in the
city of New York. Of this marriage was a son,

RAYMOND C. GRAY, b. May 16, 1849; mar. May 21,
1874, Mary Jane Eginton, an accomplished lady
who died one year after. Mr. Gray is an attorney and counsellor; residence, Covington, Ky.
He is alike a great-great-grandson of John Gray,
(3), of Sharon, Conn., of David Raymond, of
Kent, Conn., and of Rev. Blackleach Burritt,
of Revolutionary fame. A second son died in
infancy.

Cynthia Raymond Gray died at Cincinnati, O., March 28th,
1854, and John T. Gray married 2d, Dec. 1856, Sallie Tarvin.
Issue:

GEORGE T. GRAY, b. Sept. 10, 1857; married Margaret
Adelaide Williams, Mar. 6, 1883; residence, Frank-
lin, Pa.; has a son,
EDWIN DUNLAP GRAY, b. Dec. 12, 1883.

EDWIN GRAY, who d. 1861.

Sallie Tarvin Gray died in Covington, Aug. 19, 1860, and Mr.
Gray mar. 3d, Bettie H. Tarvin, (previous wife's sister,) in Covington, Feb. 12, 1862, and had:

BETTIE TARVIN GRAY, b. 1868.
EDWIN GRAY, b. 1870.

Also three children deceased. Bettie H. Tarvin Gray died
Nov. 12, 1870, and John T. Gray mar. 4th, Mrs. Addie Smith,
Sept. 18, 1873, at Franklin, Pa.

John T. Gray achieved high reputation as a Civil Engineer
and bridge builder. For biographical sketch of Mr. Gray see
pages 131 to 133. He resides at Covington, Ky.

ELISHA BURRITT GRAY, son of Alanson, mar. Aug. 1st, 1850, Margaretta R. McDowell, at Franklin, Pa. Children:

EMILY JANE (FLEMING,) born May 18, 1851, at Franklin, Pa.; married and has 2 children, Gray Fleming, born Aug. 23d, 1874, and Margaretta F., May 1st, 1879.

ANNA C. GRAY, born March 14, 1853; married Capt. J. P. Newell, (now Register and Recorder of Jasper Co., Mo.,) and has 3 children, 2 daughters and 1 son.

WM. GALBRAITH, 3d child and only son of E. B. Gray, born July 13, 1855; died Oct. 18, 1856.

MARGARETTA JOSEPHINE GRAY, 4th and last child of Elisha B. and Margaretta R., born May 24, 1858; married Henry S. Church, of New York, June 1st, 1880; has 2 children, viz: Catharine, and Henry S., Jr. Mr. Church died at Cheyenne, Wyoming, 1885.

Mr. and Mrs. E. B. Gray still continue to reside at Franklin.

ALFRED W. GRAY, 3d son of Alanson Gray, married at Cincinnati, O., 1849, Elmira Morris Bradowry, and has 1 son and 5 daughters, viz:

JANE R. GRAY.

ALANSON GRAY, born Jan. 31, 1853; unmarried, and lives at Vera, Ill.

SARAH B. GRAY, born Jan. 1855; lives with her uncle, Elisha B. Gray, at Franklin, Pa., and is an assistant in the Post Office at that place.

LYDIA B. GRAY, born Oct. 31st, 1857.

JULIA C. GRAY, born July 14, 1863.

MINNIE E. GRAY, born May, 1872.

MARTHA JANE GRAY, mar. B. B. Anderson in 1850, who died in 1881; she had a son and daughter.

ALANSON GRAY, JR., fourth son, married, 1854, Kate Reed, of Covington, Ky. They had 2 daughters, one of whom died young and the other is married. Mr. Gray died in March, 1861.

SALLIE STANTON GRAY, died in infancy.

OLIVER HAZZARD GRAY, fifth son, died in 1839, aged 6 years.

PHILANDER RAYMOND GRAY, sixth son, married July 19, 1862, Josephine C. McDowell, sister of Mrs. Elisha B. Gray, and has eleven children, three daughters and eight sons, viz :

ELISHA B. GRAY, JR., b. Jun. 25, 1865, Lewis Co., Ky.
PHILANDER R.,   "   " Dec. 8, 1866, Franklin, Pa.
WM. AYRES,   " May 24, 1868,   "   "
FREDERICK CHARLES, " Feb. 12, 1870,   "   "
FANNIE JOSEPHINE,   " Dec. 17, 1871,   "   "
ALANSON MCDOWLLL, " Oct. 24, 1873,   "   "
JOHN LATHROP,   " Feb. 6, 1875,   "   "
EMILY JANE,   " Feb. 11, 1877,   "   "
MCDOWELL,   " July 17, 1879,   "   "
THOMAS,   " Aug. 29, 1881,   "   "
JOSEPHINE,   " Oct. 11, 1883,   "   "

RICHARD TARVIN GRAY, son of Alanson Gray, mar. at Covington, Ky., 1866, Elizabeth Rood; 3 children, viz:

P. RAYMOND GRAY, b. 1867.
MOLLIE ROOD GRAY, b 1869.
SADIE GRAY, b. 1877.

Reside at Covington, Ky.

SALLIE A. GRAY, 3d daughter, mar. 1868, John Armstrong; had 5 children; d. Jan., 1881.

NANCY W. GRAY, mar. at Franklin, Pa., Oct. 10, 1860, Jas. W. Shaw, Register and Recorder of Venango Co., Pa.; one child, Mary Shaw, who died in June, 1872. Present residence, Bradford, Pa.

MARIA GRAY, youngest daughter of Elisha Gray, and sister of Alanson Gray, senior, married Dr. Charles Martin, 1819, at Sherburne, N. Y., and removed to Mason Co., Ky. Had 5 daughters, viz: Aurelia, Emily, Amelia, Cornelia, and Melissa, (the latter married Mr. George Moore and resides at Memphis, Scotland Co., Mo.,) and 3 sons: Charles, who has long resided at Carson City, Nevada, Henry Hazard, and Edward, who resides at Bethany, Mo. Maria Gray Martin died at Memphis, Scotland Co., Mo., Sept. 6, 1846.

PHILANDER RAYMOND GRAY.

A son of Alanson and grandson of Elisha Gray, in him are united the Lathrops, the Burritts and the Tarvins, while the strong Gray characteristics are still preserved. The following biographical sketch is from the *Citizen-Press* of Franklin, Pa., date of Nov. 6, 1884, it being the occasion of his removal from that city after a residence of over twenty years. It is a highly honorable record, both in public and private life; as a patriot soldier, a trusted official, an esteemed citizen, reflecting credit on himself and giving added lustre to the name of Gray:

"Our citizens were much surprised last week by the announcement that Mr. P. R. Gray had resigned the position of General Manager of the Eclipse Lubricating Oil Works. Universal regret was expressed, particularly when it was reported that he proposed to remove from this section of the country. Mr. Gray richly deserves the confidence and esteem with which he has always been regarded, and he retires from his important trust with the respect of all classes. His whole career justifies a warmth of friendship creditable alike to him and the community of which he has been for many years a valued member. Born and reared in Kentucky, where his early manhood was spent working at the carpenter trade, the petroleum excitement brought him to Franklin in February, 1861. The next spring he built a small refinery, shipped oil by water to Cincinnati, and laid the foundation for a lucrative business.

"Leaving everything in the hour of his country's peril, he enlisted in Company A., of the 121st Pennsylvania Volunteers, under Captain George E. Ridgway, going to the front with the army in August of 1862. After serving as 1st Sergeant of the Company he was promoted to 2d Lieutenant for bravery at the battle of Fredericksburg, Dec. 13th, 1862, and complimented in a general regimental order for his conduct on that hard-fought field. In October, 1863, he was promoted to 1st Lieutenant; was detailed as acting Quartermaster of the 121st Regiment and commissioned in November; in February, 1864, was detailed Quartermaster of the Brigade, serving as such until the close of the war, when he was honorably discharged. In 1865, a few months after his return from the seat of war, he was

elected as Sheriff of Venango County. It was expected he would discharge his responsible duties efficiently, and the result did not disappoint the public. During his term the Pithole excitement had its rise, lawlessness was frightfully prevalent, and the position of Sheriff was really the most arduous in the gift of the people. How faithfully the difficult task was performed is familiar to every resident of Oildom.

"Mr. Gray had cast his first vote for Lincoln in 1864, thus identifying himself with the Republican party, to which he was destined to render signal service. In 1869 he was appointed Collector of Internal Revenue for this District, holding the office five years, when he resigned to take charge of the Eclipse Refinery. The sterling qualities that marked his course in the army and as Sheriff were brought to bear in the Government service as Collector. The work was systematized thoroughly, the revenue was collected promptly, and no District in the United States could boast of better management. It is ten years since Mr. Gray became Superintendent of the Eclipse, which has grown to be the largest establishment of the kind in the world. In the supervision of the institution his energy, business tact and superior judgment have proved invaluable. To his skillful management no small share of its great prosperity is attributable. Competent in every respect to ensure the best results in each department, he took pride in bringing the works to the utmost degree of perfection. We voice the sentiment of the entire community in predicting his success in whatever enterprise he may engage. A residence of twenty years in this city has shown the staunch character of the man both in public and private life, and no citizen of Franklin stands higher in popular estimation than P. R. Gray."

Mr. Gray removed with his family to Elizabeth, N. J., in February, 1885, and became interested in the Polar Oil Refinery Co., of New York, the works being located near Bergen Point, N. J. He in the prime of life, in the fore-front of active business affairs, and the father of a very interesting family. Mrs. Gray, the mother of their eleven living children, is a woman of strong character, and is every way a worthy companion of her esteemed husband.

Ruth Gray, daughter of Nathaniel and Deborah Lathrop Gray, born at Dover, Dutchess Co., N. Y., Dec. 16, 1776, married Joel Hatch, Dec. 5, 1787, of Kent, Conn., and one of the pioneers and original proprietors of Sherburne, N. Y. Also afterwards Justice of the Peace, succeeding his father-in-law, Nathaniel Gray, to that office, and for over half a century a prominent citizen of that place. Mrs. Gray was one of the charter members of the Sherburne Congregational Church. She died Aug. 7, 1838. Mr. Hatch d. Mar. 26, 1855. Children:

DEBORAH HATCH, b. Oct. 31, 1789; d. Jan. 31. 1861.
JOEL HATCH, Jr., author of the History of Sherburne, N. Y., b. Nov. 3, 1791; d. Dec. 27, 1864.
MILO HATCH, b. Mar. 25, 1793; d. Aug. 5, 1830.
THERON HATCH, b. Nov. 21, 1795; d. Aug. 14, 1841.
JULIUS W. and JULIA HATCH, b. Jan. 10, 1801; Julia (Newton) d. Sept. 1, 1880; Prof. Julius Wells Hatch d. at Morrisville, N. Y., June 28, 1882.
RELIANCE HATCH, b. in Sherburne, July 2, 1804; married Joseph Carrier Sept. 9, 1830; residence, Elmira, N. Y.
R. C. HATCH, of Fayetteville, N. Y., b. Jan. 19, 1806.
ESTHER HATCH, b. Feb. 2, 1808; d. Nov. 9, 1863.

Bethiah Gray, daughter of Nathaniel and Bethiah Newcomb Raymond Gray, born at Kent, Conn., July 4, 1776, married Daniel Hibbard, at Sherburne, N. Y., and afterwards removed to the western part of the State, and died there.

ADDENDA.

Etta Babcock Gray, wife of Charles Austin Gray, (page 58,) died at Waterville, Minn., in May, 1885, aged 26 years.

J. Dixon Gray (page 58,) was for a term U. S. Revenue Assessor in Iowa; was member of the Presbyterian Church, and a man highly respected.

Elijah Gray and Sarai Raymond are supposed to have been married at Kent, Conn., in 1788. The statement (page 57), that he died at Jamestown, N. Y., proves to be incorrect. It was at the residence of his son Joseph Dixon Gray, Marengo, Ill. Mrs. Gray died at Sheridan, N. Y., in July, 1829. Elijah Gray enlisted in the Revolutionary army at the age of 17, and served until the close of the war. He was a man of genial nature and made many friends.

JOSEPH GRAY.

"Joseph Gray, oldest son of John Gray (3), was born in Windham, Conn., June 12, 1732, and died in Greene, Chenango Co., N. Y., March 29, 1796, leaving two sons, Jeduthan and Amos." This is the brief mention made in the Record of John Gray (4,) of his elder brother Joseph, and but for which probably the names of not one of his many descendants would have appeared in this Genealogy. With that as a starting point, by correspondence it was ascertained that there were several persons by the name of Gray residing in Greene. Letters from them stated that they were the descendants of Jeduthan and Amos Gray, but as for Joseph Gray, they had never heard of him; no such man had ever come to that part of the country. This was certainly a decided and unexpected foil. But there was the clear though brief statistical statement of John Gray in regard to his brother, made at the time of his death, giving exact date as well as place, which was not far distant, in the same county; and then there was the corroboration of the names Jeduthan and Amos, so it was determined to persistently push on investigation until the truth should be made clearly to appear.

Inquiry made in the direction of Sharon and vicinity revealed the fact that the names of Joseph Gray and Jeduthan appeared in a list of those who protested against the aggressions of the British crown, at Amenia Precinct in 1775, and the name of the latter appeared as a patriot volunteer at that place in 1776. A search of the old records of Dutchess County at Poughkeepsie, revealed the fact that Joseph Gray had given a mortgage to Mary Walton, Apr. 12, 1765, for £100, on 30 acres in Amenia Precinct, "adjoining the Oblong line, in accordance with a certain obligation dated May 6, 1762;" which fixed his residence there at that early date. It was also discovered by old tax rolls of Amenia that he was assessed continuously from 1771 to 1778, inclusive, and in the latter year the names of Jeduthan and Amos Gray, both also appear as each taxed on £1.

These facts all taken together were strongly corroborative of the relationship of father and sons, as stated in the record of John Gray. But there was also another clue. The Jeduthan

Gray who was at Greene, N. Y., was a Baptist Elder of note. Elder Jeduthan Gray was found to have previously been the pastor of a church at Great Barrington, Berkshire Co., Mass., for many years, and had removed from there to Greene. Amos Gray, his brother, had also lived at Great Barrington during that period.

The old town records of Amenia show that "Joseph Gray, his ear mark is a swallow tail in each ear, slit the upper side left ear. Recorded this 18th day of April, 1762." Also, "Joseph Gray bought land in Lot No. 35," (30 acres), in 1762, and sold the same in 1769. He must have continued to reside in that town until 1779, as a daughter, "Sarah Gray, of Amenia," was married at Sharon, Sept. 14, 1779, and also her brother Jeduthan, same time and place. After this time all trace of him seemed to be lost. A determined, thorough personal search however, finally, almost by accident, disclosed him again, in an interesting connection on the records of the old Baptist Church at Millerton, N. Y., formerly a part of Amenia Precinct. At an Ordaining Council held there Dec. 17, 1788, it appears that Joseph Gray was present from the Baptist Church in New Canaan, Columbia Co., N. Y., and was appointed to make the opening prayer; that Elder Jeduthan Gray, then of Great Barrington, Mass., was appointed "to preach the sermon and give the right hand of fellowship." Father and son met together in such delightful and sacred companionship! There was and is the original record, and it was a great pleasure to look upon it, and to stand upon the spot where it was made. The lost was found in that venerable old tome, so happily preserved, with other treasures.

New Canaan was at that time the residence of John Gray, brother of Joseph, and what more natural than that he should have gone there from Amenia, as the tendency of migration was in that direction? It was a great disappointment however, to the writer, that thorough search afterwards made in New Canaan, failed to find further evidence of Joseph Gray there. The records of that old Baptist Church, itself now extinct, alas, are lost! And with them doubtless much of interest concerning Joseph Gray. The site of the old church, a wild and rocky height, with a few marked and unmarked graves about it, and nature's baptismal pool in the mountain stream near by, are all that remain. The voices of the past are silent, and give no sign other than here recorded.

That Joseph Gray did remove to Greene, N. Y., and died there as stated, there is no reasonable doubt. Two of his brothers, John and Nathaniel, had removed to Sherburne, also in the Chenango Valley, and only about twenty miles distant. It was natural that he should go in the same direction. Again, his son Amos was at Greene, in 1794, two years before the period of his father's death. The evidence on that point is conclusive, and must be taken as final. But in regard to the personality of the father of Jeduthan and Amos Gray, there is other and absolutely convincing testimony, that of the living witness, the venerable Dr. Joseph Gray, of Cambridgeboro, Crawford Co., Pa., son of Elder Jeduthan Gray, who after long search was found, and when communicated with informed the writer that his grandfather, the father of Elder Jeduthan Gray, was Joseph Gray, and he, Dr. Joseph, was named after him! That was certainly a finality from which, with all the corroborating circumstances, there can be no appeal.

Yet one important fact eluded and still eludes all research: The personality of the mother of Joseph Gray's children. Nowhere does her name or identity appear; not among the records nor even in the traditions of the family is there the least trace of when or where or who Joseph Gray married, or when or where she died. Not even the living grandson had the most indistinct recollection in that regard. In vain were the old records of all that vicinage carefully conned over for the missing link. It could not be found. This was not slight cause for regret, but the search revealed the fact that there were daughters as well as sons, and a numerous family of descendants, particulars of which follow. The father and mother of such a race must have been possessed of decided character and strong individuality, though their deeds unheralded, they sleep in nameless graves. And this tribute to their worth may well be accorded to them by their descendants to the remotest generation, in all time to come.

JEDUTHAN GRAY.

Elder Jeduthan Gray, the oldest son, and probably oldest child of Joseph Gray, was born in the year 1756. This much appears in the old family Bible record made by his own hand, in the possession of the writer, but the month and the day of the month are too faded and indistinct to be deciphered. The inscription on his memorial stone corroborates the above, in that it is inscribed thereon that he died Mar. 2d, 1830, "In the 74th year of his age." As to the place, his living son, Dr. Joseph Gray, of Cambridgeboro, Pa., says it was in Conn. Probably at Sharon, as that was his father's early home. The next mention of him is his signing of the Patriot protest against British aggression, at Amenia Precinct, 1775, and in 1776 he enlisted in the Revolutionary army, and was a Sergt. in Capt. Wheeler's Co., Col. Hopkin's N. Y. Regt. The History of Amenia says that "Jeduthan Gray was honorably noticed for bravery at the battle near Fort Independence, (vicinity of Peekskill, N. Y.,) in 1777." His name appears on the tax list of Amenia for 1778, and the Church records of Sharon, Conn., show that he was married to Anna Warren of that place, a niece of Lieut. James Warren, a prominent citizen of Sharon, and probably daughter of Nehemiah Warren, by Rev. Cotton Mather Smith, Sept. 14th, 1779. The records of the Probate Court of Sharon show that Jeduthan Gray and Anna his wife conveyed to Jehiel Rowley, Feb. 27, 1795, all their right, title and interest in the real and personal estate of Lieut. James Warren, dec'd, which had been given conditionally by will to Deborah Warren, his wife, on his decease, May 14, 1788. Consideration, £20.

Jeduthan Gray having become prominent in after years as an Elder and Baptist preacher, it was of interest to discover if possible his church connection and the date and place of his ordination. Search was made in the old records of that region, however, without avail. Only two Baptist churches were found of date early enough for such record, and a personal examination of one of these, that now at Millerton, N. Y., formerly Amenia Precinct, failed to disclose anything except the fact that Elder Jeduthan Gray had been present at an Ordaining Council there held Dec. 17, 1788, on which occasion he preached the ordaining sermon and gave the right hand of fellowship. Also according to the record Elder Gray was there present on the preceding Sabbath, "and gave advice and sweet counsel both to the church and to the candidates."

At this time he was preaching at a place called Seekonk, in the town of Great Barrington, Mass., and about two miles westwardly from the present village of that name. This unquestionably was his first pastorate, but where did he come from; where did he receive ordination; and where did he reside after his marriage in 1779 and prior to his appearance as a Baptist preacher at Great Barrington in 1785? These are interesting queries, and in this connection the following statement made by one of his sons, many years ago, the original of which, an interesting old record, is now at hand, is pertinent:

Warren Gray, born Dec. 23, 1784, in Columbia Co., N. Y. Moved to Great Barrington, Mass., the year following, where he resided until his tenth year, when he removed to Egremont, where he resided until his twentieth year, when he emigrated to Greene, Chenango Co., N. Y., where he has since resided.

This is a very significant record. "Born in Columbia Co., N. Y." Doubtless in the vicinity of the New Canaan first Baptist Church, which was the only church of that denomination then in existence in that county, or region, and near where his father resided, who afterwards represented that church in the Ordaining Council in the old Baptist church in the then Amenia Precinct, 1788, to which reference has already been made. In all probability he resided there during that period, and becoming interested in that church, was in due course of time set apart to the ministry as an Elder. Unfortunately the records of that old church, which has since ceased to exist, have been lost, and therefore the exact data, so desirable, cannot be verified. From that place—the old church was located on the heights of what is now Austerlitz, near Red Rock and the town of Canaan—he very likely followed down the valley of Green River, and finding the western part of Great Barrington and the plains of Egremont fair to look upon, and the people without a shepherd, he set about to build up the walls of Zion there, and to found a new Baptist church and society. His first appearance there must have been in 1785, and in that place and vicinity he successfully labored for twenty years, building up a church in that rural region that had in 1803, according to the published reports of the Shaftesbury Association, a membership of 121 communicants.

Although it is eighty years since Elder Gray removed from that neighborhood, his memory is still cherished there, and many traditions of him remain. Oliver Watson, aged 91, who resides near Seekonk, on being interviewed said he remembered him well, and also his sons. He pointed out the site of the old church, which was a large barn-like structure, since removed, and also a mound in the midst of a fertile field where had stood the house in which Elder Gray lived. David Olmstead, aged 90, also well remembered Elder Gray; had heard him preach many times. and thought a great deal of him. Hon. Daniel B. Fenn, now of Stockbridge, Mass., whose father resided in that vicinity in those early days, says Elder Gray was frequently at the house of his father, who was a prominent Methodist, and he describes him as a man of fine presence, and kindly, genial countenance; social, and good company. Others had alike pleasant recollections of him.

The public records at Great Barrington show that Elder Gray bought 40 acres of land there in 1787, for which he paid £140, and sold the same in 1799, for $900. In 1788 he paid taxes on personal and real, 4s. 9d. About 1796, Elder Gray moved to Egremont, two or three miles to the westward, that being a more central and convenient place for his congregation, and they met for worship afterwards at what is now North Egremont, where the church is located to this day, and the records from 1791 are still preserved. The old house where Elder Gray lived, near there, is still pointed out. It appears that though "fervent in spirit," he was "not slothful in business," but was a man of substance as well as a preacher of the Gospel, was active and prosperous. His salary, however, was only £40 per annum. He bought 30 acres of land in Egremont, in 1804, for $120, and sold the same in 1805 for $330. He also sold 70 acres there Aug. 19, 1805, for $1,800, and Nov. 6, 1805, sold 12 acres for $125; all of which was preparatory to his removal to Greene, N. Y., which took place the following year, 1806.

While pastor of the Great Barrington and Egremont church, Elder Gray attained much prominence as a Baptist preacher. He was frequently called to Hillsdale, N. Y., and regularly supplied the pulpit of the North Hillsdale Baptist church, on alternate Sundays, during a part of the year, 1796. Afterwards, in 1802, he was moderator of a stormy council held there to consider the question of dividing that church; also again January 27, 1803, on which occasion the record says "Elder Gray manifested a burthen against bro. Richard Kenyon for his disorderly conduct in railing against him in the church;" which was bad for Richard, for though slow to wrath Elder Gray evidently was not a man to be trifled with.

Elder Gray was present at Flat Brook church, Canaan, N. Y., at a meeting of the Shaftesbury Association, Sept. 1, 1790; and at an Ordaining Council held at the same place, May 27, 1795, and he preached the opening sermon before the Stephentown Association at Union Village, N. Y., June 7, 1797. His report of a case of discipline referred to him by the Baptist Church at Flat Brook, found among the archives, is so original and unique, that a part of the testimony, and the findings in the case, all in his own characteristic calligraphy, is here given as a rarity. It is on a well preserved sheet of foolscap, brown with age, closely written, viz:

Sisters Esther and Sally Beech saith, that they believe that Br. Brownson has given just occasion of Burthen by showing too much fondness toward Sister Priscilla Church.

Deacon North saith, he believed that Br. Brownson's conduct toward Sister Priscilla Church was wounding to the cause of religion,

Sister Sabra North saith, she did withdraw from communion because she did believe that Br. Brownson and Sister Priscilla did wound religion.

Capt. Tiler and wife saith, they believe that Br. Brownson and Sister Priscilla did conduct with that fondness toward each other that was wounding to religion.

Br. Thomas Marshal saith, he believeth that Br. Brownson's conduct towards Sister Priscilla was that which gave great occasion to gainsayers to speak reproachfully of religion.

Sisters Elizabeth and Mary North saith they believe that Bro. Brownson and Sister Priscilla did show that fondness for each other that gave great occasion of Burthen.

A true copy, attest, JEDUTHAN GRAY, Cl'k.

To the 2d Baptist Church at Canaan: Whereas, we have received a request from you to send Brethren to give the reasons why Ashbel Brownson may not with propriety join with you in Church relation; these are the Reasons which we hold as a bar of fellowship until his Brethren are satisfied with him, or made to appear that they ought to be satisfied with him. JEDUTHAN GRAY.

And so at last Elder Gray bade farewell to the people with whom he had lived and labored for upwards of twenty years, and to whom he had become so strongly attached, to journey to his new home in the Chenango valley, and to a new field of labor. The following sketch of his life from that period onward, is quoted from the early history of Greene, written by the late Dr. W. D. Purple, of that place, and is full of interest:

"In the year 1806 Elder Jeduthan Gray located on the farm now owned by Philo Webb, east of the Genegantslet Creek. He was from Berkshire Co., Mass., where he had been well and favorably known as a clergyman of the Baptist denomination. Immediately on his arrival among us he commenced the work of gathering a church which was called the 2d Baptist Church of Greene. It soon became respectable both in character and numbers, and extended over that part of Greene and the eastern part of the adjoining town of Lisle. Elder Gray was the moving spirit in this extensive organization. His clerical duties were not confined to a central point, but extended to every neighborhood and hamlet in the vicinity. His unremitting attention to the sick, the dying and the disconsolate elicited universal praise. His talent and ability were of a high order, and not only in his pastoral duties but in every relation of life incident to a new settlement his advice was sought and his agency required. Our early settlers fully appreciated his services and sacrifices in their behalf; his councils and admonitions are recorded in grateful remembrance by his cotemporaries, and the plandit of a good and faithful servant embalms his memory. He died at Sugar Grove, Warren Co., Pa., in 1830."

Elder Gray removed from Greene to the town of Concord, Erie Co., Pa., in 1823. Some of his family had preceded him thither, and the settlement they made was called "Grays." The Post Office address is Spartansburg, Pa. There he continued his labors as a pioneer preacher, and was actively so engaged until the time of his decease.

The following letter giving account of the death of Elder Gray was written by his son, Dr. Joseph Gray, to a brother at Greene, N. Y.:

ROCKDALE, April 1st, 1830.

Dear Brother: Yours of the 18th inst. was duly received. We were glad to hear that you were all well. Almira has been very low in health. I almost despaired of her recovery, but through the goodness of God she is recovering her health in a measure. I have not heard from Concord since I left there, the day after father was buried. Father was taken unwell on the Canisteo, about forty miles from Ketchum's, and continued to get worse until he arrived at Sugar Grove, Warren Co., Pa., 22 miles from Concord. He stopped at Capt. Phelps', three-quarters of a mile from Hiram's, and was unable to be removed from there, until he died, which was one week. His complaint was the pleuresy and inflammation of the lungs. He was carried into the neighborhood where he lived, and buried. He retained his senses to the last, and died triumphing in the faith of that Gospel he has preached to others rising of half a century. I asked him if he was sensible that he was but a short time for this world, perhaps ten minutes before he breathed his last. "Oh, yes; but I go with a hope of glorious immortality beyond the grave. Come, Lord Jesus! Oh, come quickly! Not my will but thine be done, Oh, Lord!" and died without a struggle.

The devoted pastor, the faithful friend, the patriot soldier, the loving husband and father, the able preacher, and beloved Elder, his work well done, his warfare accomplished, had fallen asleep.

"Servant of God, well done!
Rest from thy loved employ;
The battle fought, the victory won,
Enter thy Master's joy."

Anna Warren Gray, Elder Gray's beloved and worthy consort, died Jan. 28th, 1837, in her 77th year, and was buried by his side.

DESCENDANTS OF ELDER JEDUTHAN GRAY.

Silas Gray, oldest son of Elder Jeduthan Gray, was born March 23d, 1781; mar. Polly Hare; died at Spartansburg, Pa., Aug. 19, 1849. Children:

LEVI GRAY, b. Apr. 15, 1803; mar. Lucy Lewis; children:
WILLIAM GRAY, dec'd.
PATTY GRAY,
LEWIS GRAY,
SILAS GRAY.

EMELINE GRAY, b. July 14, 1804.

WILLIAM GRAY, son of Silas Gray, was b. Aug. 23; 1808; mar. Dolly Rose, July 3, 1831; she d. May 1, 1853; mar. 2d, Louisa Akin, May 7, 1854; he died April 14, 1885; children:

> ALBERT GRAY, b. Oct. 23, 1833; mar. Rosine Akin, Jan. 1, 1856; Concord, Pa.; children:
>
>> FLORA GRAY, b. Mar. 23, 1858; mar. Edward Baker; children: Velna and Mary Baker.
>>
>> WILLIAM GRAY, b. Feb. 16, 1860; mar. Etta ———one child,
>>
>>> NINA GRAY, b. Nov. 1881.
>>
>> ISRAEL GRAY, b. Nov. 7, 1867.
>>
>> JEAN W. GRAY, b. Mar. 11, 1879.

> CORDELIA GRAY, daughter of William Gray, was b. Mar. 14, 1835; mar. Harvey Davis, Sept. 10, 1854; widow; four children; two sons, Weldon and Forrest; two daughters, dec'd.

> ALONZO GRAY, of Titusville, Pa., son of William Gray, b. Jan. 25, 1838; mar. Lottie Droun, Sept. 8, 1864; children:
>
>> ALTON L. GRAY, b. June 22, 1865.
>>
>> DOLLY R. GRAY, b. Sept. 21, 1872.

> MARY ANN GRAY, b. June 8, 1839; mar. Frank Murdock, Mar. 26, 1860; d. Nov. 11th, 1883. Children: Irving, William, and Stella.

> JOHN GRAY, Dr., b. Dec. 9, 1840; mar. Agnes Baker, June 27, 1866; d. at Findley's Lake, N. Y., Mar. 7, 1873; two children:
>
>> WILLIE GRAY, dec'd.
>>
>> NELLIE GRAY.

> PASCHAL GRAY, Dr., of Rochelle, Ill., b. Feb. 5, 1844; mar. Lydia Carpenter, Mar. 15, 1865; mar. 2d, Agnes Cannings.

> SARAH GRAY, b. Jan. 25, 1846; mar. D. D. Carpenter, July 3, 1864; five children: Delbert, Mamie, Stella, Arthur, and Willie, dec'd; residence, McPherson, Kansas.

> LUCY GRAY, b. July 2, 1847; mar. Lyman Murdock, May 30, 1868; d. Feb. 3, 1878; one child, Eddie.

> SILAS GRAY, b. June 30, 1849; mar. Elda Howard, Sept. 10, 1872; Concord, Pa.

JEDUTHAN GRAY, b. May 27, 1851; mar. Rossie
Thomas, Aug. 26, 1879; children:
BYRON W. GRAY, b. Oct. 6, 1881.
ZETTIE A. GRAY, b. Nov. 11, 1885.
DOLLY CECELIA GRAY, b. Nov. 10, 1852; d. June
14, 1874.
EMMA GRAY, b. July 7, 1857; mar. Bruce Miller,
Aug. 29, 1875; one child, Ernest; residence,
Elgin, Pa.
ADDIE GRAY, b. Nov. 20, 1861; mar. Frank Hyde,
Feb. 14, 1886. Residence, Spartansburg, Pa.

William Gray died at his residence in Concord township, Pa.,
of Paralysis, April 14, 1885. The following sketch of his life is
from the Corry *Herald:* "Mr. William Gray, our esteemed
friend who has just passed from among us, settled on the farm
where he died, in 1834. Few men have possessed the confidence and respect of his fellow citizens to the extent that he
did. For 35 years he was Justice of the Peace, and for many
years was School Director. He was a member of the Spartansburg Baptist Church 22 years, having the confidence and christian sympathy and fellowship of his brethren."

BETHEL GRAY, b. Nov. 22, 1814; mar. Eliza Cummings;
dec'd; no children.
ANGELINE GRAY, b. July 28, 1816; mar. Converse Higgins;
one child, James Higgins; Freehold, Pa.
LYMAN GRAY, b. Dec. 13, 1819; mar. Mary Bills; d. July
16, 1884. Children:
PARNEY, dec'd.
ELLA, dec'd.
LAVERN.
FRANKLIN, dec'd.
FRANCIS.
JEDUTHAN GRAY, b. May 8, 1823; mar. Emeline Blakeslee;
mar. 2d, Adeline Droun; Spartansburg, Pa.; children:
ERNEST, dec'd.
DELIA, b. Oct. 20, 1861.

POLLY GRAY, daughter of Elder Jeduthan Gray, b. Mar. 1,
1782; united with the Baptist Church of Great Barrington and Egremont, Apr. 21, 1799; mar. Eli Webb; d.
at Greene, N. Y., July 27, 1854.

WARREN GRAY.

Warren Gray, second son of Elder Gray was born in Columbia
Co., Dec. 23, 1784, and removed from Egremont, Mass., to
Greene, N. Y., in 1805. The following biographical sketch was
published at the time of his decease, Jan. 9, 1869: "In the
death of our aged fellow citizen, Warren Gray, Esq., our whole
community feels a shock. He has been for years the most prominent landmark in our midst, a link in the chain that unites us to
a past generation. He has fallen like the stately oak that has
long survived the primeval forest, the observed of all observers,
which at last yields to the decay of time, and falls to mingle
with its native dust. He came to this town in 1805, settling on
the East of the Genagantslet, and amid all the hardships and
privations incident to pioneer life, bore his full share of its trials,
and aided largely in converting a wilderness into the abode of
civilization and refinement. He was buried the 11th of Jan'y,
1869, by the members of Eastern Light Lodge, of which he had
been a member for 55 years, and twice its Master, assisted by
large delegations from all the adjacent Lodges, and attended by
a guard of honor from Malta Commandery of Binghampton, N.
Y., of which he was a member." Mr. Gray was appointed Justice of the Peace by Gov. Clinton, and held the office for fifty
consecutive years, and until the time of his decease.

Warren Gray married Laura Beach, 1805; she died Nov. 12,
1821, and he married 2d, Lucretia Ashcraft, Nov. 15, 1828, who
died June 14, 1880. Descendants:

> ALVIN GRAY, son of Warren, b. Oct. 14, 1807; mar. Lydia
> Ann Foot, Jan. 17, 1832, of Aurora, N. Y., who was
> b. at Homer N. Y., Feb. 3, 1812. Children:
>
>> HELEN, b. Apr. 8, 1833; mar. Joseph D. Josslyn,
>> of Boston, Mass., Dec. 4, 1860, now of Bar-
>> ker, Broome Co., N. Y.; two sons, Archie and
>> Josie, both dec'd.
>>
>> LAURA, b. Mar. 2, 1837; d. June 9, 1853.
>>
>> JENNIE, b. Jan. 13, 1839; mar. Cyrus J. Reynolds
>> of Corning, N. Y., Apr. 3, 1867, where she
>> and her husband and two sons, Herbert and
>> Harry, reside.

Mr. and Mrs. Alvin Gray now reside with their daughter and son-in-law, Mr. and Mrs. Josslyn; P. O. address, Chenango Forks, N. Y.

HARRIET GRAY, b. June, 1812; mar. Timothy Winston; had two sons, Curtis, and Chas. G. Winston, of Greene, N. Y. She d. July 4, 1843.

LUCY ANN GRAY, daughter of Warren, b. Jan. 27, 1815; mar. Stephen A. Race, May 30, 1833; two sons, Warren B., of Irving Park, Ill., and James Race, of Brooklyn, N. Y.

ELIZA A. GRAY, daughter of Warren, b. Feb. 3, 1817; d. July 4, 1858.

LAURA J. GRAY, b. June, 1819; mar. Stephen W. Davis; May 16, 1847; one daughter, Sarah, who mar. Smith Hotchkiss, June 5, 1867.

CHARLES GRAY, son of Warren, b. Sept. 28, 1821; mar. Mardula Carter, Oct. 21, 1843, who d. Mar. 8, 1855; mar. 2d, Mary J. Ramsay, Aug. 30, 1858. Residence, Greene, N. Y. Children:

FRANK E. GRAY, b. June 30, 1848; mar. Lydia M. Carter, Oct. 26, 1870; is a Dentist, and resides at Greene, N. Y.; one child,
MARDULA C. GRAY, b. Jan. 29, 1873.

LUCY A. GRAY, daughter of Charles Gray, b. Sept. 30, 1850; residence, Greene, N. Y.

CHARLES W. GRAY, b. Nov. 13, 1859; is an attorney and counsellor at Greene, N. Y.; mar. Anna M. Russell, Oct. 17, 1883; one child,
AGNES R. GRAY, b. Jan. 4, 1885.

ANN ELIZABETH GRAY, daughter of Warren, b. Nov. 27, 1832; mar. Chas. H. Barnard, July 17, 1861, who d. March 27, 1864; she mar. 2d, Frederick E. Barnard, Jan. 23, 1873.

BETHEL GRAY.

Bethel Gray, third son of Elder Jeduthan Gray, was born in Great Barrington, Mass., Jan'y 24th, 1787. May 24th, 1811, he married Cornelia Carter, who was born Jan. 22, 1794. A kinsman still residing at Greene, N. Y., says of him: "Bethel Gray lived in this, and the adjoining county of Broome, where it might be truly said of him that he made the wilderness to blossom like the rose. He raised a large family, most of whom are yet living. He was a man of stern integrity, and many noble traits of character; was looked up to in all the relations of life." Bethel Gray died Feb. 4th, 1866; his wife died July 7th, 1869. Children and descendants:

MIRIAM GRAY, b. Sept. 18, 1812; mar. John Aldrich, Nov. 21, 1831, at Ithaca, N. Y. He d. Aug. 16, 1871. Had two children: William, b. Aug. 15, 1832, mar. Mary M. Haupt; have a son and daughter. Mary A. Aldrich, b. Feb. 2, 1836, mar. John D. Weed, Mar. 8, 1869, who d. Aug. 21, 1872. Mrs. Aldrich is now a widow and resides with her son William at Wyoming.

MARY ANN GRAY, b. July 13, 1814; mar. Herman C. Reed of Ithaca, N. Y. Had three sons and one daughter. Two of the sons died of disease contracted in the war for the Union. Mr. Reed is deceased and Mrs. Reed now lives with her surviving children at Brockton, N. Y.

JULIA ANN GRAY, b. Sept. 23d, 1816; mar. Joel Parcell, of Ithaca, N. Y., Sept. 21, 1834; four sons: William T., b. July 18, 1835; Charles E., b. Feb. 2, 1839; Frank G., b. Sept. 20, 1844; Ambrose W., b. Mar. 19, 1851. The three oldest are married. Frank and Charles live in Florida, William in Colorado, and Ambrose, unmarried, lives with his parents at Fremont, Neb.

HIRAM T. GRAY, oldest son of Bethel, was born Jan. 21, 1818, and married Susannah Minsker, Oct. 1, 1843, at Jersey Shore, Pa. Present residence, Big Rapids, Mich. Four sons living, and one daughter, who died in infancy, as follows:

SYLVESTER H. GRAY, son of Hiram T., b. Feb. 3, 1846, at Jersey Shore, Pa.; mar. Antha Gray. daughter of Dr. W. S. Gray, of Freeport, Ill., June 16, 1875. Removed to Big Rapids, Mich., 1873, and is engaged in the lumber business. One child,
VIVIAN BYRON GRAY, b. Nov. 17, 1876.

JEROME B. GRAY, son of Hiram T., b. Sept. 27, 1848, at Jersey Shore, Pa.; mar. Kate M. Darlington, daughter of Hon. Wm. Darlington, at West Chester, Pa., Feb. 6, 1873, where he now resides, and is a member of the firm of Hooper Bro. & Darlington. Children:
NORMAN D. GRAY, b. May 16, 1874.
ISABELLA GRAY, b. May 1, 1876; d. May 8, 1876.
CHARLES P. GRAY, b. July 4, 1880.

EUGENE W. GRAY, b. May 1, 1858, at Lock Haven, Pa.; mar. Jennie L. Stevens, at Big Rapids, Mich., Nov. 22, 1881; residence, Roscommon, Mich.; one child,
SUSIE E. GRAY, b. July 1, 1883.

GEORGE C. GRAY, youngest son of Hiram T., b. March 18, 1860; unmarried; resides at Big Rapids, Mich.

Susannah Minsker Gray died Aug. 21, 1875, and Hiram T. Gray married 2d, Hannah A. Phillips, May 10, 1877.

LUCINDA GRAY, daughter of Bethel Gray, b. July 29, 1822; mar. Luther A. Bliven, Jan. 30, 1844; he dec'd, since which she has twice married; resides at Unadilla, N.Y., with her only surviving daughter.

LAURA A. GRAY, daughter of Bethel, b. Sept. 24, 1824; mar. Lyman Frost, of McDonough, N. Y., in 1846; has had six children: Cornelia, mar. Henry Blakesly, of Lincoln, Neb., and has two children; Alice, the second daughter, mar. Prof. E. Howard, of the University of Nebraska; Sumner Frost, d. in Colorado; Flora, living with her parents, at Lincoln, Neb.; Lincoln Frost, and Fremont Frost, dec'd.

CHARLOTTE J. GRAY, dau. of Bethel, b. July 26, 1827; mar. LeRoy A. Casterline, Oct. 9, 1851; has four sons: Orrin D., b. 1853, and mar. Mary D. Webster, at Lansing, Mich., 1876; Warren B., b. 1855, mar. J. M. Webster, 1881; Herbert L., b. 1861, mar. Clarie Hallock, in 1880; Fred S., b. 1861 —all of Maple Rapids, Mich.

MARGARET M. GRAY, dau. of Bethel, b. Sept. 2d, 1829; mar. Samuel L. Vars, April 5, 1845; d. July 26, 1861,

ORRIN D. GRAY, son of Bethel, b. June 16, 1832; mar. Margaret E. Wolcott, of Corning, N. Y., Jan. 30, 1855; moved to Nebraska, 1879; d. Sept. 6, 1879; children:
FRED B. GRAY, b. Jan. 19, 1856; mar. Ida S. Gage, March 10, 1875; residence, Lisle, Broome Co., N. Y.; children:
GEORGE W. GRAY, b. Jan. 23, 1877.
FLORENCE S. GRAY, b. Aug. 19, 1884.
MARY L. GRAY. b. May 22, 1858; mar. Martin Joyne, Mar. 15, 1882; residence, Lisle, N. Y.
CHARLES M. GRAY, b. Nov. 27, 1860; Fireman on R. R.; residence, Corning, N. Y.

HORATIO N. GRAY, b. Oct. 13, 1835; d. April 11, 1836.

HEMAN C. GRAY, youngest son of Bethel Gray, b. Sept. 8, 1838; mar. Eveline N. Gates, Sept. 14, 1867; residence, Broome Co., N. Y.

WILLIAM S. GRAY.

Dr. William S. Gray, son of Bethel Gray, and grandson of Elder Jeduthan Gray, was born June 26, 1820, and married Margaretta Hill, of White Deer, Lycoming Co., Pa., Apr. 27, 1848. Dr. Gray attended lectures at the Philadelphia Medical College. After marriage, removed to Stephenson Co., Illinois, in 1848. Practised medicine there seven years, after which he engaged in mercantile business. Was elected County Treasurer in 1857, serving three terms— six years. Was engaged in the manufacture of woolen goods for a number of years, and operated several farms. He removed from Freeport, Ill, to Big Rapids, Mich., in 1876, where he entered into partnership with his son-in-law, S. H. Gray, constituting the firm of S. H. Gray & Co., engaged in the manufacture of lumber and shingles. Has served seven years as Alderman from the Fourth Ward in the City Council of Big Rapids.

Dr. Gray has had three daughters and one son. Antha, eldest daughter, born April 8, 1849, married S. H. Gray, son of Hiram T. Gray, June 16, 1875, and has a son, Vivian Byron Gray, born Nov. 17, 1876. Next daughter died in infancy. Third daughter, Ida, died at the age of ten.

WILLIAM BYRON GRAY, only son of Dr. Gray. born March 24, 1866, at Freeport, Ill., was drowned in the Muskegon river, at Big Rapids, Mich., July 5, 1878. The following brief extracts from an account of the noble life and tragic death of this gifted youth, published at that date, is here given:

"Monday, July 8th, at 8 o'clock in the evening. a hearse, followed by a long line of carriages, passed along Michigan Avenue bearing the remains of Byron Gray to the Cemetery. He came to this city a little more than two years ago with his parents, Dr. and Mrs. Gray. Last Friday, July 5th, toward evening, he went to the river to bathe with two companions. By inadvertance he got into a swift current, beyond his depth, and being unable to swim, his companions came to the rescue, and the older one swam with him almost to a place of safety, when Byron letting go his hold was swept away by the rapid current, and despite every effort was drowned. Our city has never, per-

W S Gray

haps, been more profoundly stirred, than when the sad news passed from one to another, Byron Gray is drowned!"

"The awful grief of father and mother can be conceived only by those who have passed through great sorrows. He was the only child remaining at home, and he was to his mother the most loving friend and companion. Indeed, the whole city mourns the sudden ending of so beautiful and promising a life."

HIRAM GRAY.

Hiram Gray, fourth son of Elder Jeduthan Gray, was born in Great Barrington, Mass., Feb. 14th, 1789; mar. Eliza Ketchum, at Greene, N. Y., Feb. 22, 1810; he died at Sugar Grove, Pa., July 28, 1833, and she died at same place, May 4, 1836. Children and descendants:

HESTER GRAY, b. Nov. 12, 1810; mar. Alvin E. Buel, in Jul, 1829; d. July 5, 1865; Mr. Buel resides in North Clymer, N. Y.; children: Eliza, Edwin, Hiram, Sally, Elizabeth, John, Julia and Minerva.

CAROLINE GRAY, b. Sept. 27, 1812; mar. George McIntosh, March, 1833; d. Feb. 12, 1871; eight children.

MIRETTA GRAY, b. May 22, 1815; mar. Anson Stilson, Sept. 24, 1837; residence, Matthews Run, Pa.; children and descendants: Emma E. Stilson, b. Dec. 22, 1838, mar. Henry Pilling, Sept. 13, 1854, and has five children and three grandchildren; Emeline Stilson, b. May 18, 1840, mar. Hilary Wentz Apr. 20, 1866, and has five children; Franklin Stilson, b. Jan. 23, 1842, mar. Sept. 12, 1868, has four children; Hester E. Stilson, b. Nov. 10, 1843, mar. Thomas P. Page, May 2, 1863, and has four children; Gilman G. Stilson, b. Sept. 17, 1845, mar. Lydia Harlow, Nov. 28, 1870, no children; Nancy S. Stilson, b. May 9, 1850, d. Mar. 3. 1857; Irena I. Stilson, b. April 28, 1857, mar. Wm. D. Baker, 1872 and has three children.

ELI GRAY, b. Sept. 18, 1817; mar. Sophie Lewis, June 1, 1843; d. June 26, 1848; three daughters: Perlina, Lovina, and Cornelia.

HORACE GRAY, b. Nov. 12, 1819, Caneadea, Allegany Co., N. Y.; mar. Emeline A. Merrill, Nov. 9, 1841, at Birmingham, Mich. Children:

> ADELINE M. GRAY, b. Nov. 2, 1842.
>
> ALBERT ROLLIN GRAY, b. Dec. 23d, 1844; mar. Laura Markley, Aug., 1874; two children.
>
> ABELBERT WARREN GRAY, b. June 9, 1847; mar. Martha Carpenter, Aug. 26, 1865; children:
>> HORACE ALBERT GRAY, b. in Pontiac, Mich., May 28, 1866.
>> MATTIE BELL GRAY, b. at Taylor's Falls, Minn., Aug. 29, 1869.
>
> ALVIN CORTIS GRAY. b. Oct. 26, 1851.
>
> AUGUSTA EMELINE GRAY, b. in Pontiac, Mich., Oct. 28, 1856; d. Mar. 19, 1860.

CYRUS and SILAS GRAY, twin sons of Hiram Gray, b. Nov. 3d, 1823; Silas d. Nov. 3d, 1824; Cyrus, a bachelor, d. Oct. 15, 1873.

WARREN GRAY, b. Oct. 26, 1826; d. May 13, 1828.

GEORGE ALBERT GRAY, b. Aug. 13, 1830; d. Feb. 6, 1831.

WILLIAM HOYT GRAY, b. July 14, 1832, at Sugar Grove, Pa.; mar. at same place Dec. 25th, 1856, to Mary Ellen Whitely who was b. in Freehold, Pa., Jan. 21, 1840; present residence, Eagle Grove, Wright Co., Iowa. Children:

> WILLIAM JAMES SEYMOUR GRAY, b. at Forest Lake, Minn., Dec. 15, 1857.
>
> MERRITT ALONZO GRAY, b. at Columbus, Anoka Co., Minn., Jan. 7. 1860.
>
> INEZ ESTELLA GRAY, b. at Middle Branch, Chisago Co., Minn., Apr. 21, 1862; mar. A. A. Godfrey at Ft. Dodge, Iowa, in July, 1880; resides at Luverne, Iowa.
>
> JOHN ELMER GRAY, b. at Wyoming, Chisago Co., Minn., June 25, 1864.
>
> CHARLES CYRUS GRAY, b. at Taylor's Falls, Chisago Co., Minn., March 8, 1867.
>
> THOMAS MERTON GRAY, b. at Forest Lake, Minn., April 29, 1869.
>
> ERNEST OWENS GRAY, b. at Taylor's Falls, Minn., Oct. 16, 1872.
>
> NETTIE EMELINE GRAY, b. June 3, 1874.
>
> EDWIN GRAY, b. at Rock Creek, Minn., Mar. 1, 1876.

Mary Ellen Gray, wife of William H. Gray, died at Forest Lake, Minn., May 13, 1876, and he mar. second, Sarah Northrup, at Webster City, Iowa, Sept. 2d, 1878. She d. July 28, 1884. Children by this marriage:

GRACIE GRAY, b. July 17, 1879, at Troy, Iowa.

OTTO SHERMAN GRAY, b. June 11, 1882, Troy, Io.

ANNE (NANCY) GRAY, daughter of Elder Jeduthan Gray, b. at Egremont, Mass., May 25, 1791; mar. John Hayes; d. at Spartansburg, Pa., Nov. 24, 1867; among the children, Ann Eliza, Almira, Orland, Rebecca Rose.

SABRA GRAY, dau. of Elder Jeduthan Gray, b. at Egremont, April 19, 1793; mar. George Ketchum.

BARNUM GRAY, son of Elder Jeduthan Gray, b. Jan. 17, 1795; d. Jan. 30, 1797.

DR. JOSEPH GRAY.

Dr. Joseph Gray, son of Elder Jeduthan Gray, and at this date, the only surviving child, was born at Egremont, Mass., Aug. 17, 1797. He married Almira Bristol, at Greene, N. Y., Feb. 27, 1816. Studied medicine with Dr. Bradly, at Waterford, Erie Co., Pa. Practised there, in Madison, Wis., and in Cambridgeboro, Pa., where he still resides, over 30 years. Was twice elected a Member of the Pennsylvania Legislature, 1844 and '45, and was also U. S. Marshal in Wisconsin. Though suffering from the infirmities of age, is still in the fair possession of his faculties. Children and descendants:

POLLY GRAY, died at the age of twelve.

CAROLINE GRAY, b. Sept. 3, 1819; mar. Peter Pettecord, Oct. 4, 1835, who d. Apr. 30, 1871. Children: John Morris b. Jan. 31, 1836, d. March, '38; George, b. July 1837; d. Aug. '39; Amos, b. May 20, 1840; Almira, b. Dec. 6, '41, d. Mar. '45; James E., b. May 10, 1843, mar. widow Bloodgood, May, 1880; Caroline A., b. Apr. 25, '45, mar. John King, Sept. 25, '65; Andrew J., b. Nov. 24, '46; Wm. Henry, b. Apr. 27, 1845, left ship at Valparaiso in 1860, and not heard from since; Virginia, b. July 1, '50, d. Apr. '52; Joseph, b. Feb. 28, '53, d. Jan. 20, '82; Franklin P., b. Nov. 21, '53, and d. Sept. '54; Amanda, b. Mar. 21, '55; Clarissa, b. Apr. 23, '57, d. Oct. '58; Sarah Jane, b. Aug. 20, '58, d. Dec. 20, '59.

Dr. JOHN HAYES GRAY, of Cambridgeboro, Pa., oldest son of Dr. Joseph Gray, was born in Concord, Pa., April 24, 1824, and married Sophia R. Wheelock, Dec. 10, 1848. Was appointed to a position on the Staff of Governor Shank, of Pennsylvania, with the rank of Lieut.-Col., when only 19 years of age. Attended medical lectures at the Berkshire Medical College, Mass., in 1847. Practised medicine about forty years where he now resides, and has retired in favor of his son, Dr. M. D. Gray. Is at present giving his attention to developing valuable mineral springs and the building up of a remedial institute on his estate near Cambridgeboro, Pa. Dr. Gray was a Member of the Pennsylvania State Legislature for two terms, 1871 and 1872, and was a candidate for Member on the Prohibition ticket, in 1885. In his own terse language, he is "a *Gray*, a Baptist, a Prohibitionist, and Anti-Secret Society man." Children and descendants:

> MARY ALMIRA GRAY, b. Oct. 29, '49, mar. Dec. 5, 1871, to Henry E. Lefever; children: Harry D., Sept. 28, '72, Ida, b. May 23, '74, d. Oct. 9, '81, Jessie, b. Feb. 23, '76, d. Oct. 2, '81, Geo. L., b. Feb. 29, '80, d. Oct. '81, Harvey J., b. Mar. 18, '82.

> MYRON D. GRAY, Dr., of Cambridgeboro, Pa., b. Feb. 5, 1852; mar. Esther Allen, Sept. 10, 1874; one son b. Aug. 15, '76, d. Nov. 1881.

Dr. M. D. Gray studied with his father, attending one course of lectures at Cleveland, and two courses at Philadelphia, where he graduated. He has the distinction of being the third in succession in the line of physicians of direct descent in the family of Gray, the representatives of the three generations all there living at this date.

> MARTHA ALICE GRAY, b. Aug. 27, '56; mar. Perry A. Gage, Sept. 9, 1880; a son, John Gage, b. Aug. 15, 1882.

> CLARA B. GRAY, b. Oct. 20, '59; mar. Frank W. Hyatt, July 3, '76; a daughter, Pearl, b. Sept. 26, 1879.

> CARRIE D. GRAY, b. Oct. 20, 1859; mar. DeElmer Kelly, Dec. 13, 1884.

> HATTIE A. GRAY, b. Jan. 9, 1862.

> NELLIE M. GRAY, b. May 8, 1868.

Hon. ALMON D. GRAY, son of Dr. Joseph Gray, was born Feb. 16, 1829; married Adelia C. Allen, daughter of Col. B. Allen, of Bristol, Vt., Nov. 1, 1855. Mr. Gray engaged in the study and practise of the law. Was elected the first Mayor of the city of Hudson, Wis., District Attorney of St. Croix Co., Wis., Member of Assembly of St. Croix Dist. in Wisconsin Legislature, also District Attorney of Pepin Co., Wis., member of Board of Supervisors same county, and County Judge of Pepin Co., Wis. Has now gone west "to grow up with the country," and has established himself at Bismarck, Dakota, as the senior member of the law firm of Gray & Gray.

Mr. Gray enlisted as a private in the 16th Regt. of Wisconsin Volunteers in Nov., 1861. Was appointed Sergt. Major of the Regt., and in March following commissioned as Capt. of Co. H. Served with honor until discharged on account of serious illness. Children:

CALISTA A. GRAY, b. July 4, 1856.

ALMON J. GRAY, son of Almon D., was b. Sept. 27, 1857; studied law, and was admitted to the bar Feb. 27, 1883, at Alma, Wis. Removed to Bismarck, Dak., and engaged in the practise of the law with his father, under the firm name of Gray & Gray.

GEORGE BENJAMIN GRAY, b. July 14, 1859; has been engineer on Missouri river steamers; now in the jewelry trade.

EFFIE A. GRAY, b. Nov. 10, 1865; mar. Orlando Murray, at Pepin, Wis., Feb. 5, 1885.

ADELBERT B. GRAY, b. Sept. 23, 1867.

NORMAN A. GRAY, b. Aug. 27, 1870.

ARCHIE H. GRAY, b. Oct. 11, 1875; d. June 2, 1877.

LOVETT M. GRAY, b. Feb. 8, 1878.

RALPH D. GRAY, b. March 1, 1882.

AMOS S. GRAY, youngest son of Dr. Joseph Gray, was born in Waterford, Pa., June 25th, 1835; married Mary E. Munson, at Hudson, Wis., Feb. 22d, 1858. He was P. M. of the Wisconsin Assembly in 1856; Register of Deeds of St. Croix Co., Wis., 1858-9; Dep. Sheriff, 1860-61; P. M. of Farmington, Wis., '62 and '63; County Commissioner and Clerk of Circuit Court, '63 and '64; Capt. of Osceola Guards 1863, and promoted to Major of 1st Bat. 5th Regt. Wis.; Member of the Wisconsin Legislature

1863; Town Clerk of the town of Pepin, and Police Justice of the village of Pepin, Wis. Children:

ADDIE M. GRAY, b. Sept. 17, 1860; mar. A. C. Tucker, Feb. 22, 1882; a daughter; Lucilla, resides Rapid City, Dak.

HENRY F. GRAY, b. Dec. 22, 1862.

MEDA M. GRAY, b. Sept. 14, 1868.

GEORGIA A. GRAY, b. May 31, 1871.

MYRON H. B. GRAY, son of Dr. Joseph Gray, was born in Waterford, Pa., 1827; married Harriet Jackson ,1845; was in the Mexican war; went west, raised a large family, and died in Hudson, Wis. Children:

ALMIRA GRAY.

CHARLES GRAY.

ELI GRAY.

Eli Gray, son of Elder Jeduthan Gray, was born in Egremont, Mass., Sept. 18, 1799; married Sally Bates; he died at Black Creek, Ohio, June 20, 1852; she died at Shreve, Wayne Co., Ohio, Feb., 1878. Children and descendants:

GEORGE KETCHUM GRAY, b. Jan. 13, 1822; mar. Charlotte M. Tuttle, Mar. 17, 1850; removed from Ohio to Missouri in 1863; d. at Allendale, Mo., where his widow still resides, in April, 1874. Children:

PRUDENCE ALICE GRAY, b. Aug. 13, 1851; mar. Newton Maudlin, Dec. 23, 1875; 3 children.

SALLIE REBECCA GRAY, b. Sept. 28, 1852; mar. Lewis B. Imus, Apr. 18, 1875; 6 children.

NANCY ANN GRAY, b. Dec. 22, 1853; mar. Wm. Cavin, Apr. 18, 1876; d. Feb. 4, 1877.

ELI BISHOP GRAY, b. Sept. 17, 1855.

ABIGAIL GRAY, b. March 17, 1857; mar. Miles Brown, Sept. 25, 1881; one child.

HENRY CLARK GRAY, b. Sept. 15, 1858.

BETHEL HIRAM GRAY, b. July 16, 1860.

BYRON LEMUEL GRAY, b. July 16, 1860; d. Mar. 6, 1861.

LAURA MELVINA GRAY, b. Ang. 18, 1862.

DANIEL PARDEE GRAY, b. Sept. 22, 1864.

MARY MARGARET GRAY, b. Sept. 27, 1866.

Eli, Henry C., and Bethel Gray are at Leadville, Colorado, engaged in mining.

LAURA ANN GRAY, b. Sept. 8, 1823; mar. Elisha Henderson, Apr. 1845, who died Sept. 1854; two sons who reside at Iola, Kansas; she mar. second, David Yarnel, and resides at Shreve, Ohio.

SABRINA GRAY, daughter of Eli Gray, b. Aug. 6, 1825; mar. Thos. B. Harris, 1848; three children; residence, Allen Co., Kansas.

HENRY BATES GRAY, son of Eli Gray, was born March 8th, 1827; married Barbary Ann Donald, March 16, 1852; she died Dec. 24, 1864, and he married second, Rachel E. Tarrh, Feb. 18, 1866; residence, Black Creek, Holmes Co., Ohio; children:

ARVILLA E. GRAY, b. Feb. 1, 1853; mar. John G. Smith, June 14, 1871; two children.

RACHEL S. GRAY, b. Sept. 3, 1854; mar. John Kaylor, Apr. 8, 1875; two children.

SALLY L. GRAY, b. June 26, 1856; mar. Albert Wachtel, March 26, 1884.

JOHN M. GRAY, b. June 16, 1858; mar. Biddy Naven, Nov. 15, 1882; residence, Creston, Wayne Co., O.; a son,

HENRY B. GRAY, b. Sept. 19, 1883.

WILLIAM S. GRAY, b. Sept. 1, 1860.

GEORGE V. GRAY, b. May 31, 1863.

EMMA E. GRAY, b. June 11, 1867.

LLEWELYN D. GRAY, b. Apr. 8, 1869.

HEMON E. GRAY, b. Feb. 26, 1872.

CHANNING L. GRAY, b. Aug. 26, 1874.

WADE H. GRAY, b. Dec. 10, 1876.

WALTER GRAY, b. Aug. 30, 1879.

HENRY B. GRAY, JR., b. Sept. 8, 1883.

ABIGAIL B. GRAY, daughter of Eli Gray, b. Apr. 20, 1829; mar. Samuel Bevington, Aug. 1847; no children; residence, Iola, Kansas.

HERMON CARTER GRAY, son of Eli Gray, was born May 30, 1831, in Erie Co., Pa.; married Almedia J. Booth, in Valparaiso, Indiana, March 20th, 1856; children:

JOSEPHINE A. GRAY, b. Dec. 31, 1856; mar. John Dole, Nov. 17, 1881; two children.

LAURA ELLA GRAY, b. Feb. 23, 1858.

CARRIE BELL GRAY, b. Dec. 20, 1859; d. Aug. 6, 1865.

HERBERT C. GRAY, b. Nov. 11th, 1861.

ALFRED A. GRAY, b. June 19, 1860.

IDA M. GRAY, b. June 19, 1860.

SILAS B. GRAY, b. Oct. 8, 1870.

BURTON B. GRAY, b. July 3, 1873.

Mr. H. C. Gray enlisted as a private in the war for the Union, Co. G., 29th Regt. Iowa Vols.; was a Sergt. when discharged. Was in the service three years, and in several battles. Present residence, Oak Grove, Powesheik Co., Iowa.

> HIRAM P. GRAY, youngest son of Eli Gray, b. Feb. 17th, 1835; mar. N. J. Harger, at New Buffalo, Mich., Nov. 4th, 1858; residence, Iola, Kansas; children:
>
>> ABBIE GRAY, b. Aug. 31, 1859.
>> NELLIE GRAY, b. May 10, 1861.
>> SAMUEL GRAY, b. Sept. 13, 1866; d. Nov. 23, 1877.
>> IDA GRAY, b. Dec. 27, 1878; d. Apr. 18, 1879.
>> SUSIE GRAY, b. June 10, 1870.
>> ADDIE GRAY, b. April 1, 1876.

AMERALZAMON GRAY.

Ameralzamon Gray, youngest son of Elder Jeduthan Gray, was born at Egremont, Mass., July 18, 1802; married Anice Blakeslee; died at Black Creek, Ohio, April 20, 1849; she died at same place, Oct. 1867. Children:

> MARYAMNA GRAY, b. May 14, 1827; mar. Jonathan Parsons, Oct., 1842; three sons; is a widow, and resides in Indian Territory.
>
> HELEN GRAY, b. July 5, 1838; mar. Oliver Spurgeon; died July, 1872; one daughter.
>
> CELENA GRAY, b. Aug. 1848; mar. Joseph Nider; lives in Indian Territory.

AMOS GRAY.

Amos Gray, son of Joseph Gray and grandson of John Gray (3) of Sharon, it is claimed by some of his descendants, who certainly ought to know, was born in 1761. In view of the fact that the public records show the name of Amos Gray on the tax list of Amenia Precinct, in 1777, the presumption is very strong that he was born at an earlier date. And again, the date of birth, 1777, well substantiated, of his oldest son, makes an earlier period for his own birth almost absolutely necessary. That he removed to Berkshire Co., Mass., there is abundant evidence, although the fact does not appear on the church or town records of that place. He married Eunice Kellogg, who died at Greene, N. Y., 1815, to which place he had previously removed, one account says in 1794, and another, 1798. But before that period he had met with a very serious accident. It appears that he was a mason, and while engaged in blasting out the rocky foundation of a house for Conrad Sharpe, near Egremont, the site of which is still easily ascertained, a premature blast put out both of his eyes, making him totally blind the rest of his life. And yet after that, he removed to the Chenango Valley, was among the pioneers of that section, and became the owner of a large and desirable farm which remains in part in the possession of his descendants unto this day. After the loss of his first wife, he married again, and made a will disposing of his property; all the while totally blind. He also revisited Great Barrington and Egremont, and an old gentleman residing in the latter place, Mr. Joshua Clark Millard, informed the writer in 1885, that he well remembered Amos Gray, then blind, being at the residence of his father, for a few days, when he, the narrator, was a boy, and he had led him about. He must have been a man of solid, substantial parts, and it is said of him that he weighed three hundred (300) pounds. Eunice Kellogg Gray, the mother of his children, was probably the sister of Elder Nathaniel Kellogg, who had married Mr. Gray's sister Anice. Amos Gray died at Greene, Chenango Co., in 1828, having resided there for a period of over thirty years, leaving the homestead to his youngest son, Amos Gray, Jr.

DESCENDANTS OF AMOS GRAY.

JOSEPH GRAY, oldest son of Amos Gray, was born 1777; married Miriam Hubbell at Greene, N. Y.; removed to Washington Co., Indiana, and died there Feb. 18, 1854, "aged 76 years, 11 months." Mrs. Gray died Sept. 23, 1844, "aged 67 years, 2 mos. and 10 days." Children:

> LEWIS GRAY, d. on Green River, Ky.; forty years since.
>> HORACE GRAY, of Chestnut Hill, Ind., son of Lewis Gray, declined to furnish any information of his own or of his father's family.
> RILEY GRAY, b. 1802; d. in Mempis, Ind., Sept. 8, 1870.
> ALBERT GRAY, d. in California, 1850.
> MALINDA GRAY, b. July 2, 1806; mar. John C. Pixley, Mar. 25, 1825; d. July 18, 1864; children: Mariah, b. Jan. 21, 1828; Emeline, b. Nov. 13, 1830; Angeline, b. Sept. 4, 1833; William S. Pixley, b. Nov. 20, 1836.
> LAURA GRAY, b. 1807; mar. Mr. Sturdevant; d. at Otisco, Ind., Feb. 26, 1879; five children.
> MABEL GRAY, mar. a Mr. Dailey and removed to Missouri.
> NELLIE GRAY, mar. Peter Dailey.
> PALMYRA GRAY, d. in Washington Co., "50 years ago."
> ZILZANNETTA GRAY, d. in northern Indiana, 1879.
> AMBROSE GRAY, moved to northern Ind.; "died 20 years ago."

JEDUTHAN GRAY.

Jeduthan Gray, second son of Amos Gray, was born in Berkshire Co., Mass., probably in Egremont, in 1780; married Ruth Loomis at Greene, N. Y., and removed to Washington Co., Indiana, 1819; married 2d, Clarissa Grosvenor; resided in Franklin township until his death, 1849. Children and descendants:

> HULDAH GRAY, b. Nov. 13, 1798; mar. Charles A. Bartle, Aug. 2, 1815; d. at Bartle, Ind., Sept. 9, 1843; children: Ruth Ann, b. Apr. 5. 1817, now widow Buckley; resides at Stony Fork, Pa.; Warren Bartle, b. Sept. 28, 1818, and resides at Bartle, Ind.; Loomis, b. 1822, d. 1856; Elizette, b. Aug. 2, 1824, d. 1872; John Henry, b. May 2, 1827, d. Dec. 20, 1858; Amanda, b. Dec. 24, 1830, d. May 23, 1846; Loren M., d. Dec. 27, '32; Orrin C., b. Apr. 17, 1838; Caroline A., b. Aug. 12, 1841, d. Oct. 27, 1842.
> LOOMIS B. GRAY, b. in N. Y., and d. in Ind.

ORRIN C. GRAY, son of Jeduthan Gray, b. Aug. 17, 1807;
mar. Alvina B. McClellan, Oct. 30, 1825; she d. Nov.
18, 1871; he d. Nov. 23, 1884; children:
JEDUTHAN GRAY, b. April 29, 1827.
CHARLOTTE RUTH GRAY, b. Jan. 11, 1829.
ABIGAIL GRAY, b. Oct. 5, 1831.
CHARLOTTE RUTH GRAY, 2d, b. Aug. 5, 1833.
ABIGAIL GRAY, 2d, b. Feb. 3, 1836.
CHARLES GRAY, b. April 12, 1838.
ANNIE H. GRAY, b. Jan. 15, 1840.
PERLINA GRAY, b. Oct. 20, 1842.
LODISCA GRAY, b. Dec. 2, 1850.
ORRIN MILLARD FILLMORE GRAY, b. Jun. 11, 1853.
ABIGAIL GRAY, daughter of Jeduthan, b. in N. Y.; mar
John Moore, of Madison, Ind.; four children:
PHILO P. GRAY, son of Jeduthan, b. 1813; mar. Marian F
McClellan, 1835; residence, Bartle, Washington Co.,
Ind.; children and descendants:
MARCUS GRAY, b. Mar. 19, 1837; mar. Marietta
Younkin, Oct. 18, 1860; children:
LILLY F. GRAY, b. June 6, 1861; mar.
John R. Humphrey, June 4, 1880;
has 3 children, b. '82, '83, '84.
HENRY H. GRAY, b. Aug. 30, 1863; d.
Sept. 6, 1864.
EMMA F. GRAY. b. June 25, 1865; mar.
LaFayette McAdams, Sept. 3, 1884.
MINEY E. GRAY, b. Oct. 3, 1867.
JAMES P. GRAY, b. Jan. 2, 1870.
WILLIAM E. GRAY, b. Feb. 4, 1873.
NELLIE G. GRAY, b. May 18, 1875.
CHARLES C. GRAY, b. Apr. 29, 1879.
BERTHA P. GRAY, b. Nov. 11, 1882.
HARRISON GRAY, son of Philo P., b. May 17th.
1840; mar. Emeretta Owens, who d. July 22,
1874, and he mar. 2d, Jane A. Warman, July
27, 1876; children:
ANNIE BELLE GRAY, b. Nov. 29, 1877.
NETTIE MAY GRAY, b. July 6, 1879.
OLIVER PALMER GRAY, b. June 8, 1881.
BLANCHE PEARL GRAY, b. Apr. 17, 1883.
Harrison Gray enlisted Aug. 16, 1862, in Co. B, 81st Indiana
Vols., in the war for the Union ; was wounded at the battle of
Chickamauga, Sept. 19, 1863, in the thigh ; ball not extracted;
is a pensioner. Residence, Bartle, Washington Co., Ind.

DENIS GRAY, son of Philo P., b. 1842; mar. Dec. 31, 1868, to Amanda F. Bartle, daughter of Mr. Warren Bartle of Bartle, Ind.; children:
REUBEN M. GRAY, b. Nov. 6, 1869; d. July 26, 1870.
OTTO F. GRAY, b. Oct. 9, 1871.
PHILENA S. GRAY, b. Nov. 1, 1875.
LULU C. GRAY, b. Feb. 10, 1880; d. July 22, 1881.

Denis Gray enlisted in Co. B, 81st Indiana Volunteers, was in the battles of Perrysville, Stone River, Chickamaugua, Missionary Ridge, Kenesaw Mt., and at Atalanta, where he was seriously wounded. Is Postmaster of Bartle, Ind.

MARTHA J. GRAY, dau. of Philo P., b. Apr. 9th, 1845; mar. James Weller, Sept. 1, 1861; children: Amanda Rosanna, b. July 17, 1862, mar. Chauncey Humphrey, Mar. 12, 1879; Flora Bertha, b. Apr. 13, 1874; Estelle Magdeline, b. Feb. 7, 1878; Itaska Madline, b. May 10, 1882.

PARMER GRAY, of Salem, Ind., son of Philo P., b. Sept. 17, 1847; mar. Mary A. Sides, Aug. 20, 1868; children:
IDA GRAY, b. June 12, 1869.
LIZZIE GRAY, b. Aug. 2, 1877.

AMOS GRAY, Jr., b. Jan. 9, 1849; mar. Violana Weller, March 17, 1873; children:
ROSEA T. GRAY, b. July 11, '74; d. 1875.
HERBERT ELNOR GRAY, b. May 26, 1879.
ELBERT LEONARD GRAY, b. Mar. 18, '82.
MILLARD FILLMORE GRAY, b. Dec. 1, '83.

MARY GRAY, dau. Philo P., mar. Mr. Hosea, of Spencer, Ind.

CLARISSA GRAY, dau. Philo P., mar. Mr. Kenedy.

ELIZA ANN GRAY, daughter of Jeduthan Gray, b. July 19, 1818; mar. Jonathan Hosea, Mar. 7, 1834; children: Margaret, b. Oct. 21, 1835; Violana, b. Sept. 12, 1840; Romulus Hosea, b. Nov. 12, 1844.

AMOS T. GRAY, son of Jeduthan, b. April 25, 1820; mar. Mary A. Miller, Mar. 22, 1842; she d. 1880; he resides at Bartle, Ind. Children:
ISABELL R. GRAY, b. June 11th, 1843; mar. Wm. A. Richardson, Oct. 1864.
EMILY R. GRAY, b. Sept. 25, 1845; mar. W. Howell, 1861.

SARAH M. GRAY, b. Jan. 8, 1849; mar. James
    Howell, in 1864.
WILLIAM R. GRAY, b. May 5, 1852; mar. Isabell
    Shields, 1873; a son,
        CLYDE ELGIN GRAY, b. May 14, 1883.
ELIZA ANN GRAY, b. July 19, 1854; mar. Jerome
    Weir, 1873.
HULDAH E. GRAY, b. Nov. 12, 1862; mar. Frank-
    lin Shields, 1879.

Amos T. Gray was a member of the 58th Indiana Regt. in
the war for the Union, and participated in "Sherman's march to
the sea." He is a Deacon in the Baptist Church.

JEDUTHAN GRAY, Jr., son of Jeduthan and Clarissa Gray;
    mar. Levina Hardesty; was killed at the battle of An-
    tietam in the war for the Union; left three children;
    unable to learn their names; the widow married again.

MARY GRAY, dau. of Jeduthan Gray, Sen.

GEORGE R. GRAY, son of Jeduthan and Clarissa Gray, was
    born March 29, 1838; mar. Mary E. Weller, in Octo-
    ber, 1855; she d. in Aug. 1862, and he mar. 2d, Eliza-
    beth Callaway, Sept. 28, 1865; children:
        JULIA A. GRAY, b. Nov. 25, 1856.
        CLARISSA E. GRAY, b. Jan. 9, 1858.
        SARAH S. GRAY, b. Dec. 30, 1860.
        JOSEPH J. GRAY, b. Aug. 14, 1867.
        ALPHEUS M. GRAY, b. Feb. 8, 1870.
        NANCY J. GRAY, b. May 3, 1872.
        MARY M. GRAY, b. Aug. 4, 1878.
        WILLIAM F. GRAY, b. Dec. 22, 1881.
        GEORGE R. GRAY, Jr., b. Mar. 24, 1883.

George R. Gray enlisted in the war for the Union, Aug. 27th,
1862, and was discharged the same year by reason of an acci-
dental wound while on the skirmish line near Lancaster, Ky.; residence, Spencer, Ind.; 7 grand children by first wife's daughters.

ADELINE GRAY, dau, of Jeduthan and Clarissa Gray, resides
    in Kansas City.

ALPHEUS GRAY, son of Jeduthan and Clarissa Gray, resides
    at Spencer, Ind.; was a soldier in the war for the Union.

ELIZABETH (BETSEY) GRAY, daughter of Amos Gray, was born
Oct. 13, 1782, in Berkshire Co.. Mass., and removed first with
her father's family to Greene, N. Y., and afterwards with her
brothers and their families to Washington Co., Ind., where she
continued to reside until her decease.

ENOCH GRAY.

Enoch Gray, third son of Amos Gray, was born in Berkshire County, Mass., 1783, and removed with his father in his boyhood to Chenango Co., N. Y., where he grew up to manhood and married in 1813, Sarah Hurlburt, who was born in Litchfield Co., Conn., Mar. 12, 1792. He taught the first school kept in the town of Greene, and continued to reside there, an esteemed citizen, until his decease, Dec. 13, 1857. Children and descendants:

ANGELINE N. GRAY, b. June 19, 1815.

ELIJAH R. GRAY, b. Oct. 17, 1819; mar. Catharine E. Burroughs, at Greene, Sept. 27, 1843; she d. Aug. 8, 1848, and he mar. 2d, Mary B. Smead, at Hudson, O., Oct. 19, 1855; he d. at Junction City, Kansas, Aug. 24th, 1868. Children:

> GEORGE E. GRAY, b. Aug. 13, 1844; resides in Bolivar, Allegany Co., N. Y., married but no children.
>
> EMMA C. GRAY, b. Dec. 29, 1847; d. Aug. 6, 1848.
>
> MARY B. GRAY, b. Dec. 9, 1856; d. Apr. 29, 1861.
>
> CHARLES GRAY, b. Oct. 6, 1858; drowned Aug. 8, 1868.
>
> FRANK GRAY, b. Mar. 21, 1860; d. Aug. 5, 1860.
>
> HENRY GRAY, b. Aug. 7, 1861; resides at Des Plaines, near Chicago.
>
> FANNIE L. GRAY b. Aug. 27, 1863; mar. James C. Barry, of Des Plaines, Ill., Dec. 6, 1885.

FREDERICK H. GRAY, b. May 28, 1820; unmarried; resides at Des Plaines, Ill.

WILLIAM D GRAY, b. May 28, 1824; d. in California, 1860.

GEORGE G. GRAY, b. Nov. 15, 1827; d. Nov. 25, 1840.

JULIETTE E. GRAY, b. June 7, 1832; mar. John Garland, at Chicago, Nov. 15, 1870; residence, Des Plaines, Cook Co., Ill.

JAMES M. GRAY, b. May 12, 1834; mar. Ettie Woodruff, May 16, 1875; d. at Fergus Falls, Minn., Aug. 2, 1884.

HELEN J. GRAY, b. Feb. 28, 1840; mar. Geo. C. Roberts, Editor and Publisher of the Chenango *American*, at Greene, N. Y.

AMOS GRAY, JR.

Amos Gray, Jr., son of Amos Gray, and grandson of Joseph Gray, was born in Berkshire Co., Mass., Feb. 2, 1790, and married Christina Tenbrook, who died at Greene, N. Y., April 14, 1832. He died May 1, 1868. Children and descendants:

MARANDA GRAY, b. Sept. 11, 1811; d. Mar. 27. 1882.

SAMUEL J. GRAY, b. Oct. 28, 1813; d. at Greene, N. Y., Feb. 19, 1885; children and descendants:

HENRY S. GRAY, b. March 13, 1837; removed to Nevada, Iowa, mar., and had the following children:

LILLY GRAY.
GEORGE GRAY.
AUSTIN GRAY.

S. D. GRAY, son of Samuel J., b. Oct. 16, 1838; mar., children:

GEORGE P. GRAY, b. Sept. 11, 1867.
ELISHA GRAY, b. Aug. 16, 1878.

CHARLES D. GRAY, b. Sept. 4, 1840; mar.; residence, Brisbin, Chenango Co., N. Y.; children:

JERRY H. GRAY, b. Feb. 27, 1862.
DELILAH GRAY, b. May 11, 1864.
C. W. GRAY, b. May 6, 1874.
STIRA GRAY, B. Aug. 19, 1883.

LUCINA GRAY, b. Dec. 14th, 1842; mar. Will Wheeler; two children, Jerry and Emily.

GEORGE W. GRAY, b. Aug. 19, 1849; residence, Greene, N. Y.; mar., a son,

BRAINARD GRAY, b. Jan. 14, 1871.

JANE GRAY, b. June 16, 1852; mar. Garry Wheeler; children: Celia and Lena.

RHODA GRAY, daughter of Amos Gray, Jr., b. Oct. 28th, 1814; d. Nov. 19, 1874.

JAMES M. GRAY, b. Jan. 7, 1816; d. 1826.

SARAH M. GRAY, b. Sept. 20, 1820; mar. Thos. A. Kathan; mar. 2d, Henry Balcolm.

NANCY T. GRAY, b. Dec. 27, 1822; mar. Townsend D. Welch; d. March 17, 1885.

JAMES P. GRAY, b. March 29, 1828; mar. 1849, Mariette Kendall; no children; residence, Brisbin, N. Y.

DAUGHTERS OF JOSEPH GRAY.

There were three daughters born to Joseph Gray, sisters of Amos and Elder Jeduthan Gray,—Sarah, Anice and Tamor. No record of their births has been found, but they will be considered in the order named.

SARAH.

The old church records of Sharon, Conn., show that Sarah Gray, of Amenia, N. Y., was there married to Reuben Barnes, Sept. 14, 1779, conjointly with the marriage of her brother Jeduthan Gray to Anna Warren. There were three children born of this marriage, Celia, Reuben, and Joseph Barnes. The family removed to the Chenango Valley, and the last obtainable information of her was, that she was, years ago, residing with a son somewhere between Greene and Oxford, N. Y.

ANICE.

Anice Gray married Elder Nathaniel Kellogg, a Baptist preacher of some note, mention of whom is made in the old Baptist Church records of Amenia, now Millerton, N. Y., as having been present at an ordaining council there held December 17, 1788, at which his father-in-law, Joseph Gray, then of Canaan, Columbia Co., N. Y., and his brother-in-law, Elder Jeduthan Gray, were both also present and participated. No record of the family found.

TAMOR.

Tamor Gray first married a Mr. Ames, and had seven children; four sons and three daughters; he died, and she then married second, Job Thompson, and had one daughter, and a son, Robert Thompson. The latter part of her life was spent in Union Township, Erie Co., Pa., where she died many years ago. She had considerable medical skill and practise.

The descendants of Joseph Gray, as will be seen, far outnumber those of either of his brothers, although the full list is not given, owing to the great difficulty which indifference and lack of interest interposed in some branches of the family, remotely situated. They are mainly Baptists, with which religious denomination their immediate ancestors were prominently identified, and are a vigorous, virile race, with the strong family characteristics predominant.

DARIUS GRAY.

Darius Gray, son of John Gray (3) and Catharine his wife, was born in Sharon, Conn., Jan. 18, 1752, and married Abigail Ashley of that place, who died May 16, 1812. He died Aug. 12, 1816. There are strong indications on the public records that Darius Gray became the owner of the John Gray homestead, described as being east of and adjoining the Gould place, so called, in the history of Sharon, still easily located, on what is designated "the Mountain," although only an elevated plateau which is overlooked by the high range of hills eastwardly, near the summit of which, he afterwards made his home, on a farm now owned by Mr. Peck, his father having purchased it from the heirs of Darius Gray after his decease. All the other sons of John Gray, with the possible exception of William Gray, had removed from Sharon prior to 1790, and he alone remained to perpetuate the family name and to preserve the family traditions on that historic spot. And when he died how much of family history was lost, some of it never to be reclaimed. How easily he could have pointed to the place where his father and mother were buried, and his brother William, and have solved the mystery concerning his missing brother James. A surviving grand child, Mrs. Anne M. (Gray) Beebe, who is his only descendant in the direct line now residing in the town of Sharon, remembers him as "a large, noble looking man." He was buried near the farm house where he had lived, and died, and afterwards removed to a pleasant cemetery near the eastern borders of the town.

There were four daughters and two sons, all of whom married and had families, as follows:

DESCENDANTS OF DARIUS GRAY.

CYRUS W. GRAY, Rev., son of Darius, b. Aug. 3, 1784; mar. Belinda A. Smith, of Hadley, Mass.; he d. at Stafford, Conn., Aug. 20, 1821; she d. at Peabody, Mass., Feb. 17, 1859; four daughters and one son.

SILAS A. GRAY, son of Darius, b. Aug. 3, 1784; mar. Lucretia C. Wadhams, of Goshen, Conn., Nov. 1, 1809; she d. July 12, 1853; he d. Mar. 5, 1867.

Mr. Gray always resided in Sharon, and was a highly respected citizen of that town. He was a deep thinker as well as a man of affairs, and wielded an able pen. His polemic passages with the late President Taylor of Yale, when the controversy between the Old and New School Presbyterians was in progress, he espousing the cause of the former, attracted no little attention in the religious press. As will be noticed, he was a twin brother of Rev. Cyrus W. Gray. The following is a list of his children and descendants:

AUGUSTUS B. GRAY, son of Silas A., b. Nov. 10, 1811; mar. Sally B. Butler, March 4, 1838; d. July 29, 1852, on the Pacific Ocean, while on his way to California. Sally B., his wife, d. Feb. 12, 1868. Children:

FRANKLIN D. GRAY, dec'd.

JULIET L. GRAY, "

DELPHINE L. GRAY, b. Aug. 30, 1839; mar. James S. Baldwin, of Cornwall, Conn., Dec. 31, 1863; residence, Pittsfield, Ohio.

SILAS A. GRAY, b. in Sharon, Conn., Oct. 16, 1848; mar. Ella J. Taylor, of Minneapolis, Minn., Jan. 1, 1882; residence, Mitchell, Dakota.

ANNE MARIA GRAY, daughter of Silas A., b. Feb. 23, 1814; mar. Orrin Butler, Dec. 25, 1834, who d. Aug. 5, 1847; four daughters, Anne M., Lucretia A., Amelia A., and Maggie A. Butler, all deceased; and two sons, Calvin and Moses Butler, with the latter of whom, in the eastern borders of Sharon, near West Cornwall, Mrs. Beebe resides. She mar. 2d, William Beebe, who d. Nov., 1878.

BETSEY GRAY, b. May 4, 1816; mar. Daniel Scoville, Aug. 30, 1838; two sons, John and Eugene, and a daughter, Isabel. Mr. Scoville d. May 13, 1858; she d. June 6, 1869.

FRANKLIN DARIUS GRAY, of Chicago, Ill., b. May 19, 1818, in Sharon, Conn.; mar. Ann O. Phelps, daughter of Jeremiah Phelps, of Norfolk, Conn., July 4, 1843; an adopted daughter,

ISOBEL CLIFTON GRAY, b. May 16, 1859.

Mr. F. D. Gray has been a resident of Chicago since 1840, and is President of the National Safe Deposit Company of that city.

CYRUS WINTHROP GRAY, son of Silas A., b. May 7, 1821; mar. Dollie Hyde Everett, of Ellsworth, Sharon, Conn., April 17, 1843; d. at LeRaysville, Pa., Oct. 21, 1874. Children:

> ANNIE AMELIA GRAY, b. Oct. 3, 1845; mar. Jasper Perkins Bosworth, of LeRaysville, Pa., Sept. 25th, 1867 ; children: Winifred Gray Bosworth, b. Sept. 24, 1880, d. Mar. 18, '81; Marjorie Lee Bosworth, b. July 21, 1885.

> LILLIE AUGUSTA GRAY, b. May 3, 1855 ; married Frederic Edward Stevens, of Hooksett, N. H., Feb. 22d, 1882; a son, Gray Stevens, b. July 23, 1883.

MOSES W. GRAY, of Chicago, son of Silas A., b. in Sharon, Conn., Apr. 10, 1824; mar. Mary L. Gaylord, daughter of Joseph I. Gaylord, of Goshen, Conn., May 22, 1850. Children:

> CLARA LUCRETIA GRAY, b. in Goshen, Conn., May 20, 1856; mar. Frederick P. Miles, of Salisbury, Conn., Feb. 24, 1881, a daughter, Loraine, b. July 16, 1884, died March 16th, 1884, at Lakeville, Conn., where the parents reside.

> FREDERICK GAYLORD GRAY, b. May 7, 1859; mar. Susan Williams, Jan. 1883, at Marshalltown, Iowa.

> FRANK M. GRAY, b. May 23, 1866.

Moses W. Gray is a member of the firm of Gray, Burt & Kingman, wholesale grocers, Chicago. He has a summer residence at Goshen, Litchfield Co., Conn., and there all of his children were born.

> BETSEY GRAY, dau. of Darius, mar. Joseph Barstow; moved to Wisconsin, and died there; two sons, John and Wallace, and a daughter, Laura.

> MARY GRAY, daughter of Darius, mar. Joseph Sutliff, removed to Ohio, had 3 children, and died there.

> ABIGAIL GRAY, dau. of Darius, b. 1794; d. in Sharon, Aug. 2, 1869; unmarried.

> CAROLINE GRAY, dau. of Darius, mar. Rev. Mr. Miller, and lived in Ohio; he died, when she mar. Mr. Bignal, removed to Berlin, Wis., and is still living there.

REV. CYRUS W. GRAY.

Rev. Cyrus W. Gray, son of Darius Gray, and twin brother of Silas A. Gray, was born in Sharon, Aug. 3, 1784, and pursuing a course of study, he entered Williams College, from which he was graduated with honor in 1809. Having decided to devote his life to the Christian Ministry, he attended Andover Theological Seminary. At the close of his first year there, his studies were in part interrupted by his being called to the office of Tutor in Williams College, which position he filled with much credit for two years. In the latter part of this time he had obtained license to preach, and commenced his labors in the ministry.

In January, 1813, a few months after Mr. Gray had taken his final leave of College, he began to preach in the first parish, at Washington, Litchfield Co., Conn., and was ordained as pastor April 4th of that year. In Sept. 1815, he was dismissed at his own request. After that he visited western New York, and labored in that State and New England, till the spring of 1817, when Providence directed his course to Stafford, Conn. There he continued in the work of his Master, as a faithful preacher of the Word, and the beloved pastor of his people, until suddenly stricken down in the midst of his usefulness. The following inscription copied from his tomb, is a just and fitting tribute:

Sacred to the Memory of
REV. CYRUS W. GRAY,
Pastor of the First Church in East Stafford;
Who with a mind cautious and profound,
Rather than rapid in its operations;
Strong in its conceptions;
Original in its views;
Disciplined by science and well furnished with knowledge;
Uniting in his character
Uncommon decision, with a heart formed for friendship;
In his manners simple;
In the avowal of his sentiments, undisguised;
In his doctrine uncorrupt;
In his piety fervent and steadfast;
In his preaching, instructive, earnest, and deeply penetrating;
Indefatigable in his labors;
And continually advancing in the high career of usefulness;
Was summoned by a divine voice, from the charge of a
Youthful family, and an affectionate flock, to the
Society of the redeemed in glory, on the 20th day of
Aug., A. D., 1821, and in the 37th year of his age.
"Behold an Israelite, indeed, in whom is no guile."

E. H. Gray

FREDERC EUGENE WINDSOR GRAY.

A son of Rev. Cyrus W. Gray, the subject of this sketch was born in Washington, Litchfield Co., Conn., May 2, 1814. When only seven years old his father died, and he was adopted by Dr. Porter, of Hadley, Mass. After suitable preparation Mr. Gray commenced the publication of a paper at Ipswich, Mass., in 1837, called the Ipswich *Register*. This he so ably conducted that in the spring of 1840 he received an urgent call to take charge of the Lynn *Freeman*, which he accepted, and he so admirably filled the place that, on the election of President Harrison, he received an offer to take charge of an Administration organ to be established at Washington, which however, was prevented by the early demise of the President.

Always a staunch Whig until the death of that party, in 1845 he took the position of Editor of the New Jersey *Advocate*, published at Rahway, N. J., which position he continued to fill until 1856, when he removed to Newburgh, N. Y., where he edited for a time the *Gazette*, and then became editor of the *Telegraph*, the weekly and daily editions of which he continued to conduct, until the failure of his health.

Mr. Gray held the pen of a ready writer, and as a conversationalist he was rarely equalled. He possessed a remarkable memory, and as an instance of this, when a child in the Sunday School, the members of his class being requested to see which could commit the most of Scripture to memory, he greatly surprised his teacher, when the test came, by correctly reciting three thousand verses ! He could repeat a sermon, or address, years after having heard it, almost verbatim, and his mind was richly stored with historic and other treasures of knowledge.

Mr. Gray was earnest and zealous in whatever he undertook; he threw his whole soul into every good enterprise, and labored for the improvement of every place in which he resided. He was an Episcopalian, and dearly loved that Church. He cared for the widow and the orphan, and the blessing of more than one that was ready to perish, was upon him. In 1864 he had removed to Vineland, New Jersey, with his family, for the improvement of his failing health. He was suddenly stricken down with apoplexy while visiting a daughter in Brooklyn, N. Y., where he died, April 6, 1871. His remains were taken to Newburgh for interment, where he was buried with the services of the Episcopal Church, and with those of the Masonic fraternity, of which he had long been a faithful and honored member. His beloved pastor, closed a sketch of his life published at that time, with the following beautiful and affectionate eulogy: "Short as was my acquaintance with our departed brother, I had early learned to respect and love him. His purity of character, his singleness of mind and heart, and exemplary christian life, endeared him to me greatly. It was with profound sorrow I heard the news of his death. It is but a small wreath to his memory that I now lay upon his tomb, but it is the offering of a pure pastoral love."

It is needless to add that such a man was greatly missed in the circle where he moved, but especially in his family and home. Mr. Gray was married at Ipswich, Mass., Aug. 8th, 1839, to Elizabeth Kimball, daughter of Rev. D. T. Kimball, who was for over half a century the pastor of the Congregational Church at that place. Miss Kimball was graduated at Ipswich Seminaary, and a lady of high character and rare worth. She was the lifelong and beloved companion of Mr. Gray, and still survives, actively engaged in church work and interested in every good cause. Her residence is at Franklinville, N. J. One son and three daughters were born to Mr. and Mrs. Gray, as follows:

ELIZABETH KIMBALL GRAY, b. Aug. 28, 1840; mar. Capt. H. S. Spaulding, Aug. 31, 1878; a son, Henry Seville, b. Sept. 16, 1880, in Franklinville, N. J.

Mrs. Elizabeth Kimball Gray Spaulding is much interested in literary work, and has a regular engagement with the N. Y. *Examiner*, the noted Baptist paper, besides she occasionally contributes both of verse and prose for other journals and publications. When her father's health was impaired, she went into his office and for several months conducted the business of both a weekly and daily paper with credit to herself and satisfaction to all parties. She has also been a useful and honored teacher for for years, and is still so engaged. Her present residence is at Iona, N. J. She is a very interesting and gifted lady.

ELIZABETH KIMBALL GRAY SPAULDING.

MARY EUGENIE GRAY, b. July 5, 1846, in Rahway, N. J.; d. June 16, 1868, at Vineland, N. J.

FREDERIC EUGENE GRAY, b. at Rahway, N. J., Nov. 26, 1848; d. Sept. 16, 1851.

The father bereaved thus touchingly portrayed his grief at the loss of his loved and only son: " In the full flush of his innocence he fell with the first leaves of Autumn, and the Autumn winds sigh out mournfully his requiem; but mingled with its sadness there comes a voice which sweetly whispers peace and consolation to the bruised hearts which yet linger behind him."

JULIA VIRGINIA GRAY, b. at Rahway, N. J., Dec. 18, 1852. Is a successful teacher; unmarried, and makes her home at Vineland, N. J.

DAUGHTERS OF REV. CYRUS W. GRAY.

ELIZABETH ASHLEY GRAY, dau. of Rev. Cyrus W. Gray, b. at Hadley, Mass., March 19, 1816 ; mar. William H. Smith, at Hadley, June 16, 1841; a daughter, Julia Gray Smith; residence, Chelsea, Mass.

JULIA AUGUSTA GRAY, dau. of Rev. Cyrus W. Gray, b. Oct. 22, 1817; mar. Justin L. Ambrose, 1840; no children; residence, Boston.

CATHARINE AURELIA GRAY, dau. of Rev. Cyrus W. Gray, b. Feb. 14, 1819; mar. Samuel Newman, of Peabody, Mass.; dec'd.

MARY ANN B. GRAY, dau. of Rev. Cyrus W. Gray, b. at Stafford, Conn., Sept. 19, 1820; d. at Sharon. Aug. 10, 1822.

DANIEL GRAY.

Hon. Daniel Gray, or "Judge Gray," as he was rightfully called by his neighbors and fellow citizens in his later years, was the seventh son of John Gray (3) of Sharon, and was a manly and noble character. There is a slight discrepancy between different authorities concerning the date of his birth, the official town records of Sharon having it as June 4, 1756, while the records of the Surrogate's Court, same place, in noticing the appointment of his mother, Catharine Gardner Gray, as his guardian, in 1763, give the date of his nativity May 4, 1756; and his age, as given on the memorial stone at his grave, taken from the date of his death, would make his birth on July 4th. In any case he was of good parentage, and from a hardy, vigorous youth developed a brave and patriotic manhood. Born during the continuance of the French war, and near the borders exposed to its ravages, he grew up with instinctive patriotism pulsing in his dauntless heart that needed but the occasion to bring it forth. The Revolutionary spirit was there; the might to do, the courage to dare. War raised its horrid front, the summons to duty came, and young Daniel Gray, like many another noble youth, went bravely forth to risk his life if need be on "the perilous edge of battle," to meet the foes of his country and of mankind. To what dangers he was exposed, by what disaster he was overcome, and how he bore himself through it all, is so well told in the annals of Rensselaer County, which became his later home, that the account is here given entire:

"Daniel Gray was one of those young men who enlisted their all in the cause of Independence. He had volunteered in Col. John Pathson's Regt., which was sent North, toward the Canada lines, to attend to the Indians, and in a battle with them at a place called 'The Cedars,' on the Sorel River, and not far from Montreal, Col. Pathson was surprised and defeated with the loss of about 60 taken prisoners, besides the killed and wounded. Among the prisoners so taken was Daniel Gray. The first night after their capture the Indians threw them on the ground on their backs, and then having extended their limbs to the full extent fastened them with staddles. Then they cut poles eight or ten feet in length which they laid on them transversely. Indian

guards with arms in their hands lay on either side of each prisoner, and on the poles, bending them to the ground. In this position Mr. Gray lay through the night, with an innumerable mul-
titude of mosquitos feasting on his blood. He was often heard
to say that it was the most insufferable night he ever experienced.

"The Indians were often insulting and abusive to their prisoners. At one time Mr. Gray was sitting quietly on a log, when
a young Indian coming along, without provocation insultingly
proceeded to spit in his face; whereupon Gray gave the youthful
savage a vigorous kick, knocking him down and causing him to
'squall' at the top of his voice. The Indians thereupon rushed
out with their tomahawks uplifted, and would have made short
work of dispatching the unarmed prisoner, but just at that mo-
ment an old squaw who had witnessed the affair interposed, and
the captive's life was saved.

"Another incident: Some days after the commencement of
their captivity, the Indians asked Gray to show them how to
wrestle. He complied with their request, easily throwing one
Indian after another as fast as they came up. At last the great
bully of the tribe came, and he threw him also. This greatly an-
gered the burly savage, but he was not allowed to injure Mr.
Gray, who afterwards received many favors and privileges from
the Indians not granted to the other prisoners.

"The capture took place in May, 1776, and a year from the following September, after many months of captivity, the prisoners were for a consideration turned over to the British authorities, and closely confined on the prison ship at Halifax, where
they suffered more severity than they had at the hands of their
barbaric captors. To add to the horrors of the situation, the
small pox broke out, devestating the ranks of the ill-treated prisoners. The following April the survivors were exchanged, and
Mr. Gray returned home."

That he afterwards re-enlisted and did good service for the
Patriot cause is evidenced by the fact that his name appears on
the records in the State archives of New York, as a Lieutenant
in Col. Van Rensselaer's Regiment.

Soon after the close of the Revolution, Daniel Gray removed
to the Hoosick Valley, and settled in the north part of what was

then Stephentown, but that portion was afterwards set apart and designated as the the township of Berlin. And there he continued to reside until his decease, May 23, 1830.

The records show that Daniel Gray was Captain of a Company in Col. Van Rensselaer's Regiment of N. Y. State Militia in 1788. In 1789 he gave a mortgage to Sephen Van Rensselaer for £50, on 128 acres of land in Stephentown, which shows that he had become a land owner; and in 1791, he was appointed as one of the first Justices of the Peace in the County of Rensselaer. He was elected Member of Assembly in the State Legislature, which then convened in the city of New York, in 1794; was re-elected Member of Assembly in 1796, 1797, 1798, and 1799; was again elected to the Assembly in 1821, and participated in the Forty-fifth Session; as will be seen, being honored by being so elected six times to the Legislature of the State of New York. In the meantime he had served several consecutive terms as Justice of the Peace, and Associate Judge of the County, and had also been repeatedly elected Supervisor of the town of Berlin. In the troublous anti-rent times, Mr. Gray was one of the Commissioners delegated to confer with the Patroon, and he was efficient in securing a just and satisfactory settlement. He was a member of the first Board of Trustees of the Baptist Church of Berlin, and continued to fill the position until his decease. In this connection it is happily said of him by a cotemporary, "The honorable distinction shown him in this his place of residence, is all sufficient to show the character and talent of the man."

With all the world before him Mr. Gray chose for his home a retired spot afar from the bustling highways, and the activities of more ambitious life. Up a narrow valley to the eastward, down which flows a rapid running stream, until near where the border of Berlin is bounded by the Massachusetts line, and the Hoosic Mountains seem to shut it in with walls of living green, presenting a scene of rare wildness and picturesque beauty,— there in such seclusion, and amid such romantic surroundings, was the ideal place that he had chosen, and chosen well; there, for nearly half a century he lived, there he died, and there he was buried. There in that unpretentious farm home up among the mountains, were born to him thirteen (13) children, who went forth into the world to become useful and honored citizens, men and women of force and character, most of whom lived to over four score, and all of whom were living when the youngest was nearly sixty; two still survive. From that seclusion he was called forth almost continuously to fill positions of honor and public trust, as already herein recorded. And this soldier of the Revolution was pre-eminently a man of peace, often acting as an arbiter to settle differences between neighbors, and an aged citizen still there residing who remembers often to have seen him in his youth, and was a familiar friend of the family, recently remarked to the writer that it was a very perverse man who would not submit to the arbitration of Judge Gray, as his fellow townsmen commonly called him. What a priceless legacy such a good name, which is still remembered and bears fruitage in that community after more than fifty years. That is the greatness grown upon the granite rock of character, and it endures.

Mr. Gray married for his first wife, Sarah Harris, June 1, 1783, whose parents were Quakers, and resided in Stephentown, of which Berlin was then a part. She was the mother of six children. "Sarah, the Amiable Consort of Daniel Gray, died Mar. 30, 1798," in the 34th year of her age, is the simple inscription at her grave. Mr. Gray married second, Jemima Rix, of Preston, Conn., who was the mother of seven children, and after the decease of her husband removed to Barry, Pike Co., Ill., where she died Aug. 19, 1840.

Mr. Gray was the last survivor of his father's family, his brothers and sisters having all gone before him. A patriarch indeed, his children still clustered around him, loth to leave those familiar scenes and the family fireside; but how soon and how widely to be scattered. Mr. Gray died May 23, 1830. The following brief epitaph recorded at his tomb well commemorates his worth:

"All that was mortal has here found an end,
Of a Patriot, a Statesman, a Christian and Friend;
On earth having finished the labors assigned him,
Heaven called for its own and men had to resign him."

DANIEL H. GRAY.

Daniel H. Gray, oldest son of Daniel and Sarah Harris Gray, was born in Berlin, (then Stephentown), July 25, 1785, and married first, Naomi Thomas, who died at Berlin, N.Y., Feb. 23, 1822. She was the mother of six children,—four sons and two daughters. Mr. Gray married second, Phebe Godfrey, who was the mother of eight children,—four sons and four daughters; she died at Cedar Hill, Dallas Co., Texas, Feb. 22, 1855. Mr. Gray, as will be seen, was the father of fourteen (14) children, nine of whom were born at Berlin, two in Pike Co., Ill., and three in Texas. He was the owner of a farm at Berlin adjacent to the old homestead, and after his father's death, in 1830, he removed to Atlas, Pike Co., Ill., then on the borders of the far distant west; no slight undertaking with his large family, making the long journey in the huge emigrant wagon of those days, and taking his household goods with him; but it was in due time, after some stirring incidents by the way, safely accomplished. There he remained near kindred, some of whom had preceded, and others who had followed him, until the fall of 1839, when he again moved on for the new El Dorado, Texas, where he arrived Dec. 1, having crossed the Red River and the Arkansas, and braved the dangers of the wild frontier, then swarming with Indians and outlaws. There he stuck his stakes and built a house of pine logs, and set about establishing a home. The surroundings just suited his courageous, adventurous spirit.

For more than twenty-five years, and until his death, he remained a citizen of Texas, and participated in the stirring scenes that marked that stormy period of its history. That he was a man of great physical strength and personal prowess, is abundantly evidenced. And that he was a loyal citizen in the time that tried men's souls, that he fearlessly upheld the Flag of the Union when Secession and Rebellion would have trampled it in the dust; and when armed Traitors stalked abroad with fire and sword threatening death and destruction to all who opposed their mad schemes, Daniel H. Gray, let it forever be said to his honor, let it be recorded as the crowning glory of his life, in the midst of the storm and the tempest was true.

As evidence of Daniel H. Gray's steadfast patriotism, the following quotation from a letter written by his brother, Stephen R. Gray, of Pittsfield, Ill., date of July 14, 1861, to friends at Berlin, N. Y., is good testimony. It says: "Daniel's health is good, and his letters interesting. The old man is a true Patriot, God bless him! He says, 'I am for the old Star Spangled Banner, come life or death!'" And again, what is still more emphatic is the following vivid portrayal by his own hand of a scene which came near being a tragedy, in which he bravely repelled a band of Texan rebels who essayed to take his life. The letter was written to his brother Stephen, and the original is now at hand:

CEDAR HILL, DALLAS CO., TEXAS, }
June 12, 1866. }

Dear Brother Stephen:—Through the goodness of an allwise God I am yet on earth. I will give you a short sketch of my life for the last four years. You had heard that I was married the third time. The lady thinking that my two sons living with me would be compelled to go into the army, (Rebel,) thought if she could only get rid of me, horses, cattle, all would be hers at a blow; so 'she raised the hue and cry that I was Abolition. All knew I voted Union. Let me say right here, my dear brother, how would my conscience have wrung with despair, to have turned against our fathers, the veterans of the Revolution! "Union!" yes, that is my motto, and will be in my dying moments. They came with a rope, and one of them put his hand on my shoulder with the threat that they had come to hang me. I turned, and strength came to me like it did to Sampson, for I exclaimed in my heart, "God help me!" In an instant I seemed stronger than in my young days. I grabbed him by the throat, and said, "You shall die first!" He was in a vice from which he could not break away, and was struggling for life, but my strength was like iron. Three more ran to assist him. Before they could get me loose the fellow fell down; half a minute more would have done the work for him. I told them they were a set of cowards. "Hang me if you dare! My boys will be home after awhile and they will lie 'round your cabins till they get the last dog. I am an old Texan and have seen bears, panthers, wolves; I have never turned out the way yet, nor for such a set of rascals as you are!" More than 2,000 have been put to death for being Union men. I was robbed of thousands of dollars of property. * * *

Farewell, dear Stephen, and don't forget to write.

Your Brother,   D. H. GRAY.

Mr. Gray died at Cedar Hill, Dallas Co., Texas, Feb. 11th, 1867, less than a year from the date of the preceding letter. At the time of the desperate encounter therein recorded he must have been nearly eighty years of age. A grand old man; what metal there was in him. The descendants of his fourteen children may well rise up and salute his memory.

DESCENDANTS OF DANIEL H. GRAY.

HENRIETTA GRAY, dau. of Daniel H., b. 1811; mar. D. W. C. Varey, of Stephentown, N. Y. Removed to Texas and died there; no children.

DANIEL W. GRAY, son of Daniel H., b. 1813; mar.; d. in 1864, leaving one daughter and five sons, to wit:
> IRA GRAY.
> HORATIO GRAY.
> DANIEL GRAY.
> CHARLES GRAY.
> WILLIAM GRAY.
> ROBY GRAY; mar. Professor John N. Dewitt, of Barry, Ill.

SARAH GRAY, dau. of Daniel H., b. 1815; mar. Dr. David Seeley, of Pike Co., Ill.; removed to Texas, where he died in 1854, leaving a son who was killed in the Rebel army at Shiloh, and two daughters; also a large property, comprising 15,000 acres of land, six negroes, and 600 head of cattle. The widow was afterwerds twice married.

HAMILTON GRAY, son of Daniel H., b. 1817; removed to Ill., and d. at Rockport, Aug., 1837; an excellent young man and much beloved.

DARWIN P. GRAY, DR., son of Daniel H. Gray, b. at Berlin, N. Y., 1818; removed to Texas with his father's family in 1839; studied medicine; graduated in 1845; entered the U. S. Army as Surgeon in 1846, and served until the close of the Mexican war, since which he has been engaged in civil practise in Texas. Dr. Gray married Miss M. Lamkin, Dec. 24th, 1847, at Cameron, Milan Co., Texas; she died March 6, 1885, at Grape Vine, Tarrant Co., Texas, Dr. Gray's present residence. Children:

IONE GRAY.
WILLIAM GRAY.
FRANK GRAY.
SEELEY GRAY.

BURTON T. GRAY, son of Daniel H., b. June 1, 1821; mar. Sophronia Babcock, Feb. 28, 1850; she d. Dec. 27, 1859, and he mar. second, Mrs. Maria Brown, Oct. 25, 1862. Residence, Barry, Ill. Children:

ELLEN GRAY, b. Jan. 12, 1853.
FRANK GRAY, b. May 9, 1856.

RUSSEL F. GRAY, son of Daniel H. and Phebe Godfrey Gray, b. 1824, in Berlin; removed with his father's family to Texas; mar. Mrs. Ferguson, 1848; she died and he mar. again; residence, Llano, Llano Co., Texas; children:

DELILAH GRAY, b. Jan., 1849.
ROBERT GRAY, b. Feb., 1850.
WASHINGTON GRAY, b. 1851.
WILBURN GRAY, b. March, 1852.
LIZZIE GRAY, b. 1855.

MARY GRAY, dau. of Daniel H., b. 1826; mar. Rev. Mr. Crawford; residence, Calvert, Texas.

JAMES SCHUYLER GRAY, son of Daniel H., b. 1828; mar. Mary E. Green, Nov. 26, 1868; residence, Handley, Tarrant Co., Texas; children:

ADDIE GRAY, b. Oct. 25, 1869.
MARGARET P. GRAY, b. Nov. 4, 1871.
DELLAH GRAY, b. Nov. 1, 1873.
MILAN H. GRAY, b. Jan. 10, 1876.
MARY EMILY GRAY, Nov. 22, 1877.
SUSIE GRAY, b. Dec. 23, 1879.
PEARLE EURENE GRAY, b. March 16, 1881.
MYRTLE D. GRAY, b. Aug. 9, 1884.

CLARENDON ROSS GRAY, son of Daniel H., b. 1833; mar.
Jane Glass, Feb. 1869; d. at Austin, Texas, Oct. 26th,
1877; two children deceased, and one living:

JANE GRAY, b. March, 1870.

The name of Clarendon Ross Gray should be written high on the
scroll of honor among those who deserve well of the Republic.
In the midst of disloyalty and Treason, the fires of patriotism
still burned in his breast. The following quotation is from a letter written by him to kindred date of Jan. 21, 1865: "For nearly three years I have been a wandering exile from my home and
dearest kindred, driven to the necessity of leaving my native
land to save my life, simply because I held to my patriotism with
a tenacious grip. On the 7th of Oct. '63, I entered on the task
of leaving the confines of rebeldom for Mexico. All my troubles heretofore sank to nothing in comparison to the undertaking
I now proposed. Four hundred and twenty miles of principally
an arid plain, three rapid rivers winding their way across the disconsolate wanderers's path, which challenge the strenuous efforts
of the boldest swimmer, and passage must be made while night
holds its dark mantle over the earth and hides the refugee from
view of the treacherous murderers who guard the banks,—this
vast plain must be traversed with little hope of success. I trust
it may never fall to my lot again during life's pilgrimage to perform such a journey." On reaching the Union lines, via Mexico,
he enlisted, Nov. 10th, '63, as a private in the 1st (loyal) Texas
Cavalry, in which he did good service for the Union cause, and
on the 23d of Dec. following was promoted to Lieutenant. All
honor to his memory!

MARGARET P. GRAY, dau. of Daniel H., b. 1837; d. March
20th, 1875.

MILAN H. GRAY, son of Daniel H., b. Jan. 24, 1840, in Texas; d. in Louisiana, Aug. 7, 1863.

ADELAIDE GRAY, dau. of Daniel H., b. 1842; mar. Mr.
McPherson; residence, Colorado City, Colorado.

AMANDA M. GRAY, dau. of Daniel H., b. 1843; mar. Mr.
Jaques, Bremont, Texas.

CLARENDON ROSS GRAY

SARAH GRAY, dau. of Daniel Gray, b. Apr. 18, 1787; mar. Hezekiah Hull, of Berlin, N. Y.; children: Daniel Gray Hull, who was drowned in the Mississippi while out on a fishing excursion; Dr. Hamilton Hull, of Sandlake, N. Y.; Ferdinand Hull; Laura Hull, who mar. Dr. Philander Thomas of Berlin; Sarah Hull; Arvilla Hull; Ferdinand Hull; Egbert Hull, an officer in the Union army, and died in Libby Prison from the effect of wounds received in battle; Pardee Hull, who lives on the old homestead; Halbert Hull, and Cleber Hull; Mrs. Sarah Gray Hull d. at Berlin, N. Y.

ROBY GRAY, dau. of Daniel Gray, was b. Sept. 27, 1789; in 1812 she mar. Clarendon Ross, of Hancock, Mass. Removed to Pike Co., Ill., where he d. Aug. 7, 1820; in 1823 she mar. Capt.Leonard Ross, a younger brother of her deceased husband. Her only son, Schuyler Gray Ross, d. Jan. 14, 1833, in his 20th year. Her second husband d. in 1836. Mrs. Ross afterwards removed to Barry, where she continued to reside with her kindred until her decease, Sept. 18, 1880, only lacking 9 days of reaching 91 years. To the last she retained her mind and memory to a remarkable degree. A contemporary says of her: "Sunshine and hope seemed to beam in her countenance and cheer her heart. Most nobly and wisely has she filled her sphere, and she now rests from her labors. Long and lovingly will be cherished the memory of 'Aunt' Roby Ross."

BETSEY GRAY, dau. of Daniel Gray, was born at Berlin, N. Y., April 1st, 1791; mar. Alonzo G. Hammond, at that place, July 18, 1811; he was a Member of the N. Y. State Legislature in 1828, and 1833; was appointed one of the Commissioners of Brooklyn in 1834; elected Judge and Surrogate of Kings Co., 1845; was also appointed one of the Supreme Court Commissioners for the State of New York. Judge Hammond d. Dec. 21, 1859; she d. Feb. 18, 1864. Children: Adelia Maria, b. Apr. 1, 1812, mar. John J. Ross, at Berlin, N. Y., July 4, 1829; he d. 1855; Mrs. Ross re-

sides at 168 Duffield St., Brooklyn, N. Y. Eliza A.
Hammond, b. Aug. 28, 1814, mar. Tunis Bergen, at
Flatbush, N. Y.; Dec. 18, 1855; d. in April, 1869.
Burton G. Hammond, b. July 30, 1816; unmarried, d. in
Brooklyn, N. Y., Feb. 18, 1873.

ELSIE GRAY, dau. of Daniel, b. April 8, 1794; mar. Dexter
Wheelock, of Hancock, Mass.; removed to Pike Co.,
Ill., 1819, in company with the Ross families; she d.
at Payson, Ill., Aug., 1880, leaving a married daughter,
Eliza Harrington, wife of Dr. Harrington, at that place,
and a son, John Gray Wheelock, of Kinderhook, Pike
Co., Ill.; Mr. Wheelock d. in California, 1851.

POLLY GRAY, dau. of Daniel, b. April 30, 1796; mar. Eliphalet Jones; removed to Aurora, Erie Co., N. Y.; children: Henry was a boot and shoe dealer at Baton
Rouge, La.; Albert, who was a druggist at Mobile,
Ala., was in the Rebel army and d. from a wound received at Shiloh; William and Mary, who reside on
the old homestead at Willink, N. Y.

PHEBE GRAY, dau. of Daniel, b. Mar. 24, 1798; mar. Lang-
ford Greene, of Berlin; removed to Illinois 1830; had
three children: Jay, who mar. Victoria Gray, dau. of
Schuyler Gray, and lives in California; Sarah; Warren
Greene, of Benton Co., Missouri. Phebe Gray Greene
d. in March, 1865.

HANNAH GRAY, dau. of Daniel and Jemima Rix Gray,
b. 1802; mar. Harry Hull of Berlin, N. Y., June 30,
1824; d. Dec. 6, 1872; children: Lucy Jane Hull, b.
Oct. 22, 1826; John Henry, b. Oct. 21, 1828; Kleber,
b. Aug. 20, 1830; James Kleber, b. Oct. 6, 1832; Tracy Darwin, b. April 2, 1834; Ulberto Franklin, b. Feb.
12, 1836; Nelson Gray, b. Nov. 14, 1837; Caroline
Victoria, b. Dec. 5, 1839; Hannah Mary, b. Jan'y 21,
1843.

CAROLINE GRAY, dau. of Daniel, b. March 5, 1806; mar.
Orlando Babcock, at Barry, Ill., 1846; he d. in Sept.
1874; she d. Feb. 5, 1881; no children.

Stephen R. Gray

STEPHEN RIX GRAY.

Stephen R. Gray, son of Daniel and Jemima Rix Gray, was born at Berlin, N. Y., Jan. 9, 1804, and was married to Sabrina Bentley at that place, June 16, 1825. In July 1837, he removed to Illinois with his family, having previously made a prospecting tour to that then far western State. On arrival they stopped in the Mississippi bottom until Feb., 1838, when they moved to Barry, Pike Co., Ill. He was the first Postmaster of Barry, and held that office until 1850, when he was elected Sheriff, and removed to Pittsfield, which was the county seat of Pike. He was several times elected Justice of the Peace of Barry, and in 1844 was appointed one of three Commissioners to appraise and divide in equal portions one hundred and sixty quarter sections of land in the military bounty lands of the State, belonging to the estate of William James of Albany, N. Y. While examining these lands he witnessed the destruction of the anti-Mormon Press at Nauvoo, Ill. In 1863 he was elected Supervisor of the township of Pittsfield, and superintended the erection of a new Jail building and Sheriff's residence. For several years he was also successfully engaged in mercantile business under the firm name of Wells & Gray.

Mr. Gray still survives, and that fact softens the voice of praise of some delightful traits of character in him. Noticeably one of these is his kindly and affectionate interest in his kindred. It was the privilege of the writer not long since to peruse his correspondence extending over a period of years, with a member of the family, and through it all was manifested a kindly, sweet and beautiful christian spirit overflowing with loving, affectionate interest. Every evil he deplored, every good cause advanced. Many interesting family facts here presented were gleaned from those pages. In a letter written by him to his kinsman, Col. Reuben Gray, a sketch of whom appears in this volume, and dated at Barry, Ill., April 3, 1846, concerning family matters, occurs the following: "I now hope to be able to form new acquaintances of the Gray family, which will be ever dear to me, if on no other account than through the respect I hold for my father."

Mr. Gray is described by one near to him, as "a fine looking old gentleman, tall and straight, with hair as white as snow." His beloved wife, Sabrina Bentley Gray, died in Oct., 1877, after they had lived together over fifty-two years. Nine children were born to them as follows:

DESCENDANTS OF STEPHEN R. GRAY.

CHARLOTTE ELIZA GRAY, b. June 1, 1826; d. at Barry, Ill., Jan'y 13, 1847.

CYRUS WINTHROP GRAY, b. Oct. 29, 1827; mar. Sarah Anne Elizabeth Long, at St. Louis, Mo., Oct. 26th, 1851; she died 1861, and he married second, Mrs. Kate W. Matthews, at Perry, Ill., May 21, 1868; residence, Carlinsville, Ill.; a grain dealer; children:

GEORGE P. GRAY, born June 1853; d. Aug. 1854.
ROBERT E. GRAY, b. April 1855; d. April 1855.
MARY L. GRAY, born 1860; mar. Will C. Bush, of the Pike Co. *Democrat*, Sept. 3, 1880; a daughter, Helen Gray Bush.
SARAH A. GRAY, d. May, 1862.
PAUL W. GRAY, b. April 19th, 1870.
FLORENCE ISABELLE GRAY, Oct. 28, 1872.
HELEN LUCILLE GRAY, b. Dec. 31, 1874.
FRANK MERRILL GRAY, b. Dec. 26, 1877.

DANIEL DARWIN GRAY, b. May 21, 1830; mar. Sarah Jane De Haven, at Barry, Ill., 1850; a carpenter and builder; a soldier in the Mexican war and in the war for the Union; d. at Barry, March 20, 1871; the widow and family reside at Decatur, Ill.; children:

CHARLES EDWIN GRAY, dec'd.
HENRY STEPHEN GRAY, b. Nov. 1, 1854; married Clara Burch, Dec. 25, 1878; is a Palace Car Conductor between Chicago and St. Louis; children:
LE MAR A. GRAY, b. Aug. 30, 1879.
ELMER S. GRAY, b. June 28, 1884.
MARY LOUISE GRAY, b. Dec. 31, 1856; mar. E. C. Haak, Sept. 30, 1877; children: Mabel, b. Apr. 26, 1879; Harry, b. Feb. 1, 1882.
JOHN DE HAVEN GRAY, b. Feb. 19, 1858.
ALONZO W. GRAY, b. Feb. 2, 1860.
ELMER AND ELLEN GRAY, (twins,) dec'd.
ANTOINETTE GRAY, b. March 25, 1868.
MARION FRANCES GRAY, b. April 11, 1871.

WILLIAM HENRY GRAY, son of Stephen R., was b. Sept. 24, 1833; mar. Virginia Louise Browne, at Pittsfield, Ill., Sept. 15, 1858; removed to St. Louis, Mo., and successfully engaged in the wholesale and retail grocery trade; was killed by a blow from a drayman while trying to prevent a conflict between him and one of his own employees, April 17, 1871. He had the following children, of whom all those living reside at St. Louis, Mo.; also Mrs. Gray:

> EFFIE DOUGLAS GRAY, b. July 4th, 1859.
>
> WILLIAM HENRY GRAY, Jr., b. March 26, 1861; mar. Tennie Heidel, Apr. 28, 1886.
>
> CORA VIRGINIA GRAY, b. March 19, 1863.
>
> ARTHUR PIERCE GRAY, b. Aug. 8, 1864; dec'd.
>
> MONTROSE ERASTUS GRAY, b. Jan. 15, 1869.

MARY FRANCES GRAY, b. April 7, 1836; mar. Milan Smith Coxe, June 21, 1866; he had a large book and stationstore at Cairo, Ill., where he d. 1875; she then took a position in the public schools at Jerseyville, Ill., which she still occupies; no children.

ROBY GRAY, b. Oct. 26, 1839; mar. Mason Foster, June 10, 1868; residence, Barry, Ill., her father, Stephen R. Gray, making his home with them. Mr. Foster is a native of Sullivan, N. H., where he was born Aug. 28, 1839; he has charge of the hardware establishment of Seeley, Lloyd & Co.; no children.

VIRGINIA GRAY, b. April 17, 1842; d. June 13, 1846.

JOHN BENTLEY GRAY, b. March 12, 1845; mar. Laura Appleby, at St. Louis, June 18, 1867; was City Weigher; d. leaving one child,

> ADDIE GRAY, of St. Louis.

ELEONORA VIRGINIA GRAY, b. Aug. 26, 1848; mar. Joshua Pike, July 21, 1869. Mr. Pike is Superintendent of the public schools of Jerseyville, Ill., and is considered one of the best educators in that State. One child, Frederick William Pike, b. May 25, 1871.

SCHUYLER GRAY.

Schuyler Gray, son of Daniel, was born at Berlin, N. Y., Apr. 5, 1810. He married Amanda M. Streeter, at Berlin, Sept. 6th, 1834, and removed to Pike Co., Ill. He was a master builder, and his work in Rensselaer Co., N. Y., and Barry, Ill., will long remain to attest his skill and workmanship. He died at his residence in Barry, Sept. 6th, 1874, on the fortieth anniversary of his marriage. His widow still resides there. Children:

FLORA AUGUSTA GRAY, b. June 18, 1835; married David Pike May 21, 1868; resides at Vandalia, Missouri.

EDGAR S. GRAY, b. Jan. 1, 1837; mar. Eliza Elam, Dec. 24, 1862; residence, Downey, Cal. Children:

NETTIE M. GRAY, b. Aug. 18, 1867.
ROBERT GRAY, b. 1871.
ALMA GRAY, b. 1873.
MARY V. GRAY, b. 1875.
EUGENE GRAY, b. 1878.
ALFRED GRAY, b. 1880.
EMILY GRAY, b. 1884.

OLIVE VICTORIA GRAY, b. Aug. 25, 1838; mar. Jay Greene Aug. 5, 1859; residence, Black's Station, California. Children: Phebe A., Schuyler, Harry, Charles, David, Germain, George, Minnie H.

EMMA E. GRAY, b. Jan. 8, 1841; d. March 24, 1842.

HARVEY ROMEYN GRAY, b. Aug. 29, 1842; unmarried; is a painter; residence, Downey, Cal.

SARAH D. GRAY, b. April 17, 1844; mar. Lorenzo Smith, April 22, 1862; removed to Perry, Mo.; d. Dec. 13, 1883. Children: Olive V., Luttie, Frank, and Harvey.

CHARLES SCHUYLER GRAY, b. Mar. 1, 1846; d. June 21, '46.

MARY VESTA GRAY, b. Oct. 9, 1848; mar. Fred. Hawkins, Dec. 31, 1868; residence, Downey, Cal. Children: Daniel, Jessie, Halmer, Bulah, and Fred Hawkins, Jr.

MARTHA F. GRAY, b. Feb. 9, 1850; unmarried, resides at Los Angeles, Cal.

CARRIE AURORA GRAY, b. Dec. 27, 1853; unmarried, and resides at Barry, Ill.

JESSIE M. GRAY, b. Nov. 2, 1857; mar. John A. Smith, March 5, 1877; residence, Vandalia, Mo.; children: Floyd P., Edna E., and Nellie Smith.

FLOYD GRAY, b. Sept. 3, 1859; commercial traveller for Gray, Burt & Kingman, Chicago; residence, Barry, Ill.

HORATIO NELSON GRAY, son of Daniel, was born at Berlin, N. Y., Feb. 2, 1808. Removed to Pike Co., Ill.; afterwards to California; died at Barry, Ill., April 2, 1881; unmarried.

THOMAS TRACY GRAY.

Thomas T. Gray, son of Daniel Gray, was born at Berlin, N. Y., April 23d, 1812, he being the youngest of the thirteen children. Born and raised on a farm, he followed that occupation until after his father's decease, on the old homestead, so dear to him and to the family. On reaching his 21st year he entered the village store of Mr. Bentley at Berlin, as clerk, and there continued several years, making his home with his sister, Mrs. A. G. Hammond. In 1835 he purchased of Chancellor Walworth of Saratoga, 160 acres of land situated adjoining the town of Worcester, Pike Co., Ill., afterwards changed to Barry, where he now resides. On the 20th of October, 1838, Mr. Gray was married to Mary Frances Crandall, of Berlin, who is the mother of all of his children, and still survives. The following spring, May 20th, 1839, they removed to their new home in the far west, where the most of his brothers and sisters had already preceded them, and settled on his farm near the present town of Barry. Followed farming for a few years and then engaged in the mercantile business; then farming again, and then Railroad contracting. Was for several years Station Agent for the Wabash R. R., at Barry. Has held the office of Town Clerk, School Inspector, etc., in Berlin and Barry, but has never been an office seeker. Of his political principles, he says: " I started out as a Democrat. Martin Van Buren was the first President 1 voted for, but as time passed on I left the Democratic party and stepped into the ranks of the Republican party, where I now remain."

Mr. Gray has been from the first quite interested in the Gray Genealogy, and has furnished much important and interesting information concerning his father's branch of the family. He has the distinction of being one of the three surviving grandchildren of John Gray of Sharon, and is the youngest of them. In personal appearance he is said to bear a strong resemblance to his honored father, as will be seen by accompanying portrait. Mr. and Mrs. Gray have ten children, all living at this date, and all married but a son and a daughter, and have several grandchildren, as appears in the following list of descendants:

EUGENE GRAY, b. Sept. 5, 1839; mar. Lydia Wier, of Barry, Jan. 8, 1867; is a merchant in the town of New Canton, Pike Co., Ill.; no children.

MELISSA GRAY, b. Dec. 24, 1842; mar. Joseph E. Haines, a nephew of Mrs. Chas. M. Gray, of Chicago, Dec. 10, 1869; reside at Barry; have five children: Howard, Roand, Bethuel, Ralph and Bertha.

HENRY T. GRAY, b. Jan. 8, 1844; was a soldier in the war for the Union.

CHARLOTTE GRAY, b. Jan. 20, 1846; mar. Bethuel Roand, June 11, 1866; reside in Barry, Ill.; one child, a daughter.

HALBERT N. GRAY, b. Jan. 15, 1848; mar. Emily R. Scribner, of Griggsville, Ill., May 1, 1876, where they continue to reside; he is a dealer in stock and grain; children:

> SHIRLEY EUGENE GRAY, b. April 4, 1877.
> MOLLIE BLANCHARD GRAY, b. May 30, 1880.

JOSEPHINE GRAY, b. Dec. 15, 1850; mar. James P. Cassidy, Sept. 18, 1872; he is Asst. Supt. W. U. Telegraph Office at Minneapolis, Minn., where they reside; children: Halbert and Margaret Cassidy.

FANNIE I. GRAY, b. April 14, 1852; mar. William E. Stitt, of Chicago, May 26, 1880; he is a grain dealer and member of the Board of Trade of that city; no children.

HARRIET GRAY, b. May 12, 1854; married Frederick Chas. Ottowa, April 16, 1880; reside at Barry; a son, Frederick Leon Ottowa.

FLORENCE GRAY, b. Dec. 21, 1856; mar. Harry Breeden, Nov. 10, 1876; he is a machinist; they reside in Chicago and have two children: Herbert and Tracy Breeden.

GERTRUDE GRAY, b. May 6, 1862; resides with her parents at Barry, Ill.

CAPT. SILAS GRAY.

Capt. Silas Gray, son of John Gray (3) of Sharon, and Catharine Gardner Gray, was born May 19, 1748, and was the first child by the second marriage of his father. The copy of his application for a pension made in 1818, as furnished by the Pension Office, and herewith published, would make his birth three years later, but the above date, copied from the town records of Sharon, and corroborated by the records of the Surrogate's Court at that place, is assumed to be correct. He had chosen his elder brother, John Gray, for his Guardian, Feb. 7, 1764, and the records show that he purchased a piece of land in the east part of Sharon, of Simeon Smith, Jan'y 20, 1769, for £78, and re-sold the same to Smith for same price, Dec. 11, 1773.

The Revolution soon followed, and with others of his brothers, at least four of them, he early enlisted in the Patriot cause, and marched with that hazardous expedition to capture Canada, that culminated in disaster when the gallant Montgomery and his compatriots fell in their rash but heroic assault upon the citadel of Quebec. Of that, and his subsequent highly honorable career as an officer and soldier, the following sketch has been kindly furnished from the records of the Pension and War Department at Washington:

"In his application for a Pension, dated in April, 1818, he states that he was then residing in Guilderland, Albany County, N. Y., and would be 67 years old on the 19th of the next May. That he entered the service about May 1, 1775, in the 4th New York Regiment, commanded by Colonel Henry B. Livingston, and that he continued in service as Captain until discharged, June 23, 1783, at Newburgh, N. Y. That his discharge, with his commission, and the muster rolls, had been destroyed by fire. That he was at the capture of St. Johns, (November 3d, 1775), Montreal, (Nov, 13, 1775,) the battle of Quebec, (Dec. 31st, 1775,) the surrender of General Burgoyne, at Saratoga, (Oct. 17, 1777,) the battle of Monmouth, New Jersey, (June 28, 1778,) and others which he did not mention. Peter Swart, a witness, testifies that he saw Silas Gray in 1782, at Schoharie, N. Y., with a Company under his command.

"As Captain Gray does not mention the respective grades to which he was appointed, with dates, the following history has been compiled from documents on file in this office:

"In a printed list of the names of officers, not including Ensigns, assigned to the four Regiments raised in New York, as reported in August, 1775, by a Committee of the Provincial Congress of that Colony, the name of James Holmes appears as Colonel of the 4th Regiment, with Henry B. Livingston as Captain of the 1st Company, but the name of Silas Gray is not in that printed list, nor has it been found as an officer in the muster rolls on file, (which however are not complete,) prior to his appointment November 26, 1776, as 2d Lieutenant in Captain Benjamin Walker's Company, 4th Regiment, of which Henry B. Livingston was Colonel from Nov. 21, 1776, to January 31, 1779. Lieut.-Col. Peter Regnier was temporarily in command of the 4th Regiment from February, 1779, until April 26, 1779, from which date Colonel Weissenfels appears to have commanded until he was 'deranged,' January 1, 1781.

"Silas Gray was promoted from 2d Lieutenant in Captain Walker's Company to 1st Lieutenant, to rank from March 13, 1777, and transferred to Captain Jonathan Pearsce's Company, January 9, 1778, the Regiment being stationed at that time at Valley Forge. He was promoted Captain, April 11, 1780, but the muster rolls of his Company are not on file. After his promotion, it is reported that in the re-organization of the army he was 'deranged,'* Jan'y 1, 1781. After that date, it is not probable that he had a regular command in the army, but it is probable that the Company which Mr. Swart testifies to having seen under his command at Schoharie in 1782, was a Militia Volunteer Company on a short tour of duty in that vicinity to protect the inhabitants of the frontier from Indians.

"While Silas Gray was 2d Lieutenant, his Company, early in September, 1777, is reported at Stillwater, New York, and during the winter of 1777–8, at Valley Forge. After the enemy evacuated Philadelphia he must have joined in the pursuit through New Jersey to Monmouth, where the battle took place, and then toward New Brunswick. From there the 4th Regi-

---

*In Revolutionary parlance, supernumerary, or transferred.

ment turned north across the Hudson River and encamped at North Castle, then at White Plains, until the fall of 1778, and winter of 1778-9, when he was on duty in Central New York, viz: Fort Plank, Stone Arabia, and Canajoharie. In the winter of 1779-80, he was encamped at Morristown, New Jersey. During the period from May, 1778, when encamped at Valley Forge, to the time of encamping at Morristown, he was the only officer in his Company, except in May, 1779, when an Ensign was transferred to his Company, and remained with him until going into winter quarters at Morristown, New Jersey, which is the last report of his Company on file."

SILAS GRAY'S WILL.

The following is a copy of the Last Will and Testament of Silas Gray, on file in the Surrogate's Court at Schenectady, N. Y.:

In the name of God, Amen: I, Silas Gray, of the town of Princetown, and County of Schenectady, though weak in body, but of sound and perfect mind and memory, blessed be Almighty God for the same, I do make and publish this my last Will and Testament in manner as following, that is to say: First, I give and bequeath unto my daughter Peggy, wife of Turney I. Sturges all my devise and lands belonging to me lying in the town of Hector, and County of Seneca; and I also give and bequeath unto my daughter Peggy, wife of Turney I. Sturges, a bond and mortgage against one McEntyre, left in the hands of David Sacia for collection; and I also give and bequeath unto my daughter Peggy, wife of Turney I. Sturges, all my pension which I draw from the United States.

And I also give and bequeath unto my daughter Caty, wife of Peter Biste, twelve dollars and fifty cents; and I also give and bequeath unto the daughter of Peter Biste, named Gainet, a gown's cloth; and also I give and bequeath unto Turney I. Sturges all my wearing apparel of all denomination.

And also I do will and ordain and nominate and appoint, Aaron Von Wormer and Calvin Cheeseman, Jr., of Duanesburgh, and Turney I. Sturges, my lawful executors and administrators for the true and intente of my Last Will and Testament.

Given under my hand and seal November the 28th, 1818.

In the presence of   SILAS GRAY, [L.S.]

Michael Von Wormer.
Aaron Von Wormer.
Wm. R. Ward.

The records show that the Will was proved Feb. 28th, 1820. He had died on the 19th of Jan., 1820, and not in April, as has been stated. The records of Seneca County show that "Silas Gray, of Middleburgh, Schoharie Co., by Edward Gray his Attorney, deeded 600 acres of land in Hector (now a part of the Co. of Schuyler,) to William McIntire, Sept. 28, 1816." The mortgage referred to in his Will is doubtless one he held on this property, but the records do not show that it was ever assigned or satisfied. So Capt. Gray had lived in Middleburgh, as well as in Guilderland and Princetown, and previously, probably at Rensselaerville, Albany Co., as the records show that "Silas Gray and Sally Gray his wife sold a farm of 110 acres in the town of Rensselaerville, Sept. 19, 1814." This is of interest as being the only record of her name found. They had previously lived in Egremont, Berkshire Co., Mass., where he had purchased land July 14, 1806. But to go back further : The records of the old Congregational Church at Sharon, Conn., show that "Silas Gray and wife united Sept. 6, 1789. Children of same baptized same date." This shows that he had returned to that place after the Revolution, and probably continued to reside there several years.

It might seem an easy task, with the foregoing data, secured by much painstaking labor, to trace his descendants; but it has not proved to be so. In fact, it has been found very difficult, if not impossible of attainment. No one has been found by the name of Biste in all the region adjacent to where Silas Gray is known to have lived and died, and none by the name of Sturges who are descended from, or related to, or any person whatsoever who has knowledge or recollection of the said Turney I. Sturges, who had married Peggy, the daughter of Capt. Silas Gray; notices in the press, personal search, including a large collection of genealogical statistics of the Sturges family, all failed of the desired result. It appears, however, that the families of Sturges and Turney are of Fairfield, Conn., where some of them still reside, and that there have been intermarriages. Capt. Silas Gray was a typical soldier of the Revolution; a grim and stalwart Continental. Traditions of his personal prowess are still handed down in the family, and his name is perpetuated on the rolls by a score or more of kindred.

WILLIAM GRAY.

William Gray, son of John Gray of Sharon, was born May 22, 1754, and was the sixth son of his father. The first record of him after his birth is the fact that his mother, Catharine Gardner Gray, was appointed his Guardian on the 25th of April 1763; and on Jan. 18, 1768, having arrived at suitable age, he chose Ebenezer Hutchinson for his Guardian. In the diary of his elder brother John, is found the meagre statement that he died in Sharon, and the most diligent search has failed to find other record of him, except in Sedgwick's History of Sharon, which gives account of some of his Revolutionary war record, from which we learn that he participated in the battle at Lexington, and received favorable mention for his heroic conduct on that occasion. The above mentioned history says: " A Company was formed in Sharon in 1775, and marched northward for the conquest of Canada, under Gen. Montgomery. Before St. John was taken, it was determined to make an attempt on Montreal with a few troops. The troops were paraded, and Allen marching in front of the Connecticut line invited volunteers to join him. William Gray was one of the few who stepped forward to share in the perils of this expedition." The story of the failure and repulse of the rash assault, in which many were killed, and the rest of the heroic band, including William Gray, were taken prisoners, is retold. The prisoners, loaded with irons, were sent to England, for the avowed object of punishing them as traitors. The threat of retaliatory measures prevented such summary proceedings, and after being kept in close confinement in England and Ireland during the ensuing winter, they were brought back to New York in the spring of 1776, and confined in an old church. From this place the Sharon prisoners planned to escape. There was a high fence around the church, and " William Gray managed to loosen one of the long planks of which it was built, and through this opening he and his companions made their escape as soon as it was dark enough to conceal their operations. They soon found means to land on Long Island, and thence over the Sound to the continent, and so returned to their friends in Sharon."

There is no further trace of William Gray other than the mention of his death, reference to which has already been made. No date is given, but it was probably during or soon after the Revolution. He sleeps in an unmarked, unknown grave, but it is the grave of a brave patriot soldier who loved his country and served it well.

JAMES GRAY.

James Gray, the youngest son of John Gray of Sharon, was born Aug. 3, 1759, and his mother, Catharine Gardner Gray, was appointed his Guardian on the 25th of April, 1763, his father having died in 1761. Though he was doubtless a soldier of the Revolution, it is not easy to exactly place him there. There was a James Gray who was a member of a Company of Minute Men organized in Great Barrington, Mass., and which marched for Boston April 21, 1775. He was quite young then for such service, but it might have been he. At best, however, it is only a surmise. The records of Sharon show, that on Feb. 5, 1785, James Gray bought ten acres of land of Israel Pennoyer, on the road leading from Sharon to Middle Bridge, for £26, and that he resold the same to Pennoyer Jan'y 19, 1786; and the church records show that he married Parthenia White of Sharon, March 26, 1786, after which he mysteriously disappears, the only trace of him being the following statement or tradition handed down in the John Gray branch of the family, and given to the writer by the late Chas. M. Gray, Esq., of Chicago: "Another of my grandfather's brothers located in lower Virginia; his name was James, and his descendants are numerous in that section of the State." He had received this information from his uncle, Col. Reuben Gray, who had given much attention to the history of the family. Considerable research however has been made in that direction without avail, and regretfully the unsuccessful search was given up. There are numerous Gray families in Virginia, some mention of which appears in this Genealogy, but the task of finding the descendants of James Gray, must devolve upon the future historian of this family. What generations may have been born to him during these hundred years!

J. Gray

JOHN TARVIN GRAY.

The following autobiographical sketch of John T. Gray, grand son of Nathaniel Gray, and great grandson of John Gray of Sharon, whose family record appears on page 63, is well worthy of a place in this family history:

"My father (Alanson Gray,) moved from Kentucky to Cincinnati, in the year 1825 or 1826, remaining there in business until 1829, when ill health compelled him to go back to the country. From twelve years old to twenty-one I lived on a farm. After passing seventeen years I took up a regular course of hard studies at home at night, odd hours and bad weather: Arithmetic, Geometry, Trigonometry, Algebra and History. I built myself a 12 x 14 hewed log study, in which I prepared myself for Woodward High School, Cincinnati, where I attended a portion of the years 1842-3, and where I was prepared for the profession of Civil Engineering.

"In June, 1844, I was preparing to go south in quest of occupation in my profession, when one beautiful, quiet evening a handsome stranger came, just at sunset, to my father's house, surrounded by miles of the grand primeval forests for which Kentucky at that day was celebrated. My father was absent. An hour later he returned home. The meeting was touching in the extreme. That stranger, unknown to the family prior to this meeting, was Philander Raymond, the schoolmate of my father in dear old Sherburne. This stranger, of whose boundless philanthropy I had heard enough from my father's winter evening recitals to make a large book, was soon as fully known personally as he had been through long years by name and fame. He was then the Manager of the large Brady's Bend Iron Works, on the Alleghany River 65 miles above Pittsburg, and had come to Cincinnati to close a contract to furnish the flat iron rails for the Little Miami R. R., from Morrow to Xenia, a distance of some 22 miles. On learning my intentions he urged me to keep out of the South, and come up to Brady's Bend in October, and he would employ me. I took his advice, and soon had charge of all surface and underground Railroads, all mines for coal, iron ore and limestone, 3,000 tons of which had to be provided weekly for four blast furnaces, one 40-fire Railroad mill and forge, foundry, and 385 dwellings. I arrived there the first week in October, 1844, and married his only daughter June 22, 1848, at which time I had been for many months Superintendent of the Rail Mill, made so by order of the Boston and New York owners. At this mill I designed the first set of T Rail rolls west of the Alleghanies, and made on them the first rails laid in Ohio, and the first in Michigan. The first in Ohio was 2,000 tons for the Little Miami R. R., from Cincinnati to Millford, 16 miles; the second, 8,000 tons for the Michigan Central from Detroit to St. Joseph, 68 miles.

"In 1848 I left Brady's Bend, and went to, and took an interest in Sugar Creek Furnace, 5 miles north-west of Franklin, Pa., which was not successful. From there I went with my young wife and baby to Pittsburg, Pa., and took charge of the construction of the Chartiers R. R., running from a point four miles below Pittsburg out into a large field of coal comprising 700 acres. This belonged, R. R. and coal, to a N. Y. and Phila. Co. I nearly completed the R. R., laid out two tunnels and partly opened up this large field of coal, and then left their service and was made Supt. of Construction of 190 miles of the Pa. & Ohio R. R., now the East end of the Chicago & Ft. Wayne R. R. After the completion of this Road, I came, in June 1853, to Cincinnati, and began the building of a Suspension Bridge between Covington and Newport, opposite Cincinnati, and the same year built one at Tiffin, 180 miles north in Ohio.

"In 1855 went to Nashville, Tenn., and up to June, 1860, built nearly 40 R. R. Bridges; one for the State of Tennessee, over the Cumberland, for the joint use of the Louisville & Nashville, and Edgefield & K'y Railroads, at a cost of $205,000. Also enlarged the Water Works for the city of Nashville. In 1860 came back to Kentucky to rest a season, but the war cut me off from returning to Tenn. Since the war have built numerous suspension and other iron bridges in Ohio.

"Have made extended surveys of the country north of Lake Superior. Have examined a great part of Texas, and made reports thereon. Partly constructed a Railroad from Flemingsburg, Ky., to reach the splendid coal fields on the valleys of the upper Licking and North Fork of the Kentucky rivers in Morgan, Wolf, Breathitt, Perry, and other mountain counties.

"In my whole life, I have built 127 bridges, nearly all for Railway use, and not one of them ever let a train or engine go through.

"By request, photos of some of my designs for suspension and other bridges, have been furnished the Austrian Minister and been sent to the College of Architects and Engineers at Vienna, Austria.

"When I was ready to leave home, the last week in September, 1844, my books and all I had were in two carpet bags. I had $57 in money, the earnings of my own hands. I gave my father, who had a large family, $55.50, and with the remainder, $1.50, paid my way to Cincinnati, from a point 20 miles above. I went to an uncle in Newport, just opposite, and borrowed $10 to take me to Brady's Bend, and on arrival there at 9 P. M., (having had no supper,) I had 5 cents left! The first to greet me at the door of my benefactor and future father-in-law, was the wonderfully bright and beautiful, rosy cheeked and blue-eyed daughter, who on the 22d of June 1848, became my wife. I used the first $1,500 of my earnings at this place to purchase merchandise to start my father in a small country store, which necessitated the postponement of my marriage one year.

"Now, at 65, I look back over a busy life of 48 years laboriously spent; free from any but simple, regular habits; mainly spent for others, many of whom still live, but many more have gone to rest."

CYNTHIA RAYMOND GRAY was born at Sherburne, N. Y., and educated in the city of New York, where she graduated in 1840. She died in Cincinnati, Ohio, the 28th of March, 1854, and was buried in the family plot near Madison, Lake County, Ohio, by the side of her kindred. She left one son, Raymond C. Gray, Esq., of Covington, Ky., another son having died in infancy.

The full genealogical record of John T. Gray's family appears on page 63, the above having been received too late for position in connection therewith.

BETHIAH GRAY HIBBARD.

BETHIAH GRAY, of whom brief record is made on page 68, is worthy of special mention as the only child that came to maturity from the marriage of Nathaniel Gray and Bethiah Newcomb Raymond, widow of David Raymond, and mother of James, Abraham, and Newcomb Raymond, of whom mention is made in this Genealogy. She was born at Kent, Conn., on the historic 4th of July, 1776, and she married Daniel Hibbard, at Sherburne, N. Y., in 1796; removed from there to Sheridan, Chautauqua Co., N. Y., in 1811, and died at Jamestown, N. Y., Oct. 24, 1854. She had four children, as follows:

LUTHER HIBBARD, born 1798; married Laura Clark, and died Feb. 19, 1843, leaving three children: Eliza, who married John Evans, and has two living children, Mary and Anna; Jane, who remains unmarried; and Daniel Hibbard, who married Aurora McManus, and has three children, Nellie, Carrie, and Arthur. Mr. and Mrs. Evans, and their daughters, and sister, Jane Hibbard, reside at Rochester, Minn., from which place Daniel Hibbard and family have recently removed to Pomona, California.

AMASA HIBBARD, the second son, died in childhood.

MARY HIBBARD, daughter of Daniel and Bethiah Gray, born in Sherburne, N. Y., July 1, 1806, married Joseph Kenyon, and had four children: Darwin, Caroline Sylva, Horace Fenton, who married Emma Rockwell but has no children, and Mary Adelaide, who resides in Buffalo with her aged mother, and is Preceptress of one of the High Schools of that city.

LAURA HIBBARD, second daughter, mar. David McCord, of North East, Pa., and had three children: George, Mary, and Frank; Mary only is living; unmarried, at North East. Both sons were in the war for the Union. George died at Andersonville.

Bethiah Gray Hibbard was an interesting, lovable character, and her memory is cherished by her descendants. It is said that Lafayette remarked, when she was presented to him during his visit to this country in 1824: "She is the most beautiful woman I have seen in America!" Perhaps he remembered that her half-brother, Newcomb Raymond, had served under him with honor at Brandywine and Yorktown!

ADDITIONAL STATISTICS.

S. D. Gray, was married to Mary J. Race, Jan. 20, 1866.

Chas. D. Gray mar. Margaret Wheeler; mar. 2d, Annis Hollenback, Dec. 23, 1872.

Samuel J. Gray married Eliza Smith.

George W. Gray mar. Melinda Wheeler.

All of the above are descendants of Amos Gray, Jr., whose record appears on page 99.

Maranda Gray, daughter of Amos Gray, Jr., whose name is in the record on page 99, married Joseph Willson, at East Greene, N. Y., Mar. 6, 1834; died in Jackson, Mich., Mar. 27, 1882. Children: Adelaide Birdsall Willson, born July 15, 1835, in Greene, N. Y.; mar. George C. Mericle, at Wellsville, Alleghany Co. N. Y., March 28, 1870; removed to Omaha, Neb., where he died June 10, 1883; Mrs. Mericle now resides at Jackson, Mich. Christina Gray Willson was born at Chenango Forks, N. Y., Sept. 7, 1836; mar. Geo. W. Baker, at Greene, N. Y., June 1, 1859; resides at Jackson, Mich. Ann Aceneth Willson, born May 23, 1840; died July 13, 1840. Joseph Daniel Willson, born Oct. 12, 1842; married and has two children; resides at Jackson, Mich.

Dr. Paschal P. Gray, son of William Gray, and great-grand son of Elder Jeduthan Gray, whose name appears with his father's family on page 78, as of Rochelle, Ill., answers a letter of inquiry there directed, as follows, from the Sandwich Islands:

Honolulu, H. I., June 29, 1886.

M. D. Raymond, Tarrytown, N. Y.

My Dear Sir:—Your favor forwarded from Rochelle, Ill., just received. The only additional information I can render relates to myself, as follows:

Paschal P. Gray, Dr., Honolulu, Hawaiian Islands, b. Feb. 5, 1844, mar. Lydia Carpenter, March 15th, 1865; she d. Feb. 12, 1871; he mar. 2d, Agnes H. Canning, Jan. 16, 1884.

I graduated at the Hahnemann Medical College, Chicago, 1879–80. You must have spent much time, patience, and not a little money in obtaining the necessary material for such a work, and, if when completed, you have copies for sale, would be pleased to know your terms, that I may avail myself of the opportunity of possessing the Genealogy of the Gray family.

Courteously Yours,   P. P. Gray.

DR. JOHN F. GRAY'S FAMILY.

The following contains some statistics of the family of Dr. John F. Gray, (6), which do not appear in the record given on page 22, being received too late for position there:

ELIZABETH WILLIAMS GRAY, b. in the city of New York, June 10, 1827; mar. Lewis T. Warner, May 30, 1849.

JOHN HULL GRAY, b. Dec. 13, 1828; d. Sept. 12, 1829.

JOHN F. GRAY, Jr., b. June 30, 1830; d. Feb. 5, 1834.

JOSEPHINE AUGUSTA GRAY, b. Sept. 7, 1832; d. Feb. 11, 1834.

GERALDINE HULL GRAY, b. Oct. 8, 1835; d. Oct. 7, 1855.

JOHN FREDERICK SCHILLER GRAY, Dr., b. Aug. 12, 1840; mar. Anna Henderson, at Baton Rouge; she dec'd; his present residence, California.

EDWARD HULL GRAY, b. Sept. 14, 1842; dec'd.

MARY LUDLOW GRAY, b. April 4, 1845; mar. to Benjamin Knower, at Trinity Chapel, New York, by Rev. Morgan Dix, March 22, 1873.

BURRITT PATCHIN SACKETT, son of Rev. and Mrs. D. E. Sackett, b. Aug. 25, 1845; d. Aug. 26, 1846.

GIFFORD NEWCOMB SEE, son of J. E. and Lizzie Raymond See, and great-great-grandson of Mabel Gray Raymond, born at Pittsfield, Mass., May 11, 1886.

NELLIE GRAY, only child of the late Dr. John Gray, and a great-great grand-daughter of Elder Jeduthan Gray, born 1870, lives at Elyria, Ohio.

DELIA GRAY, daughter of Jeduthan Gray, and great-grand daughter of Elder Jeduthan Gray, mar. Harry Proctor, Oct. 1st, 1878; one child, Ethel Proctor.

WILLIAM GRAY, grandson of William Gray, and great-great grandson of Elder Jeduthan Gray, mar. Etta Clark, June 8, 1879; one child, Nina Gray, b. Nov. 4, 1881.

FLORA GRAY, grand-daughter of William Gray, b. March 23, 1858, mar. Edwin Baker, Feb. 17, 1881; children: Velma and Mary Baker.

PATTY (MARTHA) GRAY, daughter of Levi Gray, mar. a Mr. Burdick, and resides at Tontogany, Wood Co., Ohio.

The record of this family of Grays here closes. It is not complete and perfect, but it is as nearly so as the limitations of time and expense permit. Though not in every direction entirely successful, the writer has devoted to it his best energies, and unceasing labors. In general, as will be seen, the family is divided into five branches, the descendants of five of the sons of John Gray (3) of Sharon, to wit: John Gray, (4), Nathaniel, Joseph, Darius, and Daniel; of the three other sons, Silas having no male descent, William apparently no issue, and James Gray, lost in mystery, and his descendants, if any, unknown. If some lines seem to be given more prominence than others, it is because of circumstances beyond the control of the writer. How much effort has been put forth in directions where little appears, none can know. While in general information has been freely and fully furnished, in some cases the indifference manifested has negatived the best results. None, of any degree, or however remote, have knowingly been neglected. The only wonder, perhaps, is, that it should have been possible to present in so compact a form the record of a family so widely scattered.

A summarizing of statistics presented shows the following:

NO. OF MALE MEMBERS OF THE DIFFERENT BRANCHES.

		LIVING.	DECEASED.	TOTAL.
Descendants of	John,	35	44	79
"	Nathaniel,	21	10	31
"	Joseph,	121	53	174
"	Darius,	5	9	14
"	Daniel,	37	17	54
Total, - - -		219	133	352

The above only includes those bearing the name of Gray, and not any of collateral branches, no matter how closely related. As will be seen there is a wide discrepancy between the numbers in the different branches, which would be even more marked if all the vacancies were filled. For instance: The record of the families of Nathaniel and Darius, is believed to be full, (except it may be of recent births), and of John, with one possible exception, while there are several lacking in Daniel, and a larger number still in the descendants of Joseph, already outnumbering in living members, the sum total of all the other branches put together.

Of the learned professions, there are Physicians, 16; Ministers, 4; Lawyers, 5; Editor, 1.

INTER-MARRIAGE OF RAYMONDS AND GRAYS.

The intermarriages of the Raymond and Gray families, since it was one of the direct causes that led to the production of this Genealogy, is properly mentioned here. There have been altogether seven instances, as follows:

Bethiah Newcomb Raymond married Nathaniel Gray, son of John Gray of Sharon.

Newcomb Raymond married Mabel Gray, daughter of John Gray (4).

Abraham Raymond married Betsey Gray, sister of Mabel Gray.

Sarai Raymond, sister of Newcomb and Abraham Raymond, married Elijah Gray, son of Nathaniel.

Cynthia Raymond, grand-daughter of James Raymond, brother of Newcomb and Abraham, married John T. Gray, a great-grandson of Nathaniel Gray.

Mercy Raymond, daughter of James Raymond, married Abraham Mudge, son of Abraham Mudge and Anne Gray, daughter of John Gray of Sharon.

Lyman Raymond, Dr., grandson of Newcomb Raymond, married Roselle Ryneck, grand-daughter of William Ryneck and Anne Gray, daughter of John Gray (4).

There are several marriages of cousins recorded in this Genealogy, and one instance, the marriage of Wellington Lee and Harrriet D. Gray, in which two branches of the family, John and Nathaniel were united, and in it the blood of the Grays, and Raymonds, and Lees, and Lathrops, and Wentworths, was blended. Though living in many instances in proximity with other Gray families, no instance of intermarriage with them has been found, and only one marriage of a Gray with a Gray,— Sylvester H. Gray, a great-grandson of Elder Jeduthan Gray, and Antha Gray, daughter of Dr. W. S. Gray, of Big Rapids, Mich., and a great-granddaughter of Elder Jeduthan Gray.

LARGE FAMILIES.

Philander Raymond Gray, of Elizabeth, N. J., of the Nathaniel Gray branch, takes the honor of having the largest family of living children by one mother—11—being 8 sons and 3 daughters.

Henry Bates Gray, of Black Creek, Holmes Co., Ohio, of the Joseph Gray branch, has the honor of the largest number of sons and living children (by two mothers)—14—being 9 sons and five daughters.

George Ketchum Gray, of the Joseph Gray branch, had 11 living and deceased children by one mother, who is still living.

Wm. Hoyt Gray, of Eagle Grove, Iowa, of the Joseph Gray branch, has by two mothers, 11 living children—8 sons and 3 daughters.

John Gray (3) had 13 children by two mothers—8 sons and 5 daughters.

John Gray (4) had 12 children by one mother.

Daniel Gray, son of John Gray (3), had 13 children by two mothers.

Daniel H. Gray, son of Daniel Gray, had 14 children by two mothers.

Alanson Gray, grandson of Nathaniel Gray, had 13 children by two mothers.

William Gray, of the Joseph Gray branch, had 13 children by two mothers.

So it will be seen that the record shows ten families of eleven children and upwards.

AGED ONES.

Mrs. Amanda Gray Lee, of Cedar Mountain, N. C., a granddaughter of Nathaniel Gray, has the honor of being the oldest living member of the family, as she is also older than any deceased, being near to the close of her 94th year.

Caroline Gray Bignal, of Berlin, Wis., daughter of Darius Gray, is believed to be in her 90th year.

Dr. Joseph Gray, of Cambridgeboro, Pa., grandson of Joseph Gray, is in his 90th year.

Roby Gray, daughter of Daniel Gray, lived to be almost 91.

John Gray (5) died in his 90th year.

WIDELY SCATTERED.

That this family of Grays is of the true Pilgrim stock is evidenced by the fact that the descendants of a man (John Gray 3) born 1707, should now be found (besides those NOT found) scattered in 22 States and Territories, and one family in the Sandwich Islands! And by descendants is meant those having the name of Gray, or having had that name before marriage. What a scatteration!

ILLUSTRATIONS.

The illustrations are not by any means the least interesting feature of this family history. They not only embellish these pages of perhaps somewhat dry statistics, but in the future they will have additional value as the years go by. It was hoped that some others would avail themselves of the opportunity so offered, but the number of portraits furnished much exceeds the original expectation of the publisher. No better or other evidence than these illustrations need be presented of the character of the family whose history in brief is herein set forth.

It perhaps should be stated that the main expense of producing these pictures has been at the charges of those furnishing them, though some additional cost to the publisher; thus it will be seen that no favoritism has been shown.

It is interesting to note the perpetuation of family names in the different branches, the patronymic John being carried down in the direct line without a break for eight successive generations, while in the other families it frequently appears. In this connection it will be remembered that one of the first of the Grays mentioned in history was John de Gray, recorded at Battle Abbey. But there is little in a name; in heredity, much.

About fifteen hundred names appear in the preceding lists, nearly one thousand of them representing living persons, but the number would be considerably increased if all of even the first and second degree of kin were represented. What a family of descendants for John Gray of Sharon to have contemplated!

A sketch of other Gray families, some of whom have manifested considerable interest in this work, is presented on the following pages.

SKETCHES OF OTHER GRAY FAMILIES.

SAMUEL GRAY,

Record concerning the family of Samuel Gray of Boston, Mass., and Dorsetshire, England, made by his son, Ebenezer Gray, of Windham, Conn.:

"My father's name was Samuel Gray. He was born in Dorsetshire, old England, about the year 1657. My mother's maiden name was Susannah Langdon; she was born in Plymouth, Devonshire, England. My father died in Boston in the 48th year of his age. My mother lived a widow till her death, and died in Boston, at my sister Gibbon's; she was between 80 and 90 years old when she died, I suppose. My mother had fifteen living children. Since my recollection there were ten of us living together," viz:

I. JOANNA GRAY, who married James Bolderson in Boston; she died in about the 40th year of her age and left one daughter.

II. SAMUEL GRAY, who mar. the only daughter of Maj. Edward Palmer, of New London, Conn., and died about 35 years of age, leaving no children.

III. JOSEPH GRAY, who mar. Capt. Sear's daughter of Boston, and died in about the 30th year of his age, leaving five or six children.

IV. ELIZABETH GRAY, who mar. Andrew Palmer, only son of Maj. Edward Palmer, of New London, Conn.; she died at about 50 years of age and left five sons and one daughter: Gray, Bryant, Edward, Andrew, Elizabeth, William.

V. REBEKAH GRAY, who mar. Dr. John Gibbons of Boston; was living 1766, aged about 77; had two daughters: Anne, who mar. Dr. Sylvester Gardiner, of Boston, and Lucy, mar. Mr. Leavins. Lucy d. Feb. 1, 1770; Anne d. Jan. 1772.

VI. JOHN GRAY, who mar. Mary Christopher, daughter of Richard Christopher, Esq., of New London, Conn.; died in Boston about the 40th year of his age, and left no children.

VII. WILLIAM GRAY, who died in Barbadoes, aged 22 years.

VIII. BENJAMIN GRAY, who mar. a daughter of Rev. Mr. Bridge, of Boston; died in Boston near the 50th year of his age and left four or five children.

IX. EBENEZER GRAY, "(who through the goodness of God) am now living, Nov. 5th, 1766, and on the 11th day of this month, New Style, shall be 69 years old, mar. Mary Gardiner, daughter of John Gardiner of the Isle of Wight, (Gardiner's Island,) June 28, 1720." Mary Gardiner Gray died at Lebanon, Conn. July 27, 1726, and he mar. 2d, Mary, widow of Thomas Coit, of New London, Feb. 20, 1728, who died Dec. 10, 1764. Ebenezer Gray died at Windham, Conn., Sept. 8, 1773. Children and descendants:

SAMUEL GRAY (2).

I. SAMUEL GRAY, son of Ebenezer and Mary Gardiner Gray, born at Easthampton, L. I., April 6, 1722; mar. Lydia Dyer at Windham, Conn., Nov. 7, 1742, she a daughter of Col. Thos. Dyer of that place, where she was born July 12, 1724. He died at Windham Aug. 3, 1787; she died there July 3, 1790.

DESCENDANTS OF SAMUEL GRAY SON OF EBENEZER.

EBENEZER GRAY, (2) son of Samuel, b. July 26, 1743, mar. Sarah Stamford, March 30, 1786; she d. at Hartford, Sept. 29, 1835; he was Colonel and Brigadier General during the Revolution; he d. Jan. 18, 1795. Children:

EBENEZER GRAY, Jr., b. May 16, 1787; d. at Windham, Aug. 5, 1844.

CHARLOTTE GRAY, b. March 9, 1789, mar. Patrick Lynch, Oct. 27, 1812; he d. at sea, Apr. 4, 1819; she d. in New York, Dec. 14, 1873; children: Thomas Rawson, b. Nov. 3, 1813, d. May, 1845; Anne Charlotte, b. Nov. 1815, mar. Vincenzo Botta March 31, 1855; residence, New York.

SAMUEL GRAY (3).

SAMUEL GRAY, (3), son of Ebenezer, (2), b. Feb. 5, 1792, mar. Anna Cook Smith, of Bristol, R. I., Nov. 27, 1815, and d. at Hartford, Dec. 3, 1834. She d. at Hartford, April 25, 1863.

DESCENDANTS OF SAMUEL AND ANNA C. GRAY.

JOHN SMITH GRAY, son of, born Sept. 16, 1816; mar. Mary

Watkinson, May 9, 1848. Residence, Hartford, Conn. Children:

ELLEN WATKINSON GRAY, b. July 7, 1849, mar. John H. Barbour; children: Ellen Gray Barbour, b. May 4, 1879; Mary Watkinson Barbour, b. July 27, 1884, d. July 27, 1885; Henry Gray Barbour, b. March 28, 1886.

JOHN WATKINSON GRAY, b. March 19, 1851, mar. Clara M. Bolter; children:

ROBERT WATKINSON GRAY, b. Jan. 15, 1876.
MARY BARTHOLOMEW GRAY, b. Aug. 31, 1877.
CLARA GRAY, b. Oct. 21, 1880.

ANNIE GRAY, daughter of John S., b. Dec. 7, 1852, d. Oct. 17, 1855.

CHARLOTTE GRAY, daughter of Samuel, b. June 30, 1818, mar. John Ripley Tracy, Dec. 12, 1843; he d. at Hartford, Oct. 9, 1870; children: John Frederick, b. Oct. 11, 1844; Samuel Gray, b. Aug. 31, 1846; Charlotte Gray, b. March 19, 1848; Anne Hinckley, b. Feb. 19, 1850; Newbold Le Roy, b. June 17, 1853, mar. Florence Emma Lilian Stampe, at Sidney, Australia, April 10, 1884; Sophia Dennie, b. July 12, 1854.

ANN GRAY, b. Nov. 27, 1820, mar. Thomas Jones Failes, Oct. 7, 1839; children: Alice G., b. at Mantanzas, Cuba, June 9, 1841, mar. Chas. F. Sharp.

SARAH JANE GRAY, b. Jan. 23, 1823, mar. Augustus Newbold Le Roy, at Hartford, Dec. 10, 1845; children: Jacob, b. Apr. 6, 1850; Charlotte Otis, b. Oct. 26, 1854.

MARY GRAY, b. Sept. 4, 1828, mar. William Field Staunton, Nov. 20, 1855; children: Mary Ledlie, b. at Buffalo, N. Y., Dec. 6, 1858; William Field, b. at Toledo, Ohio, Dec. 23, 1860; Gray Staunton, b. at La Porte, Ind., July 6, 1865.

MARY GRAY, daughter of Samuel, (2), b. Oct. 14, 1744, mar. Rev. Enoch Huntington, of Middletown, Conn. ; children: Enoch Huntington, who mar. Sally Ward, and had Sally, Enoch, and Mary, who mar. Wm. Hurlburt.——Mary, who mar. M. F. Russell of Middletown, and had Mary, Harriet, who mar. N. Larned, Julia Ann, Charles, Wm. H. who mar. Mary Hubbard and had Mary, Harriet, and Henrietta; Abigail, Frances M., who mar. Mr. Rush of N. Y.; Sarah M., who mar. Francis Gray

Southmayd.——Martha, who mar. Ed. Hurlburt and had William who mar. Mary G. Huntington; Samuel.——Lydia, mar. Col. Simeon North, who was born at Berlin, Conn., July 13, 1765, the son of Jedediah North, a descendant of John North who was born in 1615, and left England (or Wales) in 1635, and was one of the original land owners and settlers in Farmington, Conn. Col. North had previously married Lucy Savage in 1786, who died Feb. 24, 1811. She was the mother of Simeon North, late President of Hamilton College, who mar. Frances Harriet Hubbard, he born Sept. 7, 1802, and d. Feb. 9, 1884; she d. Jan. 21, 1881. Edward North, Professor of Greek, Hamilton College, is a grandson of Col Simeon North and Lucy Savage North. By the second marriage, with Lydia Huntington, was born Lydia Huntington North, who mar. Rev. Dwight M. Seward, in 1836, both of whom still survive, they having celebrated their Golden Wedding at South Norwalk, Conn., in May, 1886. ——Esther Huntington, dau. of Rev. Enoch, mar. Benjamin Rosecranz, and had Sally and Enoch.——Samuel Gray Huntington, Judge, mar. Mary Johnson and had Sarah; d. at Troy, N. Y., July, 1854.——Mehitable.

Lucy Gray, daughter of Samuel, (2), b. June 27, 1746, d. March 9, 1826.

Thomas Gray, son of Samuel, (2), b. May 22, 1749, mar. Abigail Wales, April 9, 1771; d. Feb. 1792; children:

> Lydia Gray, b. Mar. 23, 1773, who mar. Chas. Chambers of Pomfret, and had Thomas, Maria, who mar. Mr. Randall of Ashford, Abigail who mar. Col. Bicknell of Ashford, and Lucy.

> Elizabeth Gray, dau. of Thomas, mar. Dr. Thomas Hubbard of Pomfret, and had Frances Harriet, who mar. Rev. Simeon North, D. D., L.L. D., late President of Hamilton College, Clinton, Oneida Co., N. Y., April 21, 1835, and d. Jan. 21, 1881; Thomas G., and Russell Hubbard.

> Lucy Gray, dau. of Thomas, mar. Dr. Samuel Lee, and had Sumner, who mar. Elizabeth Woodward of New London, and had Sarah, who mar. Henry King, of Medina, Ohio, and Samuel; Charlotte Lee, who mar. Thomas Grosvenor of Pomfret, and had Thomas and Samuel; Henrietta, and Hart. Lucy Gray Lee

mar. 2d, Prof. Thomas Hubbard, of Yale College,
and had Mary, who mar. Hon. William H. Russell
of New Haven, Principal of the College Institute,
and founder of the Skull and Bones Society in Yale
College. Had Lucy Gray, Frances Harriet, Henrietta
Lee, Mary, Talcott Huntington, Thomas Hubbard,
Philip Gray, Wm. H., Edward H., and Robert Gray.
Mrs. Russell resides at New Haven, Conn.

PRUDENCE GRAY, dau. of Thomas, mar. Payson Grosve-
nor of Pomfret, who had Charles, Zara, Edward,
Mary, who mar. Chas. Matthewson of Pomfret, and
Elizabeth.

SAMUEL GRAY (3.)

SAMUEL GRAY, son of Samuel, (2), was born in Windham,
June 21, 1751. He graduated at Dartmouth 1774, in the first
class after its establishment in 1770. He was Deputy Commis-
sary General under Gov. Jonathan Trumbull during the Revolutionary war. Though not a lawyer he was Clerk of the Courts
of Windham County a great many years. He mar. Charlotte
Elderkin, July 2, 1788; he died in 1836 in his 86th year.
Children and descendants:

HARRIET GRAY, b. Feb. 1, 1790, mar. Oliver C. Grosvenor, of Rome, N. Y., and had Oliver D., and Charlotte G. Grosvenor.

MARY GRAY, b. May 31, 1792, mar. Samuel H. Bynn,
and had Samuel G., who mar. Aurelia Little, John,
Harriet, Elizabeth, and Mary.

THOMAS GRAY.

THOMAS GRAY, son of Samuel Gray (3), was b. Oct. 3, 1794;
graduated at Yale College, 1815; was often elected to offices of
honor and trust, was for several years a Clerk in the House of
Representatives at Washington, and at the time of his death was
Clerk of the Superior Court of Connecticut for Windham Co.,
and was Judge of Probate for the District of Windham. A cotemporary says of him: "Mr. Gray was highly esteemed and respected by all classes of his fellow citizens, for his useful talents,
his amiable and obliging disposition, and for his uprightness and
integrity of character." He married Mary C. Webb, who d. in
March, 1823; he mar. 2d, Lucretia Webb, May 11, 1824; he d.
Aug. 29, 1860; she d. Aug. 27, 1867; children and descendants:

HENRY GRAY, Dr., son of Thomas, b. March 13, 1825; received a degree as Physician at Dartmouth; mar. Sarah Ann Kinnie, Oct. 4, 1849; residence, Bloomfield, Conn.; children:

> ANNA L. GRAY, b. Nov. 12, 1856.
> MARY GRAY, b. May 12, 1861.

MARY GRAY, dau. of Thomas, b. 1827, d. 1838.

CHARLOTTE GRAY, dau. of Thomas, b. June 14, 1830, mar. Dr. D. W. C. Lathrop, U. S. Surgeon in the war for the Union; he dec'd; children: James, Clinton, and William.

HANNAH GRAY, dau. of Thomas, b. Sept. 2, 1837; mar. James S. Parsons, Pres. Continental Life Ins. Co., of Hartford; he dec'd; she resides at Windham; children: Walter G., Katie, and Charlotte.

LYDIA GRAY, dau. of Samuel, (2) b. Apr. 17, 1761; d. Jun. 9, '61.

JOHN GRAY, son of Ebenezer, (1), b. at Easthampton, L. I., Sept. 21, 1723, mar. Elizabeth Powell, daughter of Stephen Powell of Lebanon. A record at hand says there were ten children, but only the following, without further descent, are given:

> JOHN GRAY.
> WILLIAM GRAY.
> ELIZABETH GRAY.
> BETSEY GRAY.

MARY GRAY, dau. of Ebenezer (1) and Mary Coit Gray, b. at Lebanon, Conn., Nov. 11, 1728, mar. Russell Hubbard of New London, Jan. 30, 1755, and had Mary, who mar. David Nevins of Norwich, Conn., and had Mary, Henry, David, Russell, Fanny who mar. Chas. Thomas of Norwich; Samuel, James, Elizabeth who mar. M. Townsend; Rufus L., Richard, and Rev. William Nevins of Baltimore.——Thomas Hubbard, who mar. Mary Hallam of New London, and had Thomas, Russell who mar. Abigail Williams of Norwich; Amos H. who mar. Mary Ann Laman of Norwich, and William Hubbard.——Martha. ·——Lucretia, who mar. David Tracy, and 2d mar. Elijah Backus of Norwich, and had Thomas, and Lucretia, who mar. Nathaniel Pope of St. Genevieve.——Russell.——Martha, who mar. David Wright of New London, and had Martha, David H., Mary, William, Chas. F. and Thos. H.——Susannah, who mar. 1st, Ebenezer Bushnell, and had Lydia, Thomas, Harriet, Leon-

ard, who mar. Julia Lee; Tryphena, and Ebenezer; Susannah
Hubbard Bushnell mar. 2d, Robert Mannering and had William.

LUCY GRAY, dau. of Ebenezer, (1), b. in Lebanon, June 8,
1730, d. 1772, unmarried.

JONATHAN GRAY, son of Ebenezer, (1), born in Lebanon,
March 6, 1732, mar. Mary Mason, dau. of Samuel Mason of
Stonington, March 11, 1756. Children:

>   MARY GRAY, b. at Stonington Aug. 6, 1757, mar. Peleg
>   Dennison, and had Noyce, Peleg, who mar. Harriet
>   Eldridge of Stonington and had Hannah; Samuel,
>   Joseph, Leonard, Samuel, Mary, Elizabeth, and
>   Bridget Dennison.

>   SAMUEL GRAY, b. Aug. 4, 1759; believed to have been
>   married and had descendants.

>   ESTHER GRAY, dau. of Jonathan, b. Aug. 27, 1761, mar.
>   Zebulon Staunton, and had Taber who mar. Fanny
>   Potter of Stonington and had Fanny, Mary, Jabez;
>   Henry, Jonathan, Zebulon, George, Fanny, Frank,
>   Nathaniel G., Elizabeth who mar. Chas. Dennison
>   of Stonington and had Elizabeth, Mary and Charles;
>   Mary, Esther, Samuel.

SUSANNAH GRAY, dau. of Ebenezer, (1), b. Dec. 11, 1733, in
Lebanon, mar. John Richards of New London, July 7, 1765,
and had one child, that died; she died at New London, Feb. 20,
1768.

ELIZABETH GRAY, dau. of Ebenezer, (1), b. Dec. 11, 1733,
and twin sister of Susannah Gray, mar. Samuel Hern, Nov. 17,
1763, and had Elizabeth, b. June 29, 1765, who mar. Ambrose
Fellows and had Mary who mar. Charles Burdick, and Sally;
she mar. 2d, Thos. Steamback and had Julia; Mary, b. Dec. 18,
1766; and William, b. Aug. 6, 1768.

WILLIAM GRAY, son of Ebenezer, (1), b. in Lebanon, May 16,
1737, and d. at St. Kits, Jan. 20, 1766; unmarried.

ESTHER GRAY, dau. of Ebenezer, (1), b. in Lebanon, May 20,
1739, mar. William Southmayd, of Middletown, Nov. 25, 1777,
and had Samuel Gray Southmayd, b. Dec. 28, 1778, who mar.
1st, Sally Gill; and mar. 2d, Sarah Russell, a grand-daughter of
Rev. Enoch Huntington, whose wife Mary Gray Huntington, was
a grand-daughter of Ebenezer (1) and Mary Gardiner Gray, the
two branches of the family being so united.

Thomas Coit, stepson of Ebenezer Gray, and son of Thos. and Mary Coit, b. Aug. 15, 1725, mar. Abigail Richards, May 23, 1756, and had Abigail, Thomas, Elizabeth; she d. Aug. 19, 1761, and he mar. 2d, Mary Gardiner, dau. of David Gardiner of New London, Jan. 12, 1764, and had Thomas, David, and Jonathan Coit.

X. SUSANNAH GRAY, dau. of Samuel Gray (1), who mar. Peter Feurt, of Boston, and d. about 30th year of her age leaving no children.

Dr. Ebenezer Gray, son of Samuel and Susannah Gray, who was born in Boston, Oct. 31st, 1697, and was the ancestor of most of the line traced out on the preceding pages, was educated at Harvard, and made the practice of physics his profession. He spent his days at East Hampton, Lebanon, Newport and Windham.

There are points of interest in connection with the families of John Gray of Beverly, and Samuel Gray of Boston. Though direct relationship is not shown, they were both of English ancestry, and cotemporaneous in this country. The Beverly Grays were not only from Boston, but John Gray (3), son of John of Beverly, was for many years a resident of Windham and Lebaanon, Conn., and up to 1743, the date of his removal to Sharon, during which period Ebenezer Gray, son of Samuel, and the ancestor of most of the Grays whose names appear in the foregoing record, was also a resident of that neighborhood, where some of his descendants still remain. Friendly intercourse has also been maintained in later years between some members of the two families, on the basis of congenial tastes, and kindred associations. To the writer, there is another fact of added personal interest, in that this family of Grays intermarried with the Gardiners of Gardiner's Island, from whence his own maternal ancestry. It would have been gratifying to have given herewith the complete genealogical record of the family of Samuel Gray, if it had been practicable to have done so.

WORCESTER GRAYS.

The most numerous, probably, of all the many branches of the Gray family in America, and not the least in point of interest, is the group of so called Worcester Grays. Whether all distinctively of one family is not positively determined, but they were doubtless kindred and closely allied. M. L. Gray, Esq., of St. Louis, who is of that line, and has given much attention to ancestral research, furnishes the following interesting sketch as the result of his investigations:

"Among the emigrants, 140 families, who came from the North of Ireland in 1718, to Boston, was one John Gray. He settled with others of the colony at Worcester, Mass., same year. They were Scotch, (called Scotch-Irish), whose ancestors in 1612 went from Argylshire, Scotland, and settled near Londonderry. John Gray bought land in Worcester in 1718, and in 1722–3. There were other Grays: Robert, Samuel, William, Matthew, probably Hugh, and John, Jr., who was the son of the elder John; but whether any or all of the others were sons of John, is not certainly known. A deed made by John and Izobel his wife, conveys land in Worcester which they say was deeded to him by his 'honored father, John Gray.' This proves that John whose wife was Izobel, was the son of the elder John. Of John and Izobel his wife were Daniel, born in Worcester, 1728; Isaac, who commanded a Company in the battle of Bunker Hill, John, Elizabeth, and probably Ebenezer. Daniel begat Lamond, John, Joel, Jeremiah, Thomas, Collister, and three daughters, who severally married Amos Blackmer, James Lindsey and Daniel Haskell.

"John Gray, who came over in 1718, was one of a Committee in Ireland who wrote to Gov. Shute of the Mass. Colony in 1717, enquiring as to the encouragement emigrants would receive if they came to this country. From Lincoln's History of Worcester it appears that this elder John occupied one of the 'fore-pews' in the church, from which it may be inferred that he was a man of some position. About 1740, thirty-eight of the emigrants that were in Worcester, bought the township of Pel-

Melvin L. Gray

ham, and among them were John Gray, Jr., Samuel, William, Matthew, and probably Hugh. Robert remained in Worcester, and was the ancestor of Prof. Asa Gray, of Cambridge, Mass. Of the descendants of William, Matthew and Samuel, I have no trace, (trace however will be found on the following pages of some of them,) nor do I know anything of the descendants of Capt. Isaac or his brother John, both of whom were brothers of my great-grandfather Daniel Gray. I know that between 1785 and 1800, quite a number of families of Grays in Pelham moved to Salem, Washington Co., N. Y., and thereabouts, and that several families scattered further west in New York. Three brothers of my grandfather Lamond, named Joel, John and Collister settled respectively in Otsego, Madison, and Chenango counties; the former, at Cooperstown, where he left children. The other brothers, Jeremiah and Thomas, remained in Massachusetts, and their descendants are in Belchertown, Wilbraham and Amherst."

"My grandfather settled in Bridport, Vermont. My branch were strong Presbyterians according to the kirk of Scotland— several were Elders, and when they became Congregationalists, were Deacons in the church. Among the names of males I found at Pelham besides those already mentioned, were Aaron, Ebenezer, Nathaniel, Jonathan, Jacob, Moses, Joshua, Joseph, Amos, Adam C., Eli, Eliot, James, Jonah, &c. Names of females: Elizabeth, Esther, Elinor, Patience, Experience, Jean, Phebe, Martha, Margaret, Sarah, Anne, &c."

The foregoing is of value as a clear and reliable statement made up from the records after painstaking personal search, and the Worcester Grays are under much obligation to Mr. Gray for it.

MELVIN L. GRAY, Esq., of St. Louis, is a son of Daniel Gray, he son of Lamond, son of Daniel, son of John Gray, Jr., son of John. John, Jr., was born 1700, and died in Pelham, 1779. Daniel Gray (1) was born 1728, and married a Miss Lamond from Leicester; they had a son Lamond, born about 1753; by a second wife, Mary Dick, Daniel had sons Jeremiah, Thomas, John, Joel and Collister, and three daughters, to whom reference

152.

has already been made. Lamond, eldest son of Daniel, (1), married Isabel Conkey, widow of Lieut. Robert Hamilton, of Pelham, and about 1787 or '88, Lamond and wife emigrated from Pelham to Bridport, Vt., where he lived till 1812, and had sons, Joel and Daniel (2).

DANIEL GRAY (2).

DESCENDANTS OF.

Daniel Gray (2), had by his first marriage, Ozro Preston Gray, born at Bridport, Vt., 1806, and died there in 1882, leaving no children. By a second wife, Mary Bosworth, he had the following sons and descendants:

> EDGAR H. GRAY, b. 1813, graduated at Waterville Col-College, Me., 1838; became a Baptist clergyman; located first at Freeport, Me.; afterwards at Shelburne Falls, Mass., and then at Washington, D. C., and was for several years Chaplain of the Senate during President Lincoln's Administration. Is now settled at Oakland, Cal.
>
> MELVIN L. GRAY, Esq., second son by the second marriage, was born 1815, graduated at Middlebury College, Vt., 1839, and has practised law in St. Louis, Mo., since 1842.

DANIEL M. GRAY, now living at Columbus, Ohio.

FABIUS C. GRAY, who died in Gallatin, Tenn., in 1847.

OSCAR B. GRAY, a Broker, now living in New York City.

WM. A. GRAY, who died near San Antonio, Texas, 1859.

Daniel Gray (2) died in Bridport, Vt., in 1823.

Joel Gray, son of Lamond, and brother of Daniel (2), settled in Stockholm, St. Lawrence Co., N. Y., and died there about 1882, aged 87, leaving descendants.

JOHN GRAY

John Gray, son of Deacon Daniel Gray of Pelham, removed to Madison, Madison Co., N. Y., among the first settlers, and resided there until his decease. He was born March 1, 1770, and married, May 25, 1792, Susannah Hunter, who was born

Dec. 10, 1770. He died July 25, 1827, and she died Aug. 28, 1864. Children and descendants:

SUSANNAH GRAY, b. Apr. 12, 1793; d. Oct. 15, 1800.
COLLISTER GRAY, b. Nov. 29, 1794; d. Oct. 10, 1800.
APPLETON GRAY, b. Jan. 18, 1797; d. Oct. 20, 1800.
ANNIE GRAY, b. May 15, 1799; mar. Jonathan Maltbie, July 27, 1825.
SALLIE GRAY, b. Sept. 8, 1803, mar. Wm. Brown, Feb. 12, 1823; children: Wm. Brown, of Aurora, Ill., and Geo. Brown of Granger, Iowa.

JOHN GRAY, Jr., Dr., b. in Madison, N. Y., Sept. 18, 1801; mar. Clarinda M. Thompson, Sept. 8, 1825; studied medicine with Dr. Putnam, of Madison, and afterwards with Dr. Sweetland, Erie Co., attended lectures at Willoughby, Ohio, and was for a time at the Hospitals in New York. Was a skillful Surgeon and attained a wide reputation as a specialist in malarial fevers. He visited South America on a mining reconnoisance, and established a Hospital for Americans in Acapulco, Mexico. He was also a man of affairs as well as a physician and traveller. He built the first Factory (near Rome) in Oneida Co., N. Y., built the first breakwater in Buffalo, and furnished the lumber for Fort Dearborn, Chicago, 1826. Dr. Gray is deceased, but his widow still survives at Darlington, Wis. Children and descendants:

HAMILTON H. GRAY, son of Dr. John, b. 1826, married Harriet Peet, a daughter of Rev. Stephen Peet, at Beloit, Wis. Have seven children living:

HARRIET, b. May 11, 1852; mar. Dr. W. H. Armstrong; 3 children: Fred, James and Anna.
ANNA MARTHA, b. March 6, 1854; mar. C. S. Montgomery; 3 chidren: Charles, Gray, baby.
ADA D., b. Apr. 20, 1856.
JAMES H. GRAY, b. Feb. 16, 1858; mar. Jennet Buchannan; a son, Harry. Resides at Luverne, Minn.
MARY EMMA, b. Aug. 15, 1861; mar. C. B. Oldfield.
CLARA M., b. Apr. 3, 1868.
EUNICE T., b. March 17, 1876.

Hon. Hamilton H. Gray has been Chairman of Town Board and Co. Board of Supervisors, District Attorney, Member of the Assembly, and State Senator of Wisconsin, Member of the State Board of Regents, Delegate to National Democratic Convention, candidate for Lieutenant Governor, has served as Member of the State Board of Charities and Reforms. Mr. Gray resides at Darlington, Wis.; of his occupation, he says, "I am a farmer.'

JAMES B. GRAY, son of John Gray (3), died in Mexico; children:

> ANSLEY GRAY, a lawyer.
> HENRY GRAY.
> A daughter, mar. Mark Edgerton, Kansas City.

ADALINE A. GRAY, dau. of Dr. John Gray, mar. Isaac Decker; mar. 2d, John H. Martin.

DANIEL GRAY (3).

Daniel Gray, son of John Gray (3), was born in Madison, N. Y., May 18, 1805; married Roxy Adeline Tucker, Aug. 19th, 1830. Resided near Jerusalem Corners, East Evans, Erie Co., N. Y.; removed from there to what is now called Gray's Summit, on the Mo. Pacific R. R., 40 miles west of St. Louis, in 1841. He journeyed to Texas every winter, being engaged in business at Galveston, as well as carrying on the farm at home. He was in Houston's army of Independence, and a member of the Lone Star State Legislature. He died in 1851. Children and descendants:

> FRANCIS O. GRAY, b. July 26, 1831; mar. Miss Ennis; was a Colonel in the Confederate army; has seven living children.
>
> EDWARD PAYSON GRAY, son of Daniel (3), b. Jun. 10, 1833; at 15 commenced clerking at St. Louis, at 18 had engaged in business in his own name, and the same year, 1851, journeyed to Texas on horseback and successfully closed up his father's business, and is now the successful manager of the International Book and News Co. of St. Louis. He mar. Mary Elizabeth Stanly, Feb. 26, 1857. Children and descendants:

HORACE STANLY GRAY, b. Feb. 5, 1858; resides at Tustin City, Los Angeles Co., Cal.

MARY ADELAIDE GRAY, b. May 21, 1860; mar. Montrose L. Garnett, of Holden, Mo.; children: George Edward, and Montrose L., Jr.

SYBIL MARION GRAY, b. Feb. 16, 1864; mar. John Webster Spargo, Sept. 6th, 1883; children: Sybil Marion; and Edward Gray; residence, St. Louis.

EDNA LOVINA GRAY, b. Dec. 23, 1867.

MARY ADELAIDE GRAY, dau. of Daniel Gray (3), b. Nov. 4, 1836; mar. in Michigan; dec'd; no children.

WILLIAM H. GRAY, b. Sept. 22, 1843, mar. Binnie Harper; has three boys and two girls; resides at St. Louis.

COLLISTER GRAY.

Collister Gray, son of Deacon Daniel Gray of Pelham, married Hannah Calhoun, and removed to Lebanon, Madison Co., N. Y., and thence to Otselic, N. Y., where she died in August, 1851, and he died in Pharsalia, in same county, 1863. Children and descendants:

COLLISTER GRAY, Jr., oldest son of, mar. Lurenda Hill; d. in Otselic, Sept. 6, 1851, aged 47; she d. in Sherburne, N. Y., Oct. 10, 1883, aged 73; children and descendants:

DEWITT C. GRAY, b. 1832; d. at Arlington, Ill., Nov. 1, 1856.

LOVINA GRAY, b. 1834, mar. Jackson McMinn, 1857, and d. at Willett, N. Y., 1873.

JULIUS C. GRAY, b. June 16, 1836; mar. Helen R. Rogers, of Unadilla, N. Y., Aug. 9th, 1862; one child, a daughter, b. Nov. 1868; residence, Sherburne, Chenango Co., N. Y.

DANIEL M. GRAY, b. 1839; married Cornelia Sweet, of Lakeport, N. Y., 1864; went to Cleveland, Ohio; has not been heard from since 1866; supposed dec'd.

LUCETTA GRAY, b. 1842; d. in 1849.

HENRY C. GRAY, b. 1846; d. July 21, 1872.

NATHAN C. GRAY, b. 1850, d. in Oct., 1856.

NATHAN GRAY, son of Collister (1), removed to Arlington, Ill., where he now resides. He was a personal friend of Abraham Lincoln, and was one of the Delegates from Illinois to the Republican National Convention that nominated him for President.

ALEXANDER H. GRAY, son of Collister, moved to North Springfield, Mo., 1881, and died there 1885. He had previously resided at Otselic, N. Y., and had repeatedly been elected Supervisor of his town, serving with honor to himself and satisfaction to the public. He was about 70 years old.

There were two daughters to Collister Gray; Mrs. Phebe Davis, of Brooklyn, Iowa, and Mrs. Cornelia Newton, of Long Pine, Nebraska; both widows.

ROBERT GRAY.

DESCENDANTS OF.

Robert Gray was born in 1697, in Ireland, of Scotch parentage. He is supposed to be a son of John Gray, one of the signers of the "Shute Memorial," and one of the colony that came to America from Londonderry in the north of Ireland, arriving at Boston, Mass., Aug. 4, 1718, and settling same year at Worcester, Mass., where he was a man of prominence and property. Everything learned about Robert points toward the strong probability that he was a son of John, but it cannot be definitely proven. Robert is spoken of in the town records as an emigrant. Although he did not sign the "Shute Memorial," he was twenty-one years old at the time of emigration and settlement in Worcester. He had brothers, Matthew, (ancestor of Prof. A. L. Perry, of Williams College,) William, and Hugh; Samuel, and John, Jr., are supposed to be his brothers also, and sons of John, the patriarchal emigrant.

Robert Gray died in Worcester, Jan. 16, 1766. He was buried in the burial ground, (which is now a Common,) and his stone read thus:

Here lyes buried the body of
MR. ROBERT GRAY,
Who died Jan. 16, 1766, aged 69 years.

His wife was Sarah Wiley, whose family was also of the colony which settled at Worcester in 1718, and there is a tradition in the family that their courtship began on the voyage to America. The date of her death is not known, but she was living in 1758. Her mother lived with her, and died at the age of ninety-nine.

Robert and Sarah Gray were the parents of ten children, as follows:

EXPERIENCE,	JOHN,
JOSEPH,	SALLY,
ROBERT,	MOSES WILEY,
MOLLY,	SAMUEL,
JOHN, (2)	THOMAS.

MOSES WILEY GRAY, born in Worcester, Dec. 31, 1745, married Sally Miller of Worcester, about the year 1769. Soon after he removed to Templeton, Mass., where eight of his children were born. He was one of the "Minute Men" who responded to the call at the battle of Lexington, and he remained in the army afterward. In 1787 he removed to Grafton, Vt., where his wife died Mar. 2, 1793.

In 1794 he removed to Oneida Co., N. Y., and settled in the Sauquoit Valley, at a place now called Sauquoit, eight miles south from Utica. Here he married Anna Buckingham, who died in 1842, and by whom he had four children, as follows:

JOHN,	ANNA,	WATSON,	EPHRAIM.

The children of Moses Wiley and Sally Miller Gray were:

HANNAH,	THOMAS,	SALLY,	WARREN,	BETSEY,
MOSES,	THOMAS, (2)	ASA,	WARREN, (2)	LUCY.

MOSES GRAY was born in Templeton, Mass., Feb. 26, 1785, and died in Sauquoit, N. Y., Oct. 13, 1845. He married Roxana Howard, of Sauquoit, July 30, 1809. She was born in Longmeadow, Mass., Mar. 15, 1789, and died in Sauquoit, June 15, 1869. Their children were:

> ASA GRAY, b. Nov. 18, 1810; mar. Jane Lathrop Loring, of Boston, May 4, 1848; no children; Professor in Harvard College, Cambridge, Mass.
>
> ROXANA GRAY, b. May 17, 1813; mar. Geo. A. Cobb, Saline, Mich.
>
> ELSADA GRAY, b. June 1, 1815; unmarried.

ALMIRA GRAY, b. Aug. 4, 1817; mar. Warren Bragg, of Clayville, N. Y.

MOSES MILLER GRAY, b. Jan. 9, 1820; mar. Emily Townsend, of Sauquoit, Apr. 23, 1845; a farmer, and lives on the old homestead; several daughters; a son
> GEORGE GRAY, of Rancho Chico, Cal.; mar.; a daughter, and a son
>> RALPH MOSES GRAY, b. 1885.

HIRAM GRAY, b. June 26, 1822; mar. Delia Louisa Barnett, of Clayville, N. Y., Feb. 19, 1852; was a paper manufacturer at Sauquoit; d. Oct. 13, 1860; one daughter, and a son,
> HARRIS BARNETT GRAY, of Hastings, Iowa; mar., and several daughters.

GEORGE GRAY, b. Mar. 15, 1825; d. Jan. 9, 1848, while a student at Harvard College.

JOSEPH HOWARD GRAY, b. Sept. 25, 1828; mar. Martha Greene Ring, of New York, May 15, 1860; is a lawyer in New York city; two sons:
> WILLIAM RING GRAY.
> JOSEPH HOWARD GRAY.

PROF. ASA GRAY.

The following brief sketch of Prof. Asa Gray, the eminent Botanist, of Harvard College, is mainly from an article in the *Century* for June, 1886, entitled "Harvard's Botanic Garden and its Botanists." At the time Dr. Gray entered upon his duties as Professor at Harvard, 1842, he was thirty-two years old. He had pursued his studies at Clinton Grammar School, near his native place, and at Fairfield Academy, in an adjacent county. Then, without entering College, he had begun medical studies, receiving his degree in 1831. Although soon appointed Botanist of the great United States Exploring Expedition, and Professor of Botany in Michigan University, he did not accept either of these positions, but devoted himself to a study of American plants, and to the publication of the "Flora of North America." It was after his return from a visit to Europe in the further preparation of his work, that he accepted the Professorship at Harvard and entered upon his duties there.

Besides his other labors Dr. Gray has found time during all these years for a vast amount of studied writing, including among his lesser works that remarkable series of text books on botany, which are now used in all schools in the country. In 1862, Dr. Gray presented the University with his herbrarium, comprising over two hundred thousand plants, and his library of twenty-two hundred botanical works; a munificent contribution to that institution and to science.

In later years he has resumed in earnest his great work, the "Flora of North America," and with determined courage and untiring industry he continues at his task, not content to rest till the whole shall be complete. It is well said of him, "To few men of science come so grand opportunities; and fewer yet so nearly fulfill them as has Dr. Gray."

DAVID GRAY.

Adam Clark Gray, of Pelham, was the father of five sons: Levi, Justus, John, David and Ephraim. David was born in Pelham, (as probably all the sons were), Oct. 20, 1780. While a young man he spent several season on the Banks of New Foundland engaged in codfishing. On Dec. 23, 1805, he married Esther Clough, and must soon after have removed to Madison, N. Y., as a daughter, Phebe Gray, was born to them at that place, Nov. 5, 1806. The births of children, noted as follows, instances the dates and places of their several removals:

> CYRUS GRAY, was born in Springfield, Otsego Co., N. Y., July 18, 1808; was mar. April 5, 1830, and d. Dec. 17, 1857, in Harpersfield, Ashtabula Co., O., leaving six sons, all of whom have families, and four daughters.

> ELI GRAY was born in Madison, N. Y., May 7, 1810; mar., and has 2 daughters and ten grandchildren; has resided at Mayfield, Cuyahoga Co., Ohio, since 1840.

> MARTIN GRAY was born in Eaton, Madison Co., N. Y., May 23, 1812; mar., and had 2 girls; lives at Mentor, Ohio.

GEORGE GRAY was born in Lansing, Tompkins Co. N. Y., Dec. 18, 1814; mar., and has two boys, both of whom have families; he lives at Adams, Hillsdale Co., Mich.

DAVID GRAY, Jr., was born in Lansing, N. Y., Feb. 20, 1817; mar., and has four sons, three of whom have families; he resides in Paulding Co., Ohio.

ESTHER GRAY was born in Chardon, Geauga Co., Ohio, Nov. 17, 1819; mar. John G. Thompson, April 1, 1847; d. July 8, 1881, in St. Louis, Mich., leaving three daughters with families.

David Gray and his family had removed from Lansing, N. Y., in June, 1818, to Chardon, Ohio, where they settled in the woods and endured the hardships of the early settlers, and there they continued to reside for over forty years. She died June 30, 1861, aged 79 years. Mr. Gray afterwards removed to Mentor, Ohio, where he died May 29th, 1885, having reached the re- markable age of One Hundred and Four (104) Years, seven (7) months and nine (9) days! The son Eli, writes as follows of this worthy old patriarch and Centenarian: "He regarded the religion of Christ as the great motive for which he lived after 1815, until death. He was of steady habits, and consistent in his ways and dealings with all men."

MARTIN E. GRAY, of Willoughby, Ohio, a descendant of the Pelham and Worcester Grays, writes as follows:

Dear Sir:—Your letter asking for information concerning my ancestry, is received. My grandfather's name was Jacob Gray. He died in Pelham, Mass., 1815. I do not know how old he was. He had a daughter who died young, and four sons who lived to be old. My father was the oldest; his name was An- drew. He had eight children, all dead but three; he died in 1861 aged 80 years. My father's brother William died in Salem, N. Y., about 1840; he had eight children, and they are all dead. His brother Jacob raised six children and died in Genesee Co., N. Y., about 1860; two of his sons, Jacob and Otis, are living. His youngest brother's name was Matthew; he raised seven or eight children; he died in Michigan, about 1865, where his children now reside.

MATTHEW GRAY.

Professor Arthur Latham Perry, of Williams College, contributes the following concerning the descendants of Matthew Gray, of whom was his maternal ancestry:

"Matthew Gray and Joan his wife, were among the Scotch-Irish immigrants landing in Boston, Aug. 4, 1718. They went that autumn to Worcester, and died there. He became Scaler of leather and Hogreeve in Worcester in 1724. He bought in 1728 the nucleus of the "Gray farm" in Worcester, which remained in the hands of his descendants for more than a century. This farm was deeded to his son Matthew Gray (2) in Oct., 1735. Both Matthew and Joan make their "mark" to this deed.

"Matthew (2) was eight years old in 1718, and carried on the farm till 1772, when he deeded it to his son Reuben. Matthew (2) had two wives, Jean and Margaret, and 21 children, 11 of whose births are recorded in the Worcester records. Mrs. Jean Gray died in Dec. 1764, aged 48. The second wife was Margaret McFarland.

"Reuben Gray, born Dec. 2, 1744, married Lydia Millet, and they had 11 children. He died May 23, 1814, leaving the farm by will to Matthew Gray, his son, born Jan. 9, 1783, and died in 1858.

"Matthew (2) had (among other sons) Joseph, b. June 4, 1758. He settled in Mason, N. H., was a doctor, and died in 1812. He mar. in 1780, Lucy Bancroft, an aunt of George Bancroft, the historian. Their son, Dr. Henry Gray, lived and died in Weston, Vt. Dr. Henry Gray, of Cambridge, N. Y., was in the next generation, and Dr. Henry Gray, of Greenwich, N. Y., is now (1886) a distinguished physician of the fourth generation.

"Reuben and Lydia had Lydia, born July 3, 1789, who mar. Rev. Baxter Perry, of Lyme, N. H., and died there Nov. 13, 1875. Baxter Edwards Perry, born in 1826, a distinguished lawyer in Boston, and Arthur Latham Perry, born in 1830, Professor of History and Political Economy in Williams College, were sons of this marriage; and Lydia Ann Churchill, and Mary Clark Turner, were the daughters. Rev. Baxter Perry died in Lyme, Jan. 18, 1830.

"The following were copied from the cotemporary register of births in Worcester:

Matthew and Jean had

SUSANNAH, b. Aug. 9, 1736.
JEMIMA, b. June 24, 1742.
REUBEN, b. Dec. 2, 1744.
MATTHEW, b. March 1, 1750.
ROBERT, b. Oct. 30, 1751.
SARAH, b. Sept. 30, 1753.
JOHN, b. b. July 1, 1756.
JOSEPH, b. June 4, 1758.
ESTHER, b. Sept. 4, 1760.

Same Matthew, and Margaret Mc Farland, (second marriage) had, probably among several others,

JANE, b. March 19, 1767.
ISAAC, b. Oct. 30, 1769.

"I suppose John (1), William, Hugh, and Matthew (1), to be brothers, and all in middle life at the time of the immigration. Robert (1), may have been another brother, but I think he was son to Matthew (1). He was at any rate twenty-one years old in 1718, and was closely connected otherwise with Matthew (2), and lies buried beside him on Worcester Common.

"Experience Gray, b. Aug. 16, 1761, eldest child of Robert, Jr., who was born Dec. 22, 1734, mar. Abijah Perry, and was the grandmother of Hon. Aaron F. Perry, of Cincinnati."

George W. Gray, Esq., of Chicago, is of this line.

The issue being raised as to whether Joseph Gray, son of Matthew (2), and born June 4, 1758, was the Dr. Joseph Gray who married Lucy Bancroft, a record of whose descendants are given on the following pages, Professor Perry, gives the following as the basis for the claim that such was the case:

"I have often heard my mother say that we were related to George Bancroft through the Grays, and also have heard her say that we had Gray relatives in Londonderry, Vt., and that neighborhood. Dr. Henry Gray, who was own cousin to her, lived and died in Londonderry."

This would seem to be strong, and presumptive proof of the kinship of these two families, and especially so in view of the distinguished authority so quoted.

DR. JOSEPH GRAY.

Dr. Joseph Gray, was probably a son of Matthew (2) and Jean Gray, of Pelham, born June 4, 1758, although it is claimed by some of his descendants that he was of English origin, and born in Providence, R. I., 1751. He took an active part in the war of the Revolution, studied medicine with Dr. Mann, attended the lectures of Dr. Rush, and was one of the earliest regularly educated Physicians in Hillsboro County, New Hampshire. In 1780 he married Lucy Bancroft, daughter of Samuel Bancroft, who was the son of Samuel, son of Thomas (2), son of Thomas (1), who was born in England, 1622. (George Bancroft, the Historian, is the nephew of Lucy Bancroft, he being the son of her brother, Dr. Aaron Bancroft.) After his marriage Dr. Gray removed, 1790, to Mason, N. H., where he died in 1812; his wife in 1815. Children and descendants:

    I. HARRY GRAY, b. July 2, 1781; d. Sept. 16, 1782.
    II. HENRY GRAY, b. May 27, 1783; d. Aug. 24, 1863.
    III. LUCY GRAY, b. Feb. 5, 1785.
    IV. JOSEPH GRAY, b. Feb. 9, 1788; d. Feb. 9, 1879.
    V. JOHN GRAY, b. March 28, 1790.
    VI. LYDIA GRAY, b. May 20, 1792; d. June 10, 1792.
    VII. LYDIA BANCROFT GRAY, b. Jun. 19, 1793; d. Nov. 12, 1877.
    VIII. ISAAC GRAY, b. July 20, 1795; d. Aug., 1821.
    IX. HANNAH GRAY, b. Jan. 17, 1800; d. Sept. 29, 1822.

II. Dr. Henry Gray, second son of Dr. Joseph and Lucy Bancroft Gray, born at Nottingham West, now Hudson, N. H., married Margaret Carpenter, Nov. 23, 1808, and d. Aug. 24th, 1863. Their children were:

    HENRY C. GRAY, b. Jan. 7, 1810.
    ISAAC F. GRAY, b, Jan. 7, 1812.
    MARY GRAY, b. Nov. 12, 1813.
    LUCY GRAY, b. Jan. 22, 1815.
    DAVID B. GRAY, b. May 6, 1817.
    A. JACKSON GRAY, b. Feb. 23, 1820.
    MARGARET GRAY, b. Feb. 9, 1822.
    HANNAH GRAY, b. July 29, 1824.
    JOSEPH J. GRAY, b. December 25, 1826.
    JOHN B. GRAY, b. April 1, 1829.

Henry C. Gray, M. D., married Jeannette Bullions, of Cambridge N. Y., March 31, 1834. Their children were:

MARY B. GRAY, b. June 22, 1835; mar. Rev. John Anderson. Children: Mary Jeanette, Lizzie G., Harry G., Annie B., Grace Estey, John, and Charles Gray Anderson.

HENRY GRAY, b. April 23, 1837; d. Mar. 15, 1838.

MARGARET GRAY, b. Jan. 20, 1839.

ELIZA GRAY, b. March 27, 1840; mar. Dr. Benjamin F. Ketchum, Aug. 7, 1861; children: Lizzie, Harry, Katie, Liston, and Franklin Gray Ketchum.

HENRY GRAY, Dr., b. Sept. 6, 1842; mar. Sarah Anna Buel, May 7, 1867; a child,

> HARRY GRAY, b. Nov. 19, 1869.

ROBERT LISTON GRAY, b. at Cambridge, N. Y., Oct. 17, 1844; d. at battle of the Wilderness, May 5, 1864.

CHARLES ADAMS GRAY, Dr., b. July 24, 1846; married Nellie A. Joslin, Oct. 25, 1871; residence, Sioux Falls, Dakota; children:

> FLORENCE TEMPLETON GRAY, b. Jan. 31, 1873.
> ANNIE JOSLIN GRAY, b. June 11, 1875.
> CHARLES LISTON GRAY, b. April 15, 1877.
> MARY NELLIE GRAY, b. June 8, 1880.
> LIZZIE LEONARD GRAY, b. July 15, 1882.
> BETH ALLEN GRAY, b. Sept. 6, '84; d. Sept. 7, '84.
> BANCROFT GRAY, b. Aug. 22, 1885.

FLORENCE C. GRAY, b. Aug. 24, 1848; mar. Julius J. Estey, Oct. 29, 1867; children: J. Gray Estey. J. Harry, and Guy C. Estey.

FRANCES J. GRAY, (twin sister of Florence C. Gray,) b. Aug. 24, 1848; mar. Dr. L. W. Kennedy, Oct. 27, 1869; he d. May 18, 1873, leaving no issue, and she mar. second, Rev. Thomas Cull, Nov. 26, 1874; a son, Julius Estey Cull, b. Aug. 26, 1875.

ANNIE R. GRAY, b. March 30, 1850; mar. Marcius L. Cobb, Esq., of Sing Sing, N. Y., Oct. 8th, 1873; children: Marcius G. Cobb, b. Nov. 21, 1874; d. June 9, 1875; Henry G. Cobb, b. May 4, 1876; d. Jan. 15, 1877; James Willard Cobb, b. 18, 1880.

A. JACKSON GRAY, son of Dr. Henry Gray, b. Feb. 23, 1820, married Mary Burton, Nov. 25, 1845, at Manchester, Vermont; children:

> LOREN B. GRAY, b. Jan. 24, 1847; mar. Ida Kertz, Sept. 10, 1880; a son,
>
>> ROLLIN JEAN GRAY, b. June 16, 1881.

Henry Carpenter Gray.

JOHN B. GRAY, b. July 27, 1848.

HENRY GRAY, son of A. Jackson, b. Jan. 11, 1852, mar.
Alice Smith, March 3, 1880; a son,
HARRY SMITH GRAY, b. Dec. 15, 1880.

HANNAH GRAY, dau. of Dr. Henry and Margaret Carpenter
Gray, married, May 7, 1844, William W. Brockway; no issue;
residence, Cambridge, N. Y.

JOSEPH J. GRAY, son of Dr. Henry Gray, married Mattie W.
Putnam, July 27, 1854; residence, Cambridge, N. Y.; children:

ELIZABETH P. GRAY, b. Oct. 21, 1855.
MARY B. GRAY, b. May 28, 1862.
MATTIE P. GRAY, b. Dec. 20, 1863.
MARGARET C. GRAY, b. July 31, 1865.

Dr. Henry C. Gray, whose portrait herewith appears, died at
Cambridge, N. Y., Feb. 10, 1877. His widow still survives.

Dr. C. A. Gray, son of Dr. Henry C., who furnished most of
the statistics of the descendants of Dr. Joseph Gray, (1), graduated at Bellevue Hospital Medical College, New York, 1869,
and has recently removed from Sioux Falls, Dakota, to Hins-
dale, N. H.

———

DR. JOSEPH GRAY, (2).

IV. JOSEPH GRAY, Dr., son of Dr. Joseph and Lucy Bancroft
Gray, born Feb. 9, 1788, married Eunice Russell, at Cavendish,
Vt., July 11, 1811; she d. Jun. 9, 1859; he d. at Taftsville, Vt.,
Feb. 9, 1879, aged 91 years. Children and descendants:

PAMELA GRAY, b. Sept. 26, 1812; mar. Lyman Townsend,
Nov. 27, 1832; d. May 11, 1861; children: Lorenzo
Richmond, who mar. Harriet Benson and had
Mary Helen and Hosea Lorenzo Townsend;
Lucy Bancroft, who mar. Daniel Maxam; Ellen
F., who mar. Henry F. Ellis; Julia Ann, who
mar. James M. Preston, and had Herbert Pres-
ton; Lydia Maria, Samuel Lucian, and Frank
Lyman Townsend.

JOSEPH GRAY, son of Dr. Joseph, b. Jan. 20, 1815; mar.
Abigail Spaulding, Jan. 10, 1847 ; she d. Feb. 4,
1853; he mar. second, Maria Johnson Fuller, Apr.
16, 1854; he d. Sept. 28, 1875; children:

> JOHN BANCROFT GRAY, b. Feb. 16, 1848; mar.
> Emeline Morris, May 27, 1873; children:
>> LILLIE GRAY, b. 1875.
>> MINNEOLA GRAY, b. July 12, 1877.
> FANNIE ELIZABETH GRAY, b. June 28, 1849;
> mar. Dr. Worthington Brown, July 31,
> 1866 ; children: Francis Everett, Lilian
> Eliza, Robert Orcutt, and William Worth-
> ington.
> LYDIA PAMELA GRAY, b. Jan. 26, 1851.
> ARY GRAY, b. Jan. 27, 1853; d. Nov. 27, 1866.
> IRA GRAY, b. Jan. 28, 1855.
> EUNICE MARIA GRAY, b. Aug. 22, 1856.

LUCRETIA MARIA GRAY, dau. of Dr. Joseph, b. Mar. 13,
1817, mar. Charles Kendall Smith, July 7, 1835;
children: Margaret L.; John Russell, who mar. Mary
E. Clark, and had Ette Lucretia, Kendrick Stillman,
Floy Eliza, and Rosa Belle Smith; Silas R., who
mar. Mary M. Minor and had Walter Smith; Chas.
Kendall Smith, who mar. Mary C. Mackey and had
Silas Grant and Charles Homer Smith; Amelia Eliza Smith; Mary Jane Smith, who mar. John R. Berry; Juliette Smith, George Bancroft, and Rosa.

LYDIA EMERSON GRAY, dau. of Dr. Joseph, b. Jan. 2,
1819, mar. Henry L. Anthony, Oct. 20, 1838; children: Henry Gray Anthony, who mar. Mary R. Gil-
more, March 14, 1867, and had Hannah Lodel Anthony; twin sons, b. and d. Mar. 26, 1842; Samuel
Warren Anthony, b. Feb. 5, 1848; Eunice Elvira, b.
July 18, 1849.

ELIZA EASTIN GRAY, dau. of Dr. Joseph Gray, b. Feb.
20, 1825, mar. Herman Chandler Orcutt, Jan. 1,
1852; children: John Herman Orcutt, b. July 14,
1856; Zalmon Edward, b. Jan. 14, 1861, d. July 22,
1864; Charles Russell Orcutt, b. Apr. 27, 1864.

Dr. Joseph Gray (1) was married at Reading, Mass., and it
was at Quebec, Canada, that he died in 1812, which may ac-
connt for some confusion which has arisen concerning the date
of his birth.

KELSO GRAY.

Kelso Gray removed from Pelham to Peterborough, N. H., about 1766, '67; Phebe Gray, his wife, d. Mar. 27, 1814, aged 74 years; he d. Oct. 28, 1824, aged 86 years, which would make his birth in 1738, about the date of the removal of the Grays from Worcester to Pelham, aforementioned, and consequently he must have been a son of one of the original emigrants, and probably of Hugh, as that was the name given his eldest son. Children and descendants:

> HUGH GRAY, son of, who mar. Jennie Moore of Sharon, and removed to Montpelier, Vt.
>
> REUBEN GRAY, who removed to Montpelier, Vt.
>
> ESTHER GRAY, b. 1770; d. March 5, 1795.
>
> KELSO GRAY, mar. Anna Wilson, and re. to Montpelier.

MATTHEW GRAY, b. Dec. 9, 1772, succeeded his father on the old place. He mar. Mary Conner, of Poplin; he d. Dec. 25, 1841; she d. Jan. 8, 1846; children:

> MATTHEW GRAY, Jr., b. May 3, 1797, mar. Nancy Clark; mar. 2d, Mrs. Rhoda Hutchinson Bartlett, and removed to Milford; only a daughter survives.
>
> MARY GRAY, b. Apr. 3, 1799, mar. Wm. Miller; second, Wm. S. Smith.
>
> AZUBA GRAY, b. Nov. 27, 1801, mar. Hiram Chapman.
>
> WILLIAM CONNER GRAY, b. June 8, 1804, mar. Lucinda Parker, Jan. 23, 1834; he d. May 25, 1865; she d. Nov. 17, 1870; children:
>
>> HELEN F. GRAY, b. June 18, 1836; mar. Wm. McCain; residence, St. Paul, Minn.
>>
>> CLARA L. GRAY, b. Nov. 25, 1842; mar. Ervin H. Smith; residence, Springfield, Mass.
>
> LORINDA GRAY, dau. of Matthew, b. Nov. 14, 1806; mar. David Emerson; mar. second, Warren Woods, of Hancock.
>
> JEAN GRAY, dau. of Kelso, b. 1776; mar. John Shearer White.

WILLIAM GRAY, son of Kelso, b. Dec. 3, 1781; mar. Harriet Scott, dau. of John Scott, Esq., Apr. 4, 1811; d. Mar. 31, 1855. Children:

BETHIAH GRAY, dau. of, b. Jan. 7, 1812; mar Moses Greenfield Jan. 19, 1835; he. d. Nov. 28, 1844; she d. 1846; children: Bethiah, who mar. Lucien Alexander and had Lizzie, b. 1861; Maria, b. June 10, 1846.

JOHN SCOTT GRAY, b. June 11, 1813, mar. Elizabeth H. Flint, Dec. 21, 1842; he d, Oct. 13, 1843, and she mar. second, Samuel May, of Sharon, N. H., Apr. 3, 1863; a son,

JOHN FLINT GRAY, b. 1843; d. Oct. 17, 1848.

JANE GRAY, b. July 8, 1815; mar. Lyman Knowlton, Mar. 25, 1832.

HARRIET GRAY, b. Jan. 30, 1818; mar. Horatio Nelson, Jan. 1, 1839.

WILLIAM S. GRAY, b. Oct. 13, 1819; mar. Louisa Whitcomb; removed.

ADAM P. GRAY, b. June 10, 1823; d. Aug. 15, 1842.

CHARLES SCOTT GRAY, b. Nov. 25, 1824; mar. Lydia Ann Stevens, Nov. 4, 1847; fell from his buildings while repairing the same, and received injury from which he died Oct. 26, 1868. Children:

CHARLES S., b. Sept. 1, 1848; d. Aug. 29, 1849.
LIZZIE ANN, b. Aug. 12, 1850; d. Dec. 24, 1850.
FRED A., b. June 13, 1852.
JOHN S., b. Dec. 27, 1854.
ARTHUR H., b. Oct. 4, 1857.
ANNIE C., b. Aug. 17, 1859.
FRANZ S., b. Dec. 17, 1861; d. Sept. 12, 1870.
ADDIE L., b. Feb. 3, 1863.
JAMES S., b. Sept. 16, 1864.
CHARLES S., b. Oct. 15, 1865.
PERLEY B., b. July 22, 1867; d. Feb. 6, 1871.

JAMES S. GRAY, son of William, b. March 9, 1829; mar. Mary Ann ————, in New York city; she d. Aug. 8, 1852, and he mar. second, Ada Lewis.

SAMUEL GRAY, b. April 29, 1832; d. 1832.
SARAH E. GRAY, b. Feb. 22, 1835; mar. Reuben Baldwin.
MARY E. GRAY, " " " " d. 1836.

Among the first of the pioneers at what is now Union City, Pa., was Matthew Gray, 1797, and in 1806, a brother, William Gray, settled at Beaver Dam, not far distant. They had emigrated from the north of Ireland, were of Scotch ancestry, and similarity of names and characteristics strongly indicate their kinship to the Worcester Grays, though of a later emigration. They had previously resided in Huntington and Northumberland counties, Pa., where most of their children were born, and they had come thither by way of Philadelphia and Pittsburgh. Matthew had three children, respectively: Francis B., Eleanor, and William, the oldest of whom was born in 1790. He was also accompanied by a younger sister, Rachel, who afterwards, in 1803, married John Cook, of Union township. David Wilson, of Union City, in a history of that place, entitled the "Olden Times," says of Matthew Gray and his family: "The family were religious, and believed with the poet Thompson that God is ever present, ever felt, 'In the void waste as in the city full.' They dedicated their home to the love and service of God, and established in it the custom of keeping family worship; and this was the first germ of the Presbyterian Church in Union City."

Matthew Gray died in 1814, leaving his farm of 200 acres to his son Francis B., who married his cousin Jane Gray, daughter of his uncle William, his sister Eleanor having previously married her cousin William Gray, brother of Jane. Francis B. lived to be over ninety, and in 1881 was the only survivor of the family in Union township. His brother William married Anna Bracken and died in 1843. No record of other descendants.

William Gray, a brother of Matthew, settled at Beaver Dam, in 1806, had five sons and three daughters, as follows: James, William, Matthew, Robert and John, and Sarah, Jane and Anna. Jane, as already stated, married her cousin Francis B. Gray; Sarah married David Cook; William married his cousin Eleanor; John married Elizabeth Wilson and died in 1865, aged 62 years, having been Elder in the Presbyterian church 35 years; Robert married Jane Smith, and died in Union 1879, aged 81 years; James Gray married Mary Miles, and removed to Sugar Grove, where he died in 1859. A son, R. M. Gray, still resides there. James was almost a giant, and was said to have been the strongest man in General Harrison's army. All of the family were above the average stature, and were possessed of great force of character. William Gray (1) married the second time and had two sons: Joseph, who made a fortune in the tobacco trade in New York, and the other a printer and publisher in Chicago.

JAMES GRAY, a head-weaver from the north of Ireland, mar·ried about 1690, Mary, dau. of Isaac Williams and grand-daughter of Robt. Williams b. in Norwich, England, 1593, and came to Roxbury, Mass., 1637, where he died 1693. James Gray lived at Hadley, Mass. They had two sons: John, who died in the French War, and James Gray, Jr., who was a Major in the French War, and Colonel and Quartermaster in the Revolutionary War. He mar. Sarah Spring, who d. 1809. He d. 1782, in Stockbridge, Mass., where they had removed sometime prior to the Revolution. They had two daughters: Sarah, who mar. Thomas Hunt, had two sons, John and James, and d. in 1788; and Mary Gray, b. at Stockbridge, 1764, where she d. 1808. She mar. Barnabas Bidwell 1793; he was born 1763, graduated at Yale, and d. at Kingston, Canada, 1833. They had two children: Sarah Gray, b. 1796, d. 1864; and Marshall Spring Bidwell, b. 1799, and d. 1872, at New York, where he had lived since 1838. Mr. Bidwell was a Member of the Parliament of Upper Canada, from 1824 to 1836, and was Speaker four years, 1829–30, and 1835–36.

William Gray, son of James Gray, was born Dec. 11, 1745, in Scotland. He came to the Colony of Virginia in 1765, and settled in the "Northern Neck," in Westmoreland county. On the 9th of May, 1773, he married Catharine Dick, daughter of Robert Dick, of Scotland and Westmoreland Co., Va., where she was born Feb. 28, 1743. They resided there until 1784, when they removed to Fairfax Co., and lived a little below Mt. Vernon. They had five children, viz:

ROBERT GRAY, b. May 11, 1774.
JANE GRAY, Oct. 15, 1776.
JOHN GRAY, b. Oct. 12, 1779.
CATHARINE GRAY, b. April 28, 1783.
WILLIAM FAIRFAX GRAY, b. Nov. 3, 1787.

William Gray died March 8, 1796, and his widow, Catharine Gray, removed to Alexandria, Va., 1799, and resided with her son Robert, until 1814, and afterwards with her son-in-law, John Violett, and daughter Catharine, until she died, Oct. 5, 1829.

Robert Gray married Polly K. Nelson, of Norfolk, Va., and had only one child, which died in infancy. He removed to Fredericksburg, Va., in 1814, and died there Oct. 6, 1861.

John Gray married Ann Maria Helmbold, of Philadelphia. He died Dec. 7, 1812, and his wife, Dec. 14, 1814. They had four children: one son, who died in infancy; and three daughters—Catharine, dec'd, and Eliza and Maria, unmarried; they reside in Philadelphia.

Jane Gray mar. John Violett, in 1795, and d. Sept. 26, 1808.

Catharine Gray also mar. John Violett, and after his death removed to Pittsburg, Pa., where she died.

William Fairfax Gray married Milly Richards Stone, of Fredericksburg, Va., Sept. 24, 1817. They resided there until 1838, when they removed to Houston, Texas. They had six children who died in infancy, and six who came to maturity, viz:

> PETER W. GRAY, b. Dec. 12, 1819.
> EVALINA STONE GRAY, b. Aug. 23, 1822.
> EDWIN FAIRFAX GRAY, b. March 15, 1829.
> ALLAN CHARLES GRAY, b. Oct. 4, 1830.
> CATHARINE DICK GRAY, b. Apr. 25, 1832.
> SUSAN ALICE GRAY, b. June 12, 1835.

William Fairfax Gray died at Houston, Texas, April 16, 1841, and his widow, Milly R. Gray, died at same place, July 1, 1851.

Peter W. Gray, Judge, married Abby Jane Avery, of Stonington, Conn., in 1843. He died Oct. 3, 1874; she still survives; no children.

Evalina Stone Gray married James Temple Doswell, 1842. They reside at Fredericksburg, Va., and have several children.

Edwin Fairfax Gray married Rosalie Woodburn Taylor, at Houston, Texas, 1856. She died May, 1874; he died in Aug., 1885. They had three children: William Fairfax, Blanche, and Taylor Gray—all living.

Allan Charles Gray married Amanda Ellen Bostick, of Louisville, Ky., and they reside at Houston, Texas. Have two children: Fanny Doswell and Eb. Nichols Gray.

Catharine Dick Gray married Henry Sampson of Houston, in 1849. They reside at Galveston, and have several children.

Susan Alice Gray married Claudius W. Sears, of New Orleans, in 1854. They reside at Oxford, Miss., and have several children.

———

William H. Gray, of Astoria, Oregon, furnishes the following sketch of a detached branch of the Gray family of which he is a member, and of which it is to be regretted that a more full account could not be given, especially in the direction of early ancestry:

" I can only say, that I remember hearing my father tell about his father coming from Scotland prior to the rebellion of the American Colonists, with a Scotch kirk parson, who took his mother, my grandmother, to lead the Scotch dance, when the Declaration of Independence was proclaimed, while my grandfather Gray took the parson's wife, and had a glorious dance for Liberty ! My grandfather was next the minister, an officer of the Scotch kirk. My father, Samuel Gray, was a boy fifteen years old at that time. He had an older brother who was a soldier of the Revolution, and afterwards removed to Virginia. I have not been able to trace him. My father was born, 1761, I think in Connecticut, Mayfield. He died at 62. My father married a Miss Barber. He had learned the miller's trade, and moved from Connecticut to New York State with his wife and four children. They had altogether eleven children, seven sons and four daughters, as follows:

"Calvin Gray, the oldest, was a tinner; Bir, died at 22, unmarried; Samuel, a lumberman, died in Fulton Co., N. Y., leaving two sons and three daughters; Lyman, do not know where he went nor how much family he had; John, a Presbyterian Preacher at Moreland, Schuyler Co., N. Y., left two sons and three daughters; I come next, with four sons and three daughters, all married, and among them all 32 grand children; B. H. Gray, the youngest son, of Three Rivers, Mich., two sons and seven daughters; the married daughters of my father were Hannah More, Rhody Hull, and Maria Tiernan.

"The older members of the family all dead—none remaining except myself and younger brother. Have all been scattered, from Maine to Oregon, and from Dakota to Texas. I was born 1810. My residence in Oregon commenced Sept. 2, 1836; my wife's Sept. 6, 1838. She died 1882. For many years there was but one Gray family in Oregon, and now there are fifteen besides my own large family. A fifty years resident in Oregon, with six overland trips, and one sea trip via San Francisco and Panama, and six trips by rail; and a trip by sea to Sitka, and other journeyings around Oregon, Washington, Idaho, and a large portion of the British Territories, I can safely say that this western portion of our continent is the best and mildest portion of the whole of it, including Alaska. Am thankful that the Creator has thus far preserved me in strength and good health at 75 years of age. Respectfully yours, &c."

W. H. Gray, writer of the above, is a man of note in his adopted State, and is the author of a History of Oregon from 1792 to 1849, as well as the father of a numerous family.

M. Henry Gray, of Moreland, N. Y., and son of Rev. John Gray, of this family, sends the following valuable data, which it will be seen conflicts at some points with the foregoing statement: " The following is copied from an old record in my possession:

SAMUEL GRAY, b. Oct., 1767.
RHODA BARBER, (wife of,) b. June, 1770.
THEIR CHILDREN.
HANNAH GRAY, b. June, 1790; mar. Mr. Moore.
CALVIN GRAY, b. Aug., 1793.
SAMUEL GRAY, Jr., b. July, 1795.
BURR GRAY, b. July, 1797.
JOHN GRAY, Rev., b. Sept., 1799.
RHODA GRAY, b. Dec., 1801.
ABIGAIL GRAY, b. Dec., 1803.
LYMAN GRAY, b. Feb., 1805.
MARIA GRAY, b. Sept., 1807.
WILLIAM H. GRAY, b. Sept., 1810.
BARBER H. GRAY, b. Feb., 1815.

"My father, John, was born in Vermont. His father was a miller, at which trade my father worked. They lived in Herkimer Co., N. Y., and afterwards at Root, Montgomery Co. My father went from there to Auburn Theological Seminary in 1826. Soon after he graduated he married Mary Hoyt. His first field was at Root, thence to Cherry Valley, Wooster, Southport, and finally at Moreland, where he purchased a home and resided till his death. Mother died in 1863. They left two sons and three daughters, as follows:

"Wm. C. Gray, b. Oct., 1831; mar., but no children; Cynthia J., b. 1833, mar. E. Pease, two children; Mary E., b. July, 1835, mar. F. W. Gaylord, two children, he d. 1867 ; M. Henry Gray, b. June, 1838, mar. in 1864, no children; Hannah M., b. June, 1851, d. Feb., 1885.

"It was at Middlebury, Vt., that my father was born, and soon afterwards his parents removed to Dorset, and from thence to New York, as already stated. I have heard my father speak of the family as being of Scotch origin."

B. H. Gray, of Three Rivers, Mich., the youngest son of Samuel, was born Feb. 28, 1815, and the names and dates of birth of his children are as follows:

SARAH M. GRAY, b. Aug. 12, 1839.
MARTHA A. GRAY, b. Jan'y 20, 1842.
ELLIOT S. GRAY, b. Jan'y 19, 1844.
HARRIET A. GRAY, b. May 4, 1846.
ELLEN R. GRAY, b. July 27, 1848.
ALICE E· GRAY, b. March 27, 1853.
RHODA J. GRAY, b. October 27, 1856.
WILLIAM F. GRAY, b. Feb. 27, 1858.
CARLIE A. GRAY, b. Nov. 14, 1861.

Van Rensselaer Gray, of Hudson, N. Y., son of Samuel, Jr., is of this family, and had a brother and three sisters.

He writes as follows: "My father, at the time of his death, was a resident of Fulton Co., N. Y. His name was Samuel, which was also the name of his father. I believe they hailed from Yankeeland, but my father died when I was a mere lad, and I left home very early. My home has been in this city for thirty-five years and more."

Mr. Van Rensselaer Gray is a prominent business man in Hudson, and has been for many years extensively engaged in the hardware trade in that city.

J. M. Gray, Esq., of Allendale, S. C., furnishes the following interesting data: "The family to which I belong moved to this State between 1800 and 1810, from Trent Co., N. C.; my grandfather, Jacob Gray, and two brothers, Jos., and Parker, settled in this section; Thomas Gray, another brother, moved to Florida about that time, and I think afterwards moved to Texas; William Gray, another brother, remained in North Carolina; Parker Gray, after remaining here a number of years, prior to 1830 removed to Alabama. My great grandfather, Israel Gray, moved from Virginia to North Carolina sometime previous to the Revolution, as he was in the army in that State during that war. I do not know whether he had any brothers. He was of Irish descent, but whether born in this country of Irish parents, or born in Ireland, I do not know. I think however that there were brothers, as I have understood that a part of the family moved to Ohio, together with a family named Wells, about the time he moved to N. C. I think he married a Parker. I have an impression that he or his parents came to Virginia from Massachusetts. [Worcester Grays?]

"There is a family of Grays in Edgefield County, in this State, whom I have understood came from North Carolina, and also that came from the same family, but cannot vouch for it as I do not know any of them. There is a Gen. C. Walter Gray, living in Greenville, this State, who moved from Edgefield. The branch of the family to which I belong have been long noted for their great physical strength. Family tradition says that my great grandfather Israel Gray was once captured during the War of the Revolution and was in the charge of seven (7) men at night. By watching his chance he (having succeeded in getting his hands loose, for they had bound him to a tree) being a very powerful man, sprang upon the sentinel and disarmed and killed him without arousing the others, and then by using the bayonet before the others awoke, and the club of the musket, and shooting after they awoke, he succeeded in slaying them all. When he returned to camp and told how he had escaped and that he had killed seven of the British, his companions would not believe him until he took them to the place and showed them the seven dead bodies."

The following sketch of the Grays of Townsend, Vt., is furnished by Augusta L. Fessenden, of that place, whose mother is of that family: "After a long time I found the name of my great grandfather, Jonas Gray, and his wife's name was Susannah. Some say that she was a Gray before being married. The following is the record as full as I can at present give it to you."

JONAS GRAY, b. 1733; d. Nov. 13, 1804.
SUSANNAH GRAY, (wife of Jonas,) b. 1727; d. May 1, 1813.
CHILDREN OF.
AMOS GRAY, mar. Betsey Read Tyler; he d. March 3, 1850; she d. June 25, 1843.
JONAS GRAY, Jr., mar. Hannah Wisnell; he d. Jan. 7, 1843; she d. Oct. 11, 1838.
SALLY GRAY.
MATTHEW GRAY.
JAMES GRAY, mar. Betsey Wilkinson; he d. Jan. 15, 1856; she d. Nov. 2, 1852.

JESSE GRAY, b. Oct. 27, 1795; mar. Susannah Ober; he d. March 27, 1832; she d. May 27, 1853. Children and descendants:

ALANSON GRAY, mar. Sabrina Pool; d. at Chicago. 1863; children:
DELIA S., mar. Park Davis; two children; Mary P. and Henry L. ; residence, Sioux Falls, Dakota.
ADELBERT E. GRAY, mar. Mary Van Wie, and has two children: Florence and Mabel S. Mr. Gray is a wholesale provision dealer in Albany, N. Y.
VILLERMER GRAY, unmarried; residence, Townsend, Vt.

SUSAN and BETSEY GRAY, daughters of Jonas Gray, the latter the mother of Augusta L. Fessenden, of Townsend, Vt. Jonas had a brother Joseph.

Miss Fessenden further says: "We are of English descent. Tradition says there were three brothers and one sister came from England; the sister died soon after coming to this country; two of the brothers settled in the north part of this State and one in Mass., but do not know their given names."

And yet location and family names would seem to indicate that this is a detached branch of the Worcester Grays.

Dr. Wm. A. Gray, of Columbia, Fluvanna Co., Va., writes as follows concerning the branch of the family with which he is connected: "Having died many years ago, before this scribe was born, the christian name of his grandfather Gray has escaped his memory, but his impression is that it was John. Nor is he certain that in coming to Virginia that he first resided in one of the counties below Richmond, or in Goochland Co., 30 miles above that city. He had three sons: Thomas, Joseph, and William, and four daughters: Anna, Polly, Eudocia, and Lucy. Thomas and Joseph were unmarried and left no descendants. William, my father, married Jane Guerrant, a sister of Gen. John Guerrant. For a short period my father engaged in mercantile business at Richmond, and then located in Goochland, where he most creditably filled numerous high and responsible offices. He was Colonel in the war of 1812. His sister Anna married James McAlister; Polly married a Pledge, and moved to one of the western States; Eudocia married a Shelburne, and Lucy married her cousin Jack Gray, and moved to South Carolina. My parents had five children whom they were enabled to raise and educate in the best schools of that day. The eldest, John Guerrant Gray, was a lawyer, married Miss Lindsey, of Albemarle Co., had three sons, one of whom survives, and has a wife and several children. There were also five daughters, some of whom were married, and their descendants are in Hanover and Louisa counties. Betsey Gray, second child of my father, married Thomas Massie, and had one daughter and five sons, one of whom, Charles, is an eminent physician in Goochland. The next daughter, Susan, never married.

"The author of this sketch, the next in rotation, viz: Wm. A. Gray, was educated for a physician, and attended a full course of Lectures at the University of Pennsylvania, where he graduated in 1830, and soon after located in Fluvanna Co., where he yet resides, and for more than fifty years has been extensively engaged professionally. In November, 1831, he married Mary Ann Brooks, a most beautiful wife, and by this union have three sons and three daughters, viz: William B. Gray, who after attending a full course of Medical Lectures in the University of Virginia graduated in the Jefferson Medical College, of Phila., 1852.

After practising successfully with his father for nearly 20 years, he removed to the city of Richmond, where he married Lucy Susan Bowles, daughter of Judge D. W. K. Bowles, who had previously married C. C. Ettet of Richmond. He is now permanently located there with a large and lucrative practice. He has no children. My second son, A. A. Gray, is a distinguished lawyer residing at Palmyra, the county seat of Fluvanna Co. He has been twice married; his first wife a Miss Shepherd, by whom he has a lovely and accomplished daughter, Willie Blanche Gray. His second marriage was with Miss Bettie Leftwich, by whom he has two sons: Affie Leftwich, and Ernest A. Gray. My eldest daughter, Susan E. Gray, is unmarried and resides with her aged parents. My second daughter, Isabella Jane, married A. L. Shepherd of Richmond, an extensive commission merchant and lumber dealer; have two promising boys. My youngest daughter, Mary A. Gray, married E. P. Morris of Richmond; is a widow, had one son, Vivian Gray, since deceased; a noble youth. My sixth, and youngest child, John G. Gray, died in his 20th year, soon after engaging in mercantile pursuits in the city of Richmond.

"Finally, Judith Guerrant Gray, the youngest child of my beloved parents, married Dr. A. V. Payne, by whom she had three daughters and a son, most of whom removed to Missouri and died there some years since."

There was a very early emigration of Grays to Virginia, as appears in the following extract from the " Muster Roll of the Inhabitants of James City and Iland," made in 1624:

"Thomas Graye, Margaret his wife, William their son aged 3 years, Jone their daughter aged 6 years."

The foregoing interesting family is probably one of the branch·es of this ancestral tree which was so early planted in the fertile and prolific Colony of the Old Dominion.

———

Mr. W. A. Gray, of New Boston, Va., furnishes the following concerning a family of Scotch Irish Grays of which he is a member: "I am the only son of Dr. G. R. Gray, a farmer and physician of Halifax Co., Va. He says his great grandfather came from the East and settled in Raleigh, N. C., about one hundred years ago. My father has two brothers, J. A. Gray, of Guilford Co., N. C., and Rev. Fletcher Gray, of Wilkes Co. My grandfather was Rev. Alson Gray, a noted Methodist preacher in his day. He died at his residence in Guilford Co., 1881. A cotemporary says of him: 'The writer ventures to say, that in the annals of his church, there is no record of funeral honors such as were rendered to Father Gray. Uncle Gray was truly a great and good man. He was the father of his Church in North Carolina. He lived long, and served his generation faithfully. A nobler soul, more deeply imbued with the pure and fervent spirit of Christianity, and what he thought to be right, never passed from earth to the more genial realms of immortality. He preached more than ten thousand sermons and traveled more than 100,000 miles during the 58 years of his active ministry. His name will long live in the history of the Methodist Church in North Carolina.' Two of his brothers, Rev. John, and Rev. Arington Gray, were also ministers of the same denomination. My great-grandfather, Gilbert Gray, had also two other sons, Dr. Wm. Gray, who removed to Ohio, and Elisha, a school teacher, who died when young, in Tenn. There were also three daughters. F. C. Gray, of Lewisburg, Preble Co., Ohio, is a grandson. My great grandfather had several brothers, but I cannot give their names nor the name of their father."

The above, if not of the Worcester Grays, are probably akin to them.

———

B. C. Gray, Esq., of Richmond, Va., represents still another family. He says: "My great-grandfather, whose given name I do not remember, was an Englishman, and emigrated to this country at an early period in the 18th century, and settled in this State. My grandfather, whose name was William, was born in the county of Amelia, where my father James Gray, was also born. I think that my grandfather had only one brother, and that he was a bachelor. I have a brother, Rev. Robert Gray, of Gallatin, Tennessee. This is about all the information I can give you concerning my ancestry."

Mr. B. C. Gray is an old and highly respected citizen of Richmond.

J. C. Gray, Esq., of Cortland, N. Y., furnishes the following concerning what is apparently a detached branch of the Worcester Grays, and which would have been classified directly with them, but for delay, in the hope of getting further and more full information, although, as will be seen, it is claimed that the original emigrant of this family came direct from Scotland: "By what I can learn, my great grandfather came from Scotland, when quite young, to the State of Vermont, or Massachusetts, I am not certain which, (probably the latter,) lived there, was married there, and his children born there, but while they were yet young removed to or near Fishkill, Dutchess Co., N. Y., where he and his wife both died soon after, leaving four sons, viz: John, David, Peter, and Ephraim. Their father's name, my great grandfather, was David Gray. Of his sons, John Gray, became a physician, and lived and died in Cattaraugus Co., N. Y. David lived at Delhi, N. Y. Ephraim was a bachelor, of a roving disposition; do not know where he went to. Peter, my grandfather, was ten years old at time of his father's death, 1778. He was bound out to a man by the name of Morse at Fishkill. When he was fifteen years old he ran away, crossed the Hudson to Orange Co., lived there a few years, went to Sullivan Co., was married there, and removed to Marathon, Cortland Co., about 1800, and lived there until he died, about 1850. My grandfather had four sons, and five daughters, as follows: William, Ogden, Rachel, Polly, John, Henrietta, Adaline, Elizabeth, the only daughter who still survives, and George W. Gray. The latter is the only son living; he resides in the town of Lapeer, Cortland Co., N. Y. My father's name was Ogden. He lived on the farm my grandfather settled on in Marathon, and died there in the year 1866. He left four sons: Peter N., J. C., Hala, and William E. Gray. P. N. Gray lives on the old homestead; the subscriber, J. C., is living in Cortland, N. Y., a watchmaker by occupation and still carrying on the business; Hala is a farmer at Hooper, Broome Co., N. Y.; Wm. E. is in the lumber business at Fernandina, Florida. I have two children only; Harry P., a watchmaker with me, and Charles B. Gray, traveling for the Ladd Watch Case Co., of Providence and New York."

Peter Gray was born Oct. 12, 1768; married Elizabeth Barnes

of Pike Co., Pa., 1793; he died Jan. 29, 1851, in his 83d year; she died March 22, 1863, aged 88 years.   Children and descendants:

> OGDEN GRAY, son of Peter, b. March 28, 1797; mar. Susan Barnes of Lumberland, Sullivan Co., N. Y., 1818; children:
>> ELIZABETH, b. Oct. 21, 1820; mar. S. C. Taft; d. June 28, 1846.
>> POLLY M., b. Aug. 11, 1822; mar. Nathan Underwood.
>> OGDEN GRAY, Jr., b. Sept. 1, 1826; mar. Lydia H. Watrous; d. Feb. 3, 1870.
>> ELINOR B., b. July 21. 1828; mar. Jerry Wood; d. July 3, 1882.
>> JERRY C. GRAY, b. Nov. 26, 1830; mar. Fannie A. Judd, Feb. 8, 1860; two sons: Harry P., and Charles B. Gray; residence. Cortland, N. Y.
>> SUSAN A., b. Nov. 21, 1832; mar. Emory Gee.
>> HALA B., b. Dec. 13, 1834; mar. Amy Robinson.
>> EMILY A., b. Feb. 1837; mar. Merritt Tyler.
>> WM. E., b. Mar. 29, 1839; mar. Elizabeth Pierce.
>> ADDIE L., b. Nov. 13, '41; mar. Seneca Wright.

The following additional data in regard to this family is furnished by David G. Wyckoff, of Jerseyville. Ill., a grandson of David Gray, son of David: " My mother, Elinor Gray, was born in Fishkill, Dutchess Co., N. Y., 1787; died in Jerseyville, Ill., March 17, 1871.   She was married in Blenheim, Schoharie Co., N. Y., March, 1809, to John Wyckoff. There were born of this union, ten children, viz: John A., David G., Nathan, Solomon G., Theodore T., Franklin D., Elizabeth D., Charles, Augustus, and James B.; all deceased but Elizabeth Davis, who now lives at Creston, Iowa, and myself.   My mother's father was David Gray.   He was a native of Fishkill, N. Y.   He married Deborah Hunt, and moved to Schoharie Co.. N. Y., 1796.   He was 13 years old when the British occupied Fishkill Church. David Gray and Deborah his wife had eleven children; they are now all dead.   Their names were Solomon, Betsy, Elinor, Phebe, Maria, Hiram, John, James, Abel, Matilda, Mahala."

Hiram Olmstead, Esq., of Walton, N. Y., and a grandson of David Gray, contributes the following interesting sketch: " My grandfather, David Gray, was a Quaker. It was his usual custom to sit with his hat on, and when he came to the table to take off his hat and ask a private blessing, and after the meal to put it on again. He was of a humorous disposition, and this was intensified in my mother, Phebe Gray Olmstead. David Gray died in Walton, May 6, 1855. Some of the family claim that he was 96, but I have often heard him say that he was 21 in the Spring before the Fall in which the British left New York, which would make him 94 at the time of his death. Deborah his wife, died Nov. 17, 1844, aged 73. She was blind the last twenty years of her life.

"Solomon Gray, the oldest son of David, married a Miss Hoagland, and had five daughters and two sons. He was a merchant in Catskill, N. Y., and while on his way to Athens in a small boat with his son Ogden, was capsized and drowned in the Hudson. This was in the summer of 1834. His daughter Emeline died October 17, 1835. Maria married Abram Schermerhorn and had four daughters and one son, all of whom are married and live near Moresville, N. Y.; she died June 21, 1885. Adaliza, born Dec. 31, 1828, mar. a Mr. Travell, and had Ella M., who mar. L. Clark, living near Gilboa, N. Y., and Marion E., who mar. P. C. Ranner, now of Laramie City, Wyoming Ter. James Oscar Gray, twin brother of Adaliza, and his brother Ogden, left New York on a whaling voyage, and that is the last that was ever heard of them. Melissa mar. David Zeeley, and died near Gilboa, leaving a son Charles. Elizabeth, b. at Catskill, N. Y., June 23, 1831, mar. J. S. Page, now of Delhi, N. Y., and has a son and two daughters; Jerome S., b. May 30, 1861, mar. Delia Launt and has two children, is a jeweler and resides at Delhi; Frances W., b. Oct. 27, 1864, and Lydia B., b. May 25, 1865; both living with their parents at Delhi.

"Abel Gray, son of David, lived at Catskill; had a son Willard; the family all dead.

"Betsey Gray, married John Brinkerhoff, and moved to western N Y., and had a son Richard, who left three daughters; a daughter Maria who mar. Joseph Doughty, and has three daughters, all married and now living at LaFayette, N. Y.

"Nellie Gray married John Wyckoff, and lived in New York

city. Of their seven children, John A. died two years since in New York, leaving a widow and one daughter and three grand children. David Wyckoff is a prominent merchant in Jerseyville, Ill.

"Maria Gray married a Watson, and had one daughter, who was the first wife of J. S. Page, who afterwards married Solomon's youngest daughter Elizabeth.

"Hiram Gray was struck by lightning and killed at Meredith, N. Y., 1842.

"James Gray had a family and the last I knew was living in western New York.

"Phebe Gray, my mother, married Philo Olmstead. March 9, 1817, and had four children: Debby Ann, David Gray, Hiram, and Sarah. My father was born Nov. 11. 1795, and died Nov. 17, 1874. Mother was born Aug. 7, 1794, and died June 3, 1850; and after her decease he married her sister Matilda, Nov. 8, 1850; she d. Apr. 4, 1878. Mahala remained unmarried, and d. Sept. 20, 1866. Deborah Ann. oldest daughter of Philo and Phebe Olmstead, b. Dec. 9, 1817, d. Feb. 24, 1821. David Gray Olmstead, b. July 20, 1819, mar. Maria Strong Oct. 4, 1843, d. Aug. 11, 1846, at Walton, N. Y. He left a daughter, Ella, who mar. Egbert Chamberlain and now resides at Binghamton, N. Y.

"Hiram Olmstead, son of Philo and Phebe. mar. Sarah E. Hanford, June 25, 1848. Children: Mary Olmstead, b. Aug. 30, 1850; graduated Vassar College, class of '80, and taught in the High School at Fond du Lac, Wis.. for five years. Charles Olmstead, b. Feb. 1, 1853, is a Congregational Minister, and located at Oswego Falls, N. Y.; is married and has a son Clarence J. John Olmstead, b. Mar. 23, 1856, is a merchant in Walton; is mar. and has two children, Edith, and Bertis H. Hiram Betts Olmstead, b. Aug. 10, 1859, is mar. and a farmer at Walton; has a daughter. Carrie E. Olmstead, b. Aug. 8, 1862, has been a student at Elmira Female College. Henry Olmstead, b. Sept. 24, 1864. Julian H. Olmstead, b. Aug. 25, 1868. Altogether, we have five sons and two daughters. I was born Feb. 20, 1821, and Sarah E., my wife, was born Apr. 15, 1827.

"Sarah, daughter of Philo and Phebe Olmstead, b. Apr. 20,

1823, mar. Jeremiah B. Eells, Sept. 19, 1844. Children: Junius Hiram, mar. and has four children. Frederick, mar. and has one child. Betsey Ann, mar. and has three children. James R., d. 1886, aged 21 years. Sister Sarah and her children live at Walton, N. Y., where her husband is extensively engaged in the manufacture of wagons and carriages."

R. E. Gray, Esq., Treasurer of the Keystone Paint Company of Muncy, Pa., furnishes the following data of an interesting family of Quaker Grays, with whom he is connected:

"Our grandfather died before our father was married, I think, and we never knew anything concerning him, only that he came from Chester Co., Pa., when his family was small, and settled near Mount Pleasant, Ohio, and I think near a Quaker (Friends) Meeting, called Short Creek. He was a Quaker preacher. In my early days, I recollect my grand mother; she then lived in Monroe Co., Ohio. She died somewhere between 1884 and '85 I think. They had seven children that I know of: Samuel, Esther, David, Elijah, Thomas, Elisha, and John. They are all dead except Thomas. who is about 80 years of age.

"My father's name was David. He married Christiana Edgerton, of Belmont Co., Ohio. They had nine children: Richard E., Elijah H., Joseph, Elisha, Mary, Nathan, Sarah, Jesse, and Ann. I, Richard E., live here at Muncy, Pa. Married in Ohio, 1853, to Ann McCorhing. We have had six children, of whom four are living: Alice M., Emma, Viola, Albert M., Kate L., and Mary C. Kate L. died in 1877, aged 15 years. The remaining three daughters are married. My son is single.

"My brother Elijah H. Gray, was all through the late war, and was promoted in regular order from the ranks to Major. He married in Illinois, and raised a family of several children. He died shortly after the war, and I have lost track of his family.

"Brother Joseph was also in the late war; served two years. He married a lady in New Jersey and had two children; they now live in Dakota. His children's names are Willie and Louisa Gray.

" Brother Elisha Gray, of Telephone fame, lives at Highland Park, a suburban town near Chicago. He married Miss Delia Shepperd. They have four children, two girls and two boys: Minnie, Anna, Eddie and David Gray.

"Brother Nathan died, unmarried, at about the age of 22, in the army, at Nashville, Tenn.

"Mary married Charles Muchine, at New Sharon, Iowa; is a widow and has three children. Sarah married Henry Cope, and has two children; she also lives at New Sharon, Iowa. Sister Ann died when about twenty years of age.

"My father's brothers' and sisters' families are scattered and I cannot tell much about them. Nearly the whole of them moved to Camden, Jay Co., Indiana, a great many years ago, but I do not know where they are now."

In regard to the ancestry of this family, Prof. Elisha Gray, of Highland Park, writes: "I learn that early in the 18th century two brothers came to this country from some northern shire of Ireland, being of Scotch-Irish parentage. One of these brothers settled in Mass., and the other in eastern Pennsylvania; I am of the last named branch."

The following, from Governor Gray, of Indiana, strongly indicates relationship. as will be seen, to the foregoing family of Grays:

LETTER FROM GOVERNOR GRAY.

UNION CITY, IND., Nov. 24, 1884.

M. D. Raymond, Tarrytown, N. Y.

DEAR SIR:—Yours under date of Nov. 20th, inquiring after my ancestry is at hand. In reply will say, my ancestors were from England. My great-grandfather's name was Enoch Gray, grandfather's, Anthony, my father's, John. All my ancestors, from my father up, were Quakers, and residents of Chester Co., Pennsylvania, where I was born.

Very Truly Yours,

ISAAC P. GRAY.

ISAIAH GRAY,

The following sketch of a family of Grays whose early home was at Martha's Vineyard, Mass., is furnished by Dr. A. J. Gray, of this branch:

"Father's entire life was spent in Tisbury, Duke's County, Mass. He was by occupation a farmer. His life was comparatively uneventful. He was a man of uncompromising integrity; respected the rights of others as well as his own and in every relation exhibited a religion of deeds as well as of words.

"Of his paternal grandfather, the writer can give only a few facts. His name was Abijah. He lived in Evans, Erie County, New York. He was married twice, his first wife being the mother of all his children, ten or eleven in number, most of whom lived in Erie Co., N. Y. Of those children the writer can remember the names of Harrison, Daniel, Isaiah, Mary and of course, Franklin, who was my father. One of these brothers was the father of Dr. E. P. Gray, formerly of Buffalo, N. Y.

" Isaiah Gray, (whose wife was Mary Morgan,) had a family of eight children. The third son, who was named Alfred Gray, married Sarah Brice, of York, Livingston County, N. Y., in 1855. In 1857 he emigrated to Kansas, where he achieved distinction as Secretary of the State Board of Agriculture, and where he died January 23, 1880.

"Mary Gray, daughter of Abijah, lived and died at Vineyard Haven, Mass., and was the wife of Saunders Dunham.

"It may not be out of place, to say of the writer, that he was born in Tisbury, Mass., was educated in the Common Schools of his native place, in Pierce's Academy at Middleboro, Mass.; and the State Normal School, at Bridgewater, Mass. Taught school six years, studied medicine, graduating at Dartmouth College, N. H., in Oct. 1860. Was a Medical Officer in the Army, from 1862 to 1881; then resigned, to enter civil practice, at Cheyenne, Wyoming Territory."

Dr. A. J. Gray has since removed from Cheyenne to El Paso, Texas.

ISAIAH GRAY, lived and died at Tisbury, Martha's Vineyard, Mass.

ABIJAH GRAY, son of Isaiah, born at Tisbury, Mass., March 29, 1769; mar. Dolly Foster, who was born Aug. 4th, 1775, who d. Feb. 13, 1834; he d. Oct. 6, 1846. There were fourteen children. Abijah Gray was one of the first settlers at Evans, Erie Co., N. Y., and died there.

FRANKLIN GRAY, son of Abijah, b. Nov. 8, 1804; mar. 1st, Thankful D. Luce, who d. Aug., 1850; mar. 2d, Eunice Chase, 1857; he d. Oct. 7, 1870; Mrs. Gray resides at North Tisbury, Martha's Vineyard, Mass.

SARAH D. GRAY, dau. of Franklin Gray, b. May 3, 1834; mar. Capt. Jacob L. Cleveland, in 1852; he d. in 1870; there were four children, as follows: James, who d. in infancy; Thankful, b. 1853; mar. in 1876, Shadroch D. Tilton; one child, Helen Marion, b. in 1877. Henry J. is unmarried. Josephine, b. 1864, who married William Swift, in June, 1884.

FRANKLIN GRAY, Jr., d. in infancy.

ADONIRAM J. GRAY, Dr., son of Franklin, b. Oct. 28, 1837; mar. Alice Worth, dau. of Capt. and Mrs. Alice Banning Merry, and grand niece of Gen. William Worth, of Mexican War fame. No children. Present residence, El Paso, Texas.

There were four children by the second marriage of Franklin Gray: three of whom died in infancy; and a daughter, Hattie Hazleton, born 1862, mar. Geo. W. Evans, and resides at North Tisbury, Mass.

Gilbert Gray, son of Abijah, resides at Evans, N. Y., and has a son Frank Gray.

Abijah Gray had a brother, Freeman Gray, who had a son, William Gray, who resides at North Tisbury, and a daughter, Fostina Baxter, of West Tisbury, Mass. Also two sisters, Thankful, who mar. Mr. Clifford, and has a daughter, Elizabeth Clifford, at Woods Holl, Mass., and Katy Gray Allen, who had no children.

The ancestry of Isaiah Gray, the head of this line, is not apparent, but propinquity at least indicates that he may have been of the Yarmouth or Plymouth Grays.

REV. EDGAR HARKNESS GRAY, D. D.

FAMILY AND DESCENDANTS.

Rev. Edgar Harkness Gray, D. D., was born at Bridport, Vt., Nov. 15, 1813. Most of his youth was spent at that place, and there he commenced his studies for the ministry, graduating at Waterville College, Me., in 1838, and married to Mary Jane Rice, at Augusta Me., on the 13th of December following. He studied Theology with S. F. Smith, at Waterville, Me., and has supplied the largest Baptist Churches in Freeport and Bath, Me., Shelburne Falls, Mass., Washington, D. C., San Francisco, and Oakland, Cal., where he is at present actively engaged in the ministry at the advanced age of 73 years.

He had five children by his marriage, viz:

NATHANIEL OSCAR GRAY.
WILLIAM EDGAR GRAY.
MARY ELLA GRAY.
SARAH EMMA GRAY.
AUGUSTA ANNA GRAY.

While settled at Shelburne Falls Dr. Gray had repeated calls to go to larger churches in New York and Boston, but refused them all on account of the advantages of education his children there enjoyed. At the breaking out of the war he received a call from "F." St., Baptist Church, Washington, D. C., and accepted it. About this time Rochester University conferred upon him the degree of Doctor of Divinity, in acknowledgment of his great ability.

Within a few months after his residence at Washington, the late U. S. Senator Harris, of New York, called upon him to ascertain if he would take the nomination of Chaplain of the United States Senate, and obtaining his consent, he was unanimously elected. Abraham Lincoln was then President of the United States and the friendship that sprung up between them was unbroken until his death. During Dr. Gray's chaplaincy the U. S. Senate was composed of some of the ablest intellects of the day. Dr. Gray presided at the great Sanitary Commission Meeting in the House of Representatives when Lincoln, Colfax, Beecher, and others sat on the platform, and when the country was thrilled with the news of the assassination and death of President Lincoln Dr. Gray was one of the officiating clergy-men who pronounced the funeral oration and prayer in the presence of one of the most august bodies ever assembled in this country. He also officiated at the funeral of Thadeus Stevens. Upon the expiration of his term of office he was re-elected as Chaplain and served during Johnson's administration. Dr. Gray's entire life has been one of doing good to others. His life has been pure, unblemished and unstained, and his ability has placed him at the highest eminence attainable for a man in his calling, and his good work still continues.

Nathaniel Oscar Gray, the eldest son, was born while Dr. Gray was settled at Freeport, Me., on the 9th of May, 1841. He was sent to and graduated at Philips' Academy, Andover, Mass., in 1860, and from there to Brown University, at Providence, R. I., where he graduated in 1864. Studied law with M. L. Gray, Esq., and admitted to the Bar in St. Louis, Mo., October, 1867. Married Mary Taylor Johnson (sister of the Rev. Dr. Herrick Johnson, then President of the Theological Institute, of Auburn, N. Y.) at St. Louis, Mo., Dec. 13, 1869, by whom he has one son, Herrick Johnson Gray. The industry shown in the practice of his legal profession brought N. O. Gray into notice and prominence, and the successful issue of his cases soon became known and he was sought after by the largest corporations and most prominent banks, and entrusted with their legal business. Among his clients was Myra Clark Gaines, who retained him in preference to any other attorney in the State to recover for her large properties which she was legally entitled to covering some of the wealthiest portions of the city of St. Louis. He has been repeatedly urged to enter politics and become a candidate for the Supreme Bench, but his practice is so much more lucrative than any returns he could receive in office that he has persistently refused. His integrity is unquestioned and his ability is recognized by all who have had occasion to avail themselves of his services.

William Edgar Gray, the second son, was born at Shelburne Falls, Mass., on the 10th day of Jan. 1845, and followed a business career in preference to a profession. He obtained a position in the Treasury Department at Washington, D. C., in 1863, as Prize Money Cashier in the Fourth Auditor's Office, and left this after the close of the war and established a banking business in New York City in 1867. In 1870 he went to London, England, and engaged with a number of English and French bankers to buy up the entire Spanish debt of about £30,000,000 and which was then selling at about 13c. on the dollar, and by regulating the finances and revenues of the Gov't of Spain, by changing its policy and administration, intended carrying the price of the securities to about their par value. With the view of doing this, an arrangement was privately made with Queen Isabella, of Spain, to abdicate in favor of her son, Prince Alphonso, and the consent of the Pope was obtained to give the new King his papal blessing, and all seemed working well towards the success of the London syndicate and their plans in placing in the Spanish Cabinet its own officers to collect and regulate the Spanish revenues, when Germany proposed to put the Prince of Hohenzolern upon the Spanish Throne, which was so speedily resented by France that the result was a fierce but short war between the two nations. It was about this time that he met Bonnie Balfe, and married her in London, Jan. 4, 1877, Since then he has been engaged in promoting different American enterprises and placing their securities upon the London and European markets. He is at present the Financial Agent of The United States Land and Investment Company, of 145 Broadway, N. Y. City, and has had the placing of one million dollars of their bonds and one million of their stock, one half of which he has sold in the U. S., and the balance in London.

Of the three daughters, Mary Ella Gray, the eldest, died in Washington, D. C., May, 1869.

Sarah Emma, the second, is still unmarried but noted for her genial disposition and analytical mind, and is possessed of rare beauty and great personal accomplishments.

Augusta Anna Gray, the youngest daughter, married Prof. Henry Martyn Paul, of the Naval Observatory of Washington, D. C., in Aug. 1878.

The ancestral connection of Rev. Edgar H. Gray and his family with the Worcester Grays, appears on page 152.

EDWARD GRAY.

ARMS
GRANTED TO
EDWARD AND LYDIA
GRAY,

OF
LINCOLNSHIRE
ENGLAND,
1635.

GRAY.

EDWARD GRAY,

OF LINCOLNSHIRE AND BOSTON.

EDWARD GRAY, born in Lincolnshire, England, 1673, came to this country in 1686. He served an apprenticeship with Mr. Barton at Barton's Point, Boston, as a rope-maker. When he had earned enough for the purpose, he returned to England to visit his friends. On his coming down the English Channel he was impressed on board a man of war, whence he was released through the influence of the Surgeon, who knew his family. He then returned to Boston, where he again worked as a journey-man, and soon earned enough to hire a rope-walk, in which he was so successful that in a very short time he was able to pur-chase one. His business continued so prosperous that he was thereby enabled to live genteelly and to dispense liberal chari-ties.

In 1699 Mr. Gray married Susannah Harrison, by whom were seven children. She died June 4, 1713; he married 2d, Hannah Ellis, a niece of Rev. Dr. Coleman, of the Brattle St. Church, she having come over from England for that purpose. Dr. Coleman had told his wife that he had two nieces in England, and asked her if he should send for the one called "Lump of Love." She assented, and he accordingly sent for her, and soon after she arrived Mr. Gray married her. By her he had five children. He became an opulent merchant, and died July 2d, 1757, aged 84 years. He had lived a long and useful life, and left a handsome estate. Dr. Chauncey said of him in a funeral sermon, "He was unexceptionable, and unenvied except for his goodness." He was buried in the Granary Burying Ground on Tremont St., behind the Park St. Church, in his own tomb near the gate. By his will dated Feb. 12, 1753, witnessed by James Otis, Mr. Gray gives to his son John, the rope-walk, a brick warehouse adjoining, with yarn houses, knotting house, dwelling house and land, standing the whole length of the present Pearl street, and on "Cow Lane," now High St. and Atkinson St., and valued at £1,000. The whole estate was appraised at about £5,500. By the inventory he had ten colored slaves appraised at £246.

HON. HARRISON GRAY, b. 1701; mar. Elizabeth Lewis,
1734; was Treasurer of Province; left Boston with
British troops, 1776. Had Harrison, b. in 1740,
who d. in London, 1830; Lewis, who mar. Susannah
Jackson; John; and Elizabeth, b. 1746, who mar.
Samuel A. Otis, the Patriot, whence Harrison Gray
Otis.

EDWARD GRAY, (2) b. 1703; mar. Hannah Bridge; had Edward, (3) b. 1728; and Elizabeth, who. mar. David
Cheever. He d. 1740.

ANN GRAY, b. 1705; mar. Increase Blake, 1739; children: Increase, Benjamin, Joseph, Ellis G., Mary, and
Sarah Blake.

PERSIS GRAY, b. 1706.

SUSANNAH GRAY, b. 1708; mar. Col. Jos. Jackson, and
had Joseph, Henry, and Susannah, who mar. Lewis
Gray, son of Harrison Gray.

BETHIAH GRAY, b. 1710.

JOHN GRAY, b. 1713; mar. 1st, Mary Otis, of Barnstable;
May 14, 1761; mar. 2d, Mrs. Abigail Gridley; no issue.

REV. ELLIS GRAY.

REV. ELLIS GRAY, son of Edward (1) and Hannah Ellis Gray,
born 1715, married Sarah Tyler, 1739. He was colleague pastor of the Second Church, Hanover St., Boston, where his ministrations continued until his decease, which occurred Jan. 7th,
1753. He was buried in King's Chapel, William Tyler's Tomb.
He left issue as follows:

HANNAH GRAY, b. 1744, mar. Thos. Cary of Chelsea; one of
her daughters was the wife of Rev. Dr. Tuckerman.

ELLIS GRAY, (2), b. 1845, merchant, of Boston, mar. Sarah
Dolbeau, and d. 1781; she d. 1811, leaving a large property by
will. Issue:

ELLIS GRAY, (3).

THOMAS GRAY, b. 1779; d. Aug. 17, 1820.

SARAH GRAY, mar. Judge Hall of Boston; a son, Ellis
Gray Hall.

HANNAH GRAY, mar. 1st, Judge Wilson, of Washington; 2d, Dr. Bartlett, and had Caroline.

LUCY GRAY.

HARRIET GRAY.

THOMAS GRAY.

Thomas Gray, son Ellis (2), was a shipmaster and sea captain. He went to sea from Boston when only twelve years old, and had sailed around the world three times before he was twenty-one years of age. He was then made Captain, and was considered an excellent navigator. During the time of the French Embargo, his ship was captured and scuttled in mid ocean, involving also the loss of a valuable cargo. He was placed in the hold of the French vessel and received harsh treatment from his captors. He died at New York, Aug. 17, 1820. He had married Mary Wiswall, daughter of Daniel Wiswall and Rachel Close, and she died in New York, Aug., 1822, leaving the following issue:

SARAH GRAY, b. Oct. 25, 1806; mar. David Field, of Harrison, N. Y., Dec. 31, 1823; d. Jan. 1, 1883, at Harrison; left no descendants.

JOHN D. GRAY, b. Dec. 10, 1808; mar. Eliza B. Taylor, of New York, May 7, 1831; mar. 2d, Eliza Burns of White Plains, N. Y., where he died Oct. 20, 1872. He was for many years a prominent citizen of White Plains, (the county seat of Westchester county,) was twice elected Supervisor of the town, and served three terms as a Trustee of the village. Issue:

> EMMA GRAY.
> ALICE GRAY.
> GEO. T. GRAY.
> FRANK GRAY.

THOMAS GRAY, Jr., b. Jan. 4, 1811, mar. Charity Emlitch, in New York, Apr. 25, 1830; d. at Williamsburgh, N. Y., Aug. 13, 1856. Issue:

> THOMAS GRAY, d. June 18, 1864, from wounds received in the battle of the Wilderness.
> SARAH GRAY, mar. Abram Lossee; last known residence, Brooklyn, N. Y.
> MARY GRAY, mar. a Mr. Fowler; dec'd.
> JANE ANN GRAY.
> GEO. GRAY, was a soldier in the war for the Union; residence, Brooklyn, N. Y.
> JAMES GRAY; residence, Brooklyn.

DANIEL W. GRAY, son of Capt. Thomas, b. Nov. 29, 1814, mar. Sarah Field at Harrison, N. Y., Dec. 25, 1833, with whom he still continues to live, and where he has resided from early childhood. He is a highly esteemed citizen, and has several times been chosen Supervisor of his Town, and has filled other positions of trust. Issue:

> MOSES F. GRAY, of White Plains, N. Y., b. Dec. 4, 1834, mar. Sarah J. Pickford, of Brooklyn, May 7, 1863; mar. 2d, Sarah Smith. Children:
> > DANIEL W. GRAY, b. 1866.
> > ANNIE GRAY, b. 1868.
>
> JOHN D. GRAY, b. Oct. 28, 1836, mar. Maggie J. DeVoe, Sept. 28, 1870; resides at White Plains, N. Y.
>
> WILLIAM GRAY, b. Jan'y 16, 1839, mar. Susie Julian, of Brooklyn, June 17, 1863. Issue:
> > IDA GRAY, b. Jan. 13, 1865.
> > WILLIAM GRAY, b. Nov. 9, 1867.
> > SARAH GRAY, b. Aug. 11, 1869.
>
> CHAS F. GRAY, b. July 3, 1841, mar. Lydia Carpenter; resides in Brooklyn.
>
> GEORGE T. GRAY, b. Jan. 21, 1844; unmarried, and re- resides with his parents, Harrison, N. Y.
>
> MARY F. GRAY, b. Sept. 1, 1846; mar. John R. Bates; June 18, 1879; residence, Trumansburgh, N. Y.
>
> ELIZABETH T. GRAY, b. Dec. 26, 1848; mar. Charles M. Carpenter, May 29, 1878; issue: William Fields Carpenter.
>
> SARH GRAY, b. May 14, 1854, mar. Samuel J. Barnes, Nov. 12, 1879; children: Emily and Edith.

Ellis Gray (3), brother of Capt. Thos. Gray, was a lawyer, and is said to have lived in Boston. Not traced.

Ellis Gray (4), a son of Capt. Thomas Gray, d. young in New York.

WILLIAM GRAY, son of Rev. Ellis, b. 1747.
EDWARD GRAY, " "
SARAH GRAY, dau. of Rev. Ellis mar. Samuel Cary of Chelsea.

MARY GRAY, dau. of Edward (1), b. 1717; mar. Nathaniel Loring, of Hull, 1739.

SARAH GRAY, b. 1720; mar. Jeremy Green, Poet. Children: Edward, Sarah, Hannah, Nathaniel.

THOMAS GRAY, b. 1721; a bachelor; d. Oct. 1774.

WILLIAM GRAY.

WILLIAM GRAY, son of Edward (1), b. 1724; mar. Elizabeth
Hall, dau. of Capt. Stephen Hall of Charlestown, Dec. 7, 1759;
d. May 10, 1775; she d. at Jamaica Plains, Dec. 24, 1825. Issue:

> MARTHA HALL GRAY, b. Sept. 12, 1760; mar. Dr. Sam-
> uel Danforth, and d. July 4, 1790. Issue: Caroline,
> b. Oct. 1789, and d. 1832.
> STEPHEN HALL GRAY, b. Oct. 9, 1761; d. 1782.
> WILLIAM GRAY, b. Nov. 21, 1762; d. July 9, 1805.

EDWARD GRAY, (4) son of William, was b. July 16, 1764;
mar. Apr. 15, 1790, Susanna Turell, daughter of Madame Tur-
rell, a character famous in the revolutionary days. He was a
graduate of Harvard, an "Honest Lawyer," a man of note. See
"One Hundred Orators of Boston;" she d. Sept. 10, 1806; he
d. Dec, 27, 1810. Issue:

> MARY ANN GRAY, b. Nov. 27, 1793; mar. Wm. A. Fales; d.
> Feb. 22, 1850; issue: Edward Gray Fales; Jane Minot
> Fales, who mar. Geo. Lamb, of New Orleans; Mary Tur-
> ell Fales, who mar. Thomas Gray, M. D., of Boston; and
> Caroline Danforth Fales.

EDWARD GRAY, (5) b. Dec. 15, 1792; d. Dec. 23, 1810.
ELIZA GRAY, b. 1795; d. 1851.
SUSANNAH GRAY, b. 1797; d. 1808.
JOHN GRAY, b. Dec. 5, 1798; mar. 1st, Sarah Payne, of Brook-
lyn, Conn., who d. March 16, 1853; mar. 2d, Nancy John-
son, of Newburyport, Mass.; he d. Nov. 22, 1859. Issue:

> SUSAN E. GRAY, b. at Brooklyn, Conn., March 22,
> 1834; mar. 1st, Geo. S. Thorp, and had Marion
> Gray Thorp; he d. 1860, and she married 2d,
> Leon C. Magaw, and had Leona, James, Louis
> de Vincent, and Ethel.
> EDWARD GRAY, (6) b. 1840; d. at Worcester, Mass.,
> Sept. 21, 1859.
> WILLIAM SEARLES GRAY, b. June 1, 1846; mar. Mary
> Mason Jordan, and had Elizabeth Johnson
> Gray. He died in San Francisco, 1874.
> CATHARINE SEARLES GRAY, b. March 11, 1848, at
> Worcester; mar. Elisha Dodge, of Newburyport,
> and had Robert Gray Dodge, Edwin Sherrill
> Dodge, and Lawrence Paine Dodge.
> FANNY GRAY, b. Aug. 31, 1855, at Worcester; mar.
> Henry Little, of Newburyport.

REV. FREDERICK TURELL GRAY, son of Edward (4), b. Dec. 5, 1803; mar. Elizabeth P. Chapman; d. March 9, 1855; issue:

> FREDERICK TURELL GRAY, Jr.
> ELIZABETH GRAY.
> MARGARET CHAPMAN GRAY; mar. Francis Bacon of New York.
> EMILY GRAY.
> ELEANOR GRAY; mar. Patrick Jackson, of Boston.
> MARION PHILLIPS GRAY.

JOHN GRAY, son of William, b. Feb.14, 1768; a bachelor.

ELIZABETH S. GRAY, b. 1769; mar. Jacob Eustis, who d. Aug. 23, 1839. Issue: George, Elizabeth, Nathaniel, William.

REV. THOMAS GRAY, D. D.

Rev., THOMAS GRAY, D. D., son of William, was b. at the old homestead on Portland St., Boston, March 16, 1772. He graduated from Harvard, studied theology with Rev. Samuel Stillman, D. D., a celebrated divine and orator of the Revolution, and mar. his daughter, Deborah, May 23, 1793; was ordained at the Third Church, Roxbury, Mass., March, 1793; was pastor of the Unitarian Church, West Roxbury, for many years, and there he died and was buried. Issue:

GEORGE HARRISON GRAY, of Arlington, Mass., b. 1795, who mar. Ann Wakefield, dau. of Dr. Terence Wakefield, and had

> > GEORGIANNA GRAY, who mar. Horace H. Homer, of Arlington.
> > GEORGE HARRISON GRAY, Jr., who mar. Miss Bowker.
> > THOMAS GRAY, b. 1849, who mar. Miss Stowe, of Arlington.
> > JOHN GRAY, b. 1849, who mar. Miss Hill.
> > MARIA LANE GRAY.
> > ALICE BRIDGE GRAY.

HANNAH STILLMAN GRAY, dau. of Rev. Thomas Gray, b. 1796.

ANN GREENOUGH GRAY, dau. Rev. Thos., mar. Rev. George Whitney, of West Roxbury, and had Ann G. Whitney who mar. P. W. Turney, of New York; George Whitney; Caroline B. Whitney, who mar. Wm. F. Cabot, of Jamaica Plains; Herbert Whitney, who mar. Annie L. Fairbanks, of Boston.

DR. THOMAS GRAY.

THOMAS GRAY, Dr., writer and poet, son of Rev. Thomas, b. at the parsonage, Jamaica Plains, 1801; was a member of the so called Rebellion class at Harvard; took his degree of B. A.; took his degree as Doctor of Medicine both here and in France. He mar. his cousin, Mary Turell Fales, daughter of Wm. A. Fales and Mary Ann Gray, in Brunswick, Me., 1832. He was author of "The Vestal," "A Tale of Pompeii," a prize poem on "The Settlement of Roxbury," besides many other pieces in prose and poetry, hymns, glees, etc. He died in Boston, March, 1849. Issue:

> MARY ANN GRAY, mar. Guy Byram Schott, of Phila., Pa.
>
> ALICE GRAY, mar. Gedney K. Richardson, of Boston. Children: Caroline M., Marion, and Ruth Richardson.
>
> CAROLINE FALES GRAY, mar. J. B. F. Davidge, of Washington, D. C.; he d. at Paris.
>
> T. FALES GRAY, b. July 4, 1849; mar. Elleanor Thompson Powell, dau. of Charles Powell, Esq., of County Salop, England, Feb. 4, 1885.

BENJAMIN GRAY, son of Edward (1), b. 1726; married Mary Blanchard, and had

> BENJAMIN GRAY; not traced.

The foregoing brief sketch and record of the family of Edward Gray, of Lincolnshire and Boston, is furnished by T. Fales Gray, Esq., of Boston, who is of that line:

FAIRFIELD GRAYS.

The fact that the Gray family was largely represented among
the early settlers of Fairfield County, Conn., was soon ascertained by the compiler of this genealogical record, but it seemed
probable at first that they were among other pioneers from the
Colony of Plymouth and Massachusetts Bay who had pushed on
toward the frontiers on the line of westward emigration, and so
helped to people the sister Colony of Connecticut. And this
reasonable inference found ready confirmation in the discovery
that the Grays of Beverly and Yarmouth had representatives at
an early day in Litchfield Co., and in the northern part of Fairfield, and along the adjoining "Oblong." However, further research dispelled that theory, and disclosed the fact that there
was a very early and doubtless direct emigration of Grays to old
Fairfield, Conn. The records show that there were two brothers, John and Henry Gray, among the first settlers, in 1643.
They had married sisters, daughters of William Frost, who and
his family had come with them from Nottingham, England. Henry
is said to have been a man of consequence, and represented his
town at the General Court. He had married Lydia Frost, and
was in middle life when he migrated to this country. He died
about 1658, aged probably fifty years. He left four sons: Jacob,
Henry, Levi and William Gray. John Gray, brother of Henry, had
married Elizabeth Frost, but the names of his children cannot
be definitely determined. The name of William Gray of Fairfield appears on the early records of Westchester Co., N. Y.,
as having been appointed Administrator of the estate of his
brother Levi, date of June 3, 1684, who had paid church rates
in Eastchester Mar. 30, 1678. A "home lot" had been granted
to William Gray, on the 9th of November, 1680. His name
again appears on the records of Westchester Co., as having paid
church rates in the town of Eastchester in 1692; and again, the
real estate records show that "William Gray of Fayrefield in
Conn., weaver, sold his home lot in Eastchester," date of April
23d, 1697. It is not known whether he then returned to Fairfield, but that some of his descendants remained is evidenced by
the fact that the name of William Gray appears on record there

in 1775, and on a map of Westchester County date of 1779, William Gray's place, in the town of Eastchester, is noted. None of the name of Gray, have, however, at any recent date, resided in that vicinity. The name of John Gray, as will be seen, was perpetuated in Fairfield in a line of descent that cannot be traced to Henry, and doubtless is of the descendants of John, although the connecting links do not appear. The records show that William Frost, as well as his sons-in-law, the brothers Gray, were owners of large estates, which they distributed by gift and by will among their children and descendants. William Frost's will was made Jan'y 6, 1644. It is a unique document, and is published in full in Trumbull's Colony Records, I., p. 465. The names of the three children of his daughter Elizabeth by a previous marriage are therein mentioned, viz: Luke, Susannah, and Johanna Watson. He also remembers "John Gray's own two children," without naming them. He mentions his sons Daniel and Abraham, and a daughter Mary, to whom he gave all the goods and estate he had in "old England." He gave ten pounds toward a meeting house to be built for the town of Uncowah, the aboriginal title of Fairfield. Henry Gray appears to have been the principal legatee, and he was named as executor. Francis Purdy, the ancestor of the numerous family by that name, was a witness to the will.

The following is the genealogical record of these families of Grays as far as recorded:

DESCENDANTS OF HENRY GRAY.

HENRY GRAY, mar. Lydia Frost; d. at Fairfield, Conn., 1658; issue:

> JACOB GRAY.
> HENRY GRAY (2).
> LEVI GRAY.
> MARY GRAY.
> WILLIAM GRAY.
> SARAH GRAY.

Henry Gray (2) had

> ISAAC GRAY.
> WILLIAM GRAY (2), b. 1685.
> HENRY GRAY (3).

All the above sons of Henry Gray (2), received gifts of land from their father date of 1708.

WILLIAM GRAY, (2).

WILLIAM GRAY (2), b. Fairfield, Conn., 1685, mar. 1st, Abigail Cooley, Dec. 23, 1714; mar. 2d, Elizabeth Meaker, Oct. 31, 1716. Issue:

STEPHEN GRAY, b. Nov. 7, 1715.
WILLIAM GRAY, (3), b. Aug. 17, 1717.
ABIGAIL GRAY, b. May 7, 1719.
ELIZABETH GRAY, b. Apr. 12, 1721.
EBENEZER GRAY, b. Mar. 29, 1723.
JABEZ GRAY, b. Oct. 11, 1728.
THADDEUS GRAY, b. Oct. 27, 1730.
JOSEPH GRAY, b. Oct. 11, 1732.
ELISHA GRAY, b. June 1, 1735.
JOSHUA GRAY, b. Sept. 22, 1738.

William Gray (2), d. Aug. 27, 1761, and his wife Elizabeth d. July 6, 1772. He made a will May 5, 1759, which was admitted to probate Oct. 6, 1761, and is on file in the old records of Fairfield.

WILLIAM GRAY, (3).

William Gray (3), and Sarah Disbrow, dau. of Thos. Disbrow, were mar. at Fairfield, Jan. 25, 1742; she d. Oct. 27, 1778. Issue:

MOSES GRAY, b. Aug. 11, 1743; d. Oct. 15, 1812.
ELIAS GRAY, b. Apr. 4, 1746.
OLIVE GRAY, b. Dec. 3, 1748; d. July 6, 1778.
SARAH GRAY, b. Apr. 1751; d. April 26, 1792.
AMOS GRAY, b. Mar. 17, 1753; d. Mar. 30, 1803.
ELIZABETH GRAY, b. Jan. 8, 1755; d. July 6, 1772.
LYDIA GRAY, b. Jan. 18, 1757; d. Dec. 30, 1786.

ELIAS GRAY.

Elias Gray removed to New Fairfield, and died there Nov. 27, 1826. His will was admitted to probate Dec. 16, 1826, and by it he bequeathed to his wife, Jemima, one-third of his estate. He also gave legacies to Amos Nickerson, son of his dec'd daughter Huldah, to John and Anna Wheeler, children of his dec'd daughter Sarah, to his daughter Anna, wife of Joseph Covell, daughter Polly, wife of Cyrus Gray, and daughter Olive. His sons Allan and Russell were appointed his sole executors. He also had a son William (4), and a daughter Eunice.

Elias Gray was three times married; 1st to Eunice ————,
who died August 25, 1782. He married 2d, Anna ————,
who died February 3, 1786; he married 3d, Jemima Barnum,
daughter of Richard Barnum of Danbury, who died March 27,
1828. Captain Richard Barnum was a son of Captain John
Barnum of Danbury, who was eldest son of Deacon Richard
Barnum, who was third son of Thomas Barnum, one of the first
settlers of Danbury in 1684, who was born July 9, 1663, son of
Thos. Barnum, of Norwalk.

The first marriage had taken place in old Fairfield, but
soon after the birth of the first born son the removal to New
Fairfield must have been made, as the following, copied from
the church records of the latter place evidences: "Elias Gray,
January 26, 1772, admitted to ye Privilege of Baptism for his
children on ye account of a Recommendation from the Rev'd
Mr. Reepley of Green's Farms," a Parish in the town of Fairfield.

DESCENDANTS OF ELIAS GRAY.

WILLIAM GRAY (4), b. June 24, 1767; d. Sept. 22, 1844.

HULDAH GRAY, dau. of Elias and Eunice Gray, b. June 13,
1769, mar. Mr. Nickerson; d. May 26, 1803.

SARAH GRAY, dau. of Elias and Eunice Gray, b. Sept. 4, 1778,
mar. Nathan Wheeler; d. Nov. 21, 1815.

ALLAN GRAY, son of Elias, b. May 10, 1781, lived and died at
Rhinebeck, N. Y. Had a son, Rev. Firmin Gray, a noted Meth-
odist preacher, who had a son and two daughters; lived near
Hyde Park, Dutchess Co., N. Y.

ANNA GRAY, dau. of Elias and Anna Gray, b. Jan. 27, 1786,
mar. Joseph Covell.

EUNICE GRAY, eldest daughter of Elias and Jemima Gray,
born Nov. 16, 1788, mar. Joseph Sherwood, and had a son Orrin
Sherwood who d. Mar. 31, 1839; she also had Olivia, who mar.
Henry Sturtevant of Bridgeport, Conn., and Amanda Sherwood,
both dec'd; she d. Sept. 27, 1838.

OLIVE GRAY, dau. of Elias and Jemima Gray, b. Sept. 23,
1790, d. Mar. 8, 1829.

RUSSELL GRAY, son of Elias and Jemima Gray, b. July 24,
1794, mar. Hannah Jones Sept. 4, 1817; he d. at Eddyville,
Iowa, Apr. 29, 1859; she d. same place, Aug. 23, 1877. Issue:

BENJAMIN JONES GRAY, b. at New Fairfield, Conn., June 30,
1819, d. at Sacramento, Cal., Dec. 2, 1849; "Was one of
nature's noblemen, an honor to his name."

AUSTIN GRAY, Rev., b. at New Fairfield, Feb. 28, 1821, mar.
July 18, 1847, to Sarah Elizabeth Brush. Issue:

> HIRAM BURROUGHS GRAY, b. at Washington, D. C.,
> July 16, 1848; d. Omaha, Neb., May 28, 1866.
>
> MARY ELIZABETH GRAY, b. Dec. 25, 1850; d. Mar.
> 15, 1852.
>
> EDWARD FARLEY GRAY, b. Apr. 29, 1853.
>
> GEORGE FRANK GRAY, b. Nov. 25, 1854, mar. Oct.
> 10, 1880, to Regina Hetrich, of Cowley Co.,
> Kansas. Children: Mary Mahala, dec'd, and
> Orpha.
>
> MARY AMELIA GRAY, b. at Eddyville, Iowa, Feb. 26,
> 1850, mar. Samuel W. Loughridge, Dec. 24,
> 1885.

JAMES WILLIS GRAY, b. July 23, 1824, mar. Aug. 26, 1846, to
Ann Webster; d. at Albion, N. Y., Mar. 31, 1880. "He
was much beloved by all who knew him."

HIRAM BURROUGHS GRAY, b. at New Fairfield, Conn., Oct. 13,
1828, d. at Steubenville, Ohio, April 12, 1849; a youth
of high hopes and bright promise.

POLLY GRAY, dau. of Elias and Jemima, b. Mar. 7, 1802, mar.
Cyrus Gray, at New Fairfield, May 10, 1821; he d. at Yorkville,
N. Y. She still survives, and resides with a grandaughter, Sarah
Frances Gray, at Norwalk, Conn.

WILLIAM GRAY, (4).

WILLIAM GRAY, (4), son of Elias was b. in old Fairfield,
June 24, 1767; mar. 1st, Sarah Jennings, of Danbury, Conn.,
1793; she d. Nov. 13, 1806. Issue:

ISAAC GRAY, b. in Fairfield, Co., Sept. 6, 1793.

ELIAS GRAY, b. Kent, Conn., June 25, 1795; was in naval service war of 1812, and severely wounded; d. July 26, 1818.

MARY GRAY, b. Kent, July 25, 1797; mar. John Kelley, Sept.
30, 1820; d. Providence, R. I. 1880.

ANSON GRAY, b. Ridgebury, Conn., July 23, 1799; d. Jan. 9,
1876.

EUNICE GRAY, b. North Salem, N. Y., Oct. 2, 1801; married
Geo. Eastwood, Apr. 15, 1822; d. Aug. 18, 1825.

William Gray (4) mar. 2d, Mary Higgins, of South-East, Putnam Co., N. Y., May 12, 1807; she d. Mar. 6, 1820, in the 46th
year of her life.   Issue:

> SARAH GRAY, b. Dec. 5, 1808.
> WILLIAM GRAY (5), b. Oct. 22, 1810.
> HARVEY GRAY, b. March 9, 1812.
> LEWIS GRAY, b. Feb. 5, 1814.
> ALLEN GRAY, b. April 8, 1816.

William Gray (4), mar. 3d, Annie Stevens, Aug. 22, 1821, who
survived him.   Were no children by this marriage.   Mr. Gray
spent some years in Dutchess Co., N. Y., where he owned and
cultivated a farm, and several of his children were born, but
returned to the old homestead in New Fairfield after his father's
death, where he died Sept. 22, 1844.   It is said of him, that as
a boy, during the trying times of the Revolution, he exhibited not a little of the fervor of the true patriotic spirit.   The
incursion of Gov. Tyron and his tory troops up through Connecticut to Danbury, and the destruction of that town, aroused
to arms all the patriots in that vicinity, and Elias Gray, with his
neighbors, rallied in response to the urgent call, and marched to
meet the foe, he leaving the youthful William with the panic-
stricken household, with strict injunctions not to depart there-
from; but the martial spirit of the Grays so fired the boy's
heart that, soon after the departure of his father, arming himself
with an old fowling-piece, he followed after, and having come in
sight of the retreating column of the enemy, from the secure
breastwork of a convenient stone wall, blazed away at the Brit-
ishers.   It is said that the castigation administered to this young
hopeful for his constructive disobedience on that occasion, was
the slightest ever known to have been applied by the hand of
that stern parent and valiant patriot, Elias Gray.

Sarah Gray, daughter of William and Mary Higgins Gray,
was born in Clinton, Dutchess Co., N. Y., Dec. 5th, 1808;
mar. James Vance in New York city, 1830.   They removed to
San Antonio, Texas, where Mr. Vance built Government Stores,
furnished supplies for the U. S. Army, bought real estate, and
became very prosperous.   A grand daughter, Mary Vance, of
San Antonio, only remains.

WILLIAM GRAY, (5).

William Gray (5), son of William Gray (4) and Mary Higgins, was born on Monday, Oct. 22d, 1810, in the town of Clinton, Dutchess Co., N. Y. He there grew up to manhood and spent several years learning the business of a country store in the town of Dover Plains, N. Y. In 1830 he went to New York city to engage in mercantile life, and there resided and continued in business until 1880. He then removed to Nyack-on-the Hudson, where he continues to reside, at his beautiful country-seat, "Gray Court."

Mr. Gray, gifted with tastes above his early opportunities for their improvement, redeemed many an hour from the drudgery of apprenticeship in a village store, for communion with nature, and with those poets who are her best interpreters, which he made the companion of his walks in the woods and fields of his native Dutchess, Bryant being his special favorite. And the poetic taste and temperament so developed in him, has given an afterglow to his later life, which still has much of the fire and fervor and enthusiasm of youth.

Mr. Gray's memory was always remarkably retentive, and a poem, or portion of history once read, could be repeated by him to the letter. It is said that his mother also had a wonderful memory, and that he inherited from her much of his poetic and literary taste. Though not having had the advantages of a classical education, he won and enjoyed the lifelong friendship of Bryant, and other distinguished men of letters. He has also rare comprehension of political history, and has positive and well established political opinions. He has fine business capacity, and his eight years of service as Cashier in the Comptroller's Office of the city of New York, was a sufficient test of the integrity and firmness of his character.

Mr. Gray was married to Lavinia, daughter of Rebecca Wharton and John Titus Johnson, at their residence on Rutger Street, New York, Nov. 14th, 1837. She died March 21, 1853, and he was married again, Aug. 23, 1855, to Harriet D., daughter of John Milton and Sarah A. Tabor, at Dover Plains, Dutchess Co., N. Y.

CHILDREN OF WILLIAM AND LAVINIA GRAY.

William Cullen Bryant Gray, the first born, and eldest son of William Gray and Lavinia Johnson, was born at No. 40, Rutgers St., New York, the residence of his maternal grand-parents, Sept. 15, 1839. He was named after the distinguished poet, W. C. Bryant, and himself developed much literary taste and talent. He was educated in the public schools of New York, graduating with honor at N. Y. College, 1860. On the breaking out of the Rebellion he returned from Texas, where he had been spending the winter previous with friends, and joined the army of the Union, receiving a commission as 1st Lieut. in the 4th N. Y. Artillery. He was soon promoted to the position of Aide-de-Camp on Gen. Doubleday's Staff, where he served with distinction during the campaign of 1862, participating in the engagements on the Rapidan, Rappahannock, and the second battle of Bull Run.

But the honorable career of this gallant and noble youth was cut short in the morning of his high hopes. He died at the Georgetown Hospital, D. C., Jan. 1, 1863, having been taken seriously ill about a week previous. With the delirious exclamation, "*Forward! march!*" he soon sank back into his last sleep. Bryant Gray was not only a gallant patriot soldier, ardent and true, but he was in many respects a youth of high endowments and bright promise. This shines forth on every page of the beautiful memoir of his life prepared and published by his pastor, Rev. Dr. Thompson, of the Broadway Tabernacle Church, New York. Among the tributes which there appear, are the following stirring lines written by the poet Bryant, on hearing of his enlistment, and which seem almost prophetic of his fate:

> "Think that the cause is half divine
> That girds thee with the warrior's brand,
> And be the steadfast purpose thine
> To wield it with a stainless hand.
>
> "Then when the storm of war is stilled,
> Tears warm and soft as summer rain
> Shall welcome him who, from the field
> Brings back a life without a stain.
>
> "Or should'st thou perish in the strife,
> The tears that weep thy death shall flow
> For one who gave a stainless life
> To shield his country from the foe."

MARY HIGGINS GRAY, dau. of William and Mary Higgins Gray, b. Feb. 15, 1844; resides with her father's family at Nyack, N. Y.

WHARTON J. GRAY, b. Aug. 17, 1847, mar. Fannie M. Huyler, of Nyack, N. Y., 1876; issue: Ethel Gray, b. June 14, 1877; residence and business, New York.

AMELIA GRAY, mar. in 1874 to John F. Harman; issue: Bryant Gray Harman, b. Nov. 1, 1878; Elsie Harman, b. May 19, 1882; Helen Harman, b. Oct. 5, 1884. Mr. Harman is of the firm of Handy & Harman, dealers in bullion and specie, New York, and resides in Plainfield, New Jersey.

ALICE GRAY, mar. in 1878, to William Wilson Clay; issue: Christabel Clay, b. Mar. 26, 1879; Percy Clay, April 15, 1880, d; William Wharton Clay, b. Sept. 29, 1882. Mr. Clay is an Architect in Chicago, where he has a large and prosperous business.

CHILDREN OF WILLIAM AND HARRIET D. TABOR GRAY.

BABY GRAY, b. May 20, 1862, d. April 16, 1864.
LILLIAN GRAY, b. Oct. 21, 1865.
WILLIAM GRAY (6), b. May 25, 1867, New York city.

HARVEY GRAY.

Harvey Gray was born in Clinton, Dutchess Co., N. Y., and settled in Bristol, Conn., 1836, having previously resided for a few years at Southington, Conn., at which place he was married to Mary Woodruff, Oct. 16, 1831. He continued to reside at Bristol until his death, May 8, 1883, he having with his wife celebrated their golden wedding two years previous. Mr. Gray had much mechanical genius, and was engaged in the manufacture of clocks, water wheels, etc.; was at the head of a large business. His death was much regretted by his friends and townspeople, by whom he was beloved and esteemed for his noble, consistent character, and he was honored by in memoriam notices in which his activity in organizing Young Men's Christian Associations, and interest in every good work for the welfare of his fellow men, were thoroughly recognized. Children and descendants:

HORACE GRAY, son of Harvey, was b. at Southington, Conn., July 16, 1832; was married to Julia Perry, June 26th, 1854. Enlisted under Col. Joseph Hawley, in the 7th Conn. Vols., in the war for the Union; was wounded at Fort Wagner, and d. at Charleston, S. C., July 12, 1863.

> HELEN ALICE GRAY, daughter of Horace, b. May 4, 1855, mar. C. T. Olcott, and resides at Bristol.

CHARLES GRAY, son of Harvey, b. in Bristol, Conn., May 15, 1847, was married to Harriet R. Baldwin, Mar. 29, 1871; is book keeper and cashier for Cheney Bros., New York; residence, Brooklyn; children:

> ALICE LOUISE GRAY, b. in Bristol, Jan. 20, 1873.
> MARY ARLINE GRAY, " " Jan. 30, 1875; d. in Brooklyn, Jan. 20, 1886.

The widow of Harvey Gray resides at Bristol, Conn.

LEWIS GRAY, son of William (4), b. 1814, mar. to Jane Ann Van Siclin, b. in Canada, July 14, 1822, at the city of New York, by the Rev. Dr. Sawyer, Sept. 5, 1843; she d. at Crotonville, N. Y., Sept. 25, 1883. Present residence of Mr. Gray, Jersey City. Issue:

> GEO. B. GRAY, b. Dec. 11, 1844; mar. to Antoinette See, at Sing Sing, N. Y., Sept. 4, 1864.
> ALLEN F. GRAY, b. July 1, 1846; mar. Ellen L. Hughes, in Jersey City, Sept. 14, 1876.
> FRANCIS L. GRAY, b. Aug. 8, 1847.
> MARY B. GRAY, b. March 5, 1851; mar. John J. Reynolds, in New York, June 7, 1869.

Allen Gray, son of William Gray (4), and Mary Higgins Gray, mar. Eliza Jane Smith, daughter of Gershom B., and Temperance Smith, of Norwalk Islands, Conn., Sept. 25, 1844. Issue:

> ADA BYRON GRAY, b. July 5, 1845; d. in city of New York, Dec. 22, 1857.
> ARLINE AUGUSTA GRAY, b. Nov. 17, 1846; mar. in Christ Church, Brooklyn, Nov. 19, 1873, to Jas. E. Wilson, of that city. Issue: Charles Gray Wilson, b. Aug. 27, 1874.
> LESLIE HIGGINS GRAY, b. at Little Rock, Arkansas, Feb. 4th, 1850.

Allen Gray was formerly member of the large clothing house, firm of Smith & Gray, Williamsburgh, but has now retired with a handsome competence, his son Leslie Gray, taking his place in business.

ISAAC GRAY.

Isaac Gray, eldest son of William (4), mar. Miss Conant, Jan. 2, 1813; he died at Hyde Park, Pa., in May, 1853. Issue :

JOSHUA GRAY, who died at Janesville, Wis., where his widow, Margaret Gray, and children, William, Henry, Sarah, Gertie, Charles, and Rosa Gray, are still living. A daughter Demma, d. and left two children. William is married and has a son George. Another son of Joshua, George Gray, died in the war.

SARAH GRAY, b. Dec. 5, 1808, in Clinton, Dutchess Co., N.Y.

MELISSA GRAY, dau. of Isaac, mar. 1st, a Mr. Folger, by whom she had two children: William and Parthena; she mar. 2d, David Ayers, by whom she has had Franklin and Jennie; she now resides near New Hampton, Iowa.

ABBIE GRAY, dau. of Isaac, mar. a Mr. Hoover, and lives at Weatherby, Pa.; has three children.

ELIZA GRAY, dau. of Isaac, mar. George Baldwin, and lives at Cherokee, Iowa; has a son Eugene.

HENRY GRAY, son of Isaac, is married, and lives near his sister Eliza; has one child.

ALONZO GRAY, son of Isaac, d. leaving two children: Joseph, mar., but residence unknown; Mary, who mar. Geo. N. McCullow, and resides at Sanborn, Iowa; has several children.

MARY GRAY, dau. of Isaac, mar. Henry Knight, and lives at Apple Creek, Neb.; a daughter, Louisa.

AMOS GRAY, son of Isaac, has several children; resides in Minn.

EGBERT H. GRAY, son of Isaac, was b. at Pawlings, Dutchess Co., N. Y., Oct. 18, 1821; mar. Sarah Pepper, b. at Hyde Park, Pa., Feb. 27, 1827. Children:

> PHEBE JANE GRAY, b. Centre Rock, Wis., Jan. 3, 1854; d.
>
> EFFIE A. GRAY, b. Janesville, Wis., Dec. 29, 1854; mar.
> C. E. Warren; has two children, Clarence and Pearl; residence, Postville, Iowa.
>
> BOADICEA GRAY, b. Janesville, Apr. 1, 1858; mar. P. C. Shipton, and has a daughter, Gladie; residence, Edgewood, Iowa.
>
> ALONZO B. GRAY, b. Janesville, Sept. 7, 1861; Cadet at West Point, class of '87.
>
> VIENNA GRAY, b. in Eden, Iowa, Dec. 10, 1864; mar. James Egan; residence, Waucoma, Iowa.
>
> MINNIE J. GRAY, b. Eden, Iowa, Aug. 19, 1867.
>
> BERT U. GRAY, b. at Waucoma, Iowa, Jan. 17, 1870.
>
> LULU ALTHEA GRAY, b. same place, Dec. 23, 1874.

Egbert H. Gray was instantly killed by a falling building, June 17, 1884. Mrs. Sarah Gray, resides at Waucoma, Iowa.

EBENEZER GRAY.

Ebenezer Gray, son of William (2), b. Mar. 29, 1723, mar. a Miss Lockwood, sister of John and Sarah Lockwood, and lived in Weston, Conn., where he died Sept. 20, 1777. He had lived for a time at Pawling, in Dutchess Co., N. Y., for the record shows that his son Ebenezer was born there. He had a daughter who had married a Mr. Hubbel, and died May 4th, 1813. Whether there were other children it is not easy to determine. Mrs. Gray was b. Apr. 19, 1733, and d. Mar. 4, 1810, having survived her husband nearly 33 years.

EBENEZER GRAY, (2.)

Quotation from record of Ebenezer Gray (2), "who was born in Pawling town, so called, on the east side of Great Swamp, so known at that time, in the State of New York, on the 8th day of May in the year of our Lord Christ 1766. But his parents removing when he was about two years old to Weston, Conn., he was brought up there until he was in his 21st year, and then went into Pawling town where he was born, and there found his wife, Sarah Burdick, when a girl." Sarah Burdick was a daughter of Amos and Martha Burdick, born Sept. 2d, 1774, and married to Ebenezer Gray, July 14, 1791. He had "gone abroad," as he quaintly expresses it in the voluminous diary which he kept, and which is still preserved,—on coming of age, and journeying up the country on foot he finally reached Fishkill, and so crossed over the river to Newburg, but shortly returned to the vicinity where he was born, and engaged for several years in teaching school at a place then called Franklin, N. Y. And there he found and married his wife as already related. He returned from there to Weston, Conn., in 1793, where he continued to reside for over 30 years. He was evidently a man of decided character and more than ordinary ability. He died in the city of New York, Aug. 23, 1829; she also died there Feb. 11, 1830. The following is a list of their descendants as full as it was possible to ascertain them:

JAMES L. GRAY, son of Ebenezer (2), was b. Dec. 2, 1792, at Pawling, N. Y. He had among other children a daughter Angeline, who married John Ash of New York; had two children.

CYRUS W. GRAY, son of Ebenezer (2), b. May 18, 1794, at Weston, Conn., mar. Polly Gray, youngest dau. of Elias and Jemima Barnum Gray, at New Fairfield, Conn., May 10, 1821. He died at Yorkville, N. Y., July 24, 1855; his widow, Polly Gray, resides at Norwalk, Conn. Issue:

HARRIS AUGUSTUS GRAY, b. July 23, 1823.
RICHARD SYLVESTER GRAY, b. Aug. 14, 1825, d.
KATHARINE JANE GRAY, b. Dec. 9, 1827, d. July 26, 1830.
MARY LOUISA GRAY, b. Sept. 6, 1830, d. same date.
EMILY JANE GRAY, b. Feb. 22, 1835, d. Apr. 16, 1840.
FRANKLIN HENRY GRAY, b. Aug. 17, 1837, d. Sept. 8, 1838.
WILLIAM HENRY GRAY, b. Jan. 25, 1841.
THEODORE DEWITT GRAY, b. Jan. 8, 1845, d. Feb. 19, 1849.

Harris A. Gray, son of Cyrus Wm., married Martha Jane Keller, of New York, August 20th, 1872; residence, Brooklyn; no children.

Richard Sylvester Gray, son of Cyrus, married Mary Jane Hollenbeek, Dec. 31, 1849, who d. May 28, 1856, in New York; mar. 2d, Almira L. Hollenbeek, Jan. 31, 1857, who d. Aug. 11, 1876; he d. Issue:

MARY ALICE GRAY, b. Nov. 30, 1850; mar. Martin Davis, of Wilton, Conn.; has two children, Leverda and Archibald; resides in Ridgefield, Conn.
HENRIETTA JANE GRAY, b. Aug. 8, 1852; mar. Jeremiah Slawson of Norwalk; four children : Mary, Ralph, Freddie and Edward.
SARAH FRANCES GRAY, b. Apr. 9, 1858 ; residence, Norwalk.
CYRUS WILLIAM GRAY, b. Nov. 5, 1859, mar. Anna Goodwin, Nov. 27, 1876; residence, Norwalk.
RICHARD SYLVESTER GRAY, Jr., b. Apr. 15, 1862, mar. Nellie McGonigal; residence, Norwalk, Conn.

HIRAM BURDICK GRAY, son of Ebenezer (2), b. March 22d, 1801, mar. Nancy Hager, Dec. 14, 1847, at Reynoldsville, N. Y.; he d. Jan. 27, 1872; she resides in New York with her son, John H.; issue:

JOHN HIRAM GRAY, b. Aug. 20, 1852; mar. Dec. 10, 1873, to Lizzie E. Beers, of New York; resides in N. Y. city, and dealer in real estate; children:

WILLIAM HIRAM GRAY, b. April 14, 1875.
FANNIE GRAY, b. July 10, 1877.
FLORENCE GRAY, b. Jan. 12, 1880.
JOHN GRAY, b. Oct. 31, 1882; d. Apr. 30, 1884.
KITTY GRAY, b. Dec. 24, 1884.

GEO. W. GRAY, son of Hiram B., b. Dec. 25, 1855; d. Mar. 6, 1885.

AUGUSTUS BURDICK GRAY, b. Apr. 2, 1861; mar. Mary Case, of Trumansburg, N. Y., June 23, 1882; resides at Poughkeepsie; children:

GEORGE W. GRAY, b. Jan. 17, 1885.
NANCY ISABEL GRAY, b. April 9, 1886.

WM. HENRY GRAY, son of Cyrus Wm., is married and has a family; resides in Brooklyn.

HORATIO NELSON GRAY, son of Ebenezer (2), b. Apr. 13, 1806; mar. Maria Satterlee, of Delhi, N. Y.; he d. May 27th, 1881; she resides at Yorkville, N. Y.; issue:

CHARLES N. GRAY, b, Nov. 14, 1868.

EBENEZER LOCKWOOD GRAY b. Apr. 22, 1808, d. July 14, 1816.

WARREN CORBIN GRAY, b. Apr. 26, 1810; mar. Jane E. Brower; issue : Warren Gray, of Phila.; Abram Gray, dec'd; Jennie Gray, and Addie Gray, who mar. a Mr. Douglas, and has a daughter Ella, all of Philadelphia. Warren Corbin Gray was lost at sea by the burning of the steamship *Melville*, off the coast, on the way from New York to Port Royal, Jan. 8, 1863.

SARAH BURDICK GRAY, dau. of Ebenezer (2), b. Jan. 13, 1812; mar. Rev. Gabriel Smith, of St. Joseph, Mich.

EPHENETUS CROSBY GRAY, son of Ebenezer (2), b. Apr. 17, 1816, mar. Elizabeth McDonald; issue: Mary Elizabeth, who mar. Geo. R. Tifft, of Buffalo, N. Y.; McDonald Gray, dec'd; and Leonora Gray. Mr. Gray was a lawyer in the city of New York, where he died March 7th, 1852.

Jabez Gray, son of William (2), b. Oct. 11, 1728, mar. Betty Hecox, Jan. 17, 1753, and had Betty, bapt. Feb. 23, 1755; and Polly, bapt. Apr. 24, 1757. Betty, wife of Jabez, d. Mar. 26, 1760, and he died in Maryland, of small pox, May 31, 1760.

Thaddeus Gray, son of William (2), b. Oct. 27, 1730, mar. Susannah Carley, Feb. 28, 1759, and had Dolly, bapt. Apr. 27, 1760; Louis, bapt. July 19, 1761; he d. Nov. 26, 1761.

Elisha Gray, son of William (2) b. June 1, 1735, mar. Ellen ———, and had Joseph, bapt. Oct. 11, 1761; he d. Nov. 30, 1774.

Joshua Gray, son of William (2), mar. Elizabeth Dibble, at Stamford, Conn., May 20, 1766, and had a daughter Abigail, born Feb. 9, 1769.

Joseph Gray, a brother of Joshua, also resided at Stamford for several years, but the historian of that place says " the name disappeared from the records soon after the close of the Revolution."

Stephen Gray, eldest son of William (2), and only child by his first marriage, left no records, and no trace has been found of his descendants.

ANSON GRAY.

Anson Gray, son of William (4), and Sarah Jennings Gray, born at Ridgebury, Conn., 1795, married Sarah L. Gray, daughter of Seymour Gray, and granddaughter of Moses Gray, who was a son of William (3), and a brother of Elias, Sept. 19th, 1824; she d. Dec. 3, 1870; he d. Jan. 9, 1879. Issue:

SALOME GRAY, b. Aug. 1825; mar. Thaddeus Feeks, Nov. 18, 1849; she d. Aug. 5, 1877; issue: Mary Feeks, who mar. Dr. Farrington, of New York.

CHARLES GRAY, b. June 1, 1827; mar. Ann Maria Boughton, of Patterson, N. Y., Aug. 23, 1852; d. June 1, 1853; no children.

ESTHER GRAY, b. Feb. 1, 1829; mar. Oren B. Lessey, Jan. 20, 1849; issue: Sarah Lessey, who mar. A. A. Dugar, of Worcester, Mass.

DAVID WILLIAM GRAY, b. Nov. 21, 1831; married Esther E. Field, of Patterson, N. Y., Aug. 9, 1853; resides in Danbury, Conn.; no children.

HARRIET GRAY, b. July 3, 1836; mar. Lewis Northrop, July 22, 1852; d. Feb. 23, 1863; had a son Ebenezer, who married and removed west.

SARAH N. GRAY, b. Oct. 27, 1845; d. Aug. 18, 1852.

William Gray (3), d. Aug. 30, 1793.

MOSES GRAY.

Moses Gray, son of William Gray (3), was born in old Fairfield, Conn., Aug. 11, 1743, and his name appears on the old parish records at Green's Farms in the town of Fairfield as having been baptized on Sept. 11th, same year. The same records show his marriage with Sarah Disbrow, March 19, 1767, and the baptism of his first born son, Gabriel, Feb. 15, 1768. He removed to New Fairfield, then a comparative wilderness, in the spring of 1768, in company with his brother Elias, and each took up a farm of 57 acres, side by side, on the east of Ball's Pond, so called, and about six miles from Danbury. By industry and economy they prospered, and both added largely to the extent of their original purchases.

Moses Gray was a Revolutionary soldier, holding a commission as Ensign. He was at the battle of Long Island, and afterwards at White Plains. Was at Valley Forge, and went home ill with camp distemper, and lost four of his children at one time, from that disease. He again served as a "Minute Man," and also was for a short time in the garrison at West Point. To every call of patriotism he gave a prompt and cheerful response.

He united with the King Street Baptist Society, June 24th, 1786, and was the chorister of that church for many years, continuing in connection with it until his death, which occurred Oct. 15, 1812. His grandson, Horace Gray, of Eustis, Florida, who has furnished most of the statistics of this branch of the family, says that he died of a prevailing "malignant fever, as did my maternal grandfather, Thomas Higgins, almost the same day, and many others, both of my grandfathers, and an aunt and two uncles dying within ten days." And the fact that Thomas Gray, a son of Moses, who had died with the disease, was buried at the same time and with his father, must have added to the general gloom.

Moses Gray and Sarah his wife had altogether sixteen children, of whom all died quite young, except five sons, as follows: Gabriel, Seymour, Thomas, Solomon and Jesse, all of whom had families, sketches of which are herewith given.

GABRIEL GRAY, eldest son of Moses, born Feb., 1768, died of cholera, while on his way from Albany to his home in Harpersfield, Delaware Co., N. Y. He left two sons, Moses and Orange Gray, both of whom settled in north-eastern Ohio, and "raised large families."

SEYMOUR GRAY, second son of Moses, born May 23, 1771, married Mary Comes, Jan. 26, 1791; she d. May 24, 1824, and he mar. 2d, Grace Lyon, Feb. 10, 1829. Seymour Gray died Jan. 1, 1845. Issue:

> ANNA GRAY, b. June 18, 1792; d. May 16, 1847.
> DANIEL GRAY, b. July 16, 1793; d. Aug. 1836.
> IRA GRAY, b. Jan. 6, 1795; d. Feb. 25, 1797.
> HIRAM GRAY, b. Dec. 22, 1796; d. May 13, 1873.
> RANCELL TOWNER GRAY, b. Mar. 19, 1797; d.
> RUFUS GRAY, b. Sept. 11, 1800; d. July 22, 1868.
> SARAH LUCY GRAY, b. Mar. 23, 1805; d. Dec. 3, 1870.
> SALOME GRAY, b. Dec. 19, 1807; d. Mar. 27, 1810.
> HARRIET GRAY, b. June 2, 1810; d. Mar. 24, 1877.

Harriet Gray mar. John Barr, Mar. 8, 1827; she d. Mar. 24, 1877; he d. Apr. 16, 1884; issue: Mary Ann, b. June 22, 1828, mar. George Albin, Feb. 13, 1850, who d. Aug. 14, 1883, and had George Arthur Albin b. Oct. 1, 1852, who d. Mar. 24, 1853, and Mary Isabelle Albin b. Jan. 16, 1860; Lucy C. Barr b. Aug. 16, 1831, and d. July 4, 1853; Martha G. Barr b. Feb. 28, 1834; Ira L. Barr, b. June 28, 1838, d. May 11, 1866; Jane Barr, b. May 20, 1843.

Seymour Gray was a man of "great natural ability," and his sons Daniel, Rancell and Rufus, it is said, "were able men, and led eventful lives." The greater pity that sketches of them were not furnished for this record, but to obtain the desired data much delay was required.

THOMAS GRAY, third son of Moses, married Sarah Wilkes. He died Oct. 10, 1812, at or near Harpersfield, Delaware Co., N. Y., of typhus fever, and was buried at the same time and in the same grave with his father, in the old Baptist Cemetery at King Street, near New Fairfield, Conn. He left five children, viz: Ezra, Squire, Lydia, Francis, and one other. Thomas was said to have been his father's "favorite son."

SOLOMON GRAY, fourth son of Moses, married Betsey Benham, and several years afterwards removed to Clarkesfield, Huron Co., Ohio, and was one of the first settlers of that country. He died 1851. Was a respected citizen. Left three children: Pamela, who married James Green and died soon after; George, b. 1815, married and raised a large family; and James, born after the removal to Ohio, who inherited the homestead, and is married but has no family.

JESSE GRAY, son of Moses, married Sarah Higgins, the youngest sister of Mary Higgins, who married William Gray (4), son of Elias, whose father was Thomas Higgins of Cape Cod, who had settled in South East, then Dutchess Co., N. Y., and whose mother was Marthy Manly, a sister of the Capt. Manly who took the first prize from the British in the Revolutionary war. Jesse received 20 acres of land of his father to entitle him to vote under the old King James Charter, and he afterwards bought out his brother Solomon and came into possession of the old homestead. He cared for his mother, " Grany Gray," as she was affectionately entitled, and who survived his father about twenty years. He was a successful farmer and added to the paternal acres. He served six months as a volunteer in the war of 1812. In the spring of 1837 he sold his property in New Fairfield, and followed his sons, who had gone out as pioneers the winter before to Michigan, taking his whole family, and settling in the town of Saline, Washtenaw Co. Jesse Gray was an "active, energetic man, a member of the M. E. Church for many years, a strong Jeffersonian Democrat until the passage of the Kansas-Nebraska Bill, when he united with and continued in the Republican Party,—none of the Copperhead in Moses Gray or any of his posterity. He died in Feb'y, 1861. Sarah his wife, outlived him, and was a remarkable woman." They had five children, as follows: Horace, Eunice, Ira, Thomas, and Martin.

HORACE GRAY, eldest son of Jesse, was born Dec. 19, 1808, and married to Abigail Bradley, in New Fairfield, Oct. 2, 1831, she born same place Sept. 4, 1812. Horace had no educational advantages, save what attained by himself at home, being too far from the District School to derive any special benefit from it. He succeeded, however, in mastering the common branches, with a fair knowledge for those times, of chemistry, philosophy, and most of the sciences, and a pretty thorough knowledge of astronomy. He commenced teaching school when sixteen years old, and followed it mostly at winter terms, until he emigrated to Michigan in 1837. He was almost the first to lecture on Astronomy in eastern New York, Vermont, Massachusetts, Connecticut, &c. In the winter of 1837, starting from Danbury, Conn., he "footed it" to Michigan, through southern Pennsylvania, over the Alleghany Mts., and through Ohio, with knapsack on his back, near 900 miles, at a cost of only $10.50, thereby saving in one month $65, a fortune in those days. And he did well by so emigrating to Michigan. He served several terms as Supervisor in Lennawee Co., during and since the war. Has spent several years in northern Mich., five years in Alabama, and the last five years at Eustis, Florida, his present place of residence. His wife, Abigail, died Oct. 17, 1863; he has not married again. They had four children, viz:

MARY JANE GRAY, b. Nov. 24, 1832, mar. John C. Cone, at Macon, Mich.; d. July 6, 1853.

GEORGE BADGER GRAY, b. July 11, 1835; mar. Eunice Barnes at Macon, Mich., Jan. 13, 1860; three children: Frank, aged 27, Minnie, 20, and Jesse, 7; has the old homestead at Macon, and has an orange grove in Florida, where he and his family spend their winters.

IRA GRAY, b. July 5, 1838; mar. Mary Wilson, at Dundee, Mich.; July 12, 1863; served three years in the war of the Rebellion; is an invalid and a pensioner; has an orange grove adjoining his father, at Eustis, Florida. Children: George A. Gray, aged 17, and Carrie M., 10 years.

BRADLEY EUGENE GRAY, b. Nov. 6, 1851, in Macon, Mich.; resides with his father at Eustis, Florida.

Horace Gray, who furnished the most of the foregoing record of the family of his grandfather, Moses Gray, although in his 79th year, writes a racy spirited letter, using no glasses, and is a vigorous and most interesting character. A true Gray, in all manly qualities, and genial withal, as well as virile, with engaging social qualities, and not a little taste for scientific and literary pursuits. So kindly appreciative, it is a pleasure to have known him even afar.

EUNICE GRAY, daughter and second child of Jesse Gray, born in New Fairfield, married Thomas F. Newell of New York city, where they resided many years. Removed with her father to Michigan, then back to New York, and then to Iowa, last to Kansas, where he died. She is now living at Holton, Kansas. Her oldest daughter Sarah, married Samuel Larned, and resides at Birmingham, Alabama. Her oldest son, Samuel Newell, and her youngest son, Ira, are with her. Her youngest daughter, Hattie, was accidentally poisoned when about twenty years old, while living in Iowa.

IRA GRAY, second son of Jesse, born about 1815, followed school teaching till he removed with his father to Michigan, where he died just one month after his arrival. "He was a young man of good attainments and excellent character."

THOMAS GRAY, third son of Jesse Gray, married Lucy Ann Collins. He commenced at school teaching, but after marriage engaged in farming extensively at Macon, Michigan, but afterwards sold out and removed to Douglas, Mich., where, by the lumbering, mercantile, farming, and fruit business, he has attained a handsome property. He is an able man, and has served one term acceptably in the State Legislature. He accompanied his brother Horace in the famous tramp from Connecticut to Michigan. Is now in California in very poor health. He has four children, viz: Jane, Pharo, Frank, and Thomas, "all doing well," as is said, although more full particulars would have been very acceptable.

MARTIN GRAY, youngest son of Jesse, born in New Fairfield, Conn., married Esther Kellogg, at Macon, Mich. He is of a mechanical turn of mind, and carried on a machine shop at Ypsilanti, Mich. Removed to Douglas, Mich., where he still resides. He inherited his father's valuable estate. Has served as Supervisor. Has but one child, a daughter Sarah.

And this ends the record of the families of Elias and Moses Gray, who were not only brothers, but closely allied by intermarriages and various degrees of kinship among their ancestors and descendants. Their lives ran closely together, and evidently they were brothers beloved.

HENRY GRAY, (3.)

According to the parish records of Green's Farms in old Fairfield, Henry Gray (3), was one of the corporate members of the church at that place in 1715. His brother Isaac was also there, and his death is recorded as having taken place Nov. 7, 1745. Margaret Gray, probably their sister, was a member of the Green's Farms Church, 1727, and her death is recorded date of Aug. 29, 1754. Henry Gray (3) had a son Samuel, but whether other children, if any, does not appear. The following statistics are in part from the town records of Fairfield, and part from the town records of Weston, and other sources.

SAMUEL GRAY.

Samuel Gray, son of Henry Gray (3), married Ellinor Sturges at Fairfield, Conn., Oct. 24, 1734; she d. Jan. 4, 1762; he mar. 2d, Joanna Stone, June 19, 1763; she d. Jan. 15, 1770. Issue.

SANFORD GRAY, b. Sept. 23, 1735.
HANNAH GRAY, b. Nov. 12, 1736; mar. Sylvanus Trancpher, Apr. 28, 1762.
HEZEKIAH GRAY, b. Nov. 14, 1738.
SAMUEL GRAY, Jr., b. July 10, 1742; d. Nov. 3, 1760.
SARAH GRAY, b. Feb. 11, 1744; mar. Gabriel Higgins ot Bedford, N. Y., March 2, 1763.
MARY GRAY, b. Mar. 8, 1746; mar. Joseph Gorham Jr., Nov. 16, 1763.

Hezekiah Gray, son of Samuel, and Abigail his wife, were members of the Green's Farms Church, 1767; and had there baptized daughters Abigail, Lucy, Ellen, and Hezekiah, Jr., the latter, date of July 19, 1761. Hezekiah, Sr., was probably the Hezekiah Gray who was a Lieutenant in a Company formed in Bedford, N. Y., 1776, and afterwards Captain of a Company attached to Col. Drake's Westchester County Regiment. His descendants not traced.

The Henry Gray above recorded as one of the corporate members of the Green's Farms Church, it must be admitted may have been Henry Gray (2), it being very difficult in the absence of exact data absolutely to determine. However it is believed to be correct as it stands.

ISAAC GRAY.

Isaac Gray, son of Henry (2), had a son Nathan; whether other children, this research has not determined. The grave of Isaac Gray is said to have been the first one in the old Northfield burial ground.

NATHAN GRAY.

Nathan Gray, son of Isaac, b. 1714, married Mary Holibert, at Fairfield, Conn., July 24, 1735. Issue:

NATHAN GRAY, Jr., b. Sept. 59, 1737.
ISAAC GRAY, b. May 7, 1739.
SOLOMON GRAY, b. Apr. 21, 1740.
THOMAS GRAY, b. Dec. 7, 1742.
DANIEL GRAY, b. Oct. 49, 1744.
MARY GRAY, b. March 11, 1745.
ELIJAH GRAY, b. Nov. 16, 1747.
JOHN GRAY, b. Sept. 3, 1749.
GIDEON GRAY, b. Mar. 7, 1751.
ELIPHALET GRAY, b. May 4, 1753.
JOSEPH GRAY, b. Nov. 9, 1754.
EUNICE GRAY, b. Jan. 19, 1756.
BENJAMIN GRAY, who mar. Elizabeth Waterbury; died young and left no descendants.

Elijah Gray, son of Nathan, married Esther Sturges, at Weston, Conn., Sept. 10, 1769; she d. Oct. 26, 1792, and he mar. 2d, Rhoda (Morehouse) Disbrow, she being a widow, May 6, 1793, who died Jan. 3, 1796, and he married 3d, Lydia Taylor, Feb. 19, 1797. Elijah Gray died on his 80th birthday, Nov. 16, 1827, and his wife Lydia, died same year. Issue:

STURGES GRAY, b. Apr. 15, 1774.
JEREMIAH GRAY, b. July 20, 1778.
ELIJAH GRAY, b. Mar. 21, 1781.
SAMUEL GRAY, b. Mar. 13, 1783.
WALTER GRAY, b. Dec. 15, 1785.
SOLOMON GRAY, b. Mar. 31, 1788.
HEZEKIAH GRAY, b. July 15, 1790.

There was a daughter Esther by the marriage with the widow Disbrow, who mar. Abraham Morehouse, and had Mary E., who d. unmarried; she mar. 2d, Lyman Banks.

There were three daughters by the third marriage, with Lydia Taylor, as follows:

RHODA M. GRAY, b. May 3, 1798; d. Sept. 1868, unmarried.

ABIGAIL GRAY, b. Jan. 2, 1802; mar. David Lockwood, of Weston, and d. at Bridgeport, Jan. 11, 1883, leaving three children: Rhoda A., David B., and Wakeman D. Lockwood, all of Bridgeport, Conn.

TEMPERANCE GRAY, mar. Hezekiah M. Coley, Dec. 5, 1830, and d. Jan. 12, 1864, leaving two daughters, Anna B., and Marv E., both unmarried and living at the old homestead of Elijah Gray, Westport, Conn.

Sturges Gray d. in the city of New York, leaving two children, Henry and Eliza, who removed to western New York.

Jeremiah Gray lived and died in New York; had 5 daughters; Sarah, who mar. Eben Redfield, of Clinton, Conn., where a son Charles now resides; Elizabeth, who married a Mr. Stone, and Henrietta, Mary and Almira.

Elijah Gray settled in Lansinburgh, N. Y. Not traced.

Samuel Gray, son of Elijah, mar. Hannah Ogden, of Dutchess Co., N. Y., and had three sons, Nelson, and Wakeman, who died young, and Solomon, who married Priscilla M. Smith, of Greenfield Hill, Conn., May 20, 1834, and had five daughters: Mary W., b. March 15, 1836, d. Jan. 15, 1840; Charlotte A., b. Jan. 21, 1839; Mary Eliza and Eleanor Wakeman Gray, twins, b. July 23, 1851, the former of whom mar. John W. Hurlbutt and has two daughters, Mary M., and Estelle C., and the latter, Eleanor W., married Edward Wheeler, June 11, 1874, and has Minnie E., Julia M., and Edward Gray Wheeler, all of whom reside in Westport, Conn.; Harriet F. Gray, mar. Geo. A. Wood, Sept. 24, 1871, and had Julia M., dec'd, and Georgia A. Wood. Eliza W. Gray, only daughter of Samuel Gray, married Lewis Adams, and lives in Rome, Peoria Co., Ill. Has had a son, killed on the R. R., and two daughters, both married. Her mother, the widow of Samuel Gray, resided with her, and died there in 1874. Solomon Gray died Apr. 23, 1870.

Walter Gray, son of Elijah, d. in Westport leaving six children: Henry, John, Jane, who mar. a Mr. Smith, Elijah, Jeremiah, and Esther M.

Solomon Gray, son of Elijah, mar. Abigail Thorpe of Green's Farms, April, 1820; he d. March 20, 1830; she d. Sept. 30th, 1862. Issue:

ELIPHALET GRAY, b. Jan. 10, 1821; mar. Harriet B. Coley, May 22, 1848; issue: Annie A. Gray, b. Sept. 21, 1850, mar. Wm. H. Bradley, May 22, 1879. Maurice Gray, b. Oct. 7, 1854, d. Nov. 25, 1874. Residence, Westport.

ESTHER BURR GRAY, b. March 6, 1823; mar. Austin Godfrey, Nov. 30, 1847.

MARY GRAY, b. Nov. 25, 1826, mar. John Gray, May 21, 1869.

ABBIE A. GRAY, b. March 30, 1830; mar. Horace B. Coley, Oct. 18, 1863; d. Nov. 27, 1879.

ELEANOR W. GRAY, b. Dec. 29, 1833; mar. Horace B. Coley Dec. 12, 1880.

Hezekiah Gray, youngest son of Elijah, died at West Point, N. Y., leaving eight children: Sturges, Sarah, Elijah, who resides at Fairfield, Conn., Mary, Henry, Eunice, George, and Rhoda Gray.

John Gray, son of Nathan, married Eunice Morehouse, at Weston, Conn., Feb. 4, 1774. He d. 1817; she d. April, 1837. Issue:

DEBORAH GRAY, b. Apr. 5, 1775; married Sam'l Meeker, March 5, 1798; she d. Oct. 2, 1839; a son Alva, d.

MARY GRAY, b. May 14, 1779; d. Mar. 13, 1785.

ANNA GRAY, b. Feb. 13, 1783; married Joseph Rowland, Dec. 6, 1812; she d. 1843; had a son Joseph, who d. in Brooklyn, Jan'y 1886, and left two daughters, Anna and Lena.

JOHN GRAY, Jr., b. Sept. 1, 1785; married Abigail Coley, May 3d, 1813; had three daughters: Mary, who mar. Thos. Goodsell, is a widow, two sons, John, d., and Heman; Deborah, who mar. Lewis Bradley, is a widow, six children, Randolph, d., Mary, John, Caroline, Anna, and Lewis, who d. Jan., 1884; Eliza, who mar. Henry M. Sherwood of Chicago, and has a daughter, Grace Sherwood.

MOREHOUSE GRAY, b. Dec. 22, 1787; married Clarissa Hoyt, May 4, 1817; d. Aug., 1825; left two children:

FREDERICK GRAY, now living at Southbury, Conn., b. 1822, mar. Harriet Tuttle; three children: Cyrus, Anna and Martha.

ANNA GRAY, who mar. Geo. Mumford, of New York; is a widow; children: Oliver, Laura and Mary.

ALVA GRAY, b. May 4, 1796.

ALVA GRAY.

Alva Gray, youngest son of John Gray, married Sarah C. Wakeman, Feb. 17, 1823, and died at Westport, Conn., July 3, 1876. The following sketch of his life is from the local paper of that date: " Alva Gray was born May 4, 1796, in that part of Westport called Coley town, which formed a part of this town at its origin; he was therefore a native of Westport. With the advantages which a common school afforded, he surpassed his schoolmates in study. His first noticeable political action was as one of the leaders in districting the State Senatorially, which he followed indefatigably until it was accomplished. As in this work, so in all things, throughout his life, his characteristics were energy and firmness. He was distinguished for a strong, comprehensive and vigorous intellect. The mastery of his profession, and his high position socially and politically, were achieved by his strong will and efforts. He scorned deceit, and diligently sought for truth. He was strictly honest, and whenever he had fixed his opinion he was immovable as the everlasting hills. So long as the party he represented was in power in this town, he did more for the financial prosperity of the town than any one man had done before his time, and it must be conceded by all who knew him that his watchfulness of public affairs has surpassed that of all others. In fact, the condition of our town affairs never were so clearly and satisfactorily represented to the taxpayers as when under his administration as Selectman.

" He had been for many years one of the most capable County Surveyors in the State. During more than forty years' practice he had surveyed every acre of ground in Westport, and had become so familiar with the history of farms, and home lots, as to make any decision he might be called on to pronounce, final. He was for many years the oldest Director in the Southport Bank. His natural talent would have made him one of the most prominent civil officers in the State, had it not been for his remarkable fixedness of opinion. Though identified with no church, and making no public profession of religion, the world accepted him as an upright, good man. In many respects Westport has met with an irreparable loss in the death of Mr. Gray."

ELIZABETH GRAY, b. Jan. 12, 1824, d. March 26, 1868.

EDWARD GRAY, b. Oct. 10, 1826, lost at sea, Apr. 17, 1842.

JOHN H. GRAY, b. Sept. 18, 1829, mar. Frances L. Wells, Oct. 13, 1859; his only child, Elizabeth, d. June 14, 1885; he d. April 18, 1876.

FRANCES A. GRAY, b. Feb. 14, 1833, resides at Westport.

SARAH A. GRAY, b. Sept. 3, 1837; d. Oct. 24, 1843.

———

Solomon Gray, son of Nathan, mar. Ann Disbrow, at Green's Farms, Feb. 18, 1762.

Gideon Gray, son of Nathan, married Anne, and had a dau. Anne bapt. Jan. 7, 1776.

Daniel Gray, son of Nathan, was probably the Daniel who married Prudence Waterbury at Stamford, Nov. 15, 1765, and had Mary, b. May 18, 1767; Prudence, b. Dec. 16, 1772, who mar. Henry Whitney at Darien, Conn., Jan. 8, 1789, and d. at Gt. Barrington, Mass., Dec. 11, 1822, and other children. He was a prominent citizen of Stamford, and a member of the Com. of Public Safety during a part of the Revolutionary period.

Eliphalet Gray, son of Nathan, had a daughter Lydia, and a daughter who married a Mr. Brown, both of whom lived and died in Belchertown, Mass.

———

JACOB GRAY,

Jacob Gray, son of Henry Gray (1), deeded land in Fairfield May 15, 1679, "which hath been legally given him by his grandfather, William Frost." He also deeded land to his daughter Rebekah, March 17, 1690. Jacob Gray, Jr., sold land in Fairfield date of Jan. 21, 1708, and then the records show that Jacob Gray gave land to his son Joseph in 1708. This Joseph is believed to have removed at an early day to Newtown, and to have been the Joseph Gray who was Selectman of that town in 1713, and the ancestor of many Grays in that vicinity whose lineage, owing to the meagre town and church records, it is impossible to satisfactorily trace. The records of Fairfield further show that "Sarah Gray, relict of Jacob Gray, died in Stratford, Dec. 16, 1716."

JACOB GRAY, (2).

Jacob Gray (2), according to the old records of the Greenfield Hill Parish, there entered into covenant and was baptized June 5, 1726, his wife Hannah having united with that church Apr. 1, 1722. On June 12, 1726, the Sunday following his admission to church membership, their children were baptized, as follows, the first three being classed as adults:

NATHANIEL GRAY.
SARAH GRAY.
JOHN GRAY, b. 1708.
JAMES GRAY, b. 1710.
JACOB GRAY, Jr., b. 1712.
ROBENA GRAY.
EUNICE GRAY.
MARY GRAY, bapt. March 16, 1728.

JOHN GRAY, son of Jacob (2), married Hannah Scribner, Sept. 19, 1730. They removed to Redding at an early day, where some of their children were born, and where he died May 10, 1755, as the record says, "aged about 47 years." Issue:

ANN GRAY, b. Aug. 2, 1732.
JOHN GRAY, Jr., b. Feb. 17, 1734.
STEPHEN GRAY, b. Dec. 7, 1735.
ABRAHAM GRAY, b. June 22, 1737.
HEZEKIAH GRAY, b. Oct. 1, 1738.
NATHANIEL GRAY, b. July 20, 1741.
HANNAH GRAY, b. June 25, 1744.
ABIGAIL GRAY, b. Dec. 28, 1745.
JOSEPH GRAY, b. July 7, 1753.
EUNICE GRAY, b. Dec. 21, 1754.

Ann Gray married Timothy Hull of Redding.

John Gray (2) was married to Ruama Barlow, at Redding, Aug. 7, 1759. He was Collector in that town 1768, and Selectman for years 1777 and 1783. He d. Oct. 25, 1793. Issue:

EUNICE GRAY, b. Mar. 15, 1760.
JOEL GRAY, b. July 27, 1763, mar. Phebe Smith, Mar. 18, 1784, and had Eunice Gray b. Feb. 24, 1785, and Sam'l Smith Gray b. Aug. 1, 1797, who resided in Redding, where he had a large farm, although engaged for a time in business in the city of New York. Samuel Smith had William Gray, who resides in Redding, Samuel, of Danbury, and Charles Gray of New Haven. Joel Gray made will in favor of his son Samuel, 1826.

Stephen Gray, son of John (1), married Sarah Ferry, Sept. 3, 1758; had a dau. Huldah b. Nov. 9, 1760, also a son Stephen Gray, Jr., who mar. Annis Boughton, Nov. 1792, and had Uriah Gray, b. June, 1793, and Ann. Uriah mar. Fanny Lockwood, and died in Redding March 10, 1832. His son, William Lockwood Gray, b. Jan. 1, 1818, went to sea, 1834, and has not since been heard from. Stephen Gray lived and died in the town of Redding.

Abraham Gray, son of John (1), removed to Ridgebury in the town of Ridgefield, Conn., where he married Mary Keeler, and died Sept. 13, 1776, without issue. His name appears on the Patriot list signed at the Oblong the year previous, 1775.

Hezekiah Gray lived for a time at Ridgebury, and afterwards at Danbury, where his name and that of Thankful, his wife, appear frequently in the real estate records up to 1786, when they removed to Great Barrington, Mass., and were for several years at a place called "Seekonk," a little to the westward of the beforementioned town, and lived adjoining the residence of Rev. Jeduthan Gray, a name prominently mentioned elsewhere in this record. From thence they removed to Chenango Co., N. Y., where all trace of them was lost. They are not believed to have had descendants.

Nathaniel Gray, son of John (1), married Hannah Boughton, of Ridgefield. He held the commission of Lieutenant in the war of the Revolution, and was killed in the battle at Ridgefield, April 23d, 1777, at the time of Gov. Tryon's tory raid on Danbury. All honor to the memory of the brave Lieutenant Nathaniel Gray. He left a daughter Hannah who mar. Samuel Eells, born at Canaan, Conn., Apr. 13, 1770, and removed to Walton, N. Y., 1809, and had Nathaniel Gray Eells, who was in the war of 1812, and mar. Betty St. John Sept. 21, 1817, and Hannah Gray Eells, who mar. Thaddeus Seymour St. John, at Walton, June 7, 1818.

Isaac Gray and Nathan Gray, Jr., sons of Nathan, as appears on page 219, were residents of Redding and Ridgefield, at an early day, and doubtless had families, though they can not be clearly traced on the records, and their descendants definitely determined.

JOSEPH GRAY.

Joseph Gray, youngest son of John (1), was less than two years old at the death of his father, but he grew up to a sturdy manhood and took an active part in affairs, as the records of Ridgefield give evidence. He was also a Soldier of the Revolution, and accompanied Arnold in the perilous march through the wilderness, participating in the hardships of that expedition. He married Lydia Keeler, by whom he had seven children. He died Oct. 7, 1833, and his wife Lydia, d. Nov. 7, 1839, aged 82 years. Issue:

ABRAHAM GRAY, b. Dec. 15, 1781.
ANNA GRAY.
HANNAH GRAY.
NATHANIEL GRAY, b. March 19, 1795.
POLLY GRAY.
SALLY GRAY.
JOHN COLLINS GRAY, b. Oct. 2, 1802.

ABRAHAM GRAY.

Abraham Gray, eldest son of Joseph, married Anna Starr, of Danbury, Conn., and soon after, in 1809, removed to Mamakating, Sullivan Co., N. Y., where most of their children were born. In 1825 they moved to the then far west, settling at Clarksfield, Huron Co., Ohio. There he bought a farm, but still worked at his trade of shoe-making. He died May 6, 1842, and she died July 20, 1844. Issue:

SMITH S. GRAY, b. May 31, 1807, d. Mar. 13, 1859.
PAMELIA GRAY, b. July 3, 1809, d. Sept 13, 1817.
ERASTUS GRAY, b. Sept. 12, 1810.
PETER S. GRAY, b. Dec. 22, 1812, d. Apr. 4, 1884.
DEBORAH GRAY, b. Nov. 9, 1814, d. Sept. 12, 1884.
LYDIA GRAY, b. Feb. 1, 1817, d. July 13, 1885.
PAMELIA ANN GRAY, b. Mar. 8, 1819, d. July 2, 1877.
SARAH GRAY, b. Mar. 22, 1821, d. Mar. 4, 1858.
SAMUEL GRAY, b. Dec. 15, 1823.
HIRAM H. GRAY, b. May 25, 1827.
ORLANDO GRAY, b. Feb. 5, 1829, d. Mar. 21, 1829.
HARRIET ELIZA GRAY, b. Dec. 15, 1831, d. June 3, 1837.

Erastus Gray mar, Mrs. Eliza Parker, 1867; has no children; resides in Norwalk, Ohio.

Deborah Gray married Edward E. Husted, Dec. 15, 1831, and had ten children, of whom seven are living, as follows: Edwin G., J. Franklin, Emma Gray, (now Mrs. Baker), Wm. M., and E. Le Grand Husted, Postmaster of that city, are all of Norwalk, Ohio; Elmer E. Husted, of Wellington, O., and Ella J., of Morgan Park, Ill. Mr. Husted was b. in Danbury, Conn., Dec. 13, 1805, and d. in Norwalk, O., Dec. 24, 1878.

Samuel Gray, son of Abraham, resides in Clarksfield, Huron Co., Ohio.

Hiram Gray, son of Abraham, lives at Emporia, Kansas. The neglect to answer letters of inquiry accounts for the lacking records of the families of the brothers Hiram and Samuel Gray, which, as in many other cases, is cause for regret.

Anna Gray, daughter of Joseph, married Thomas St. John, who was Member of the Legislature from his town for the years 1832 and 1833, and died March 4th, 1848. They had a son, Samuel Sidney St. John, born at Ridgebury, Sept. 6, 1806. He graduated at Columbia College, N. Y., and mar. Lucy A. Brush, of Ridgebury, and had three children: Thomas P., John W., and Mary A. St. John. Thomas P. graduated from Columbia College 1848, and was Member of Assembly from N. Y. city in 1851, and '52; d. Oct. 13, 1865. John W. died in Ridgefield. Mary A. mar. Smith G. Hunt of Brewster, N. Y., and has two children: Sidney St. John Hunt, and Emeline Keeler Hunt, who is a student at Vassar College.

Hannah Gray, daughter of Joseph, born in Ridgebury, Conn., July 4, 1792, married Zina St. John, Dec. 15, 1811; he d. at Leona, Mich., June 20, 1857; she d. at same place, Nov. 5, 1855. Issue: Polly, b. Nov. 9, 1812, d. Jan. 28, 1884, Lockport, N. Y.; Ann, b. July 13, 1814, d. at Leona, Mich., Apr. 26, 1848; Darius, b. Jan. 26, 1816; Samuel. b. Jan. 29, 1819, d. Apr. 3, 1884, at Leona, Mich.; Smith, b. July 21, 1820; Hannah, b. Oct. 16, 1821, d. Feb. 10, 1831; Caroline, b. Jan. 21, 1824, mar. Mr. Gregory of Lockport, N. Y.; Timothy, b. Mar. 17, 1825; Betsey, d.; Chloe; Cynthia; Jason, b. May 7, 1832, married his cousin, Julia Potter, Jan. 4, 1856, and resides at Hammonton, N. J.; and Hannah E., who d. Jan. 3, 1860.

NATHANIEL GRAY.

Nathaniel Gray, son of Joseph, married Millie A. Case, June 26, 1818, she b. May 13, 1801. He d. at Mill Plain, Conn., July 7, 1882; she d. at Brewster, N. Y., Mar. 1, 1883. They had lived together 64 years. Issue:

H. WESTON GRAY, d. in California, 1852, aged 30.

ABRAM GRAY, b. 1826, mar. Clarissa Segur, and had
    WELFORD A. GRAY, and
    ALFRED S. GRAY.

Abram Gray d. in Mill Plain, Aug. 20, 1859.

GABRIEL S. GRAY, son of Nathaniel, mar. S. Betsey Gardner; no children; resides in Danbury.

MARY E. GRAY, dau. of Nathaniel, mar. Rev. F. Kratz, Baptist clergyman, now located at Hagadorn Mills, Saratoga Co., N. Y.

HATTIE E. GRAY, dau. of Nathaniel, mar. Benj. C. Norris; had a son, Weston G. Norris, who d. 1869, and a daughter, Mamie C.; reside at New Preston, Conn.

Polly Gray, daughter of Joseph, mar. Minor Potter of Litchfield, Conn., May 24, 1841, and had Garry, Lydia, and Sally. Also Julia Potter, who mar. Jason St. John, and Minor Potter.

Sally Gray mar. William Grannis of Litchfield, Conn., and had Jason, Sidney, Aaron, Joseph, Lydia, and Dr. John Grannis, of Saybrook, Conn.

JOHN C. GRAY.

John C. Gray, son of Joseph, mar. Eliza Case, May 4, 1825, who was a sister of his brother Nathaniel's wife, and born at Cornwall, N. Y., 1804. He died at Mill Plains, Conn., May 29, 1872, where she still resides. Issue:

HENRY C. GRAY, b. June 4, 1827; mar. to Harriet M. Lessey, Nov. 2, 1859; residence, Danbury, Conn.; children:
    HATTIE GRAY, b. Nov. 9, 1862.
    JOHN H. C. GRAY, b. March 4, 1875.

LUCY ANN GRAY, b. June 1, 1832, d. Sept. 24, 1833.

MARY E. GRAY, b. Aug. 19, 1834; mar. F. D. Hamilton, and d. Nov. 29, 1881; no children.

WATSON C. GRAY, b. July 6, 1836, mar. Sarah M. Peck, Jan. 10, 1867; residence, Danbury. Issue:
    JENNIE GRAY, b. May 17, 1868.

James Gray, son of Jacob (2), mar. Sarah Gilbert, at Green-field Hill Parish, May, 1733. Issue:

SERIES JAMES GRAY, Jr., b. Feb. 18, 1736.
ICHABOD GRAY, b. Mar. 30, 1739.
SARAH GRAY, b. Apr. 19, 1742.
JANE GRAY, b. Nov. 28, 1744.
JACOB GRAY, bapt. in Redding, Feb. 10, 1754.

James Gray, (1), removed to Redding, and his widow, Sarah Gray, sold a dwelling and land there Feb. 1, 1783. He had made a will date of 1778. The inventory of the estate of his son Ichabod, of Newtown, who left a son Nathaniel, was filed 1771.

James Gray (2), mar. Assena ———, Mar. 27, 1760; mar. 2d Mehitable Turner, 1764.

Sarah Gray, dau. of Jacob (2), mar. John Byington, Nov. 16, 1763.

JACOB GRAY, (3).

Jacob Gray (3), and Naomi his wife, "renewed covenant" at the Greenfield Hill Parish Church, Aug. 13, 1738, and the record of their children appears there as follows:

SETH GRAY, bapt. Jan. 8, 1738.
JACOB GRAY, bapt. July 12, 1744.
ROUL GRAY, b. Aug. 4, 1747.
(By his second wife, widow of Beebe Mills:)
DANIEL GRAY, b. May 2, 1762.
NAOMI GRAY, b. March 4, 1764.
JACOB GRAY, b. Oct. 2, 1768.

Jacob Gray (3), d. Dec. 26, 1772, "aged about three score and one year."

Jacob Gray, son of James (1), was probably the Jacob Gray who was captured at Danbury at the time of Gov. Tryon's tory incursion in 1777.

Seth Gray and Sarah his wife, "renewed covenant" Dec. 12, 1762. He had married Sarah Mills, and had:

WILLIAM GRAY, b. April 5, 1784.
JOSEPH GRAY.
LEVI GRAY.
EUNICE, ABIGAIL, SARAH, and HULDAH GRAY.

William Gray, son of Seth, b. in Newtown, Conn., mar. Hannah Brintonell, in Salisbury, Jan. 7, 1806, and died March 21, 1853. Had a son William Kirtland Gray, b. in Newtown, Conn., Jan. 13, 1807, who mar. Sarah Pease, 1838, and d. in Jan'y, 1870. Issue: Wm. K. Gray, b. 1851, who resides at West Stratford, and James M. Gray, b. 1861, who lives at Lakeport, Conn.

Hannah Maria Gray, daughter of William and Hannah Brintonell Gray, was born at Salisbury, Conn., Apr. 30, 1813; married to Franklin Parsons, Oct. 9, 1839; residence, Ashley Falls, Berkshire Co., Mass.

Sarah Eloise Gray, daughter of William, b. Aug. 12, 1818, married to Jarvis Jones, Jan. 7, 1840, d. at Ashley Falls, Mass., Apr. 3, 1878.

James Madison Gray, son of William, b. July 7, 1820, mar. Henrietta Thomas, in 1844, and d. in California, April, 1879.

Joseph had a daughter Sally who married a Mr. Sheapard, and resided in Newtown, Conn.

Levi Gray had a daughter Fanny, who married a Mr. Woodruff, of Bridgeport. George W. Gray, son of Levi, lived in West Bridgeport, Conn., and had sons Mills, Theodore, and George Gray, Jr. Levi also had a son Brazilla, who resides at Ansonia, Conn., and a son Aaron, who removed to a place now called Gray's Landing, in Pennsylvania, and died there.

Beebe Mills Gray, son of Levi, married a Miss Sherman, and had a daughter Julia, who married W. S. Adams, of Stratford, Conn., and a son, Geo. S. Gray, who mar. Anna Maria Adams, of Stepney Depot, Conn., and has a son.

FRANK S. GRAY, mar. Libbie C. Cogswell, Apr. 22, 1875; had
HARRY E. GRAY, b. Jan. 27, 1876,
MIRIAM C. GRAY, b. May 12, 1881.

Frank S. Gray has resided at Sheffield, Mass., and been R. R. Station Agent at that place.

Beebe Mills Gray still survives at the age of 90 years.

Daniel Gray, son of Jacob (3) by his second marriage, was a soldier of the Revolution, and moved to Ballston, Saratoga Co., N. Y., in 1802; afterwards lived in Schenectady Co., and in Sullivan, Madison Co., N. Y., and in 1826 returned to Ballston.

The following additional memoranda concerning the Fairfield Grays was received too late for proper classification:

The wife of Hezekiah Gray, son of John (1), who was a son of Jacob (3), who has been mentioned, proves to have been Thankful Hoyt, the daughter of Jonathan Hoyt of Danbury.

Hiram H. Gray, son of Abraham, son of Joseph, son of John (1), sends the following: "I was born in Clarksfield, O., May 25, 1827. Was married to Jane Rogers, June 7, 1848; a son Ralph b. Dec. 9, 1849, who d. in Oct. 1850. Rollin M., born June 13, 1856, mar. Dora McMillan, Dec. 27, 1876. Removed from Ohio to Kansas, in 1857, and took up Government land near Emporia, where I have since continued to reside, and the following additions have been made to my family: Cora B., born Jan. 6, 1860, and mar. to A. P. Chance, Apr. 5, 1881; Frank E. Gray, b. Aug. 26, 1861, and mar. to Dora Wilhite, Nov. 21, 1882, and has a daughter Jennie, b. Nov. 16, 1883; Laura A., b. Jan. 12, 1864; and Kate M. Gray, b. Dec. 26, 1866."

Elijah Gray, of Southport, Conn., writes that his father, Hezekiah, son of Elijah, who was the son of Nathan, was twice married; first, to Rodak Sturges; 2d, to Eliza Loveless; he, Elijah, being the eldest son by the second wife, and born Oct. 25, 1821. Hezekiah Gray was accidentally killed at West Point, Feb. 28, 1829. Elijah Gray reports five sons and five daughters, not giving their names.

Mrs. Jane A. Smith, daughter of Walter Gray, son of Elijah, son of Nathan, writes that her father married Anna Archer of Norwalk, and had Henry Gray, born Nov. 28, 1811, and died in 1868, leaving a son Walter, who lives at Westport. John Archer Gray was b. Apr. 6, 1814. Jane A., was born Dec. 4, 1816, and mar. Francis Smith, Feb. 16, 1841, who d. Nov. 5, 1863. Esther Mary, b. Nov. 5, 1821, d. May 22, 1847. Elijah, b. Feb. 14, 1829. Jeremiah, b. June 2, 1831, d. Aug., 1872. Mrs. S. states that her father's brother Elijah, who removed to Lansingburgh, N. Y., had a son Walter.

Abigail Gray, daughter of Elijah, who mar. David Lockwood, had David Benjamin Lockwood, b. Jan. 7, 1827, who mar. Caroline Amelia Redfield, Jan. 11, 1856; she d. Nov. 5, 1865. Issue: Alice Redfield Lockwood, who mar. Chas. H. Baker, 1880; and Lester Burchard Lockwood. He mar. 2d, Lydia Ellen Nelson, of New York, by whom were Harriet Eugene Lockwood, Lucy Betty Josephine Lockwood, and Sidney Nelson Lockwood. D. B. Lockwood graduated at the Wesleyan University, in 1849, admitted to the practice of the law 1851, has been Judge of the City Court of Bridgeport, twice a member of the State Legislature, and City Attorney of Bridgeport.

A Thaddeus Gray, b. May 12, 1778, who lived in Brookfield, Conn., mar. Huldah Lobdell, and had Abigail, b. Feb. 15, born 15, 1807, who mar. Henry May, and had two sons, William, who mar. Belle Mills, and Julius, dec'd; she d. Feb. 19, 1882; John C. Gray, b. 1811, who mar. Mary Ann Lobdell and had two sons, one living, Henry C., who mar. Henrietta Lessey, and has three daughters; Mary E. Gray, b. March 21, 1818, mar. Charles Dauchy, 1845, and resides at Southville, Conn.; has no children. Thaddeus Gray d. 1848; Huldah his wife d. 1847. Thaddeus had a brother, Deacon Isaac Gray, who has a son Hiram living in New Haven, Conn.

There was a John Gray who mar. Esther Davis in Redding, Oct. 17, 1790, and had Sally, Laura, and Joel Gray.

A Justus Gray mar. Rachel Weed in Redding, Jan. 16, 1780, and had Eli, Edward, and Alfred Gray.

Anne Maria Gray, of Bridgeport, is the widow of a Joseph Gray b. at Weston, Conn., 1805, and who d. May 15, 1827.

A Daniel Gray and wife were admitted to the church at Redding in 1742, who were doubtless of the Fairfield Grays, though the connection does not appear. They had a son James baptized May 8, 1743, who married Mabel Phinney, Feb. 9, 1764, who had Jerry Gray, b. Jan. 11, 1765, Mabel, b. Nov. 29, 1766, and Betsey, b. Oct. 9, 1773.

William Gray of Eastchester, Westchester Co., N. Y., to whom reference has been made, was a tory, and after the Revolution removed to New Brunswick, where he was a magistrate. He died in 1824, aged 96 years, which would make his birth as of 1728. He was doubtless the grandson of the William Gray who was a son of Henry Gray (1) of Fairfield, Conn.

Nathaniel Gray, son of Jacob (2), had Elizabeth, b. Jan. 29, 1730; Abigail, b. Aug. 5, 1731; and Ebenezer, b. May 4, 1735; all of Greenfield Hill Parish, Conn.

Naomi, wife of Jacob Gray (3), d. Oct. 20, 1759, and he mar. 2d, Abigail Mills, widow of Beebe Mills, July 27, 1760; he d. Apr. 22, 1776, in his 64th year.

Seth Gray, son of Jacob (3), was mar. to Sarah Mills of Greenfield Hill, June 23, 1762, at which time the record says he was of Redding. He died in Monroe, Conn. His brother Jacob, and his half brother Jacob both d. young; his brother Roul not traced. Further statistics of the descendants of Seth are here presented:

A daughter of his son William married Harlow Benedict and resides in Newtown, Conn.

Huldah, dau. of Seth, mar. Isaac Crofoot and d. Homer, N. Y.

Abigail, dau. of Seth, mar. Joshua Tongue, of Newtown, and had Norman, Emory, Amasa, Orrin, Nelson, George, Deborah, Hannah and Minerva Tongue.

Joseph Gray, son of Seth, had Burton Gray, who has a dau. Mrs. E. M. Peck, of Newtown; Shelton Gray; Talman Gray, who mar. Nancy Shepard, and had a daughter, Mrs. Hawley Jennings, of Newtown, and a son Abel Bennett Gray, b. at Newtown, March 4, 1831, who mar. Ellen Keeler, at Danbury, and had Agnes Keeler Gray, b. Jan. 22, 1868. Joseph also had Abel, Sally, who mar. Mr. Shepard; Jane, Semantha, and Nancy, who has a dau., Mrs. Clark Blackman, residing in Newtown.

Isaac Gray, son of Nathan, son of Isaac, son of Henry (2), has been mentioned as having lived in Ridgefield and Redding, "descendants not traced." Long delayed response to inquiries has elicited the information that he was probably the ancestor of Grays who resided in Brookfield, Conn. The last mention of him in the Redding records is of the date 1776, and he next appears in Danbury as having purchased real estate in that town in 1786, and the records show that Isaac Gray of Brookfield, sold said land in Danbury in 1808. Now it appears that Isaac Gray of Brookfield had the following children: Thaddeus, b. 1778, whose family is given on a preceding page; Samuel, who mar.

Miss Williams of Philadelphia, and had two daughters; Hannah,
who mar. John Alexander and had a son; Lucy, who married a
Mr. Barnum, and had sons and daughters; and Isaac Gray, who
mar. Peninah Hurd, and had five sons: Curtis W., who removed
to Mich.; Edwin F., who removed to Pownal, Vt., and had Curtis W., Jr., Walter F., and Hiram A., Jr.; Hiram A., who resides
at New Haven, Conn.; Isaac C., who lived in Mich., and has a
grandson John P.; Abel H. Gray.

Wm. Bennett Gray, son of Daniel and Sally Brush Gray, was
born in Brookfield, Conn., Dec. 29, 1805, and mar. Mary Wild-
man; resided at 115 East 29th St., N. Y.

Benjamin Bulkley Gray, b. at Wilton, Conn., Jun. 9, 1784, mar.
Matilda Baxter, and had Benjamin Bulkley, Jr., b. at North Salem, N. Y., June 9, 1824, who d. Oct. 25, 1844; Harriet, who
mar. Mr. Riggs, and Ann Gray.

Daniel and Prudence Waterbury Gray, of Stamford, Conn.,
had in addition to the two daughters already named, the following sons: James, b. March 24, 1769; Philip, b. Nov. 24, 1770,
mar. Hannah Matthews and had Wm. M., b. Feb. 26, 1792, and
Mary and Eleanor; Daniel, b. Sept. 22, 1774; George Washington, born Nov. 20, 1776. The above James Gray mar. Elizabeth
Osborn at Weston, Conn., Nov. 5, 1789, and had Hannah, born
July 5, 1790; Lewis B. Gray, b. Sept. 7, 1793; Clarissa, and
Molly. Lewis B. Gray, Jr., of Huntington, Conn., is probably
son of above.

Joseph Gray of Stamford, mar. Hannah Leeds, and had Alfred, b. Aug. 26, 1793, Wm. Leeds b. June 24, 1796, Joseph,
Hannah, Molly, and Elizabeth.

Isaac Gray of Stamford, mar. Polly Gorham, and had Stephen,
b. Oct. 25, 1802, Isaac, b. Oct. 10, 1805, Alfred, b. Sept. 19,
1811; Henry, b. Sept. 25, 1815, and Jane, Elizabeth.

Nehemiah Gray and Sarah his wife, renewed covenant at the
Greenfield Hill Church, Feb. 14, 1768, but no further trace of
them was found.

A final search of the Greenfield Hill Parish records revealed a long sought fact, which had hitherto eluded the most painstaking research in various directions, viz: the date of marriage, and full name of the first wife of Elias Gray, son of William (3), there recorded: "Elias Gray of Green's Farms, and Eunice Allen, married Nov. 27, 1766." This discovery will be of especial interest to their numerous descendants.

———

What became of the descendants of John Gray, brother of Henry (1), for the will of his father-in-law, William Frost, distinctly specifies that he had at least two children, is not herein clearly apparent. There are here and there scattering, detached branches that cannot otherwhere be traced, neither can they be directly traced there. There was a Daniel Gray, a possible son of John, in Darien, which adjoins Fairfield, as early as 1660, and there was a Hugh Gray in Milford, Conn., prior to 1711. There were Grays on Long Island at an early date, a John Gray who had mar. Hannah, having d. at Jamaica, in 1724, and there were Grays at Newtown, L. I. There having been emigrations from Fairfield in that direction, the inference is strong that the descendants of John, or at least some of them, may have gone thither.

———

Miss Frances A. Gray, of Westport, states that there is a very old memorial stone at Compo, (the early residence of the Fairfield Grays,) near the shore of the Sound, which bears the inscription of "Henry Gray," and of a Mr. Frost,— unquestionably that is the burial place of the ancestors of this line, and a most interesting spot which should be rescued from threatened oblivion.

———

It would have been a pleasure to have given a more full and complete record of the Fairfield Grays if it had been practicable to have done so. The facts presented, however, have been obtained at no little expenditure and labor in research. A lack of prompt response has added largely to the difficulties in the way.

The ancestry of the following highly interesting and vigorous branch of the Gray family, has been to the writer an object of long and exhaustive research. Sometimes the hunt has seemed to turn in one direction, and then again in another, but steadfastly the quest has been pursued. All inquiry as to the early home of the four brothers, Isaac, Aaron, Elijah and Daniel, who migrated to Vermont from Connecticut near the close of the eighteenth century, brought responses pointing in the direction of "the vicinity of Danbury." Unfortunately the records at that place were burned at the time of the Tryon tory raid in 1777, and a search made there, and in all the towns adjoining, failed of the desired result; no trace was found of the ancestry of this family. Some of the early church and town records are deficient, or have been destroyed, and when that is the case, and family records also fail, only circumstantial evidence and conjecture remain. A communication from Col. E. B. Gray, a grandson of Elijah, stated that his ancestor was from New Milford, in Litchfield Co., but only a little removed from Danbury. Exaustive search there made of church and town records, and of the town history revealed the fact that a Hugh Gray, of old Milford, Conn., who had died prior to 1713, was one of the original proprietors of New Milford, but there was no evidence that he had ever lived there, nor could anything further be found concerning him or his descendants on the old Milford records. There was a Jonathan Gray who was a non-commissioned officer in a Company raised by Capt. Couch, attached to Col. Ward's Regt., Feb. 1, 1776, but no further trace of him could be found. And then, Clark Gray, one of the descendants of Isaac, says that he has a strong impression that his great-grandfather, the father of Isaac, Aaron, Elijah and Daniel, was named Elijah, of which the perpetuation of the name in the family for succeeding generations, is presumptive proof. But only one Elijah Gray appears in line as a Revolutionary soldier, and-he removed almost beyond the range of probabilities in distant Lanesborough, Berkshire Co., Mass. In New Milford, died Oct. 29, 1785, Mary Gray Noble, wife of Nathan Noble son of John, she the daughter of John and Phebe Gray of Provincetown, (Cape Cod) Mass., born Jan. 13, 1726, married May 2, 1748, and united

with the church at New Milford, Nov. 13, 1748. Hannah Noble, a sister of Nathan, married John Gray, then of Kent, and
doubtless a brother of Mary Gray who had married Nathan
Noble. Stephen Gray, a son of William Gray (2) of Fairfield,
was also for a time at least a resident of New Milford, having
purchased land there in 1761, which he re-sold in 1763, though
he may have remained there for a longer period. This, that all
the probabilities may be brought in view. To some of these
families it is quite reasonable to suppose these Grays to have
been akin. It is true there was a family of Yarmouth Grays
living at time on the Oblong, in the vicinity of Danbury, but no
connection with them was found, and on the other hand, their descendants, living near each other at Dorset, Vt., disclaimed even
remote relationship. As to the John Gray who married Hannah
Noble, his children were John, Jr., Caleb and Benjamin, and the
family afterwards removed to Bennington, Vt. No record of the
children of the Stephen Gray referred to appears, and his age almost precludes the possibility of paternity in that connection. So
far then as names there appear, only Jonathan remains as a possible ancestor, but the indications are that he was of the Scotch-
Irish Worcester Grays, while they claim to be of English descent.
There is no mention of him other than that his name appears as a
Revolutionary soldier from that town, and it does not necessarily
follow that he had ever lived there. In fact, none of the brothers
Gray may ever have lived in New Milford except Elijah, whose
presence there is evidenced by the fact that a family by the name
of Dunning was found among the early settlers there, of whom
was probably his wife. They may have been of Danbury, and
strong indications point in that direction. The Barnums, of
whom was Isaac's wife, were an old and numerous family there.
One branch of the Fairfield Grays had intermarried with them,
and why not another? Perhaps, they were of the branch of that
family that was early in Newtown, adjoining Danbury, but where
lost records prevent a trace. There are certainly marked indications in the similarity of names. It is a fairly reasonable
conjecture, but at the best it must be admitted that it is only
conjecture, and here the question is left for the future historian
to solve.

AARON GRAY.

Born in Connecticut, as is believed in the vicinity of Danbury, 1773, Aaron Gray was married to Hannah Higbee, at Dorset, Vt., July 20, 1799. A daughter, Laura, was born at Charlotte, Vt., July 13, 1803; twin sons, Orange and Orlin, were born in Dorset, June 15, 1805, both of whom died quite young; A. W. Gray, born Sept. 30, 1810, and Dr. W. P. Gray, now of Delevan, Wis. Aaron Gray died at Middletown Springs, Vt., 1835. Further particulars of his life will be found in the following biograhical sketch of his son, A. W. Gray:

ALBERT W. GRAY.

The following sketch is from a biographical notice published: "Albert W. Gray, after a long sickness, died at his residence in Middletown Springs, Vt., Oct. 26, 1885. He came of good New England stock, struggled upward by his own unaided efforts, and lived a long life full of hard work and practical usefulness. He was born at Dorset, Vt., Sept. 30, 1810, the son of Aaron and Hannah Higby Gray. His father was born in Connecticut, and with three brothers came to Dorset when the town was being settled. His grandfather was an officer in the revolution, and was killed in the service. His mother was born in Hubbardton, and her father was one of the patriots of the Revolution, and took part in the battle of Hubbardton. Aaron Gray moved with his family to Ohio when Albert was about nine years old, but his wife died there, other misfortunes came, and in about two years he returned to Dorset, and being very poor, sent Albert to live with his uncle, Elijah, at Charlotte. Here Albert lived until he was fifteen years old, when he was "bound out" as an apprentice to Henry Gray, a relative living in Middletown, to learn the wheelwright's trade. He served his time of five years, and at the age of twenty went into business for himself. His diligence soon won success. He was known as a careful and excellent workman. He had an inclination and genius for inventing, and gave much attention to the study and experimental application of mechanical principles, at the cost of both time and money. In 1836 he invented a corn sheller which was patented

AW Gray

and put into use and ranked as one of the best in its day. In 1844 he invented a horsepower, which was perhaps as good as anything in the line then made. He had it patented, and built a few machines, working in a small shop with one or two men to help him, but it did not prove a great success. At about the same time he invented a machine to make wrought iron nails, said to be the first thing of the kind made in the world. But Mr. Gray's crowning work as an inventor, was the improved horsepower with which his name is associated wherever machines of the kind are used, which he produced in 1856. Its merits were such that it commanded a ready sale, and its manufacture was a thriving business from the start. He bought a building in 1857, that had been used as a woolen mill, and fitted it up as a factory. The business prospered, and the profits have since been large and constant. His sons, Albert Y., and Leonidas, became associated with him, and about ten years since he went out of active work, and his sons have since managed the business alone.

"Mr. Gray was always an active, energetic man, and his own enterprises did not prevent his taking a lively interest in public affairs. He held every office in the gift of his town, went to the Legislature in 1866 and 1867, and was one of the eight representatives from Rutland County in the Constitutional Convention in 1857. He discovered the mineral Springs at Middletown which served to make the place a summer resort, and so indirectly, as well as directly, contributed as no other man has, to the material growth of the town.

"Mr. Gray was twice married; the first time to Angeline Skinner, by whom he had four children now living; two sons, Leonidas, and Albert Y. Gray, of Middletown Springs, and among the ablest and most active business men of Rutland Co., and two daughters, Mrs. O. C. Burritt of Hydeville, and Mrs. John P. Clark, of Pawlet. For his second wife he married Martha Holbrook of Sandy Hill, and by her leaves one daughter." Issue:

ABIGAIL C. GRAY, b. Apr. 28, 1833.
LEONIDAS GRAY, b. Dec. 10, 1834.
JOSEPHENE C. GRAY, b. Aug. 27, 1838.
ALBERT Y. GRAY, b. July 22, 1844.
HARRIET M. GRAY, b. July 6, 1849, d. Oct. 12, 1862.
LIZZIE M. GRAY, b. Dec. 21, 1881.

LEONIDAS GRAY.

Leonidas Gray, senior member of the firm of A. W. Gray's Sons, was born at Middletown Springs, Vt., Dec. 10, 1834, son of Albert W., and Angeline Skinner Gray. His life presents an example worthy of emulation by the youth of our country. His early years were similar to those of many of the most successful and eminent men of our time. Born to poverty, he was compelled to lend a helping hand to his father in the struggle for the support of the family, and as a consequence, his advantages for education were limited. But this severe early discipline was doubtless the foundation of all his success in life, and the stepping stone to his present high position among the prosperous and prominent men of his State. During other years, leading up to 1856, he was engaged in various work with his father, including mill-wright and saw mill work, and this proved an excellent school of preparation for the important place he was destined to occupy in the business that then commenced its slow but sure growth. In 1856 he was admitted to a partnership with his father, and they began the manufacture of their now celebrated horse-powers and threshing machines, the perfection of which has been gradual, the result of study and inventive genius, and which stand to-day without a rival. The building of these machines was, at first, necessarily slow, as most of the work was done by hand. The first manufactory was a room 16 by 34, which soon proved insufficient, and more room was from time to time added, until now they find no unemployed space in their immense building 95 feet wide by 175 feet long, four stories, and ten other buildings used for forges, storage, &c., and where more tread powers are manufactured than are made by any other firm in the world, and their machines find a market in all the grain growing countries of the world.

The honor for this large success is due first, to A. W. Gray, for his great mechanical skill and inventive genius; second, to Leonidas Gray, for perfect system adopted and still maintained in the conduct of the business. He has been the financier of the concern from its beginning, and has conducted the affairs of the firm through its long period of prosperity with a master

Leonidas Gray

hand. The firm continued as A. W. Gray & Son, until 1866, when another son of the inventor, Albert Y. Gray, was admitted to the partnership, and the firm name was changed to A. W. Gray & Sons. This firm continued until 1875, when A. W. Gray sold out his interest to his sons, and the firm name was again changed, to A. W. Gray's Sons.

Mr. Gray has held the office of Vice President of the National Bank of Poultney, Vt., since its organization; he is also President of the Gray National Bank of Middletown Springs, and was largely instrumental in getting into operation the famous Monteith Hotel. The Gray Brothers, wherever known, are highly esteemed, and the community in which they live may well feel proud of two such energetic and enterprising men. They sympathize with every proposition looking to the public good, and are liberal patrons of every worthy object.

The life of the subject of this sketch, as will be seen, has allowed him very little opportunity or time to take active part in public affairs, had he been so inclined. He represented his town however, in the State Legislature in 1880, that being the only official position he has accepted from the hands of his fellow townsmen. Leonidas Gray has been twice married. His first wife was Ellen Mosely, to whom he was married Sept. 12, 1860. She died in 1872, and he married 2d, Alice Woodruff, Dec. 15, 1875. Issue:

FRANCIS L. GRAY, b. Jan. 21, 1862.
ELLEN CORINNE GRAY, b, July 28, 1863.
ETHEL MOSELY GRAY, b. Aug. 29, 1867.
ALBERT WOODRUFF GRAY, b. Dec. 13, 1881.

Francis L. Gray married Fanny L. Hastings, Nov. 13, 1884.

ALBERT Y. GRAY.

Much that has been said of his brother, Leonidas, may also be said of Albert Y. Gray. He is Vice President of the Gray National Bank, and has represented his town in the State Legislature. He married Sarah A. Marshall, Dec. 12, 1867, and has two daughters:

SARAH ANGELINE GRAY, b. March 16, 1870.
JOSEPHINE BAKER GRAY, b. Feb. 25, 1874.

Josephine C. Gray mar. John P. Clark, July 4, 1860; issue:
Eva A., b. May 18, 1861; Emma A., b. Nov. 20, 1865; John
W. Clark, b. Mar. 31, 1871.

Abigail C. Gray mar. Oscar C. Burritt, Dec. 25, 1855; issue:
Nelson, b. May 14, 1857; Oscar C., b. July 24, 1863; Bertha A.
and Bertha L., (twins,) b. Nov. 18, 1866; William G., b. July 8,
1872; and LeGrand Burritt, b. Nov. 8, 1874.

Dr. W. P. Gray, youngest son of Aaron, resides at Delevan,
Wis., but repeated letters earnestly requesting information, having failed to elicit response, it is impossible to give the record of
his family here, other than the fact that he has a daughter, Mina
Gray.

ISAAC GRAY.

Isaac Gray, born 1764, "in or near Danbury, Conn.," married Lucina Barnum, born 1770, and "early in their married
life" removed to Dorset, Vt., where he died Oct. 18, 1840, and
she died July 19, 1846. Isaac Gray was a Deacon in the Baptist Church at Dorset, and a respected citizen. Issue:

> ELIJAH GRAY, b. Aug. 31, 1790, d. Jan. 1, 1856.
> ALVIN GRAY, b. July 14, 1792, d. Aug. 25, 1877.
> HEMAN GRAY.
> POLLY GRAY.

Elijah Gray, son of Isaac, married in 1814, Lydia Cleveland,
who was born in Salem, N. Y., May 9, 1791, and died Oct. 18,
1872. Mr. Gray always lived in Dorset, and was a member of
the Baptist Church at that place. Issue:

> ALVIN C. GRAY, b. Apr. 10, 1816, d. Sept. 5, 1839, at West
> Dorset, Vt.

> HANNAH C. GRAY, b. Oct. 5, 1817, mar. Guy Collson, Oct. 3,
> 1839, and d. Aug. 4, 1860, at Cortland, De Kalb Co., Ill.
> Issue: Mark G. Collson, b. Dec. 20, 1843, residence,
> Chicago. Augusta Maria Collson, b. Oct. 20, 1843, at
> Helena, N. Y., mar. at Dorset, Vt., Oct. 1, 1868, to E.
> Ferrand Hatch, of Sugar Grove, Kane Co., Ill., he a son
> of Elam, son of Deacon Timothy Hatch, one of the pi-
> oneer settlers and original proprietors of Sherburne, Che-
> nango Co., N. Y., he a son of Jethro Hatch and born at

Kent, Conn., Dec. 12, 1757. Issue of E. Ferrand and Augusta Collson Hatch: Burdette M., b. Feb. 27, 1870; Cora G., b. June 1, 1871; Addie M., b. Dec. 6, 1872; Lorenzo C., b. Jun. 18, 1874; Martha F., b. Dec. 6, 1876; Herbert D. Hatch, b. Oct. 8, 1883; all of Sugar Grove, Kane Co., Ill. Mylo Elijah Collson, son Hannah Gray and Guy Collson, b. June 9, 1845, d. Dec. 29, 1876, at Sugar Grove, Ill.

ARELIA MARIA GRAY, b. May 21, 1821, mar. Joseph Cross of Bombay, N. Y., (present residence,) 1844; no children.

MARVETT GRAY, b. Jan. 19, 1823, mar. Geo. Baldwin, May 6, 1860; residence, West Dorset, Vt. Issue: Bertha M. Baldwin, b. Aug. 2, 1861, d. July 11, 1866; George W. Baldwin, b. March 31, 1864.

LUKE B. GRAY, b. Jan. 15, 1825. mar. Dorsena Harrington, Jan. 1, 1848, and d. March 4, 1878. Issue: A daughter, b. Oct. 21, 1850, and mar. in August, 1869, to Robert Goff, of Broome. in the Province of Canada; children: Ephraim C., Caleb F., and Julia Maud Goff; all reside in Franklin, Franklin Co., N. Y.

LAMIRA GRAY, b. Aug. 21, 1828, d. Sept. 26, 1868, at Dorset.

Alvin Gray, son of Isaac, married Susannah Cleveland, daughter of Job Cleveland and Hannah Clark, whose father was killed at the battle of Stillwater Sept. 19, 1777. She was born June 18, 1794, and died at Dorset, Nov. 24, 1875. The issue of this marriage was:

LOUISA GRAY, b. June 13, 1813, d. June 8, 1838.
MARY GRAY, b. 1815, d. July 28, 1843.
LUCINA GRAY, b. Nov. 2, 1817, d. Aug. 31, 1884.
JOB CLEVELAND GRAY, b. May 17, 1820.
CLARK GRAY, b. July 4, 1822.
SUSAN GRAY, b. Sept. 16, 1828, d. Aug. 31, 1884.
GEORGE W. GRAY, b. May 17, 1833.
HENRY GRAY.

Job Cleveland Gray, son of Alvin, married Delight L. Sargeant, March 26, 1844. Resides at Eureka, Kansas. Issue:

ARTHUR W. GRAY, b. June 10, 1847, mar. Nellie Lowrey, Oct. 1872. Issue:

FREDDIE R. GRAY, b. Sept. 29, 1873; d.
GERTRUDE AGNES GRAY, b. Nov. 1874.
CATHARINE D. GRAY, b. Apr. 1, 1877.
ARTHUR GRAY, b. Nov. 1879.
HERBERT GRAY, b. June 10, 1882.

ELLA MARIA GRAY, b. Apr. 26, 1850, mar. Herbert F. Sheldon, July, 1877. Children: Laura, Carrie B., and Warren J. Sheldon.

AGNES MARTHA GRAY, b. Apr. 23, 1857, mar. H. A. Dales, Oct. 1878. A son, Elwin Ward Dales.

Clark Gray, son of Alvin, mar. Emily Kent, at Dorset, Vt., Sept. 22, 1847, and now resides at Townsend Harbor, Mass. Issue:

> MARTHA LORAIN GRAY, b. in Dorset, Apr. 10, 1850; mar. Dec. 31, 1874.
>
> HATTIE MARIA GRAY, b. in Sherman, N. Y., Oct. 20, 1855.
>
> HENRY CLARK GRAY, b. same place, Oct. 20, 1857.

George Washington Gray, Rev., son of Alvin, was born at Dorset, Vt., and was married Nov. 17, 1852, to Mary E. Miller of Sherman, N. Y. He was married a second time to Martha J. Hawkins, of Warren, Ohio, Dec. 9, 1886. Issue:

> WILLIAM ELIJAH GRAY, b. at Sherman, N. Y., Nov. 7, 1856.
>
> FRANCES MARIA GRAY, b. Jan. 17, 1859.
>
> EDWIN ELMORE GRAY, b. at Portland, N. Y., March 18, 1866.

Rev. Geo. W. Gray is a Minister of the Methodist Episcopal Church, East Ohio Conference, and is at present located at Ashtabula, Ohio.

Polly Gray, daughter of Isaac, married Eliazer Baldwin, and lived at Otter Creek, Iowa. Had a daughter, married Debias Hutchinson and lived at Oshkosh, Wis.

Heman Gray, son of Isaac, married Amy Chandler, March, 1809, and died in Nicholsville, N. Y. Had two children, Isaac C., and Lucina Gray. Isaac C. Gray lives in Ogdensburg, Wis.; Lucina married Eason Bacheldor, of Osceola, Wis.

ELIJAH GRAY.

Elijah Gray, brother of Isaac, Aaron and Daniel, was born June 17, 1772, and lived for a time at least in New Milford, Conn. Married Betsey Dunning, probably of that town, and removed to Charlotte, Vt.; afterwards removed to Elyria, Ohio, where he died June 7, 1848. Issue:

BURR DUNNING GRAY.

Burr Dunning Gray, only son of Elijah, was born at Charlotte, Vt., Jan. 14, 1799, and married Amy Maria Baldwin, at Hines-burgh, Vt., Sept. 8, 1818; she b. Dec. 12, 1799, died at Cold-water, Mich., Mar. 20, 1869; and he died at Constantine, Mich., Sept. 20, 1871. Issue:

SUSAN SALOME GRAY, b. at Hinesburgh, Vt., Sept. 21, 1820, mar. Hiram Hadley, at Gilead, Mich., July 21, 1839, and died at Coldwater, Mich., Jan. 6, 1878; two daughters, Emma H., b. Feb. 5, 1841, mar. Mr. Shrively and d. Feb. 22, 1873, and Ma-rion M., b. Oct. 2, 1843.

MARION AMANDA GRAY, b. Oct. 7, 1823, mar. D. N. Green, at Constantine, Mich., Sept. 30, 1850, and had Ida F., b. Feb. 16, 1852, and Gilbert Burr Green, b. Jan. 21, 1855, both living and married.

ORLO BURR GRAY, b. Apr. 6, 1834, at Cleveland, Ohio, mar. Oct. 6, 1858, Demmie Maria Amsden, of Honeye Falls, N. Y. Present residence, Lennox, Dakota. Issue:

GRACE HELEN GRAY, b. Sept. 13, 1859, at Orland, Ind., mar. J. E. Putnam, Dec. 24, 1879, and has two sons and a daughter.

JESSIE L. GRAY, b. March 21, 1869, at Girard, Mich.

LOUIE GRAY, b. April 30, 1866, d. March 4, 1868.

BIRDIE MAUD GRAY, b. Dec. 9, 1876, at Vermillion, Dak.

MARION L. GRAY, b. Aug. 11, 1878, " "

WM. JEROME GRAY, son of Burr D., b. at Gilead, Mich, May 14, 1837, d. Aug. 31, 1839.

ALFRED HENRY GRAY, b. Oct. 7, 1840, mar. Hattie E. Bur-dick, at Coldwater, Mich., Nov. 26, 1862; has a son.

246.

COL. EDMUND BALDWIN GRAY.

Edmund Baldwin Gray, eldest son of Burr Dunning Gray, was born at Canton, N. Y., June 17, 1825. In 1832 removed to Ohio with his father's family; thence, in 1838, to Michigan. Lived on a farm until 17; attended school at White Pigeon, Mich.; went to Vermont and was educated at the State University at Burlington. Was engaged as instructor and Superintendent of Schools many years, also as manager for publishers of school books in the West. Went to Wisconsin in 1855, for A. S. Barnes & Co., N. Y.

Enlisted in April, 1861, in the war for the Union. Was made Captain of Company C, 4th Wisconsin Infantry; served in that capacity in the Army of the Potomac till March, '62, when he went South with Gen. Butler on the New Orleans Expedition. Was sent home from there for disability, in April, 1862. Re-entered service as Major of the 28th Wisconsin Infantry in July, '62. In Feb., '63, the Regt. was assigned to the First Division, 13th Army Corps, in Vicksburg operations; June, '63, was made Lt. Colonel of his Regt. In August, '63, was assigned to 7th Army Corps, and engaged in the operations resulting in the capture of Little Rock. In March, '64, was promoted to Colonel of same Regiment. Was in the Red River Expedition '64; early in '65 joined Canby at Mobile; assigned to 3d Div., 13th Army Corps commanded by Gordon Granger. Participated in capture of Mobile, and in June, '65, was ordered to the Rio Grande, under Sheridan, and was there till August, '65, when the Regiment was mustered out of the service.

Col. Gray was Postmaster at Whitewater, Wis., till 1868, when he resigned to go into the school book business at Chicago. From 1875 he was for three years Asst. State Superintendent of Schools of the State of Illinois. In 1880 he returned to Wisconsin, and in Sept., 1886, was appointed Adjutant General of the Grand Army of the Republic, by Gen. Lucius Fairchild, Commander-in-Chief of that Order, with headquarters at Madison, Wis.

Col. Gray married Ada E. Turner, at Hillsdale, Mich., Sept. 9, 1854, she born at Geneva, Ohio, March 14, 1834. Issue:

MAUD EMILY GRAY, b. at Racine, Wis., Oct. 20, 1856; mar. Bronson C. Keeler, Feb. 22, 1881, and had Paul Gray Keeler, b. in Chicago, Dec. 16, 1881, and Edmund Starr Keeler, b. Dec. 27, 1884.

BURR MATTHEW GRAY, b. at Palmyra, Wis., Oct. 18, 1858, mar. Minnie Graham, Jan. 1, 1881, and had

> HELEN GRAY, b. in Chicago, Nov. 17, 1881.
> MAUD SOPHIA GRAY, b. Sept. 21, 1883.

EDMUND SHERIDAN GRAY, b at Whitewater, Wis., May 14th, 1864.

PAUL HENRY GRAY, b. May 4, 1866.

GEORGE GERRY GRAY, b. in Chicago, Nov. 25, 1869.

ALONZO MILTON GRAY, b. at Charlotte, Vt., April 2, 1829, resides at San Francisco; has a daughter.

HELEN JANE GRAY, b. July 7, 1831, mar. L. T. Hull, June 16, 1853, at Constantine, Mich., and had Lee Gray, b. Oct. 13, 1855; Fred Alonzo, b. July 21, 1858; Warren C., b. May 22, 1860, and one other son and a daughter.

SALLY GRAY, dau. of Elijah, mar. Leverett Sherman, and had Polly, Ann, Charles, and Albert W. Sherman. The first two deceased. Polly left two boys, Leverett and Charles Baldwin, both of whom live in Windsor, Ill. A. W. Sherman has three children: Mary, who mar. Wm. H. Holmes, lives in Charlotte, and has five children; Lillie, who mar. Frank L. Eastman, lives in New Haven, Vt., and has three children; and Alfred L. Holmes. A. W. Sherman resides at East Charlotte, Vt.

HARRIET GRAY, dau. of Elijah, mar. Wm. E. Sherman, and had Alma, who mar. Milo Hoyt and left a son who lives in Winnetka, Ill.; Henry, who died in New Haven, Vt.; John H., who lives at Charlotte, Vt.; Cynthia, who mar. Ezra Horford and has a son Wm. E. Horford. Mr. and Mrs. Sherman both died at Charlotte, Vt.

POLLY MARIA GRAY, daughter of Elijah Gray, was born at Charlotte, Vt., Sept. 29, 1801, and died at Lanark, Ill., Aug. 17, 1883. She was mar. to Calvin Powell, Jan. 6, 1819, and had Alma, who mar. a Mr. Rockwell and left a family of children at Elyria, Ohio; Henry and William S. Powell, the latter of whom lives at Elyria and has four children; Polly Ann, who lives in Mich.; also Harriet and Alvira Powell.

CHLOE GRAY, dau. of Elijah, mar. Nelson Burritt, and had Marcius Burritt, who has a family and lives at Hinesburgh, Vt.; Oscar C. Burritt, who mar. Abigail B. Gray, daughter of A. W. Gray, and lives at Hydesville, Vt., and has a family the records of which appear among descendants of Aaron Gray; Matilda, who mar. Servetus Needham and lives at Anamosa, Iowa; Leverett, who has a family and lives in Iowa, and Henry Burritt, who lives at Anamosa, Iowa.

DANIEL GRAY.

Daniel Gray, brother of Isaac, Aaron, and Elijah, is said to have been born in Connecticut, in 1765, and married for his first wife a Miss Borland. They had a daughter Susan, who married a Mr. Bigelow, and lived at Brattleboro, Vt., where she had nine children, and died Aug. 15, 1884, in the 86th year of her age. Daniel Gray's second wife's name was Stone, by whom he had two sons, Rileigh and Cyrus. Rileigh Gray married Lucy Lunn, and lived at Dorset; had four children: Mary, Alice, Alvah, and Alvin Gray, who are said to live somewhere in the State of New York. Rileigh Gray was born July 18, 1802, and died Feb. 16, 1875. Cyrus Gray married and lived in Hartford, Washington Co., N. Y., where he died in August, 1886, and where his widow resides with a daughter, Mrs. Nathan Hills. Daniel Gray's third wife was a Blakely. He always lived in Dorset after his removal from Conn. He died Oct. 2, 1837, in the 72d year of his age. "He had gone out one afternoon with an ox-team after a load of wood, and was found the next morning lying lifeless by the side of the sled, on his back, with his hat on, whip in hand." The widow of Rileigh Gray is said to be living at Gloversville, N. Y. This information concerning the family of Daniel Gray, as well as the record of the descendants of Elijah Gray son of Isaac, has been kindly furnished by Mrs. Geo. Baldwin, of Dorset, Vt.

YARMOUTH GRAYS.

The Yarmouth Grays, so called, are a numerous and notable branch of the Gray family. In a list of those reported as able to bear arms, at Yarmouth, Mass., in 1643, appears the name of John Gray. By Hannah his wife, probably daughter of William Lumpkin, he had: Benjamin, b. Dec. 7, 1648; William, b. Oct. 5, 1650; Mary, who mar. Benj. Ryder, 1670; Edward, John, Jr., and Gideon. John Gray, Jr., removed to Harwich, married Susannah Clark, daughter of Andrew, and had the following:

LYDIA GRAY, b. 1702.
SARAH GRAY, b. 1704.
MEHITABLE GRAY, b. Apr. 7, 1706.
ANDREW GRAY, b. Sept. 29, 1707.
ELISHA GRAY, b. Nov. 29, 1711.
JOSHUA GRAY, b. Oct. 19, 1713, d. 1735.
ANNA GRAY, b. Nov. 30, 1714, mar. Thacher Freeman, 1732.

The above are of record, and it is believed that he also had previously had Lot, Susannah, who mar. Nathaniel Sears, Oct. 10, 1712, Hannah, who mar. Thomas Hall, Feb. 8, 1721, Thomas, Samuel, and Edward.

Lydia Gray mar. Heman Stone, Sept. 21, 1743.

Sarah Gray mar. Samuel Hall, Feb., 1743.

Mehitable Gray mar. Ebenezer Nickerson, of Chatham, Feb. 24, 1746.

Samuel Gray mar. Alice Prince, Sept. 23, 1731.

Elisha Gray of Harwich, and Mrs. Susannah Davis, of Barnstable, declared their intention of marriage July 28, 1739. Elisha Gray, Jr., mar. Mary Crosby and had Edward, b. Oct. 2, 1770.

Thomas Gray, son of John, Jr., mar. Rachel Freeman, dau. of Lieut. Edmund Freeman, Oct. 2, 1729, and had:

SUSANNAH GRAY, b. Oct. 18, 1732.
BETTY GRAY, b. Sept. 6, 1734.
JOSHUA GRAY, b. Sept. 18, 1736, d. Sept. 2, 1755.
HANNAH GRAY, b. Apr. 27, 1739.
SARAH GRAY, b. Oct. 8, 1741.
RACHEL GRAY, b. Apr. 1744.
MEHITABLE GRAY, b. Apr. 1747.
MARY GRAY, b. Apr. 20, 1749.

Andrew Gray was received into Congregational Church, Yarmouth, March 31, 1745; mar. and had Joshua, and probably other children; d. Dec. 19, 1757. This Joshua is probably the Capt. Joshua Gray, b. 1743, who was a prominent figure in the local annals of the Revolution. He was in command of a company of Militia at Yarmouth, in 1776, and was one of a committee appointed to assist in drafting a new State constitution at a later period. He died in 1791, at the early age of 48, but history says of him that "he had lived long enough to perform most important services to his native town, as an officer in the field, and as a patriot in counsel, during the Revolutionary period." He had married Mary, daughter of Thomas Hedge, March 20, 1766, and had the following issue:

THOMAS GRAY, son of Capt. Joshua, b. 1766, mar. Hannah Sears, and had Anna, and Thomas, b. 1800, who mar. Mary S. Gorham of Barnstable, Sept. 21, 1823, and had Thomas, Jr., Mary Gorham, Gorham, and Alice Gray. Thomas Gray, Sr., was lost at sea. Gorham Gray mar. Harriet Webb, and had Mary Sturges and Hattie W. Gray.

HANNAH GRAY, dau. of Capt. Joshua, mar. Ebenezer Sears, Feb. 2, 1786, and had Charles, Joshua, Willard, Lucy, Hannah, · Sally, Mary, and Thomas Warren Sears.

SARAH GRAY, dau. of Capt. Joshua, b. Nov. 31, 1771, mar. David Thacher, Jr., July 4, 1786, and had Sally, Lothrop, Russel, Daniel. She died July 21, 1793.

MARY GRAY, dau. of Capt. Joshua, was b. Feb. 26, 1773.

PHEBE GRAY, dau. of Capt. Joshua, b. March 10, 1775, mar. Erving Smith, Nov. 20, 1794, and had Sally; mar. 2d, John Gray of Barnstable, Mass., and by this second marriage was a daughter, Elizabeth, who mar. Capt. John A. Baxter, of Hyannis, and had Cleone, Emma, John, and Lizzie. Sally Smith mar. John Gray, Jr., the son of her step-father by a previous marriage, and had John (3), who mar. and had two sons and three daughters; Isabel, Cleone, who mar. a Gorham and had Dingee and Frank Gorham; Sarah, Lizzie Irving, and Grace, who mar. Thos. Hallett and had Irving.

JOSHUA GRAY (2), son of Capt. Joshua, b. Oct. 3, 1777, mar. Rebecca Hallet, and had: Mary, Lydia, Rebecca, Charles, Eunice, Joshua, and Joseph Warren Gray, who mar. his cousin Lucy, dau. of Chandler Gray. Rebecca mar. Henry Matthews of Yarmouth, and Lydia mar. Edward Thacher.

CHANDLER GRAY, son of Capt. Joshua, b. Oct. 6, 1780, mar. Lucy Taylor, May 9, 1805, and had: Samuel, Lucretia, Hannah, Chandler, Thomas, Lucy, Henry, Mary, and William Gray. Lucretia mar. Chas. Noble. Hannah mar. Bartlett Gray of Yarmouth. Thomas mar. Mary L. Thacher; had Alice; d. 1866.

MARY GRAY (2), dau. of Capt. Joshua, b. Apr. 10, 1783, mar. Prince Matthews, and had: Frederick, George, Charlotte, and Prince Matthews, Jr.

ELIZABETH GRAY, dau. of Capt. Joseph, b. March 11, 1786, mar. Henry Thacher, Nov. 25, 1802, and had: Eliza Jane, Henry Gray, Winslow Lewis, Mary Burr, Sally, Maria Edith, George, Thomas, Charles, Caroline, Cornelia and Henry Charles.

The following children were born to Lot Gray, son of John, Jr., and Bethiah his wife:

JOHN GRAY, b. July 27, 1719.
LYDIA GRAY, b. May 22, 1721.
LOT GRAY, Jr., b. Feb. 24, 1722.
MARY GRAY, b. Feb. 28, 1724.
MEHITABLE GRAY, b. Feb. 20, 1726.

Bethiah Gray d. Oct. 16, 1728, and Lot mar. 2d, Jane Otis, of Barnstable, Jan. 7, 1731, and had:

NATHANIEL GRAY, b. Oct. 5, 1733.

Lot Gray, Jr., mar. Meriam Smith, June 30, 1743, and had the following:

LYDIA GRAY, b. Apr. 14, 174–.
ANTHONY GRAY, b. Oct. 19, 1745.
JONATHAN GRAY, b. Feb. 9, 1746.
MARY GRAY, b. Aug. 8, 1748.
MERIAM GRAY, b. March 1, 1750.
AZAH GRAY, b. April 13, 1752.
BETHIAH GRAY, b. Feb. 16, 1753.
LOT GRAY, 3d, b. Nov. 29, 1755.
SAMUEL GRAY, b. Aug. 3, 1762.
JANE GRAY, b. Apr. 4, 1766.
DEAN GRAY, b. July 15, 1768.

Dean Gray was the father of Dean Gray (2), born in Brewster, 1797, d. 1881, he father of Dean Gray (3), b. at Brewster, (adjoining Harwich, Mass.,) 1822, he father of W. M. Gray, b. at Rockville, Ct., Nov. 17, 1849, who resides at Springfield, Mass.

WILLIAM GRAY, believed to be son of John (1) of Yarmouth, born 1650, was married and continued to live there until about 1708, when he removed to Harwich, where he had purchased a large tract of land. He died there in 1723. The name of his wife has not been ascertained. Issue:

WILLIAM GRAY, (2), who mar. Deborah Sears of Yarmouth, October 8, 1719, was the only son, and inherited the homestead, upon which he continued to reside until he removed to Haddam, Conn., 1747, whence all trace of his family is lost. Previous to this however, a daughter, Rebecca, had mar. Jabez Berry in 1745, and removed to Dutchess Co., N. Y., and whither the rest of the family may eventually have followed. The following is a list of his children so far as known:

> WILLIAM GRAY, (3), b. Feb. 13, 1720.
> REBECCA GRAY, b. June 16, 1723.
> THANKFUL GRAY, b. Jan. 14, 1725.
> SARAH GRAY, b. Dec. 19, 1726.
> THOMAS GRAY, b. Nov. 19, 1728.
> ANNA GRAY, b. Oct. 16, 1730.
> MARY GRAY, b. Jan. 22, 1732.
> DEBORAH GRAY, b. Oct. 21, 1734.

It is also claimed that there were sons John and Silas. The only possible other trace found of any one of this family is, there was a Thomas Gray who was a tax-payer in the town of South East, Dutchess Co., N. Y., date of 1771.

William Gray (3) mar. Judith Nickerson, Harwich, Oct. 8, 1741.

The following is the record of the daughters of William (1):

HANNAH GRAY, who mar. William Penny, 1714, and removed to the Oblong, (South-East, then in Dutchess, and now in Putnam Co., N. Y.,) where her descendants continue to reside.

> DOROTHY GRAY, who mar. Josiah Swift, June 25, 1719.
> SARAH GRAY, who mar. Eldad Atwood, Oct. 23, 1718.
> MEHITABLE GRAY, who mar. Isaac Atwood, Oct. 23, 1718.
> THANKFUL GRAY, who mar. John Atwood, June 18, 1718.
> REBECCA GRAY.

SILAS GRAY.

The mystery surrounding the descendants of William Gray, as stated on the foregoing page, was happily dispelled, in part, at least, by a communication received from George Edward Gray, Esq., of San Francisco, who is of that family, just too late there to appear, but the interesting data so obtained is herewith given, as follows:

Silas Gray, son of William (2), who had removed with his father's family to Haddam, Conn., married and had four sons: Edward, Ichabod, John, and Thomas. Edward married and had four sons: Joel, Nehemiah, Riley, and Elnathan; and four daughters: Lucy, Huldah, Silva, and Abigail. Soon after the birth of Joel, the eldest son, Edward Gray removed from Connecticut to Williamstown, Mass., from whence, in 1803, he and his family moved to the Chenango Valley, in New York, and afterwards to Verona, Oneida Co., in the same State, locating in the Valley of Oneida Creek, near its junction with Oneida Lake, where Edward Gray soon after died, leaving a widow and eight children, as above named.

Joel Gray, eldest son of Edward, was born June 24, 1790, and died at Rome, N. Y., July 3, 1873. He married Betsey Resseguie, a daughter of Timothy Resseguie and his wife, Abigail Lee, a daughter of Deacon John Lee, who was born in North Hampton, Montgomery Co., N. Y., August 15, 1794, and who died at Rome, N. Y., Aug. 13, 1886. The Resseguies are one of the old Huguenot families that settled in and near Norwalk, Conn., at an early day. Joel Gray had four sons: Alexander, Joel, Jr., George E., and Noah Duane Gray; and four daughters: Caroline, who died in infancy, Betsey Ann, who married Samuel Allen and moved to Willoughby, Ohio, and died leaving a son, James A. Allen, who resides at Painesville, Ohio; Sarah Jane, who married Corydon C. Howe, and had Alvah, Joel T., and Charles; and Caroline, 2d, who died at thirteen years of age. Joel Gray, Jr., died unmarried. Noah Duane Gray married Ruth Cole, lives at Syracuse, N. Y., and has a son Edward Gray. Alexander Gray married Sarah Smith and had George W., Adaline, and Charles, since dec'd. He mar. 2d, Harriet Ferris.

GEORGE EDWARD GRAY.

George Edward Gray, son of Joel, son of Edward, son of Silas, son of William Gray (2), of Harwich, was born in Verona, Oneida Co., N. Y., Sept. 12, 1818, and received his early education in his native village. At an early age he manifested a predilection for civil engineering, and after completing his preliminary studies, he was placed under the tuition of Peletiah Rawson, M. A., one of the most noted civil engineers of his time. Under his instruction young Gray made rapid progress, and upon attaining his majority was employed upon the Black River and Erie Canals, and also upon several Railroads then being constructed in the State of New York. In 1853, the various R. R. Companies then operating between Albany and Buffalo were consolidated with the New York Central R. R., and Mr. Gray was appointed Chief Engineer. This important position he held until 1865, when he resigned to accept the position of Consulting Engineer of the Central Pacific Railroad of California, and remained in that position until 1871, when he was appointed Chief Engineer of the Southern Pacific R. R., which position he resigned in 1885. Mr. Gray also directed the location and construction of the Galveston, Harrisburg and San Antonio Railroad from El Paso to Antonio, Texas. Mr. Gray is a life member of the " Institute of Civil Engineers," of London, England, and also a member of the "American Society of Civil Engineers," of New York. He is a life member of the California Academy of Sciences, and is President of the Board of Directors of that Society. A writer in a recent number of *The Resources of California*, says: " Mr. Gray has earned an honored place among the architects of California's growth and prosperity, and well deserves the tribute of respect paid him by Senator Stamford, in appointing him one of the Trustees of his noble benefaction." Mr. Gray has been twice married. His first wife was Adaline Goodrich, of Rome, N. Y. His second marriage was with Lucinda S. Corning, daughter of Richard S. Corning, of Syracuse, and a niece of Hon. Erastus Corning, late of Albany, N. Y. By his second wife, has two children : Anna Spencer, and George Vernon Gray. Residence, San Francisco.

The widow of Edward Gray, (son of Silas) after the death of her husband, removed with three of her sons, Nehemiah, Riley, and Elnathan, to the vicinity of Jamestown, Chautauqua Co., N. Y., where she died at an advanced age. One of the sons remained there, and the two others removed to Lake Co., Ohio.

Ichabod Gray, son of Silas, resided, after the Revolution, in the valleys of the Chenango and Susquehanna. Mr. George E. Gray remembers that he came from thence to visit his father's family in Oneida Co., walking the whole distance there and return, when he was 110 years old! He was a rare character, and generally called "Uncle Nick." He had four sons: William, Silas, James and Jonathan. They are believed to have lived in southern N. Y., or northern Pa.

Thomas Gray, son of Silas, moved to Madison Co., N. Y., about the time that his brother Edward went to Chenango Co., and died there at an advanced age. The sons, Anson, John, and Jerry, settled about their father, and continued to live near the old homestead.

John Gray, son of Silas, had one son, William, residence unknown.

William Gray (1), was Sergeant in a company raised at Yarmouth for the war with King Philip, and with others received a grant of land for such service, in the town of Gorham, Me., then a part of Mass., and this land afterwards came to be the property of his son, William (2). There is no evidence, however, that he ever resided there, although there was quite an emigration thither from Yarmouth, including doubtless some of the Grays, whence the name of Gray given to an adjoining township, and many of that name who have resided in the State of Maine.

William Gray (3), it is said had one son, name unknown.

EDWARD GRAY.

The record of the family of Edward Gray of Yarmouth, believed to have been the son of John, is very meagre and unsatisfactory. The records of Harwich show that he had a son Benoni Gray, born there Mar. 15, 1680. The will of John Freeman, Jr., of Yarmouth, date of 1721, mentions a son of Edward Gray, dec'd, without giving his name. Edward Gray's first wife is believed to have been the daughter of Jonathan Sparrow. She dying, he married again, and is said to have had other children. Benoni Gray was early in Falmouth, where he died in 1732. His wife was named Sarah. He appears to have been a mariner. There was an Edward Gray who married Hannah Godfrey at Yarmouth, July 3d, 1727, who had a daughter Mary, born Oct. 18, 1728, also a daughter Priscilla, and a son, Richard, baptized 1735, but it does not clearly appear whose son he was; probably, however, the son, or grandson,—more likely the former,—of Edward (1), for he appears on the records in 1741, as receiving by entail, rights in a certain tract or grant of land of which the title had originally been vested in Edward (1). This, if not absolute proof of the lineage of the Edward Gray who married Hannah Godfrey, is certainly strong circumstantial evidence.

Edward Gray, believed to be the aforesaid, next appears at South-East, then Dutchess, and now Putnam Co., N. Y., in 1745. The Hall family, the Wm. Penney who had married Hannah, daughter of Wm. Gray of Harwich, the Crosbys, the Paddocks, and the Ryders, who had also intermarried with the Grays, all from the Cape, emigrated about that date, or soon after, to the town of South-East, and settled in the same neighborhood with Edward Gray. Others by the name of Gray appear on the records at a later date, in that vicinity, some of whom are the sons of Edward (2), and others of kindred, as follows: Edward, Jr., John, Benoni, Godfrey, Richard, and Oliver, who was from the north part of Harwich, and was in his native place on a visit in the winter of 1762. Now, it must be admitted that there is a slight discrepancy between this data and records furnished by the descendants of Edward, Jr. For instance, it is stated that he died in 1806, aged 78 years, which would make him born in 1728, whereas the Edward Gray claimed to have been his father,

was married in 1727, and the first child was a daughter, born in
1728. Probably there was an error, not uncommon, in regard to
his age, the date of his death, and not of his birth, being
given. That Edward should have named one of his sons Benoni, after his uncle or brother, and one Godfrey, after the father of
his wife, and one John, after the original pilgrim of this line, is
certainly a reasonable hypothesis, and it is believed to be correct. Oliver Gray was probably of another branch of the
same family; perhaps of the descendants of Gideon. Edward
Gray (2), probably died prior to 1772, as after that date Edward
(3) was not recorded as Edward, Jr. Edward (3) had made several purchases of lands in Berkshire Co., Mass., prior to 1770,
and was at that date living in the town of Lenox in said Co.,
on what was called the Minister's Grant. His sons evidently
soon followed, three of them, John, David, and Isaiah being en-
rolled among the soldiers of the Revolution from that town.
Mr. Gray was a man of substance and character. His name appears frequently upon the real estate records, and on July 6,
1774, he was chosen as one of the Delegates to the so called
Berkshire Congress. Dec. 26th of the same year, the town of
Lenox voted to re-imburse Edward Gray and others for expenses
incurred in "having hurried to the coast on what proved to be a
false alarm of war." So prompt was he to answer the call of
patriotism. In 1784, Capt. Edward Gray was one of the Delegates to a Convention to locate the Court House of Berkshire
County. His wife, Mary Paddock Gray, died Feb. 28, 1789,
aged about 62 years. He died at Lenox, 1805 or 1806, there
being no record obtainable of the exact date. Issue:

    JOHN GRAY, b. May 19, 1750.
    ISAIAH GRAY, b. 1752.
    SAMUEL GRAY, b. 1754.
    DAVID GRAY, b. 1757.
    MARY GRAY, b. 1759.
    RUTH GRAY, b. 1762.
    MERCY GRAY, b. 1764.
    HANNAH GRAY, b. 1766.
    ABIGAIL GRAY, b. 1769.
    EDWARD GRAY, (4), b. 1772.
    MIRIAM GRAY, b. 1774.

In addition, two daughters are said to have died young.

CAPT. JOHN GRAY.

Capt. John Gray, son of Edward, (3), mar. Susannah Rider, dau. of John Rider, Jr., Jan'y 1, 1770. He d. at Dorset, Vt., May 14, 1814; she d. Feb. 19, 1838. Issue:

Chauncey Gray, b. at Lenox, Mass., June 14, 1771, married Polly Borland, at Dorset, June 14, 1795. He. d. Apr. 28, 1820; she d. June 9, 1843. Issue: Anson Gray, b. Aug. 3, 1796, mar. Dec. 3, 1823, to Roxana Cleveland, of Salem, N. Y. Removed to Germantown, Wis., where he d. March 10, 1871, and she d. June 15, 1880, leaving four children: Chauncey, who was b. at Dorset, Nov. 12, 1824, and mar. Caroline Ostrander of Menamana, Wis., July 18, 1850. Issue:

> HARMON O. GRAY, b. Nov. 20, 1852, d. Feb. 11, 1854.
> BYRON C. GRAY, b. March 2, 1855, d. Aug. 29, 1856.
> MARY ELIZABETH GRAY, b. Aug. 16, 1857.
> SARAH JANE GRAY, b. Oct. 4, 1859.
> ANSON CLARK GRAY, b. Feb. 25, 1862, d. May 28, 1862.
> ALBERT ELLIS GRAY, b. Jan. 16, 1865.

Chauncey Gray resides at Myra, Wis.; has been County Clerk, and is a prominent citizen.

Anson Gray also had Byron Gray, b. June 17, 1828, Mark Gray, b. Sept. 10, 1831, and Mary E. Gray b. Sept. 5, 1837.

Chauncey Gray, Sr., also had Oliver, b. Mar. 13, 1798, Sally, b. Apr. 13, 1800, John, b. Sept. 16, 1804, Susan, b. Aug. 28, 1806, Almon, b. June 6, 1811.

Lorena Gray, dau. of Capt. John, b. Aug. 5, 1772, mar. Stephen Rider, June 2, 1790; she d. May 30, 1799; he d. Sept. 11, 1850; had 6 children, 22 grand children, and 63 g-g-children. A son, John Rider, had 2 daughters named Dorcas Lorena and Hannah Jane, who married brothers by the name of Taylor, the former of whom resides at Helena, Montana, and another daughter who mar. Dr. John E. Best, of Arlington Heights, Ill.

Anna Gray, bapt. at Lenox, Dec. 6, 1773; mar. Lewis Dunning at Dorset, 1792; had 7 children; she d. July 18, 1809; he d. March 30, 1833.

Elizabeth Gray, bapt. at Lenox, Oct. 14, 1775; mar. James

Borland, Sept. 13, 1797, and had 9 children; she d. July 11, 1818; he d. Mar. 15, 1841.

John Gray (2), b. at Dorset, Vt., Apr. 7, 1777; mar. Polly Farnsworth, of Rupert, Jan'y 2, 1803; had 5 children; he died Sept. 30, 1849, and she died Oct. 22, 1865.

Susannah Gray, b. at Dorset, Jan. 9, 1779; mar. Sylvanus Sykes, Nov. 27, 1799; had 10 children; he d. Sept. 25, 1840; she d. Apr. 17, 1866.

Mercy Gray, b. July 20, 1782; mar. Nathan Wilcox, 1798; had 3 children; she d. Dec. 5, 1803.

Simeon Gray, b. July 20, 1782; mar. Polly Ingham, at Green-field, N. Y., Sept. 18, 1804; had 9 children; he d. July 21, 1851; she d. July 11, 1857.

Jerusha Gray, b. Apr. 19, 1785; mar. Walter Rider, Dec. 10, 1820; had 2 children; she d. Jan. 18, 1865.

Edward Gray, b. Feb. 28, 1789; mar. Eunice Manly, Oct. 13, 1808; had 9 children; she d. Aug. 16, 1842; he d. May 31, 1849.

Paddock Gray, b. Oct. 12, 1793; mar. Elizabeth Manly, Aug. 23, 1815; had 4 children; he d. Apr. 24, 1858; she is still living, in her 97th year.

William Gray, youngest son and child of Capt. John Gray, b. Oct. 5, 1795; mar. Mercy Eastman of Rupert, Vt.; had 5 children; he d. Dec. 6, 1866.

The total footing of the descendants of Capt. John Gray, as furnished, shows the following remarkable summary: No. of children, 77; grandchildren, 268; great-grandchildren, 489; Total descendants, 834.

These statistics of the families of Edward (2) and Capt. John Gray, and some that follow, have been furnished by Mr. Alanson Gray, of Dorset, Vt., who is a grandson of Capt. John, and a son of John (2), born at Dorset, Oct. 12, 1807, and mar. to Rosetta C. Kellogg, March 24, 1831. He writes: " We have had 7 children; 4 are dec'd; our oldest son, Augustus H. Gray, born Jan. 31, 1832, is married and has a family of 10 children; is in the marble trade at Catskill, N. Y. A daughter Ellen, b. Aug. 23, 1843, mar. Amos Kilborn, of Litchfield, Conn. Our youngest, Marcia Kellogg Gray, b. Dec. 21, 1851, remains at home." Mr. Gray has collected full data of his grandfather's family, which would have appeared herewith if the conditions by him required had been within the scope of this work.

Isaiah Gray, son of Edward (3), settled in Middletown, Vt., and had 3 sons and two daughters.

David is said to have lost a leg in the Revolutionary war; he mar. Hannah Newberry and removed to Vt. He had sons Harry, John, Isaiah, Edward and David, Jr. Harry Gray had Wm. N., Eugene, Henry, and a daughter, all living at Middletown Springs, Vt. Harry Gray, it is said was b. in New Brunswick, N. J., 1787, and died in 1865.

Mary Gray mar. Ebenezer Hawkins, and had 4 children.

Ruth Gray mar. Gershom Martindale, and had 6 children.

Mercy Gray mar. Alexander Kent and had 7 children.

Hannah Gray mar. Abner Bangs, of Lenox, Mass., and had 8 sons and two daughters, Chauncey Bangs, one of the former, still survives, and others of the descendants continue to reside in that vicinity.

Edward Gray (4), mar. Rhoda Stoddard, and had 15 children.

Miriam Gray mar. Roger Hawkins, at Lenox; removed to Vergennes, Vt., and raised 12 children, one of whom, Rev. Henry Hawkins, resides at Granville, Putnam Co., Ill.

Priscilla Gray, daughter of Edward (2), was mar. to John Rainey, at the Oblong, July 4, 1773.

Godfrey Gray, son of Edward (2), made a will in 1818, giving legacies to his wife, Sarah, his sons John, Martin, Richard, and daughters Hannah and Caty. He was then at Ancram, Columbia Co., N. Y., although the will was probated in Dutchess Co., and is there on file.

Martin Gray had Morgan, and two other sons and daughters. Morgan had Samuel Martin Gray of Sugerties, N. Y., and John M. and Charles F. Gray.

Richard Gray, son of Godfrey, mar. Mary Tompkins, and had Daniel Gray, who settled in Western New York, Richard Gray,

John Gray, who always lived in the town of Pine Plains, Dutchess Co., N. Y., Hannah, who mar. Edmund Reynolds, Lydia, who mar. Abel Eldridge, Jane, who mar. a Mr. Rowe, and had a daughter Hannah, Priscilla Gray, who mar. Eleazer Conklin, and Ambrose T. Gray, who was born Jan. 24, 1788, mar. Almira Finch, dau. of Caleb Finch, Oct. 28, 1818, and had Ward B. Gray, merchant, and formerly Postmaster, of Millerton, N. Y., Louisa, who married a Mr. Douglas, and resides at Hillsdale, N. Y., and Tompkins C. Gray, who was teaching school when the Rebellion broke out, but left to enlist as a private in "Scott's Life Guards," 4th Regt. N. Y. V.; was promoted to First Lieut., honorably discharged, was war correspondent of the *N. Y. Tribune*, afterwards on the editorial staff of the *Post*, at Washington, where he died April 2, 1885. Ambrose T. Gray died May 23, 1859.

———

The researches herewith made afford almost conclusive evidence that the Grays of Tisbury, Martha's Vineyard, some account of whom is given on page 186, and following, were of the Yarmouth family, the intermarriages, and similarity of names, being an almost unmistakable indication. The Freemans had married Grays, and the Grays, Freemans, and a Freeman Gray was there found, a son of the Isaiah Gray whose family is traced on the pages referred to.

The time and labor bestowed by the compiler of this work upon the genealogy of the foregoing branch of the Gray family, incomplete as it appears, cannot easily be estimated, and no results to him commensurate are anticipated. Local histories, and genealogies, and town and church records have been carefully searched for ultimate facts, and every available source of information sought out. Rev. Frederick Freeman, author of the Freeman Genealogy, and of the "Cape Cod Annals," of whose elaborate researches avail has been made, says in the latter work, "The genealogical data of the highly respectable family of Grays, is to our mind somewhat complicated." Acknowledgment is also made to Josiah Paine, the historian of Harwich, for much interesting information furnished. In regard to the origin of the Yarmouth Grays, they were probably of English ancestry.

PLYMOUTH GRAYS.

There is early mention in the annals of Plymouth, of Edward Gray, a youth, who first appeared there in 1643. Very likely he was a younger brother of John of Yarmouth. For his first wife he married Mary Winslow, daughter of John Winslow, who was a brother of Gov. Winslow. The wife of John Winslow and the mother of Mary, was Mary Chilton, daughter of James Chilton, who came over in the *Mayflower*, and died the first winter. Edward Gray was married to Mary Winslow Jan. 16, 1650, and had Desire, b. Feb. 24, 1651, who married Lieut. Nathaniel Southwick; Mary b. Sept. 18, 1653; Eliza, b. Feb. 11, 1658; Sarah, b. Aug. 12, 1659; and a son, John Gray, born October 1, 1661, from whom are descended the Grays now of Kingston, Mass. Mary Winslow Gray died in 1663, and he married second, Dorothy Lettice, Dec. 12, 1665, by whom were three sons: Edward, Thomas, and Samuel; also three daughters, two of whom married Coles, and the youngest, Lydia, married Caleb Loring, of Plympton, Mass., from whom the Lorings in the north part of that town are descended. The oldest stone in the Plymouth Burial Ground is that of Edward Gray, on which is the following inscription : " Here lyeth a body of Edward Gray, Gent, aged about 52 years, and departed this life ye last of June, 1681."

Edward Gray (2), b. Jan. 31, 1666, removed to Tiverton, R.I., married, and had the following children:

MARY GRAY, b. May 16, 1691.
EDWARD GRAY, (3), b. Jan. 10, 1692.
ELIZABETH GRAY, b. Jan. 23, 1695.
SARAH GRAY, b. April 25, 1697.
PHEBE GRAY, b. Sept. 6, 1699.
PHILIP GRAY, b. Feb. 11, 1702.
THOMAS GRAY, b. Feb. 4, 1705.
HÁNNAH GRAY, b. Nov. 3, 1707.

Edward Gray mar. 2d, Mary, and had:

JOHN GRAY, b. Aug. 3, 1712.
LYDIA GRAY, b. May 12, 1714.
WILLIAM GRAY, b. July 17, 1716.
SAMUEL GRAY, b. Aug. 31, 1718.

Philip Gray mar. Sarah, and had the following:

PHILIP GRAY, Jr., b. Apr. 6, 1728.
PARDON GRAY, b. April 20, 1737.
PHILIP GRAY, 2d, b. June 22, 1750.

Pardon Gray mar. Mary, and had:

JOB GRAY, b. May 14, 1756.
SARAH GRAY, b. May 3, 1758.
EDWARD GRAY, b. July 8, 1759.
MARY GRAY, b. Aug. 3, 1761.
LYDIA GRAY, b. March 15, 1763.
ABIGAIL GRAY, b. Aug. 2, 1764.
PHILIP GRAY, b. Feb. 2, 1766.
PARDON GRAY, Jr., b. Oct. 11, 1767.
HANNAH GRAY, b. May 2, 1769.
JOHN GRAY, b. May 20, 1772.
THOMAS GRAY, b. Nov. 28, 1774.
MARY GRAY, b. Nov. 18, 1776.

Job Gray mar. Juliette Briggs, of Tiverton, Dec. 16, 1781.

Elizabeth Gray, daughter of an Edward Gray of Tiverton, mar. Willard Briggs, Oct. 15, 1778.

Samuel Gray, of the sons of Edward (1), also settled in Tiverton, R. I. He died unmarried.

Thomas Gray, the youngest son of Edward, settled in Little Compton, R. I. He was chosen a Deacon of the First Congregational Church established there in 1704, and died there, 1721. A large brown stone marks the place of his burial, and a large plot there is devoted to his descendants, who were numerous. Thomas Gray mar. Hannah Kent, and had several daughters, and a son, Samuel.

Samuel Gray, son of Thomas, married Deborah Peck, and had the following:

HANNAH GRAY, b. Nov. 8, 1751, d. 1755.
FALLEE GRAY, b. Apr. 23, 1754.
JOHN GRAY, b. March 20, 1756.
SIMEON GRAY, b. Apr. 15, 1758, d. 1781.
LYDIA GRAY, b. Jan. 22, 1761.
ELIZABETH GRAY, b. July 23, 1763.
SAMUEL GRAY, b. Sept. 29, 1765.
THOMAS GRAY, b. Apr. 22, 1767.
JONATHAN GRAY, b. Mar. 9, 1771.
JOSHUA GRAY, b. Nov. 10, 1773, d. 1775.
NATHANIEL GRAY, b. Mar. 20, 1776, d. 1836.
LOREN and BENJAMIN GRAY, (twins,) b. Feb. 5, 1779.

Nathaniel Gray mar. Lydia Coe, at Little Compton, March 29, 1807; she was born Dec. 30, 1785, and d. Aug. 30, 1848; he d. Oct. 6, 1836. Issue:

HANNAH KENT GRAY, b. Nov. 2, 1808, d. Dec. 27, 1822.

HARRIET GRAY, b. Aug. 18, 1811, mar. Henry Butler; resides on the old homestead, at Little Compton.

HORACE GRAY, b. Apr. 7, 1813, mar. Parthenia Easterbrook, and had

> EMILY GRAY, b. at Providence, R. I., July 31, 1843, mar. Chas. Rossitter, at Fall River, Mass., Dec. 30, 1866, and had Ada H., and Mabel Gray Rossitter, both deceased; she d. Mar. 7, 1885, and he resides at Brooklyn, N. Y.
>
> HOWARD GRAY, son of Horace, lives at Taunton, Mass.

Horace Gray died at Philadelphia, Jan. 12, 1865.

DIANA COE GRAY, dau. of Nathaniel, b. Aug. 17, 1815, mar. Wm. S. Wood, and had a son, Theodore Wood; she resides at Fall River, Mass.

FALLEE PALMER GRAY, b. Feb. 24, 1818, mar. Jedediah Shaw and had Horace Gray Shaw, who is in business in New York, and resides at South Orange, N. J.; and Anna W., who mar. Frank Brownell of Little Compton, and resides there. Mrs. Shaw died April 26, 1854.

CORNELIUS BRIGGS GRAY, b. Aug. 31 1820. ⎱ d. Sept. 2, 1823.
JOHN GRAY,   "   "   " ⎰

BEJAMIN COE GRAY, b. Feb. 17, 1823, d. Sept. 18, 1823.

GEORGE GRAY, b. Aug. 1, 1824, mar. and had Nancy, who mar. John Sebrey; Elva, George, Jr., and Don; he mar. 2d, and had Elwood Gray; resides at Elmore, Vt.

CHARLES HENRY GRAY, youngest son of Nathanel Gray, born July 23, 1827, mar. but no children; died in California, Feb. 12, 1873.

AMASA GRAY, a son of John Gray, brother of Nathaniel, inherited his father's farm, and at this date is still living there, being the only one residing in that old town of Little Compton, bearing the name of Gray, once so familiar there.

A Thomas Gray, said to have been a brother of Edward, died at Plymouth, June 7, 1654, but there is no evidence that he left descendants.

ASA GRAY, of Tiverton, was Town Clerk for many years from about 1820; also Justice of the Peace, and was called 'Squire Gray.

The Grays were among the early settlers of Tiverton and Little Compton, in company with other Plymouth families, on a grant from the Plymouth Company, which at that time laid claim to all that territory, and which was maintained up to the date of 1746, when the Crown decided that jurisdiction of that section of the east main rightfully vested in Rhode Island.

The Capt. Robert Gray who first crossed the bar at the mouth of the Columbia River, 1790, and consequently regarded as its discoverer, upon which fact the United States successfully based its claim to all the contiguous territory, in the great contest with Great Britain over the North-Western boundary line, and who on his return from that expedition was received with much honor at Boston and other cities, was of the Tiverton Grays, and a descendant of Edward Gray of Plymouth.

There are strong indications that Edward Gray of Plymouth, (and consequently John Gray of Yarmouth,) was a descendant of the Edward Gray mentioned on page 5, as father of Mrs. Desire Kent, who is claimed to have been the first woman of the Pilgrims who landed at Plymouth Rock. This probability is strengthened by the fact that Edward of Plymouth, as will be seen, named his first born daughter, Desire, while his son Thomas married Hannah Kent. Who Edward Gray the father of Desire Kent was, careful search of English annals would doubtless disclose. Perhaps he was the Edward Gray of Lincolnshire who was Knighted and granted Arms in 1635, and who was the ancestor of Edward Gray of Boston, 1686, whose portrait, with Arms, appears at page 191.

It would have been very pleasing to have given a more full record of the Plymouth Grays, but it was not easily obtainable; yet even this fragment of history is sufficient to demonstrate that the field is a most interesting one, which will well repay the researches of the future historian. And these leaflets are thrown in as a contribution to that end.

SALEM GRAYS.

ROBERT GRAY.

Robert Gray, the ancestor of the Salem Grays, must have been at Salem prior to 1651, as the records show that he had a daughter baptized there date of March 9, of that year. His ancestry does not clearly appear, but probably before his marriage, he was an armorer or gunner in one or more voyages with one Capt. Wall, between England and the English Colonies in New England and the West Indies. He married Elizabeth, a kinswoman or connection of Thos. Wickes of Salem. He died at Salem Jan. 11, 1662, and his will, made Jan. 1, 1661-2, names his wife Elizabeth, Executrix. She married 2d, Capt. Nicholas Manning, June 23, 1663, and had Thomas, Nicholas, Margaret and John. Capt. Manning, with others, was presented to the Court for wearing periwigs in Salem, 1679. In 1677 he was commander of the man-of-war "Ketch," which was fitted out at Salem. Was made a Judge in Maine, and afterwards imprisoned there. Living with second wife, Mary, at Richmond, S. I., 1709.

Issue of Robert Gray by Elizabeth his wife:

ELIZABETH, bapt. 1st ch. March 9, 1651; mar. June 25, 1672, John Priest, and had Elizabeth.

JOSEPH GRAY.

JOSEPH GRAY, bapt. May 9, 1652; mar. Deborah Williams, Aug. 10, 1675. He was a gunsmith. Made will May 17, 1690, and proved June 24, following. She mar. 2d, June 14, 1690, James Holgate, Surgeon, of Salem, and had James and Deborah. Issue of Joseph Gray and Deborah his wife:

BENJAMIN GRAY, son of Joseph, b. 167-, made will Dec. 14, 1716, which was proved Jan. 17, following. He was a turner. He mar. Mary Beadle, Mar. 31, 1699. Issue:

BENJAMIN GRAY, (2), b. Oct. 3, 1701.
JOHN GRAY, b. June 21, 1703.
ROBERT GRAY, b. Dec. 15, 1704.
MARY GRAY, bapt. Apr. 15, 1722, (with her mother.)
JONATHAN GRAY, b. 1709.
SARAH GRAY, bapt. April 15, 1722; mar. Benj. Rull.

Benjamin (2) mar. Sarah Cash Nov. 16. 1722; died at Salem Jan 27, 1761. Was a chair-maker, alias turner. Issue:

BENJAMIN GRAY, (3), b. Mar. 29, 1724; lived at Salem and Gloucester; a painter; mar. March 31, 1745, Elizabeth, dau. of Wm. Curtis, of Lynn; d. May 10, 1765.
SARAH GRAY, b. Dec. 14, 1725; d. Mar. 6, 1749.
WILLIAM GRAY, b. Oct. 26, 1727; d. Dec. 24, 1805.
ELIZABETH GRAY, b. Oct. 15, 1731; d. Aug. 19, 1732.
HEPZIBAH GRAY, b. Oct. 12, 1733; mar. Thos. Rice, Dec. 11, 1759, of Boston.
MARY GRAY, b. Oct. 12, 1735.
ELIZABETH GRAY, b. Nov. 18, 1738; mar. Wm. Lander, Mar. 26, 1761, and had Samuel, Elizabeth, Jona, Robert.

William, son of Benjamin (2) and Sarah Cash Gray, b. Oct. 26, 1727, mar. Sarah Mattoon, 1749; was a chair manufacturer; had

WILLIAM GRAY, Jr., b. July 5, 1750; d. Nov. 11, 1819.
SARAH GRAY, Dec. 17, 1753; d. May 23, 1787.
JOHN GRAY, b. Jan. 12, 1761.
BENJAMIN, · " " " d. Jan. 24, 1761.
RICHARD MATTOON GRAY, b. Oct. 5, 1763.

William Gray, Jr., mar. 1st, Susannah Shepherd, Nov. 5, 1772; she d. Apr. 25, 1796, and he mar. 2d, the wid. Hannah Young, Oct. 2, 1796. Issue:

WILLIAM SHEPHERD GRAY, b. July 30, 1773; was Cashier of Essex Bank, Salem, which position, for certain reasons, he abruptly abandoned. He d. about 1830, in Roxbury, Mass. Issue:

WM. MORLAND GRAY, bapt. Jan. 1, 1800; d. young.
HARADEN GRAY, bapt. Aug. 2, 1801.
FREDERICK WALLACE GRAY, bapt. June 5, 1803.
JOHN MORLAND GRAY, bapt. Apr. 15, 1805.
GEORGE ALEXANDER GRAY, bapt. Apr. 5, 1807
WM. MORLAND GRAY, 2d, bapt. July 9, 1809; d. 1810.
ANN AUGUSTA GRAY, bapt. Aug. 30, 1812.
JOHN GRAY, b. June 9, 1775; d. Feb. 8, 1776.
SARAH GRAY, b. Dec. 19, 1776; d. June 28, 1777.
JOHN GRAY, 2d, b. Apr. 24, 1778.

John Gray, son of William, (1), (Benj.-Benj.-Jos.-Robert,) born Jan. 12, 1761, was an accountant and teacher; mar. 1st, Elizabeth Archer, Nov. 18, 1783; she d. Aug. 17, 1814, and he mar. 2d, Mary Holman, Feb. 19, 1815; he d. at Salem, Dec. 9, 1838. Issue:

SARAH GRAY, b. Oct. 25, 1784; d. May 3, 1830.
ELIZABETH GRAY, b. Feb. 17, 1787; d. Jan. 7, 1792.
LUCY GRAY, b. June 21, 1789; mar. Francis H. Board-
man Nov. 29, 1810, and had Elizabeth, George, Ed-
ward, Caroline, Edward, 2d, (lived Portland, Me.,)
Mary N., Emily, Benj. A., of Salem, Wm. A., who
mar. Lucy N. Dodge, dau. of Rev. Wm. B. Dodge,
and 2d, Alvord, of Waukegan, Ill.
Richard Mattoon Gray, son of William, (Benj.-Benj.-Jos.-
Robert,) b. Salem, Oct. 5, 1763, mar. Elizabeth Needham; issue:
RICHARD GRAY, b. July 18, 1786; d. Sept. 5, 1787.
RICHARD GRAY, 2d, b. June 19, 1788.

––––––

John Gray, son of Benj. (Jos.-Robert,) b. in Salem, June 21,
1703, d. in or before 1751. He lived in Provincetown and Sa-
lem. He mar. Phebe, (?) who d. in or before 1761. Issue:
JOHN GRAY.
SARAH GRAY, mar. Charles Adee, or Eddy, of Salem,
March 10, 1768.
RACHEL GRAY.
JAMES GRAY.
There was a Mary Gray, said to have been the dau. of John
and Phebe Gray of Provincetown, b. Jan. 13, 1726, who mar.
Nathan Noble of New Milford, Conn., May 2, 1748. He was
killed at the battle of Saratoga, Oct. 7, 1777; she d. Oct. 29,
1785.
John Gray, son of John, (Benj.-Jos.-Robert,) lived in Salem;
a cordwainer. He mar. Mary, and had:
WILLIAM GRAY, mar. Sarah Smith, of Salem, Aug. 13,
1787; lived at Beverly.
MARGARET GRAY, mar. Sam'l Bell, Apr. 26, 1785, who
had previously mar. Abigail Foster.
MARY GRAY, who mar Dec. 26, 1786, James Snow,
prob. son of James and Edith, who sold to Benjamin Gray land in Salem Jan. 11, 1760.
JOHN GRAY, mar. Elizabeth Brown, Nov. 13, 1794.
Rachel, dau. of John Gray, son of John, &c., mar. Simon
Gordon, Oct. 5, 1755, and had James Gordon, b. 1760, who afterwards took the surname of Gray. He lived in Beverly; mar.
1st, Mary, dau. of Capt. Robert Foster, and 2d, Mary Gage of
Beverly, Apr. 1, 1790; he d. 1792. Had Sarah, b. 1786, who

mar. Andrew Mansfield and resided at Nobleborough, Me., 1861; son Jacob, and dau. Sarah, wife of Hon. Elisha Clarke, Bath, Me. Elizabeth, dau. of James Gordon Gray, b. Beverly, July 21, 1788, mar. Dea. Richard Manning Chipman, Nov. 30, 1805, and had Richard Manning Chipman, bapt. May 6, 1810, also Andrew M., Mary E., Eleazer Moses, Sarah C., Betsey Gray, Thomas, Henry, who d. of disease contracted in the army in 1865, Susan P., James, who d. from wound received in the battle of the Wilderness, and Ward Chipman, who d. 1855.

James Gray, son of John, (Benj.-Jos.-Robert,) lived in Beverly and Salem; a fisherman. Appears to have been a Rev. soldier; mar. 1st, Priscilla Cressey; mar. 2d, Sarah Whitefoot; d. Sept. 25, 1810.

———

Robert Gray, son of Benj. (Jos.-Robert,) b. Salem, Dec. 15, 1704; was a blacksmith; mar. Margaret Glover, Mar. 24, 1726–7; issue:

> ROBERT GRAY, bapt. Sept. 22, 1728.
> BENJAMIN GRAY.
> EPHRAIM GRAY, mar. Aug. 28, 1757.

Benjamin Gray, son of Robert, (Benj.-Jos.-Robt.,) lived in Salem; a ship-wright; mar. Mary Callum, June 21, 1752; she and all her children baptized and received to 1st Ch., Apr. 9, 1769; he d. 176–. Issue:

> ANDREW GRAY, b. 1754; mar. Mary Mugford, May 14, 1780.
> ELIZABETH GRAY, b. 1759.
> BENJAMIN GRAY, b. 1761.
> REBECCA GRAY, b. 1763; mar. Benj. Pede, Apr. 27, 1783; received from her mother, Mary Gray, wid., Oct. 5, 1790, land in Salem.

———

Robert Gray, son of Joseph (Robert,) will made Sept. 5, 1731; mar. 1st, Dorothy; 2d, Abigail; lived in Lynn; issue:

> DOROTHY GRAY, b. Aug. 23, 1701; mar. John Tarbox, at Lynn, Oct. 30, 1718.
> DEBORAH GRAY, b. Nov. 24, 1704.
> ROBERT GRAY, b. June 27, 1708.
> SARAH GRAY, b. Nov. 25, 1713.

Robert Gray, son of Robert (Jos.-Robert,) b. in Lynn, mar. Elizabeth Allen, 1732; issue:

ROBERT GRAY, mar. Dec. 11, 1755, Anna Newhall.
JOSEPH GRAY.

Joseph Gray, son of Robt., (Robt.-Jos.-Robt.,) lived in Lynn; mar. Rebecca Farrington, May 4, 1756; issue:

HANNAH GRAY, b. June 9, 1757.
REBECCA GRAY, b. Mar. 9, 1759.
WILLIAM GRAY, b. Mar. 26, 1761.
JOSEPH GRAY, b. July 13, 1763.
SUSANNA GRAY, b. July 5, 1765.

William Gray, son of Jos. (Robert,) b. at Salem, and lived in Lynn, where he initiated the manufacture of shoes by operatives. He married Hannah; will proved Sept. 17, 1743. Issue:

JOSEPH GRAY, b. Jan. 8, 1707–8.
WILLIAM GRAY, b. Aug. 30, 1710.
HANNAH GRAY, who mar. Sam'l Calley.
JEREMIAH GRAY, b. Dec. 16, 1712.
ABRAHAM GRAY, b. Jan. 13, 1714–15; d. Feb. 11, 1791.

Abraham Gray, son of William, (Joseph-Robert,) b. Lynn, d. in Salem, where he was about 1758. Was a shoe manufacturer and dealer; Deacon of 1st Ch. of Salem. In his will, made 1790, he mentions "my grandsons, Sylvanus and Winthrop Gray, my gr. daughters, Lydia Clough and Jane Williams, my three children, William, Samuel, and Hannah Gray," with John Chipman, Christopher Osgood and Asa Pierce. He mar. Apr. 1, 1742, Lydia Calley, who d. Nov. 27, 1788, aged 65. Issue:

MARY GRAY, b. Jan. 5, 1743; mar. Oct. 11, 1764, her cousin, Winthrop Gray; d. Nov. 27, 1788.
LYDIA GRAY, b. Nov. 3, 1744; mar. Joseph Clough, Mar. 28, 1766, and had Joseph, who d. about 1817.
HANNAH GRAY, b. Nov. 13, 1746; d. July 1, 1751.
JANE GRAY, b. July 31, 1748; mar. Benj. Williams and had Jane, bapt. Mar. 11, 1770, who mar. Cotton Brown Brooks of Haverhill, Dec. 13, 1794.
WILLIAM GRAY, b. June 27, 1750; d. Nov. 3, 1825.
HANNAH GRAY, b. May 23, 1752; d. Sept. 14, 1791.
ABRAHAM GRAY, b. Aug. 21, 1753; d. Aug. 6, 1788.
ABIGAIL GRAY, b. Sept. 1, 1755; d. Nov. 6, 1790.
SAMUEL GRAY, b. Aug. 2, 1760; d. Jan. 21, 1816.
FRANCIS CALLEY GRAY, b. Dec. 19, 1762; d. Apr. 27, '90.

HON. WILLIAM GRAY.

Hon. William Gray, son of Abraham, (Wm.-Jos.-Robert,) was born at Lynn, June 27, 1750; lived in Salem until 1811, after which at Boston, where he died Nov. 3, 1825. His early education was only such as the common schools in his childhood afforded. His precocity at eleven years of age led Samuel Gardner, an eminent merchant of Salem, to offer him a mercantile apprenticeship. In answer to inquiry as to what compensation should be given, the father learned that Mr. Gardner could receive six guineas for such a position from the best apprentice in the country. The latter, however, received the lad gratuitously, and he so won upon his employer, especially by exemplifications of diligence and veracity, that he obtained additionally to instruction, his clothing, and other favors testifying esteem. He afterwards was the clerk of Richard Derby, another prominent and successful merchant of Salem. He showed his patriotism by serving in the troops that under Col. Timothy Pickering's command reached Lexington by a severe forced march, in season to discharge their muskets on the British soldiers retreating from the conflict there, April 19, 1775. Mr. Gray, on commencing business soon after attaining majority, was completely accomplished for the work. In the Revolutionary war he had vessels privateering. In the prosecution of that business as a shipping merchant, the fleet of commercial vessels owned by him at one time amounted to the number of forty-four, (44), many of them the largest ships constructed. Doubling the Cape of Good Hope with vast funds, they would return with immense cargoes, that were distributed throughout our own, (country) or re-exported to foreign countries. "In twenty-five years after he began business he was a millionaire; but to accomplish that degree of success, he was compelled to abandon himself to his commercial pursuits as totally and exclusively as Hercules to his labors, or Ixion to his wheel. Very fortunately for him, he was enabled to do this to his entire satisfaction by exonerating himself from all his domestic affairs and engagements and consigning them to the management of his highly talented and accomplished wife." "Most auspiciously, Sunday unfailing shone for him a day of absolute and exclusive rest and devotion. He was a constant attendant at church, asked a blessing at his table, and the Bible was habitually read in his family. He had the good sense to abstain from tobacco in every shape." His self-command was great otherwise. Many of his apprentices became eminent merchants. Among pupils to him, after their graduation at Harvard, in 1796, and in 1806, were Francis Dana, and Jos. G. Coggeshall, Ph.D., and LL.D., Librarian of Harvard College, and of the Astor Library, N. Y. Mr. Gray was in 1810-11, Lieut.-Governor of Massachusetts. He married, Mar. 28, 1782, Elizabeth, daughter of John Chipman, Esq., of Marblehead, who was born June 9, 1756, and died Sept. 29, 1823. Mr. Chipman graduated at Harvard, 1738, was a barrister-at-law, and the eldest son of Rev. John Chipman, formerly pastor of the Congregational Church in North Beverly. It is said of Mrs. Gray, that "with her experience as a teacher, she was perfectly qualified to conduct all their domestic concerns, and superintend the education of their children."

Mr. Gray was one of the most distinguished personages of his time in New England, and his name is among the most illustrious of the family of Gray in America. The following is a list of his children, and in part of his descendants, so far as obtained:

WILLIAM RUFUS GRAY, son of William, born June 23, 1783, died July 29, 1831. He graduated at Harvard, 1800; resided in Boston; was a merchant. Married, Oct. 19, 1809, Mary, eldest dau. of Hon. and Rev. Joseph Clay, who was born at Savannah, Ga., 1764, and was Judge of the U. S. Dist. Court, Ct., 1796, and pastor of Bapt. Churches at Savannah and Boston. She d. Nov. 15, 1867.

LUCIA GRAY, b. 1788; died 1844. She mar. Aug. 25, 1807, Col. Samuel Swett, who grad. at Harvard, 1800, and d. Oct. 28, 1866. Resided in Salem and Boston; a topographical engineer U. S. A.; a merchant and author, whose children, graduates of Harvard, were Benjamin, who d. 1823, and Wm. Gray, who was pastor of Church at Lexington, 1836-9, and at Lynn, 1840; mar. Charlotte Phinney of Lexington.

HENRY GRAY, b. Jan. 17, 1784; mar. Frances Pierce, Oct. 28, 1810; d. 1834.

FRANCIS CALLEY GRAY, b. 1791; d. Dec. 1856; LL.D., grad. Harvard 1809; lived Boston; admitted to the bar but devoted himself to literary pursuits. A Fellow of H. C.; unmar.

JOHN CHIPMAN GRAY, b. Dec. 26, 1793; LL.D.; grad H. C., 1811; lived in Boston; a literateur; for many years a Senator of Massachusetts, and member of Council; mar. May, 1820, Elizabeth Pickering, dau. of Samuel P. Gardner, of Boston.

WARD GRAY, died in childhood.

HORACE GRAY, b. Aug. 25, 1800; d. 1873; grad. at Harvard 1819; merchant, lived in Boston; mar. Hannah, dau. of Phineas Upham, of Brookfield, 1827, who d. Oct., 1834; mar. 2d, July 3, 1837, Sarah R , dau. of Samuel P. Gardner, of Boston.

Hon. Horace Gray, of the U. S. Supreme Court, is of the descendants of Hon. William Gray, who was his grandsire.

———

Samuel Gray, son of Abraham, (Wm.-Jos.-Robt.,) lived in Salem, Boston, and Medford; merchant and banker; mar. Oct. 27, 1787, Anna Orne, who d. June 2, 1797; mar. 2d, Apr. 25, 1799, Mary, dau. of Rev. Edward Brook, whose wife Abigail, dau. of Rev. John Brown, was a sister of Elizabeth, wife of John Chipman, and mother of Elizabeth Chipman, wife of Hon. William Gray. Issue:

SAMUEL CALLEY GRAY, b. Sept. 7, 17—; d. Nov., 1849; grad. Harvard, 1811; resident of Boston; Pres. Atlas Bank; mar. July 1, 1829, Elizabeth Stone White, dau. Jos. White, Jr.

LYDIA GRAY, b. July 27, 1788; d. 1874; mar. Nov. 15, 1810, Thos. Wren Ward, of Salem and Boston. Issue: Martha Ann, Mary Gray, Sam'l Gray, William, Mary Gray, John G., George Cabot, and Thos. William Ward.

ANNA GRAY, b. July 27, 1789; d. Dec. 20, 1816; mar. Apr. 9, 1815, Andrew Hall, of Medford, and had Sarah.

SARAH GRAY, b. May 28, 1791; d. Sept. 16, 1805.

MARY GRAY, b. Aug. 30, 1794; mar. Nov. 3, 1816, Wm. Ray.

CATHARINE GRAY, b. Apr. 1, 1797; mar. July 22, 1823, Jonathan Porter, who grad. Harvard, first in class, 1814, admitted to bar, Middlesex Co., 1817, and d. at Medford, 1859. Issue: Geo. D. Porter, who grad. Harvard, 1851, and d. 1861.

ELIZABETH GORHAM GRAY, b. March 4, 1800; mar. Dec. 2, 1822, Franklin Howard, son of Dr. Elisha Story, and had Horace Cullen, who d. 1847, and Franklin H., b. Feb. 12, 1825, who mar. Adeline Wainwright, of N. Y., and had Elizabeth G., b. Oct. 16, 1855, and Marion W., b. Jan. 30, 1857. Mr. Story resides in Boston; trustee real estate.

CHARLOTTE GALLISON GRAY, b. Jan. 18, 1802; d. Feb. 1804.

WINTHROP GRAY, b. Apr. 18, 1804; d. Mar. 26, 1830.

FRANCIS ABRAHAM GRAY, b. Aug. 4, 1806; d. June 17, 1809.

SARAH CHARLOTTE GRAY, b. Apr. 7, 1809; mar. Ignatius Sargent, and had Sarah Ellery, who mar. Winthrop Sargent, Phila.

HENRIETTA GRAY, b. Oct. 1, 1811; mar. May 16, 1835, Ignatius Sargent, the husband of her deceased sister Sarah.

FRANCIS ABRAHAM GRAY, 2d, b. Oct. 5, 1813; mar. June 2, 1857, Helen Wainwright, of New York.

ROBERT GRAY, (2).

Robert Gray (2), son of Robert, b. Salem, May 10, 1658; will proved Oct. 22, 1725, in which he names wife, Sarah, sons Samuel and Benjamin, and dau. Sarah, with son John, to whom for reasons "sorrowful," he only gives a small legacy. He married Sarah Glover, or Grover, of Beverly, Aug. 7, 1685; was a gunsmith; lived in Salem. Issue:

JOHN GRAY, b. May 2, 1686.

ROBERT GRAY, (3), b. May, 18, 1689; d. May 3, 1697.

SAMUEL GRAY, b. Apr. 15, 1691.

HANNAH GRAY, b. Sept. 16, 1693; d. 1695.

SARAH GRAY, b. Aug. 22, 1695; mar. Nov. 4, 1714, Capt. Michael Driver, of Salem, and had Michael, Sarah, Michael, 2d, Elizabeth and Thomas.

JONATHAN GRAY, b. May 12, 1697.

JOSIAH GRAY, b. Feb. 22, 1699–1700.

BENJAMIN GRAY, b. Feb. 16, 1702–3.

JAMES GRAY, b. July 29, 1704.

John Gray, son of Robt.-Robt., was a gunsmith; mar. Abigail Masury Dec. 23, 1710; mar. 2d, Dec. 16, 1717, Susanna Jones. Issue:

Robert Gray, b. Nov. 27, 1711.

William Gray, b. Sept. 21, 1713.

Abigail Gray, b. Nov. 3, 1715; mar. July 21, 1735, Zachariah Curtis, and had Ebenezer and Samuel.

John Gray, b. Sept. 11, 1718.

Susanna Gray, b. Sept. 13, 1723.

Robert Gray, son of John, (Robt.-Robt.,) lived in Salem; a shipwright; mar. Ruth Deal, Nov. 20, 1733; she was granted letters of administration on his estate Feb. 6, 1771. Issue:

Abigail Gray, bapt. Aug. 31, 1735.

William Gray, bapt. Oct. 16, 1737.

Also Robert, Sarah, and Hannah who d. unmarried, Nov. 1809.

William Gray, son of Robert, (John-Robert-Robert,) bapt. at Salem, Oct. 16, 1737, d. 1780; a shoemaker; mar. Mary Moses, and had: William; Benjamin; Margaret, who mar. Benj. Trask; Richard; Samuel; Hannah, who mar. Caleb Cook, Dec. 10, 1796, and had Caleb, Mary Gray, and William; Abigail, who mar. Peter Pickman Frye; Mary, who mar. Samuel Cook.

William Gray, son of the foregoing William, mar. a Jones and had Ebenezer, Samuel, Robert, James, and Abigail.

Samuel Gray, son of William, (Robt.-John-Robt.-Robt.,) born June 7, 1765, d. Oct. 11, 1850; was a shoemaker; mar. Dec. 15, 1787, Ruth Ropes, and had Sarah, b, 1790; Robert, bapt. Feb. 19, 1792, mar. Sarah Ela, resided at Portsmouth, N. H., and had three sons and three daughters; Samuel, bapt. Jun. 22, 1792, killed by lightning, while sailing in Salem Harbor, 1836; Ruth, who d. aged 32, unmar.; William, bapt. May 31, 1797; Sarah R., who mar. Nathaniel Frothingham, and d. by suicide at the Asylum in Worcester; Margaret Cook, who d. unmar. at Taunton, Jan. 25, 1864; George, b. 1804, who mar. Lydia Barden of Dover, N. H., where he resided, and had George Frederick, Ruth, and Elizabeth Gray; Elizabeth S., who mar. James Chamberlain Jan. 6, 1829; Priscilla, who d. unmar.; and Samuel, died young.

John Gray son of John, (Robert-Robert,) lived in Salem; mar. Oct. 13, 1742, Sarah Dodd, of Boston, and had John; Jane, who mar. Benjamin Williams, Mar. 30, 1769; Anna, who mar. June 17, 1770, John Williams; and Sarah, who mar. Aug. 22, 1773, Daniel Pease.

John Gray, son of foregoing, mar. March 30, 1769, Lydia Crowell, and had Lydia, who mar. Joseph Cook, Dec. 30, 1792; and another daughter.

Samuel Gray, son of Robert, (Robt.,) b. Salem Apr. 15, 1691, d. 1730; a gunsmith; mar. March 23, 1721, Elizabeth Ward, dau. of John and Jehoidan (Harvey) Ward. Issue: Sarah, bapt. Apr. 28, 1728, Elizabeth and Hannah.

"Antiquarians at Salem and elsewhere have confounded Robert Gray (1), with another Robert Gray, of which latter is known what here follows: A grant of land was made to him at Salem, Apr. 5, 1662. He was in 1669, fined for attendance at Quaker Meetings. He mar. March 8, 1668-9, prob. at Andover, Hannah, dau. of Nicholas Holt, Sr., and had Catharine, Jemima, Henry, Hannah, Edward, Robert, and Breviter. He received land from his father-in-law, in Andover, 1679, and died there 1718, aged 84 years." He was the ancestor of the so called Andover Grays.

Samuel Gray of Salem mar. Abigail Lord, Dec. 28, 1671. He was probably the Samuel Gray who gave testimony in the witchcraft trials, 1692. Samuel Gray mar. 2d Susanna Buster, of Boston.

There was also an Arthur Gray of Salem who mar. Hannah Hide, Nov. 17, 1668, and had Christian, Joseph and Mary.

Query: Were not Robert Gray, (1), of Salem, Robert of Andover, Arthur and Samuel of Salem, related, as brothers or cousins, and all descendants of the Thomas Gray who was the purchaser of Nantasket, 1622, and afterwards of Salem, or Marblehead?

The foregoing sketch and record of the Salem Grays is made up from Ms. of Rev. R. Manning Chipman, of Phila., with additions by Perley Derby, Genealogist, of Salem, a copy of which was kindly furnished by the latter for this purpose.

CAPT. ISAAC GRAY.

It is stated on page 150, under head of the Worcester Grays, that John Gray, Jr., and his wife Izobel, who afterwards removed from Worcester to Pelham, Mass., had three sons, viz: Daniel, John, and Isaac, who commanded a Company at Bunker Hill, but of whom it is there said, that there was no further trace of him or his descendants. Happily, however, during the progress of this work the missing links have been discovered, and the record of Capt. Isaac Gray's family is herewith nearly in full presented. He had married Mary McLain, and had the following children : Elihu, Daniel C., Isaac, Jr., Patience, Tirzah, Margaret, Sarah, and Mary. It is said that there was also a son Andrew, who was lost at sea. The family had removed to Hebron, Washington Co., N. Y., prior to 1795, but whether Capt. Isaac went thither, and when and where he died, does not appear. Patience Gray mar. Billings Stocking, of Lisbon, N. Y., and had a large family, and some of her descendants still reside there. Tirzah Gray, born in 1775, mar. John Flack, of Lisbon, and had ten children, five of whom are still living, mostly in St. Lawrence Co., N. Y. Margaret married William Crosset, and removed to Canada; had several children. Sarah mar. a Mclanathan, and had several children; lived in Clinton Co., N. Y.

DANIEL C. GRAY.

Daniel C. Gray, son of Capt. Isaac, married Susanna Crawford, of Hebron, N. Y., and had seven children: Anna, Andrew M., Isaac, John K., Daniel C., Jr., Mary, and Tirzah Gray. Anna was born in 1796, married Wm. Foster, of Lisbon, N. Y., and died in 1836, leaving five children, of whom only Levi H. and Elizabeth survive, residing on the old homestead; Tirzah married James B. Armstrong of Lisbon, and died in 1834, leaving two daughters, Mary, who mar. G. H. Platt and resides in Lisbon, and Tirzah Armstrong, who resides at Ogdensburg; Mary Gray, youngest daughter of Daniel C., mar. David Foster, of Lisbon, and had Margaret, Tirzah A., Lewis C., who resides in Lisbon, and George Foster. Daniel C. Gray was b. June 26, 1766, and d. July 19, 1825; his wife, b. May 16, 1773, d. July 22, 1845.

Isaac Gray, eldest son of Daniel C., was born in 1798, and was mar. to Elizabeth Brown, in 1823. He possessed a strong constitution and had great energy of character. He was for some time engaged in the lumber business between Ogdensburg and Montreal, successfully running the rapids of the St. Lawrence. He afterwards purchased a farm in the town of Oswegatchie, where he continued to reside the remainder of his life. When the M. E. Church was about to be established at Heuvelton he entered heartily into the movement, aiding with his means and his counsel. He was for more than half a century an efficient member of that church, forty years of which he was classleader, and a part of that time held the offices of trustee and steward as well. He died at the age of eighty-one, his wife having died nine years previous. Their family consisted of six children: Mary Ann, who married W. H. Finney, of Colborne, Canada, and died in 1852; Tirzah N., who married Samuel Hanna, of Ogdensburg, and had a son and daughter; Sarah E., who was born in 1832, and married Col. L. H. Rowan, of Boonville, N. Y., 1860, has a daughter Florence, and resides at Franklin, N. J.; Jane L. Gray, born in 1834, mar. John Allison of Morrisburg, Ontario, in 1885, and resides at the homestead, near Heuvelton, N. Y.

Daniel C. Gray (3), son of Isaac, mar. Harriet Dings of Lisbon, Dec. 25, 1860, and resides on a part of the homestead. Issue: Isaac, Alida J., who mar. Geo. Hanna, of Lisbon, 1885, and Annie Gray.

James N. Gray, son of Isaac, b. 1829, taught school at Lisbon and at the West; d. 1870.

Andrew M. Gray, son of Daniel C. Gray, (1), was born Jan. 16, 1801, in Hebron, N. Y., and removed to Lisbon, St. Lawrence, Co., with his father's family in 1812. Upon reaching his majority he purchased a tract of land in the adjoining town of Oswagatchie, and at once commenced erecting buildings and clearing up a farm. His brothers and brothers-in-law also settled in the same neighborhood. He assisted in organizing the First Congregational Church at Heuvelton, and was for many years one of its officers. He subsequently joined the Presbyterian Church at Lisbon, and was made a Ruling Elder. He died Sept.

22, 1868. He had married Sarah Hanna, a native of Salem, N. Y., who had removed to Lisbon, Sept. 26, 1826, and by this marriage there were three children: Mary M., who mar. Rev. D. J. Patterson, of Brooklyn, N. Y., and died June 4, 1854; Agnes, who mar. Dr. W. H. Cruikshank, and removed to Carthage, N. Y., where he d. 1886. Mrs. Gray d. Dec. 17, 1867.

Walter R. Gray, only son of Andrew M., was born Aug. 13, 1831, and continues to live upon the homestead. In October, 1861, he mar. Mary J., eldest daughter of John Chambers, merchant, of Prescott, Ontario, and has five children: S. Mina, b. Nov. 22, 1862, and mar. Charles J. Fuller, of Governeur, N. Y.; Mary L., b. July 22, 1864, who resides with her parents at Heuvelton, N. Y.; Charles Oliver Gray, b. June 3, 1867, and is a student at Hamilton College, Clinton, N. Y.; Alfred W. Gray, b. Dec. 21, 1868, who is preparing to enter College in 1887; and Justin Clarence Gray, b. Nov. 5, 1872. Mr. Gray has decided literary taste, has had charge of the Agricultural Department of the Ogdensburg *Advance* for several years, and has contributed articles for publication in various papers. Has been a Democrat, and is now a Prohibitionist, and in 1887 declined the nomination of both these parties for Supervisor of his town. He has evinced much interest in this work, and thanks to his labors the family of his ancestor, Capt. Isaac Gray, so fully appears.

John K. Gray, son of Daniel C. Gray (1), mar. Mary E. Platt, of Lisbon, and removed to Ogdensburg, where he died, 1877, and she a year later. They had two children, Augustus H., and Edward P. In 1860 they were engaged in business with their uncle, J. E. Platt, of Manitowoc, Wis. Edward went to Milwaukee, purchased a bill of goods, ordered them shipped, and took the boat for home, after which he was never heard from, and it is supposed that he was foully dealt with. Augustus H., died at Ogdensburg, previous to his father's death.

Daniel C. Gray, (2), was born in Lisbon, N. Y., May 27, 1815. He married Julia Armstrong, July 31, 1839, and has a daughter, Marinda L., born May 19, 1841, who mar. W. K. Chambers, of Elkhorn, Wis., Sept. 14, 1865, and has a son and daughter. Mr. Gray is of a humorous disposition, and is called the jolly member of the family. Resides at Elkhorn, Wis.

ELIHU GRAY.

Elihu Gray, eldest son of Capt. Isaac, had six children, viz: Thurza, who mar. John Cooper, and had several children; Martha, who mar. a Gibbons, and lived at Hermon, N. Y.; Mary, who mar. Lotun Simons; Elizabeth, who mar. a Mr. Green; a son Worlin Gray, who mar. Elizabeth Ballentine, of Lisbon, N. Y., removed to Fremont. Ill., and died there, leaving a married daughter; and Daniel C. Gray, (4.)

Daniel C. Gray, (4), Elihu's eldest son; was born in 1796, and married Mary H. King, who died in 1839; he died in 1876. They had eight children, viz:

Henry A. Gray, b. March 19, 1821; mar. Mary M. Weston, Feb. 10, 1853, and had a son Vernon H. Gray, b. Oct. 6, 1859; resides at Canton, N. Y. An upright and esteemed citizen.

Lucy E. Gray, b. May 19, 1823, mar. Chester K. Clark, of North Russell, N.Y., and had two sons, one of whom d. young, and the other, Chester A., resides there.

Jane E. and Martha M. Gray, who died unmarried.

Daniel C. Gray (5), b. Feb. 8, 1833, mar. Sarah E. Winslow, July 16, 1858, and have Frederick A., b. Feb. 27, 1860, and mar. Justine E. Knox, June 23, 1883, who d. Nov. 20, 1886; Charles F. Gray, b. Feb. 25, 1863, mar. Carrie M. Towner Feb 23, 1887; and Gertrude M., b. Mar. 14, 1871. They reside in North Russell, N. Y.

Elial D. Gray, b. June 6, 1836, mar. Lucy A. Conant, Apr. 7, 1859, who d. Aug. 16, 1880, leaving four children: Merton J., b. Jan. 17, 1862; Frank E., b. May 8, 1863, mar. Nora Welch, Aug. 30, 1885, and have a child b. May 24, 1886; Eugene C., b. Nov. 7, 1868; Edith A., b. Aug. 29, 1873. Elial D. Gray mar. 2d, Rettie H. Irish, and had Henry D., b. Feb. 4, 1885. Resides at Canton.

John K. Gray, b. Aug. 12, 1838, mar. Elvira E. White, Feb. 20, 1866; no children; resides at Canton, N. Y. Was a soldier in the war for the Union, in Sixtieth N. Y. Regt., and afterwards in the 11th N. Y. Cavalry, and served till the close of the war.

Worlin Gray, brother of John K., resides in Kansas.

ISAAC GRAY, (2).

Isaac Gray, (2), youngest son of Capt. Isaac, was born at Pelham, Mass., Dec. 15, 1772, and married Elizabeth Baker, dau. of an officer of the Revolution, at Salem, N. Y., Sept. 13, 1793; he died at Sandy Creek, N. Y., Feb. 2, 1822; she d. at Geneva, Wis., Dec. 7, 1855. Issue:

Dorothy Gray, b. at Hebron, N. Y., Nov. 9, 1795; mar. Alexander Turner, and d. at Lisbon, N. Y., Oct. 2, 1824.

Phebe Gray, b.May 3, 1798; mar. Wm. Chambers, and has five children now living, three in Colorado, one in Nebraska, and Wm. K., with whom, at the advanced age of 89 years, she resides at Elkhorn, Wis.

Isaac H. Gray, born Feb. 26, 1800, mar. Augusta Morris, and d. at Lisbon, April 15, 1845, leaving the following children, viz: Lumon M., Timothy, Isaac, Francis M., Francis, 2d, Sylvester, Preston K., and Augusta, all deceased but Isaac, who is in New Mexico.

Elihu Gray, b. at Lisbon, Dec. 18, 1802, mar. Elizabeth Armstrong, and d. at Elkhorn, Wis., Sept. 23d, 1885, having had six children, of whom three are living: Clarinda and Delia, at Elkhorn, and Samuel Gray, at Geneva, Wis.

David C. Gray, b. at Hebron, N. Y., Feb. 6, 1804, mar. Agnes Armstrong, March 1, 1827, and d. May 10, 1846; she was b. March 18, 1802, and still survives; resides at Lisbon, N. Y. Issue:

DAVID H. GRAY, b. Jan. 15, 1828; resides at Flackville, St. Lawrence Co., N. Y.; unmarried.

WM. A. GRAY, b. July 13, 1881; mar. July 13, 1878, Lina A. Stocking, who was b. Feb. 9, 1853. He settled in Minnesota at an early day, and with the exception of a year in California, and his army life, he has continued to reside there, holding many offices of trust, and has also represented his District in the State Legislature. Present residence, Farmington, Minn. Issue:

ROY ELIHU GRAY, b. June 27, 1879.
JANE A. GRAY, b. Nov. 18, 1882.

JANE I. GRAY, twin sister of Wm. A. Gray, b. July 13, 1831, d. at Lisbon, May 10, 1851, unmarried.

GEORGE GRAY, b. April 11, 1836, mar. Mary Lovina Wilson, Dec. 31, 1868; served in 7th California Infantry in the war of the great Rebellion; resides at Northfield, Rice Co., Minn. Issue:

SARAH AGNES GRAY, b. Aug. 18, 1870.
WILLIAM HERBERT GRAY, b. Apr. 9, 1872.
NELLIE WILSON GRAY, b. Sept. 24, 1874.
SILAS WRIGHT GRAY, b. Sept. 17, 1877.
LEONARD ALDEN GRAY, b. Feb. 20, 1880.
GEORGE EARLE GRAY, b. June 28, 1886.

JEANETTE GRAY, twin sister of George Gray, d. Aug. 25, 1836.
ALBERT M. GRAY, b. May 26, 1843, d. Feb. 23, 1845, at Lisbon, N. Y.
SILAS WRIGHT GRAY, twin brother of Albert M., b. May 26, 1843, served in Co. A., 14th N. Y. Heavy Artillery, till the war closed, and d. at Lisbon, N. Y., Aug. 26, 1865, of disease contracted in the service. Unmarried.

This family of seven children, as will be noticed, includes three pair of twins; a phenominal occurrence, even in the Gray Genealogy!

Thomas B. Gray, son of Isaac (2), born at Lisbon, Oct. 20, Feb. 1, 1806, married Jane Armstrong, and had six children, viz: Baker F., of Eureka, Nev.; Elihu W., married, and lives at Geneva, Wis.; one of the daughters died soon after marriage leaving an infant child; and another is married and has several children; Mr. Gray and family removed west about 1845. Mrs. Gray died May 24, 1874. He resides at Geneva, Wis., and the following pleasant notice of him is copied from a paper there published, of recent date: " Mr. Thomas B. Gray has informed us that he will not be a candidate for the office of City Treasurer this spring. He is over 81 years of age, and has been honored by the people with various offices for over thirty years. For thirteen years he was Treasurer of the town, and the past year of the city. During these years he has received over $260,000 of town and city money, every nickel of which has been fully accounted for. He desires to retire in peace, with friendship towards all, malice towards none. He has the esteem and friendship of every man who knows him, and that he may live to enjoy many more years of blessings and happiness, is the expression of all."

Alexander T. Gray, brother of Thomas B., born Dec. 3, 1807, married Susan Castle, and had one son, supposed now to be living. Mr. Gray resided at Ogdensburg; he died at Albany, Sept. 2, 1842, while on his return from a trip to New York for the benefit of his health. His widow resides at Ogdensburg.

Elizabeth Gray, dau. of Isaac (2), b. Feb. 4, 1810, mar. John Armstrong, and had eight children; d. Oct. 18, 1877, at Fort Howard, Wis.

Tirzah Gray, b. March 15, 1813, mar. James Gray, and resides at Elkhorn, Wis. One of her kindred writes of her: "Although Mrs. Gray is quite aged, yet she is a thorough worker in the church, and in the Prohibition cause, which indicates that she is still living in the spirit of the age." Mr. Gray is a son of a Robert Gray who came from Ireland, and who died in Wis., in 1865. Robert had a brother, Rev. James Gray, a Presbyterian minister who was located for a time at Phila., and afterwards at Baltimore; he also had a brother John, and two sisters, one of whom married an Alexander and lived at Pittsburgh. Robert Gray, had besides James, Maria, Rachel, Jane, Robert, Jr., Agnes, Alexander, and William. They are probably of the same ancestry as the Worcester Grays, though the connection cannot readily be traced.

Agnes Gray, dau. of Isaac (2), b. Sept. 13, 1815, mar. Wm. Whitney, and had two children; d. at Morley, N. Y., May 6, '48.

John F. Gray, b. Jan. 13, 1818, mar. Wealthy Heath, and has two sons, Henry and Frank Gray, both married, and each has two children; residence, Vincent, Osborne Co., Kansas.

Asahel B. Gray, youngest son of Isaac (2), b. Oct. 9, 1820, mar. Abby Coult, and had one daughter; was a R.R. Conductor, and was accidentally killed by the cars at Mansfield, Ohio, Mar. 28, 1854. His widow and daughter reside at or near Niagara Falls.

Mr. W. R. Gray, of Heuvelton, N. Y., who has assisted much in the preparation of the foreging statistics of the descendants of Capt. Isaac Gray, thus summarizes their characteristics: "'The family is not remarkably strong and hardy, and not long-lived, and consequently not very numerous. The prevailing temperaments are sanguine and nervous, with the nervous predominating. In matters of religion, they are almost without exception of what is termed the orthodox faith. They are usually temperate, industrious and economical, without being excessively so, and in most cases succeed in accumulating a fair amount of property, and live in the enjoyment of all the necessaries, and of many of the luxuries of life. And in behalf of their good citizenship, be it said: I have never known of a member of any branch of the family, or of any of their descendants, who was ever a subject of indictment, or had a criminal process served upon him."

It is very pleasing to present the foregoing addenda to the record of the Worcester Grays.

Samuel Kerr Gray, of the Lake County Bank, Painesville, O., writes: "My father was James Gray, born near Londonderry, Ireland, 1780. Emigrated to America 1798, lived in different places in eastern Penna., and finally made a permanent home in Pittsburgh, where he resided until his death in 1857. He was married three times and had children by each wife. Children by the first wife are all dead. One son remains of the second wife, Wm. A. Gray, of St. Paul, Minn. Of the third marriage, only two children remain, Cornelia H. M. Gray, and myself, both of this place. A half brother of my father, Andrew Gray, resided at Peoria, Ill., but died several years before him."

John Gray of Gray, Dakota, writes: "My ancestors are Scotch. They came from a place called Circaldy, a seaport on the coast of Scotland, and settled in London, England, about 1790. My grandfather Gray died there, leaving two sons, Thomas and James. Thomas died in 1824. James Gray left London about 1800, and went to America; lost all track of him. John Gray son of Thomas, born in London, 1812, left there 1848; came to the States; has been a citizen many years. The following are the names of my living children: Robert and John, born in London, Ellen, George, Sarah, and Lewis Gray, born in the United States."

The following brief sketch of the Grays of Herkimer, N Y., is furnished by A. M. Gray, of that place: "My greatgrandfather came from Ireland when a boy, in 1744. Was bound out on his arrival at New York by his consent and the Capt. of the vessel, until he was 21, which was about three years. He was a 'stoaway.' He married at Stone Arabia, where he came on his arrival to this part of the country. He had five sons: Adam, Nicholas, Samuel, Robert, and Andrew. Adam was a bachelor; Nicholas was killed at the battle of Oriskany; Samuel, Robert, and Andrew all raised large families, and they are now scattered all over the world. I am a descendant from Andrew. My great grandfather's name was Adam, my father, son of Andrew, was named Adam, and each of the sons of the original Adam had a son by the name of Adam."

Frederick A. Gray, a son of the aforementioned A. M. Gray, has recently been appointed Postmaster at Herkimer.

Hon. George Gray, U. S. Senator from Delaware, is a son of the late Andrew C. Gray, and was born at New Castle, Del., May 4, 1840. He graduated at Princeton when nineteen years of age, and received the degree of A. M., in 1862. After studying law with his father, he spent a year at the Harvard Law School, and was admitted to practice in 1863; was appointed Attorney General of the State of Delaware in 1876, and reappointed in 1884; was a delegate to the National Democratic Conventions in 1876, 1880, and 1884; was elected United States Senator to fill the vacancy caused by the appointment of Bayard as Secretary of State, and has been re-relected for a full term. Senator Gray's ancestral record would have been given more fully, if it had been furnished, and it might have been of general and particular interest.

Robert Gray died near Londonderry, Ireland, 1744, leaving an infant son Robert, born 1743. This son grew up and emigrated to America in 1765. He enlisted under General Israel Putnam and served three terms in the revolution, being among those who captured Burgoyne. He emigrated to Ohio in 1800, locating near Cincinnati. His son Jonathan took part in the war of 1812. Jonathan's son William C. Gray, was born 1830; was educated and admitted to the practice of the law in 1852; in 1853 entered upon the profession of journalism. He remov- from Cincinnati to Chicago to take the position of editor-in- chief of *The Interior*, and under his able management it has achieved a large success. A cotemporary says of him: "Dr. Gray has rare incisiveness and vigor of style, with freshness of humor. He is one of the very ablest editors on the religious press, and is second to none. He is a strong antagonist, is per- fectly fearless in the expression of his convictions, and is one of the most competent and best known editors in the country." Frank Gray, son of William C., is publisher of *The Interior*.

James Gray born at Bangor, Ireland, Jan 17, 1781, married a Sarah Gray, and had Margaret Cummings, Hugh Barr, b. 1805, John, Sarah, Isabella, Charles, Henry, Ann Jean. Hugh Barr Gray mar. Letitia Patterson, dau. of Robert and Letitia Patter- son, in 1834, and had the following, all born in the city of New York: Sarah, Mary Jane, Robert Patterson, Margaretta Louisa, and Charles A. Gray. Robert Patterson Gray, son of Hugh Barr, b. Sept. 7, 1838, mar. Elizabeth Jane Burns, 1866, and had Jennie Letitia, b. May, 1867, Rufus E., dec'd, Robert Pat- terson, Jr., Norman Ellwood, Raymond Hugh and Rutherford B., twins, dec'd, and Gertrude C. Gray. dec'd. Robert P. Gray resides in New York, and his place of business is 176 E. 120th St.

Reference has been made to an Isaac and George Gray, who were cotemporaneous with John Gray of Beverly, Mass., and are believed to have been his brothers. The record of them is brief, and does not reach down to the present living generations. The Isaac referred to, mar. Dec. 19, 1706, Rebekah Woodbury, b. July 2, 1684, (whose mother's father was Roger Haskell), at Beverly, and had Hannah bapt. 1707, who mar. Robt. Morgan, and lived at Spencer, Mass.; Isaac, Jr., bapt. June 25, 1710, mar. Anna, probably dau. of John Sallows, and was a member of the church at Beverly, where he continued to reside until 1761, having ad- ministered upon his father's estate there that year, but the fact that

he sold his property there about that time, and there being no further mention of him on the records at Beverly, is presumptive evidence that he soon after removed elsewhere. No record of any children. Jacob, son of Isaac, was born 1816; no further mention of him or descendants. Lydia, b. 1717, mar. John Bond, and was living 1761. Rebekah Woodbury d. 1736, and Isaac Gray mar. 2d, Martha Ellithorpe, Apr. 13, 1738, who survived him. He died Mar. 23, 1760, and the stone at his grave in the old churchyard at Beverly is still to be found.

The George Gray of Beverly referred to, mar. Bridget, dau. of Humphrey and Elizabeth Horrill, Nov. 14, 1701, and had Geo. Jr., bapt. Apr. 4, 1703, who mar. Apr. 8, 1725, Emma Williams, b. March 29, 1703. George Gray, Sr., was a mariner, and died prior to 1729.

William Gray, born at or near Cambridge, N. Y., was captured at Whitehall, N. Y., when about 17 years old, and taken to Canada. He afterwards married an Indian girl, and being adopted by the St. Regis tribe, became one of their Chiefs, and continued to reside with them. He was recognized as their representative by the State of New York in treaties afterwards made with that tribe, and a considerable tract of land was so ceded to him. He lived at what is now Hogansburgh, N. Y., and left descendants. In the war of 1812, he was taken prisoner, and died at Quebec, May, 1814. Lineage not traced, but he is believed to have been of the Worcester Grays.

The following is gleaned from a quaint little pamphlet published by Asa Gray, of Ledyard, Conn., date of 1851: "Phillip Gray and Benjamin Gray, two brothers, whilst boys, were enticed or came aboard a vessel lying at the island of Guernsey, and detained and brought to Boston. Were there bound out to pay their passage. It is said they were of Scotch descent." Benjamin remained in Boston. Phillip mar. in Boston and had two children; she d. and he removed to what is now Ledyard, Conn., where he mar. Widow Button, whose maiden name was Stoddard and had Pillip, Jr., Benjamin, Ezekiel and Elijah, and d. in April, 1780, aged about 90.

Phillip, Jr., b. 1739, mar. Hannah Latham, and had Jonas b. 1770, mar. Lucy Spicer and had Phillip, (3), Winthrop, Oliver, Abisha, Hannah, Mary, and Althea; Lucy d. and Jonas mar. 2d, Mary Gardner, soon after which he moved to Pa., and died there. Latham Gray, son of Phillip, Jr., b. 1772, mar. Amy Brown, and had Henry, Latham, b. 1798, who mar. Julia Pendleton, and had William and Henry; moved west. Latham Gray d. 1821. Ezekiel, son of Phillip, Jr., b. 1775, was lost at sea. Stephen, son of Phillip, Jr., mar. Lydia Stedman, and had Stephen, b. 1800, mar. Caroline Babcock, and had Stephen, Jr.; Austain, mar. Betsey Smith, and had Austain, Lydia E., and Julia F.; Norman, b. 1810, moved west, twice mar., and had four children; Lydia, b. 1802, mar. Chas. Dean, and Ardelia, b. 1812, mar. Ethan O. Barber. Stephen Gray d. 1841. Hannah, wife of Phillip, Jr., d. and he mar. 2d, Mercy Chapman, and had Asa, b. 1786, who mar. Susannah Wilcox, and had Asa, Jr., b. 1802, mar. Lusanna Prosser, and had Asa F., Denman, George, Montgomery, who, d. May 3, 1886, Mercy, Susan and Sarah.

Phillip, son of Jonas and Lucy Gray, b. 1798, mar. Maria Hewlett and had a son Phillip who is said to have been shot as a deserter about 1840. Winthrop, b. 1802, Oliver, b. 1805, and Abisha, b. 1810, sons of Jonas and Lucy, all moved west.

Benjamin Gray, son of Phillip (1), b. 1740, mar. Temperance Baxter and had Thomas B. and Phillip. Thomas B. mar. Katurah Stanton, and had Benjamin, Thomas, John, Surviah, and Temperance. Benjamin moved west and it is said died 1830.

Elijah Gray, son of Phillip (1), b. 1743, mar. Candis Perkins, and had Elijah, Jr., Prudence, Hannah, Eunice. Elijah lived in the time of the Revolution, and being wounded and taken prisoner, died aboard the Jersey prison ship near New York. Elijah, Jr., b. 1771, b. 1771, mar. Abby Hilliard, and had Ezekiel, Jonathan, Hilliard, Caroline, Phebe, Sally, and Abby. Ezekiel, b. 1798, mar. Hannah Perkins and had Nelson and Delia, who both d. young. Jonathan, b. 1811, mar. Mary A. Thorries, and lived in New York. Hilliard, b. 1814, d. 1832. Sally mar. Silas Sterry, and Abby mar. Lester Perkins.

Ezekiel, youngest son of Phillip (1), b. 1745, went to sea and was lost, aged 18.

NEW JERSEY GRAYS.

The records of the office of the Adjutant General of the State of New Jersey show that at an early period of the Revolutionary struggle five brothers by the name of Gray had enlisted in the army of the Continentals, viz: Garrit, John, William, Isaac, and Robert. On the establishment of American Independence, four of the brothers removed southward, John settling in Virginia, and Garrit, William and Isaac removing to South Carolina. Their father went with them. His name is believed to have been Garrit, and his wife, Hannah. It is not known to the writer in what part of New Jersey they had resided.

ROBERT GRAY one of the five brothers aforementioned, was born in New Jersey, Sept. 25, 1745, and was in the war of the Revolution. He came to the city of Albany about 1777, and there married Susannah La Grange, on May 7th of that year. He afterwards established and conducted business in Albany until 1800, when he removed to his farm in the western part of of Albany Co., and there continued until his death. When the town of Guilderland was formed in 1803, he assisted in that work, and was chosen one of the first town officers. He was subsequently its Supervisor. Issue:

GARRIT GRAY, son of Robert and Susannah La Grange Gray, b. in Albany, N. Y., May 2, 1783, mar. Margarita Vanderpoel, dau. of John M., and Isabella (Douglas) Vanderpoel, March 1, 1804; resided in Guilderland, where he d. Mar. 30, 1836. Issue:

    SUSANNAH GRAY, b. Aug. 29, 1805, d. Sept. 12, 1805.
    ROBERT GRAY, b. Feb. 11, 1807, d. July 27, 1835.
    ISABELLA GRAY, b. Jan. 23, 1809, d. Feb. 10, 1813.
    SUSANNAH GRAY, 2d, b. Dec. 10, 1811.
    ISABELLA GRAY, 2d, b. Dec. 25, 1813.
    CATHARINE GRAY, b. Feb. 24, 1816.
    JOHN GRAY, b. Mar. 20, 1818, d. July 15, 1818.
    MARY GRAY, b. June 16, 1819.
    MARGARET GRAY, b. Aug. 28, 1821.
    HANNAH GRAY, b. March 18, 1824, d. April 28, 1886.
    STEPHEN VAN RENSSELAER GRAY, b. Mar. 1, 1827.

STEPHEN VAN RENSSELAER GRAY, son of Garrit, mar. Charlotte Comstock, Jan. 23, 1872. He resides at Albany, and is a highly esteemed citizen of that city, where he is extensively engaged in the stationary and book trade. He has furnished the data for this branch of the family, and in many ways has shown his kindly appreciation of this work.

JELLIS GRAY, son of Robert, b. Jan. 9, 1789, in the city of Albany, mar. Sarah Osterman; d. July 25, 1854. Issue:

ROBERT E. GRAY, b. in Guilderland, N. Y., Jan. 9, 1809, mar. Catharine Van Aernan, Oct. 6, 1827, d. June 8, 1838.

CHRISTIAN GRAY, b. Jan. 27, 1811, in Guilderland, mar. Barbara Ostrander, d. at Salina, Ill., April 5, 1860. Issue:

ELIAS GRAY, b. Dec. 1, 1829, mar. Louis Beebe.

SAMUEL GRAY, b. Apr. 18, 1832, mar. Eliza Powell, of Salina, Ill.

STEPHEN GRAY, b. in Knox, N. Y., Sept. 20th, 1834, mar. Lucy Bird, of Limestone, Ill.

PETER GRAY, b. in Knox, Sept. 20, 1836, mar. Mary J. Baker of Aroma, Ill.

ADELIA GRAY, b. in Knox, June 3, 1838, mar. Aaron Sheffler of Limestone, Ill.; d. 1872.

CHRISTIAN GRAY, Jr., b. in Knox, Dec. 14, 1846, mar. Harriet A. Baker at Aroma, Ill.

JOSHUA GRAY, b. in Knox, Dec. 14, 1846, (twin of Christian,) mar. Luella M. Baker, Aroma, Ill.

MARY J. GRAY, b. in Knox, Dec. 18, 1849, mar. Myron Webster at Aroma, Ill.

ELIZABETH S. GRAY, dau. of Jellis, b. March 11, 1813, d. Sept. 12, 1826.

PETER GRAY, son of Jellis, b. June 9, 1815, mar. Mary Ann McLean, and d. Aug. 13, 1846.

WILLIAM E. GRAY, son of Jellis, b. July 25, 1817, mar. Ann Shoudy, and d. Apr. 23, 1884.

ELIAS GRAY, son of Jellis, b. Nov. 4, 1819, mar. Jane Fryer.

CATY ANN GRAY, dau. of Jellis, b. Jan. 3, 1822, d. May 23, 1825.

SARAH GRAY, dau. of Jellis, b. Feb. 29, 1824, mar. James Helme.

JONATHAN BURR GRAY, son of Jellis, b. Oct. 25, 1826, mar. Mary Ann Ostrander, and d. Sept. 21, 1882. Issue:

ENDRESS GRAY, b. Oct 20, 1850.

HENRIETTA B. GRAY, b. Sept. 14, 1852, mar. Aaron F. Blessing.

SARAH GRAY, b. July 25, 1854, mar. John F. Shirtz.

WALTER GRAY, b. Sept. 28, 1858, mar. Ellen Clyckman.

MILLARD FILLMORE, b. Apr. 11, 1860, mar. Sarah Blessing.

EMMETT GRAY, b. March 20, 1862.

ANNA GRAY, b. Aug. 22, 1863, mar. Stephen Ostrander.

CORA GRAY, b. Feb. 26, 1865.

FRANK GRAY, b. Aug. 25, 1869, d. Oct. 4, 1869.

ELIZABETH GRAY, dau. of Jellis, b. July 22, 1829, Jacob Benschoten.

CHRISTINA GRAY, dau. of Jellis, b. May 21, 1836, mar. Alfred T. Dennis.

SUSANNAH, dau. of Garrit and Margaret Gray, b. Dec. 10, 1811, mar. John Marcellus, Jan. 31, 1838, and had: Robert Gray, b. March 15, 1839, Geo. W., b. Oct. 26, 1841, and Anna Margaret, b. Sept. 23, 1846, and d. Nov. 22, 1868.

CATHARINE, dau. of Garrit and Margaret Gray, b. Feb'y 24, 1816, mar. Conrad Oliver Dec. 9, 1838. Children: Margaret, b. Dec. 1, 1840, d. April 16, 1859; Conrad, b. Aug. 17, 1843, Mary, b. Nov. 15, 1844, d. July 26, 1859; Garrit, b. Aug. 1, 1846, d. Sept. 9, 1846; Garrit, 2d, b. April 15, 1848, Eveline, b. Oct. 1, 1850, mar. Stephen B. Littell, Stephen, b. Mar. 6, 1854, d. Mar. 14, 1854.

HANNAH, dau. of Garrit and Margaret Gray, b. Mar. 16, 1824, d. Apr. 28, 1886, mar. Nicholas Swart, Jan. 27, 1847. Children: Jacob Henry, b. Nov. 2, 1847, Stephen Gray, b. Jan. 27, 1850, d. Mar. 18, 1877; Edward Rosa, b. June 12, 1854, Franklin Oliver, b. Nov. 18, 1861, Emma Margaret, b. Aug. 22, 1858.

LYDIA GRAY, dau. of Robert and Susannah Gray, mar. Peter Bloomingdale, and had: John, who mar. Magdaline Crounse, Susannah, mar. Aaron Waldron, Jane, mar. Daniel Fryer, Caroline, mar. John S. Vanderpoel, Mary Ann, mar. Dow F. Slingerland, Lydia, mar. John Crounse, Robert, and Peter, who mar. Frances Pratt.

HANNAH, dau. of Robert and Susannah Gray, b. March 17th, 1781, mar. Charles Scrafford, d. Oct. 31, 1830. Issue: Susannah, George, Eve, Margaret, Elizabeth, Catharine, Lydia, Sally, Robert, and Martin.

CATHARINE, dau. of Robert and Susannah Gray, b. Nov. 15, 1794, mar. Ira C. Brand, in Guilderland, Dec. 18, 1819, and d.

June 25, 1867. Children: Susan Maria, b. May 6, 1821, d. Aug. 24, 1830, John C., b. July 17, 1823, d. Feb. 14, 1848, George Scrafford, b. Mar. 24, 1826, mar. Almena Dolph, Feb. 17, 1847, William Gray, b. Feb. 28, 1828, mar. Alida A. Van Hoesen, Jan. 7, 1868, and has a son Clarence b. Sept. 7, 1872.

SUSANNAH, dau. of Robert and Susannah Gray, b. Oct. 26, 1797, mar. James Van Aernan, and d. about 1872. Children: Susannah, Jacob Henry, Lydia, Elias.

ELIZABETH, dau. of Robert and Susannah Gray, b. about 1806, mar. John Westfall.

WILLIAM GRAY, son of Robert and Susannah, mar. Sarah Van Aernam; d. June 14, 1860.

———

GARRIT GRAY, (brother of Robert,) and Susannah Gray his wife, were living in Newberry Co., S. C., 1803, and had Hannah Gray, who mar. Nathan Oliver in Virginia, John Gray, William Gray, Lydia Gray who mar. Jesse Johnston, Mary Gray b. 1789, Isaac Gray, Susannah, who d. young, Garrit Gray, Jr., James Gray, Robert Gray, and Nathan Gray b. 1802.

WILLIAM GRAY, (brother of Robert,) and Sarah his wife, lived in Newberry, Co., S. C., 1803, and had: Garrit Gray, who died young, Abraham Gray, Mary Gray, Robert Gray, James Gray, Naomi Gray, Sarah Gray, and Isaac Gray, who mar. Elizabeth Wilson and had William Gray, who removed to Missouri, Benjamin Gray, who removed to Indiana, Jane Gray, who mar. Mr. Kelso and lived in Ky., Sally Gray, Rosa Gray, and Mary Gray, who mar. a Mr. Brown and lived in Tennessee. Isaac Gray is said to have removed to Wadesborough, Calloway Co., Kentucky.

ISAAC GRAY, (brother of Robert,) was living in Newberry or Lawrence Co., S. C., 1803, and had nine children, names not given.

THOMAS ROBERT LAFAYETTE GRAY, who resides at Lanford Station, Laurens Co., S. C., is son of Robert Gray who died in 1864, son of John Gray, (probably son of Garrit,) who married his cousin Zana Gray, dau. of Abraham who was son of William Gray, brother of Robert, Garrit, Isaac, and John.

O. B. Mayer, Jr., M. D., of Newberry, and Pres. of the State

Medical Society of South Carolina, furnishes the following: "Catharine Dewalt mar. George Gray, (believed to be of the foregoing families,) and had Rebecca Gray, Susannah Gray, Simon Peter Gray, Benj. H. Gray, and Fred. Gray. Rebecca Gray mar. David Dewalt, and had Carrie, Amelia, Catharine, Rebecca, David and George. Carrie Dewalt mar. Dr. O. B. Mayer, and I am his son."

JOHN GRAY, brother of Robert, lived in Virginia, 1803, and was married and had a family. The descendants of this branch of the family not traced. It seems possible if not probable, that this may have been the John Gray who was the grandfather of Dr. Wm. A. Gray of Virginia, a sketch of whose family is given on pages 177–8. Strength is given to this supposition by the fact that a daughter of Dr. Wm. A. Gray's grandfather, Lucy, is spoken of as having married her cousin "Jack," probably John, and gone to South Carolina, for that is where the brothers of John did go after sojourning for a time in Virginia. Again, a marked resemblance between at least one of the descendants of Robert, S. R. Gray, Esq., of Albany, N. Y., and Dr. Wm. B. Gray, (son of Dr. Wm. A. Gray,) of Richmond, Va., whose picture elsewhere appears in this record.

That there were other Grays in New Jersey is evidenced by the following from Mr. L. D. Cary, of Glasco, Kansas, date of Feb. 23d, 1887: " My mother was a granddaughter of Daniel Gray, who was born in Essex Co., N. J., March 20, 1749. He married Phebe Butler, in same county, 1775; emigrated to Warren Co., Ohio, 1809, where he died Feb. 19, 1843. He served through the Revolutionary war, and drew a pension as long as he lived."

Very likely the above Daniel was akin to Robert Gray and his brother, and all probably descendants of the John Gray who was at Elizabethtown, then of Essex Co., as early as 1670.

It is a regret to leave this interesting field so lightly touched, where there is so much promise of interest. But even these few gleanings may at least serve to stimulate research on the part of those more directly interested, and if so, the labor will not have been in vain.

Dr. John P. Gray, so long at the head of the N. Y. State Asylum at Utica, and who died Nov. 29, 1886, was born at Half-Moon, Center Co., Pa., Aug. 6, 1825, his father, Peter B. Gray, being a farmer, and a local preacher in the Methodist Episcopal Church for many years. Four brothers survived Dr. Gray, viz: Wm. S. Gray, a merchant at Stormstown, Center Co., Pa., G. W. Gray and Jacob Green Gray, who are farmers in Half-Moon Valley, Pa., and Rev. Dr. Edward J. Gray, who is President of Dickinson Seminary, Williamsport, Pa.; there are also four sisters.

Dr. Gray achieved great and well deserved eminence in his profession, and was second to none in the specialty which he made his life work. He was for 35 years connected with the Utica Asylum, and for the most of that period was its Superintendent. The Utica *Herald*, in an able summing up of his life and character, says: " Dr. Gray was at the very head of his profession as an expert in insanity, and he was also an administrative officer of the first rank. The asylum was directed with excellent system, and with a large and generous spirit. He took it with the methods of the past generation; he introduced into it every humane and elevating method favored by modern science. A leader in thought as well as in practice, he has helped to broaden,—almost to create a science and a literature relative to insanity, and to write his name in enduring characters on the history of our public charities." And again from the same: "His social attractions were marked, and in his intercourse with men in all stations, he impressed himself strongly, not merely as a physician and specialist, but as a man of affairs and a molder of events. He had no mean elements in his nature; his was a liberal soul, and magnanimity underlay all of his theories and policy. Conscious of his own integrity, firm in the wisdom of his own management, engrossed with the truth of his theories of insanity, which determined his whole policy, he met criticism with courtesy and with courage, and stood as the sturdy champion of the patient, and of the humanity which cared for them."

Dr. Gray was married Sept. 6, 1854, to Mary B., daughter of Edmund A. Wetmore, of Utica, and to them were born six children, of whom three survive: Dr. John P. Gray, Jr., William Wetmore, and Cornelia L. Dr. Gray was for many years, and until his death, a communicant in the Reformed Church, and he was a firm believer in the Christian faith, as he exemplified it in his walk and life.

DR. EDWARD J. GRAY married Dec. 26, 1861, Eva V. Emery, daughter of Josiah Emery, Esq., and they have had five children: William E. Gray, b. Feb. 7, 1763, graduated in classical course at Dickinson Seminary, Williamsport, Pa., and in Mechanic Art course at Cornell University, married, and in business at New London, Conn.; Edith Gray, b. Dec. 15, 1871, d. Aug. 1872; Grace Gray, b. May 15, 1874, d. July, 1874; Eva C. Gray, b. July 29, 1876; Edward P. Gray, b. July 16, 1877.

REV. PETER B. GRAY, father of Dr. John P., Dr. Edward J., and others, was the son of Peter and Mary Gray, who had besides Peter B., George, who died young, John L., Mary Ann, Eliza, and Jacob, who still survives. Peter B. Gray mar. Elizabeth Purdue, daughter of Dr. John Purdue, a distinguished physician then living near Bellefonte, Pa. "She was a woman of decided character, with remarkable tact in training children, and venerated, almost worshipped by her family." Peter Gray, Sr., and a brother John, were among the first settlers of Half Moon Valley, Centre Co., Pa., where they lived and died. Peter Gray it is said, established Methodism in the neighborhood, his house being the preaching place for many years. Dr. Edward J. Gray writes: "I remember grandfather as a genial old gentleman. His father came from Holland." Perhaps a descendant of the Abraham Gray who was at Leyden, 1622.

———

DR. JAMES E. GRAY, of Brooklyn and the N. Y. City Asylum, Blackwell's Island, writes: "I am descended from Scotch ancestors. My father was born in Canada, the eldest of a family of eleven. I am the sixth in a family of nine. My ancestors have all been landowners; for generation after generation the property was handed down, and we still derive an income from Scotland. As far back as I am able to remember is my great-great-grandfather, Daniel Gray. My grandfather, John Gray, about sixty-five years ago came to this country, locating in a beautiful section near London, Ontario, Canada."

GEORGE GRAY.

The following is a sketch of the ancestry of George Gray, Esq., of Dubuque, Iowa, as by him furnished:

"George Gray, merchant, teacher, session clerk, and land surveyor, resided in the village of Currie, a few miles west of Edinburgh; was born early in 1700, and was married, as I am informed, to a farmer's daughter of the same place, named Gray, and probably a relative. They had three sons: John, David, and George. The eldest, John Gray, was a butler in Grass Market, Edinburgh. He married Barbara Newton, and had a large family of sons and daughters, the former of whom all died unmarried. The father and mother died about 1822.

"David Gray, son of George (1), was a grocer. He married Anne Sommerville, July 13, 1769, and d. Feb. 6, 1806; she d. July 13, 1824, aged 73. They had the following children: John, James, David, Jr., George, Walter, Mary and Ann, and others who d. in infancy. John Gray was born May 21, 1772, and was married Sept. 24, 1795, to Elizabeth Sime of Edinburgh. They had three children who died and left no descendants. Mrs. G. d. Dec. 22, 1840, and he a few years later.——James Gray in early life went to Jamaica, and afterwards to Baltimore, and to Philadelphia, where he was married, and taught school; no children.——David Gray, Jr., was a commercial traveller, and lived at Cramond, near Edinburgh; he mar. Margaret McLean, dau. of James McLean, ironmonger, Edinburgh; he was b. 1778, and d. in Jan., 1842; his widow d. in Buffalo, N. Y., 185-. They left James Gray, Phillip Cardell Gray, Jane Gray, John M. Gray, Margaret, Ann, and William M. Gray.——George Gray was a Surgeon in Prince St., Edinburgh; he was b. 1782, and was mar. to Mary Butler of Edinburgh, Jan. 15, 1801; he d. Dec. 12, 1810, and his widow, in 1856. They had two sons, each named James, that d. in infancy, and a daughter Mary Ann, and a son, George Gray; the former died some years ago, and the latter is a lawyer at Dubuque, Iowa.——Walter Gray was a Surgeon in the British Navy; mar. an Irish lady; had one child; all dec'd.

"George Gray, (2), the third son of George (1), was a Surgeon in Grass Market, Edinburgh; mar. the daughter of Mr. Allen, Banker, of Princes St., and had four daughters and a son."

SAMUEL GRAY,

A fortuitous circumstance occurring near the close of this work adds materially to the data of the family of Samuel Gray of Dorsetshire and Boston, as it appears at and following page 141. While a nearly full list of the children with their marriages is there given, only the descendants of one of the sons, Dr. Ebenezer Gray, are traced out. The following is the family of another of the sons, and the only one other than Ebenezer who is believed to have had male issue. But which one? That is the perplexing query. The letter below published, written by Joseph Gray, a great-grandson of Samuel, distinctly says that his grandfather, son of Samuel, was named William, and that he was the eldest son of his father. Now this statement seems reasonable on the face of it, but it is seemingly put in conflict with the record purported to have been made by Ebenezer, which says that his brother William "died in Barbadoes, aged 22 years;" and since he mentions the marriages of his other brothers and sisters the natural presumption would be, considering this, that he was unmarried. And then this statement of Ebenezer is fortified by at least three old and elaborate family trees which have been carefully examined for verification. The assertion that he might have been married and left issue at 22, is met by the further averment that the said William had three sons. The proof on either side seems to be ample and sufficient, though apparently so conflicting. It would seem that a man ought not to be mistaken about the name of his own grandfather, and certainly one ought to know the material facts concerning the life and death of a brother. However, the one or the other of these statements is incorrect. If William was the grandfather of Joseph, then he could not have died as stated; on the contrary, if the statement of his death is correct, then the grandfather of Joseph could not have been William, but probably Joseph Gray (1). And there the perplexing question is left.

The very interesting letter so referred to, was written by Joseph Gray (3) to his son William, who then resided at Halifax, N. S., and was dated at Windsor, England, Feb. 8, 1799, viz:

" As soon as I received yours respecting our family Arms, I attempted to comply with your wishes, but have been prevented by Justice's business, but hope this will reach you in time for the Liverpool vessel. My ancestors, on my father's side, were from very ancient noble descent. I have somewhere, but cannot find it, our pedigree from the first of those who emigrated to America. Since my recollection, a great uncle of mine, Benjamin Gray, about the year 1738 or 1739, received letters from England, from a favorite uncle of his, John Gray, of Westminster, London, inviting him to go to England, informing him that he was the next heir to the title and estate; but this great uncle, being a very great, famous, bigoted New Light, who though not much beforehand, yet sufficient to support himself in his advanced age, would not quit his New Light system to be made King of England. He died without male issue about the year 1742.

"My father and my grandfather both being the eldest sons of their respective fathers, I am of course the eldest male heir in the line of the senior branch for five generations back. In the following pedigree I shall go no further back than my great grandfather, first explaining that the wife of Dr. Gibbons of Boston, was mother of Dr. Gardiner's wife.

" ——— (Samuel) Gray, my great-grandfather; William Gray of Boston, my grandfather; Benj. Gray of Boston, my great uncle; Dr. Ebenezer Gray of Connecticut, my great uncle; John Gray of Connecticut, my great uncle; wife of Dr. Gibbons of Boston, my great aunt; wife of Capt. Henry Aitkins of Boston, my great aunt; mother of Col. Snelling of Boston, my great aunt. * My father had only two brothers, both dead upwards of 64 years; one of them in the West Indies, without issue, and the other having only Samuel, and Alexander Gray, who lived with me as clerk in my counting house at Halifax. And I had only two brothers, viz: Samuel, who served his time with Capt. Aitkins, at the north end of Boston, and then married his daughter. He died in Boston about the year 1776, having issue male and female. My brother John, when out of his time, about 1768 or 1769, went to England, and when returned went into the Custom House at Boston as first clerk with a deputation to sign as Deputy Collector in the absence of the

Principal, and where he was much liked." He further says of his brother John, that "at the breaking out of the troubles in America he quitted the Custom House and engaged in the commission business in South Carolina," where he purchased a plantation; but "political disputes running high," he left this country, and returning to England from there went out to India, where he engaged largely and successfully in the cultivation of Indigo, attracting the attention and patronage of the East India Company. He died there suddenly, without issue, in 1782; supposed to have been poisoned by the natives.

Joseph Gray further says in this letter: "Our family arms by the name of Gray, viz: A lion passant, topaz between three fleurs de lis pearl. Crest on a wreath, a dragon's head, erased diamond ducally gorged and chained gold."

And again: "My family and all the Grays of Connecticut are from one stock."

From the foregoing, the interesting fact appears that Samuel Gray of Dorsetshire had a brother John, of Westminster, London. Joseph Gray (3,) the writer of this letter, was evidently a loyalist, (as was also his brother John,) and at an early period of the Revolutionary struggle removed with his family to Halifax, and finally to England, where he died. The larger part of this branch of the family are still in England and the Provinces, while some of the descendants as will be seen are in the United States.

This very interesting family claims great antiquity and ancient descent, and that they can trace back to, or near the time of the Conquest. The Grays of Dorset were certainly of renown in the olden time, and titles still remain in that distinguished branch of the family.

JOSEPH GRAY.

JOSEPH GRAY (2), the father of Joseph Gray (3), and son of William or Joseph (1), and a grandson of Samuel, mar. Aug. 22, 1728, Rebecca West, dau. of John West, a wealthy farmer who lived at Bradford, near Haverhill, Mass. Record of his family does not appear other than that he had three sons.

JOSEPH GRAY, (3), son of Joseph (2), and great-grandson of
Samuel, b. in Boston, Mass., July 19, 1729, in 1759 mar. Mary
Gerrish, who was b. June 27, 1741, and probably a descendant
of Benj. Gerrish, who sailed for Boston in the Ketch Mary,
Mar. 22, 1678. She d. July 13, 1838. Issue:

> MARY GRAY, b. Jan. 14, 1760, d. Aug. 1760.
> REBECCA GRAY, Jan. 1761, d. Sept. 1761.
> ELIZABETH BRENTON GRAY, b. Dec. 24, 1761, d. Feb. 26,
> 1843.
> JOSEPH GERRISH GRAY, b. Jan. 31, 1763; drowned July
> 20, 1785.
> MARY GERRISH GRAY, b. May 4, 1765.
> AMELIA ANN GRAY, b. Sept. 23, 1766.
> WILLIAM GRAY, b. Nov. 8, 1767, d. Aug. 28, 1768.
> BENJAMIN GERRISH GRAY, b. Nov. 22, 1768.
> LYDIA HANCOCK GRAY, b. Mar. 20, 1771.
> ANN SUSANNAH GRAY, b. June 9, 1773, d. Dec. 28, 1791.
> SUSANNAH GRAY, b. June 20, 1774.
> WILLIAM GRAY, b. May 2, 1777, d. Oct. 16, 1847.
> SARAH GRAY, b. Jan. 2, 1779.
> ALEXANDER GRAY, b. Aug. 26, 1780, d. July 1, 1800, of
> yellow fever, at Norfolk, Va.

Mary Gerrish Gray, dau. of Joseph, mar. Loftus Jones, and
had: Loftus, Fanny, Lewis, Mary, Jeremy, John and Jane Jones.

Rev. Dr. Benjamin Gerrish Gray son of Joseph, mar. Mary
Thomas, and d. at St. John, N. B., Feb. 18, 1854. Issue:

> BENJAMIN CHARLES THOMAS GRAY.
> JOHN WILLIAM DERING GRAY, b. July 23, 1797.
> MARY GRAY.

Elizabeth Brenton Gray, dau. of Joseph, mar. John Fraser,
and had Eliza, who d. June, 1862, and Alexander Fraser.

Benjamin Charles Thomas Gray mar. Eliza Brownlow, and
had: Chas. William, Samuel Brownlow, Benjamin Gerrish, Dr.
William, and Wentworth Gray.

> CHARLES WILLIAM GRAY, who mar. Rosalie T. Butterfield, at
> Tunbridge Wells, Eng., and had Charles Butterfield Gray,
> who mar. Marion Robinson; Mary Gray; Alice Gray;
> Catharine Louisa, who mar. Wm. H. Lawson; Rosalie,
> who mar. Edward Pitcairn Jones, R. N.; Lewis Gray;
> and Robert Stannus.

Samuel Brownlow Gray, LL. D., son of Benjamin Chas. Thos.
Gray, mar. Mrs. E. Williams, at Bermuda. Issue: Elizabeth

Brownlow, Brownlow Trimmingham, and Mary Gray Gray.
REGINALD GRAY, LL. D., son of Samuel Brownlow Gray, mar.
at Bermuda, Jeanette Gosling, and had Reginald W.,
Annie B., Edmund, and Gerald H. Gray.

Benj. Gerrish Gray, son of Benj. Chas. Thomas Gray, mar.
Annie Wiggins, and had Stephen, who mar. and d. without issue;
Elizabeth Brownlow Gray Gray, Charles, who married Florence
Carr and had Viola, and Margery Gray; Brenton, Frederick,
Annie St. John, and Wentworth Gray.

———

Rev. Dr. John W. Dering Gray, son of Rev. Dr. Benj. Gerrish
Gray, of Kings College, Windsor, N. S., and Oxford University,
Eng., mar. 1820, at Gravesend, Eng., Avis Phillips Easson, dau.
of Wm. Easson and Mary Muffat, who was b. in Jamaica, Oct.
22, 1797, and d. in N. Y., Nov. 26, 1884. Issue: Mary Thomas,
b. and d. at Amherst, N. S., 1821; Avis, b. at Amherst, N. S.,
1824, and d. in England, July, 26, 1843; William, Benj. Gerrish,
Sarah Elizabeth, Eliza Isabella, Charles, who was b. 1834, and
d. 1835; and Henry Martyn Gray, b. June 28, 1837, and d. at
New York, Sept. 3, 1878. Rev. Dr. J. W. D. Gray d. at Halifax,
N. S., Feb. 1, 1868.

DR. WILLIAM GRAY, son of Rev. Dr. J. W. D. Gray, was b. at
St. John, N. B., Apr. 1, 1826; grad. at Windsor College,
N. S., and mar. 1849, Sophia Temme; d. without issue,
at Jamaica, W. I., March, 1850.

BENJ. GERRISH GRAY, LL. D., son of Rev. Dr. J. W. D. Gray,
b. at St. John, N. B., June 18, 1828, grad. at Windsor
College, and mar. Mary Josephine Clinch, at Boston,
Oct. 2, 1861, and had Philip Easson, R. A., b. at Hali-
fax, N. S., June 15, 1863; Mary Griselda, b. July 25,
1865; Wentworth Morton, b. 1868; Frances Elizabeth
Uniacke, b. Oct. 5, 1873, and Victor Gerrish Gray, b.
Aug. 14, 1875, at Halifax, N. S.

SARAH ELIZABETH GRAY, dau. of Rev. Dr. J. W. D. Gray, b.
at St. John, N. B., Sept. 18, 1830, mar. Aug. 15, 1849,
Alfred Gilliat Gray.

ELIZA IZABELLA GRAY, dau. of Rev. Dr. J. W. D. Gray, b.
at St. John, N. B., Oct. 2, 1832, mar. Dr. Francis Robin-
son, of Annapolis, N. S., and had Augusta, Avis, Henry
Campbell, and Sarah Elizabeth.

WILLIAM GRAY.

William Gray son of Joseph, b. May 2, 1777, at Halifax, Nova Scotia, mar. at Richmond, Va., July 1, 1809, Sarah Scott, b. at London, Eng., July 10, 1780, and d. at Norfolk, Va., Sept. 4, 1838; he d. at Liverpool, Eng., Oct. 16, 1847. For many years he was H. B. M. Consul at Norfolk, Va. Issue:

> MARY GILLIAT GRAY, b. May 18, 1810, d. July 16, 1883.
> ELIZABETH SCOTT GRAY, b. Sept. 8, 1811, d. Apr. 20, 1812.
> JOHN HAMILTON GRAY, b. Jan. 16, 1814.
> WILLIAM HANCOCK GRAY, b. Nov. 26, 1815.
> An infant female, b. and d. July 17, 1817.
> ALFRED GILLIAT GRAY, b. July 2, 1818, d. Nov. 10, 1876.
> ANDREW BELCHER GRAY, b. July 6, 1820.
> THOMAS GILLIAT GRAY, b. May 7, 1824, d. July 10, 1854.

Mary Gilliat Gray, dau. of Wm. Gray, b. at Bermuda, May 18, 1810, mar. Nov. 6, 1845, at St. John N. B., to Major John Harris, U. S. M. C., and d. July 16, 1883, at Washington, D. C., without issue.

Judge John Hamilton Gray, Hon. Chief Justice, Vancouver, British Columbia, son of William, b. Jan. 16, 1814, at Bermuda, mar. May 29, 1845, to Eliza Ormond, at Dublin, Ireland. Issue: Charlotte Elizabeth Ormond, Florence Mary, John Hamilton, Scott William Alfred Hamilton, R. N., Gertrude Mabel, Sybil, and Pierpont Hamilton Mundy Gray.

> CHARLOTTE ELIZABETH ORMOND GRAY, dau. of John Hamilton Gray, mar. Henry Hallowes, R. A., and had Beatrice.

William Hancock Gray, son of Wm. Gray, b. at Richmond, Va., Nov. 26, 1815, mar. Feb. 17, 1853, Gertrude Du Guard, at Shrewsbury, Eng. Issue: Gertrude, who mar. Loftus Jones, R. N., and had Lewis Tobias, Wm. Loftus, Edith and Winifred Jones; Mary, who mar. Evelin Rich; and William Du Guard, R. A. William Hancock Gray d. in Isle of Wight, England, June, 1883.

Alfred Gilliat Gray, son of William, and grandson of Joseph, b. July 2, 1818, at Richmond, Va., was mar. Aug. 15, 1849, at St. John, New Brunswick, to Sarah Elizabeth Gray, dau. of Rev. Dr. J. W. D. Gray. Issue:

> MARY HARRIS GRAY, b. Oct. 17th, 1852, at St. John.
> HENRY SELDEN GRAY, b. Dec. 18th, 1855.   "

ALFRED GILLIAT GRAY, b. Oct. 20, 1858, Brooklyn, N.Y.
WILLIAM GRAY, b. Jan. 11th, 1861.   "
ANDREW GRAY,   }   d. Oct. 18, 1866.
AVIS EASSON GRAY, } b. Oct. 1864.   d. Jan. 12, 1865.
SARAH SCOTT GRAY, b. Sept. 13th, 1867.

Mary Harris Gray, daughter of Alfred Gilliat Gray, b. Oct.
17th, 1852, at St. John, N. B., married, Oct. 8th, 1876, at
Brooklyn, L. I., to Rufus Hatch. Issue:

ROSCOE HATCH, b. July 27, 1881.
BERTHA GRAY HATCH, b. Nov. 28, 1883.
MARY BROWNLOW HATCH, b. Aug. 31, 1886.

Andrew Belcher Gray, C. E., son of William, b. July 6, 1820, at
Norfolk, Va., mar. June 23, 1856, at New Orleans, La., Apolina
Leacock. Was a Colonel in the Confederate service, and killed
at Fort Pillow, April 16, 1862. Issue:

MINNIE GRAY, b. May 27, 1857, at New Orleans, La.
HELEN GRAY, b. Nov. 10, 1859, Brooklyn, L. I.
ANDRIETTE ELIZA GRAY, b. June 11, 1862, N. O., La.

Dr. Thomas Gilliat Gray, son of Wm., mar. Dec., 1852, at
St. John, N. B., Bessie Ormond, and had Harry Hamilton Gray,
b. May, 1854. Dr. Thos. d. at Chicago, Ill., of cholera, July 10,
1854.

Henry Selden Gray, son of Alfred Gilliat, resides at Chicago,
and is interested in the cattle ranch business. His brother Alfred Gilliat, is also in same business at Medicine Creek, Texas.
William Gray, C. E., youngest son of Alfred Gilliat, is engaged
in the service of the city of New York, on the new Aqueduct,
with headquarters at Tarrytown, N. Y., and to his kindly and
efficient aid this branch of the family is indebted for representa-
tion in this volume.

———

The following is a list of the dates of birth of the children of
Samuel and Susannah Langdon Gray, as fully as obtained:
Elizabeth, b. Dec. 31, 1685; Joseph, b. Dec. 6, 1686; Susannah,
b. Jan. 3, 1688; Rebecca, b. Jan. 26, 1689; John, b. Aug. 16,
1692; Ebenezer, b. Oct. 31, 1697. This from the Boston Records, and as the names of Samuel, Benjamin, and William do
not there appear, the presumption is that they were born elsewhere, perhaps in England, it being claimed that William was
the eldest son.

LEVI GRAY.

The following is the record of the family of Levi Gray, whose name appears on page 159, as one of the sons of Adam Clark Gray of Pelham, Mass. Levi mar. Abigail Robins, and had 12 children, viz:

EUNICE GRAY, who mar. Hyde Brown.

SALLY GRAY, who mar. Mr. Rose.

MARY GRAY, who mar. Hawley R. Carey, and has a son Hawley Carey residing at Springfield Centre, N. Y.

MATILDA GRAY, who mar. Franklin Cloys, and resides at Cazenovia, N. Y.

ALMIRA GRAY, who mar. Mark Walby, and resides at Burlington Flats, N. Y.

CAROLINE GRAY, who mar. F. Farrington.

EPHRAIM GRAY, who mar. Almira Nichols, and had Dr. R. H. Gray of Oneida, N. Y.; Levi Gray, of Portland, Me.; and Dr. Ed. Gray, of Colorado.

SIMON GRAY, who mar. Hannah Walwrath, and had Rev. S. P. Gray, of Jordansville, N. Y.; D. W., and Chas. Gray, of East Springfield, N. Y,; and Rev. L. B. Gray, of Earlville, N. Y.

LEVI GRAY, who mar. Almira, and resides at Starkville, Herkimer Co., N. Y.

CHESTER GRAY, who mar. Pernal Stannard.

CLARK GRAY, who mar. Almira Walch, and resides at East Springfield, N. Y.

DANIEL GRAY, who mar. Catharine.

It is said that all raised families.

Adam Gray emigrated from Pelham, Mass., in 1805 or 1806, to Springfield, N. Y. He was a Presbyterian, and his son Levi a Methodist. Both are buried at Springfield. This information was all furnished by Rev. L. B. Gray, of Earlville, N. Y.

Dr. AMOS GRAY, b. in Townsend, Vt., Feb. 2, 1804, son of Amos and Betsey Tyler Gray, and grandson of Jonas Gray, as appears on page 176, of the Townsend Grays, mar. Dec. 11, 1833, Sally Jennette Noble, dau. of Sylvanus Noble, b. in New Lisbon, N. Y., May 28, 1813. Dr. Amos Gray attended lectures at Castleton, Vt., and at Pittsfield, Mass., 1829, and engaged in the practice of medicine at Dexter, Mich., 1832. Issue: Chas. Gales Gray, b. Nov. 13, 1834, mar. June 19, 1861, Elizabeth R. Bruce, res. St. Clair, Mich.; Augusta Noble Gray, d.; Helen N., who mar. Jas. B. Farrand, and res. at Port Hudson, Mich.; Emily S., who mar. Samuel C. Cook, of St. Paul, Minn.; and Cora Evelyn Gray, b. Aug. 2, 1855, at Dexter, Mich.

INDEX

APPENDIX.

ADDENDA.

There was a Benjamin Gray, printer, at Boston, 1715.

Joseph Gray of Boston, bought lands at Andover, 1735.

A John Gray was Lieut. at Castle William, near Boston, 1723.

There was a Nathaniel Gray at Saybrook, Conn., 1674.

There was a Walter Gray at Hartford, Conn., 1644.

Henry Gray, of Boxford, Mass., mar Alice Peabody, 1736.

A Joseph Gray mar. Rebekah Hill at Taunton, Mass., Feb. 25, 1667, and had Joseph, b. Dec., 1667, and Mehitable, b. 1668.

A Henry Gray was at Boston, 1638; probably the Henry who was afterwards of Fairfield, Conn.

There was a Francis Gray at Piscataway, 1660.

There was a Wm. Gray at Esopus, Ulster Co., N. Y., 1676.

Mary Gray, dau. of Absolom Gray, mar. Ebenezer Benedict Nov. 13, 1762, and settled at Pawling, N. Y.

A Rev. Archibald Gray was living at Troy, N. Y., 1800.

John Gray and wife Buelah, and son Eliphalet were at Rindge, N. H., 1776.

Luther Gray paid taxes at Gt. Barrington, Mass., 1788 to 1808.

George Gray, Esq., of 15 Broad St., New York, native of Tyron Co., Ireland; res. at Grand Rapids, Mich., before the war; was Colonel of the 6th Mich. Cavalry.

Thos. and Thankful Winslow Gray of Watertown, N. Y., had Joseph Gray, of Tecumseh, Mich., Horace Gray, of Grand Island, Jesse Gray of Kalamazoo, and Alexander Gray of Detroit.

John Gray of Saco, made allegiance to Com. of Mass., 1653.

Andrew S. Gray, of Stone Arabia, N. Y., Assemblyman, 1847.

Daniel Gray of Wheeler, Steuben Co., N. Y.,   "   1860.

Norman H. Gray, Tannersville, N. Y., Assemblyman, 1852.

/ John Gray, Member of Assembly Washington Co., N.Y., 1807./

David Gray,   "   "   Rensselaer   "   1796.

John C. Gray, Co. Clerk, Tioga Co., N. Y., 1877.

Hugh Gray, Sheriff of Suffolk Co., N. Y., 1704; perhaps the Hugh who was afterwards of Stratford, Conn.

Thomas S. Gray, Warrensburg, N. Y., Surrogate, 1845; Member of Assembly 1856, and '62.

Hiram Gray, of Elmira, N. Y., Ex-Member of Congress and Judge of the Supreme Court, and Com. of Appeals.

A Lockwood Gray who mar. Polly Riggs, and lived at Ridgefield, Conn., was b. in Delaware, 1783, son of Gilead and Sarah Beers Gray.

Later investigations have elicited the fact that the church trial in which Elder Jeduthan Gray took prominent part, and in which Ashbel Brownson and sister Priscilla were defendants, page 75, took place at Torrington, Conn. Elder Gray also officiated at the dedication of the Baptist church in that place in 1789.

The descendants of Caty, dau. Capt. Silas Gray, who had mar. Peter Best, (page 127,) were found after a long search, at Toronto, Canada, whither they removed from Schoharie Co., N. Y.; but the descendants of his dau. Peggy, who had married Turney I. Sturges, were not found.

Rev. Christopher Bridge, one of whose daughters married Benjamin Gray, (pages 142 and 298) a son of Samuel Gray of Dorsetshire and Boston, and probably another, Hannah Bridge, Edward Gray (2), son of Edward Gray (1), of Lincolnshire and Boston, (p. 192) and who was for a time rector of King's Chapel, Boston, accepted a call to Christ Church, at Rye, Westchester Co., N. Y., his commission bearing date the 19th day of Aug., 1709, and there he continued his labors until his decease, which took place on the 23d of May, 1719, in the 48th year of his age. Greenwood's History of King's Chapel, pays him high encomium, and says his death was very much lamented.

ERRATA.

Tamar Gray–Ames mar. 2d, Abel Thompson, and not Job as appears on page 100.

On page 108, Col. John Pathson's should be Patterson's.

On page 131, in biographical sketch of John Tarvin Gray, he is spoken of as the grandson of Nathaniel Gray, when it should be great-grandson, etc.

Mercy Raymond is noted on page 138, as the daughter of James Raymond, when it should be Abram Raymond.

Two Samuel Grays (3) appear in the family of Samuel Gray of Dorsetshire and Boston; the one on p. 143 should be Sam'l (4.)

Peter Biste on page 127 should be Peter Best, but it there appears exactly as copied from the will of Capt. Silas Gray.

Sarah Dolbeau, on page 192, should be Sarah Dolbeare.

Several typographical errors are apparent, and possibly there are some errors of fact, but careful, conscientious effort has been made to keep the errata down to the minimum. In this connection it may be pertinent and of interest to add, that nearly all of the type setting, as well as the proof reading has been done by the author, and therefore the errors which appear are rightfully chargeable to him and not to another.

IN MEMORIAM.

In the progress of this work some have silently dropped from the ranks and have gone over to join "the great majority." This has been a source of sadness to the writer, and has caused him to hasten on to the conclusion of the work lest others still should fall by the wayside ere it was accomplished. Among those who have so passed away, not already noticed, is Mrs. Rev. Calvin Gray, of Fort Dodge, Iowa, record of whose family appears on pages 38 and 39. A dear old lady, ripe in years and ripe in Christian experience, her memory is blessed to all of her kindred.

Also Mrs. Juliette E. Gray–Garland, of Des Plaines, Ill., whose family appears on page 98, and who had manifested great interest in this work. On the 19th of Aug., 1886, she received injuries from being overturned in a carriage by a fractious horse, which resulted in her death the second day following; a sad tragedy.

And then a dear little grandson of the writer, Gifford Newcomb See, whose birth is noted on page 136, and who died at Pittsfield, Mass., March 11, 1887. A sweet human blossom plucked while yet the fresh dawn of morning was upon it.

NOTES.

The division of families which occurs in some instances may give occasion for criticism. This came from the work being necessarily done in parts, and from the determination to have all obtainable data somewhere appear up to the closing of the work. This would be obviated if the demand should warrant the publication of a second edition. Any correction of errors or additional information, will be welcome with that possibility in view.

Pages from 297 to 304, inclusive, are not indexed for the reason that they were kept open as long as possible for additional data.

ACKNOWLEDGMENT.

Many thanks to all who by their kindly interest and assistance have made the publication of this work possible. Much avail has also been made of the records of the N. E. Genealogical Society, and of State and National records, and of town and county and church records and histories, and of a large number of family histories and genealogies.

LAST WORDS.

So the last words must finally be spoken, and yet though the end has been so long looked forward to with eager interest, they are regretfully spoken. The writer has given so much of his heart to this work, that he cannot lightly put it aside as a tale that is told; he cannot easily turn away from that which has so long engaged his intense attention; he cannot soon forget those in whom he has come to feel such a deep and personal interest. But last words must be spoken, and so dear friends, farewell.

THE AUTHOR.

www.ingramcontent.com/pod-product-compliance
Lightning Source LLC
Chambersburg PA
CBHW030901270326
41929CB00008B/520